INFECTIOUS NIETZSCHE

Studies in Continental Thought

John Sallis, general editor

Consulting Editors

INFECTIOUS
NIETZSCHE

DAVID FARRELL KRELL

Indiana University Press
BLOOMINGTON AND INDIANAPOLIS

The paper used in this publication meets the minimum requirements of
American National Standard for Information Sciences—Permanence of
Paper for Printed Library Materials, ANSI Z39.48-1984.

Manufactured in the United States of America

Library of Congress Cataloging-in-Publication Data

Krell, David Farrell.
    Infectious Nietzsche / David Farrell Krell.
        p.   cm. — (Studies in Continental thought)
    Includes bibliographical references and index.
    ISBN 0-253-33005-X (cl : alk. paper). —ISBN 0-253-21039-9 (pa :
alk. paper)
        1. Nietzsche, Friedrich Wilhelm, 1844–1900.   2. Nietzsche,
    Friedrich Wilhelm, 1844–1900—Influence. 3. Philosophy,
Modern—20th century.   I. Title.   II. Series.
B3317.K725   1996
193—dc20   95-30669

1 2 3 4 5 01 00 99 98 97 96

for Elena Sophia

Du hast mehr Eltern. Wo gehn wir denn hin? Immer nach Hause.

You have several parents. Well, then, where are we heading? We are always heading home.

—Novalis, *Heinrich von Ofterdingen*, Part II

CONTENTS

Preface

Need big books on Nietzsche be breaches of good taste? Need good taste always apply? The studies that constitute the present book were written during the years 1969–1994, twenty-five years separating the earliest pieces from the most recent ones. Good taste did demand that I throw away all the early essays, and I followed the dictates of good taste 75 percent of the time. Yet the three chapters on genealogical critique, whatever their weaknesses, seemed to me the proper starting point for the book, if only because they are where I started. Whatever came after them—studies on Heidegger's *Nietzsche* in the 1970s, on Derrida's challenges to Heidegger and Nietzsche in the 1980s, and on Nietzsche and the German Romantics in the 1990s—continued to rest on the conviction that Nietzsche, even as the thinker and poet of eternal recurrence of the same, remains first and foremost a genealogist.

It is clear to me, of course, that genealogy today is an enterprise far more complex than it was a quarter of a century ago: the brief section on Gilles Deleuze and Michel Foucault that I have added to chapter 2 scarcely suffices; a serious reading of Deleuze's *Différence et répétition* is missing from chapter 3; a serious reading of Foucault's work from beginning to end appears here only as a promissory note and as hope in a generous future; finally, Derrida's deconstruction of the *possibility* of genealogy receives no serious treatment in the present book. Here it is a matter of Nietzsche confronting many thinkers— among them Plato, Descartes, Kant, Hegel, Novalis, Heidegger, Gadamer, Philippe Lacoue-Labarthe, Derrida, Irigaray, Pierre Klossowski, and Sarah Kofman—yet remaining the one he is, a genealogist who even in a vast and vastly interesting crowd is easy to find and difficult to lose. Infectious, and hard to shake off, is this Nietzsche.

It is precisely the infectious Nietzsche who dominates my most recent work, which also invokes Novalis and the German Romantics in general as background to Nietzsche's genealogical project. What unifies the book is the preoccupation with questions touching health and illness throughout—both as material for genealogical critique and as a challenge to the genealogist. For issues of health and illness seem to impinge on the life of every writer, from Plato to Pierre, whether what is written is genealogical analysis, historical study, philosophy, or fiction.

Unless otherwise noted, I cite Nietzsche's works (KSA) and letters (KSAB) in the *Kritische Studienausgabe*, edited by Giorgio Colli and Mazzino Montinari (Berlin and Munich: Walter de Gruyter and Deutscher Taschenbuch Verlag, 1980 and 1986, respectively). I cite them by volume and page in the body of my text.

A number of the chapters in my text appeared elsewhere in another form, and I would like to thank the editors of the following journals and anthologies for their support and encouragement and the publishers for permission to reprint this material in adapted form: R. Lloyd Mitchell, who edited *Topic: A Journal of the Liberal Arts*, no. 28 (Fall 1974), for chapter 4; Daniel T. O'Hara, who edited *Why Nietzsche Now?* first for *boundary 2* in 1981 and then for Indiana University Press in 1985, for chapter 5; John Sallis, editor of *Research in Phenomenology*, where chapter 6 first appeared in 1985 (vol. 15); Diane P. Michelfelder and Richard E. Palmer, eds., *Dialogue and Deconstruction: The Gadamer-Derrida Encounter* (Albany: State University of New York Press, 1989), for chapter 7; David Wood, who co-edited with me *Exceedingly Nietzsche: Aspects of Contemporary Nietzsche-Interpretation* (London and New York: Routledge, 1988), for chapter 11; and Peter J. Burgard, ed., *Nietzsche and the Feminine* (Charlottesville and London: University Press of Virginia, 1994), for chapter 12. My thanks to Janet Rabinowitch for her encouragement over the years, to John Sallis for his friendship and his readerly skills, and to Joel Shapiro, Ferít Güven, David Thomas, and Anna Vaughn for help with the text and the proofs. Thanks also to Monika Herlt of the Wilhelm-Busch-Gesellschaft in Hanover for her friendly assistance with "the mole" of chapter 5.

D.F.K.

Introduction

When my mother first caught me reading Nietzsche's *Beyond Good and Evil*—I was in high school, a teacher had given it to me, I did not understand a word—she admonished me: "People go crazy reading that sort of thing." As in all important matters, my mother was right.

The only response I can muster in my addled state is that the competing lunacies are so dependably boring that one is driven back to Nietzsche willy-nilly again and again. One is afflicted with him, as with the common cold, or the uncommon cold, or something else equally infectious. Nietzsche is like laughter from a beautiful mouth or in dancing eyes—soon everyone in the room is swept away by hilarity or hysteria, where the line that separates good health from noxious influence is obliterated.

Philosophy is divine mania, says Plato in *Phaedrus*. Yet if in our time the divine is moribund, whether piously or miserably, philosophers will need to know what sort of madness they have caught, or what sort of lunacy has caught them, simultaneously dragging them down and puffing them up. Nietzsche remains the thinker who best meets this need. It is as though he never quit his *Diakonissendienst*, never stopped being a medic—albeit an infected and infectious one. (Nietzsche served as a medic for one week in the Franco-Prussian War, at the end of August 1870, near Metz: he himself was infected almost immediately with dysentery and diphtheria by the wounded and dying soldiers he treated, so that he was forced to return to his mother and his professorship).

It would be far more grand to celebrate Nietzsche as the end of metaphysics, or the first philosopher of style, the grand; for the moment it may be best to stick with the more sober thought that he is a carrier. Even Nietzsche's enemies, after all, combat him only by infecting their readers with some other form of virulence or fanaticism, subjecting them to yet another strain of infection or strand of asceticism.

The present book consists of twelve chapters. The first three deal with Nietzsche's genealogical critique, *including* the thought of eternal recurrence of the same. (For a summary of the characteristics of genealogical critique, see the section entitled "Transcendental versus Genealogical Critique" in chapter 1.) Chapters 4 and 5 treat of Nietzschean genealogy in relation to Plato's *Phaedo*, Descartes's *Meditations*, Kant's *Critique of Pure Reason*, and Hegel's *Phenomenology of Spirit* and *Lectures on the History of Philosophy*. Heidegger's *Nietzsche* then takes center stage, albeit slightly off-center, inasmuch as Gadamer, Derrida, and Lacoue-Labarthe, as respondents to Heidegger, are the focus. A close reading of Nietzsche's notebook M III 1 (from the summer and fall of 1881) introduces the final turns of the book. Questions of health and illness, orality, the oneiric, the feminine-thalassic tendency, biography, autobiography, and fiction bring the book to its end.

A more detailed outline of the chapters may help to clarify the itinerary. The first chapter asks whether Nietzsche's genealogical critique—like Kant's transcendental critique—can yield an *inventory* of its concepts and categories, its canon and practice. Further, it asks in what such an inventory could be *grounded*. It concludes, though not by means of a transcendental deduction, that the genealogical method of *suspicion* subverts all grounds, abandoning us to a realm that can only be *underground*. The impossibility of inventories in and for genealogical critique becomes, in chapter 2, the *decadence* of all such projected inventories. That is to say, it becomes clear that the sciences and disciplines on which genealogy depends are those that thrived throughout the history of metaphysics and morals. Moreover, the drive that underpins the sciences shows a fatal affinity to the drives that propel the ascetic ideal. Both Gilles Deleuze and Michel Foucault touch on this problem of the radical recoil of genealogical critique, a recoil that occurs whenever genealogy turns to its own genealogy. Yet even if an inventory of Nietzschean genealogical critique should prove both impossible in its execution and unsavory in its origins, we are left with what Deleuze calls the "bipolar standard" of will to power. Even if we deny that will to power is an ontological "ultimate fact" for Nietzsche, as Heidegger insists that it is, will to power remains the single most important factor in genealogical analysis. Will to power as *art*, rather than as *knowledge*, soon takes us to the experience of eternal recurrence of the same, but not before an inquiry into Nietzsche's genealogy of the *language* of metaphysics and morals—and into the language of his own genealogy. Finally, chapter 2 examines the life-style of the genealogist, that is, of the *writer* of genealogies: it is the proximity of such a life to life-destructive decadence that remains disturbing in the "case" of Nietzsche, as in the cases of so many other genealogists.

Nietzsche usually writes of eternal recurrence of the same as a *burden* and a *task*: the task of overcoming decadence and the burden that will crush the decadents. Yet sometimes he appears to experience the thought as a *consolation*, as a guarantor of permanence and of an at least cyclical continuity for things. Even though Nietzsche is exquisitely aware of the decadence of the redeemer type, he does not shrink from calling eternal return a redemptive thought, a thought in which the world is "redeemed for the first time." The only way to temper one's suspicions concerning the decadence of such redemption in the thought of eternal return is to deepen one's sense of the *tragic* character of the thought. The third chapter therefore asks about Nietzsche's experience of Dionysos, especially as Zagreus, the fragmented divinity, in relation to his creation of Zarathustra as the teacher of eternal return. The problem of the decadence of redemption culminates in that of the relation of eternal return to will to power: what does it mean to *will* the recurrence of the "it was" of time; that is, what does it mean to will-to-will the redemption of the past? Only in the radiant affirmation of will to power as art can eternal return as paltry consolation be overcome. Yet the precise character of such affirmation remains elusive, if only because affirmation is mortal, its divine patron fragmented and consumed, if not altogether mortified. One must learn to think eternal recurrence of the same as *downgoing*, thinking the thought within the parameters of a *descensional reflection*, a thinking that in its most soaring affirmation *goes down*.

However, to go down is to resist two millennia of ascensional thrust in the West—the craving, whether in religion, science, or art, to go up and up. Plato, the philosopher of ladders and wings, seems the primordial opponent of Nietzsche's descensional reflection. Chapter 4 therefore poses some questions about the chances of our *reading* Plato after Nietzsche—and after all those whom Nietzsche has infected. Nietzsche's ambivalence with regard to Socrates is well known. Yet his ambivalence with regard to Plato is equally pronounced: Plato is the artist and thinker of the mixed style, yet his synthesis of epic, lyric, comedy, and prose is unparalleled in the ancient world. Although Plato may have been seduced by Socrates, there are moments when he seems to maintain the upper hand. The chapter culminates in several readings of Plato's *Phaedo*, one of them a genealogical-critical response to the Platonic paean to "dying and being dead," another a more positive response to the comedy, dream, myth, and music of the Platonic dialogues. *Phaedo* is the dialogue in which Socrates pledges a cock to Asclepius. It is the life-affirming or life-denying character of that antique cock that Nietzsche—here with the assistance of Herman Melville—compels us to examine.

In chapter 5 the cock of antiquity meets the mole of modernity—that is to say, the mole that announces itself in Kant and Hegel, two thinkers that we will already have encountered in the chapters on genealogy. That Kant, Hegel, and Nietzsche all have a mole up their family tree, or rooting about beneath the bole, was a discovery of the years 1974–1976. The resulting essay, first written in German, then translated (more or less) into English, appeared during the years in which I was teaching—among other things, Melville—at the universities of Freiburg and Mannheim; these were also the years in which I was translating and editing Heidegger's *Basic Writings* and his *Nietzsche*, the latter dominating chapters 6 and 7 of the present book. Chapter 5 discusses the three major moles of modernity. Kant himself does not champion the mole, but laments the damage that the traditional metaphysical mole has wreaked on the metaphysico-moral building site. Nevertheless, Kant's own desire to dig down to bedrock in order to provide a solid foundation for the edifice of metaphysics and morals necessitates the very burrowing that Kant condemns. Hegel, for his part, identifies the historic march of spirit as the upward-tending path of the mole; yet it is difficult to fathom Hegel's upward-bound, *victorious* mole, especially when it is identified as the murdered king of Denmark. Nietzsche's mole is both more modest and more relentless, less ascensional and less glorious, than Hegel's: it subverts past systems of metaphysics and morals, yet is never truly victorious, not even when it seeks consolation in the thought of eternal return. Nietzsche's mole does not crow so loud.

At this point in the volume a major shift occurs, away from genealogy, Plato, Kant, and Hegel to Heidegger's history of being and, in the wake of Heidegger, to Derrida, Lacoue-Labarthe, and Gadamer. Both chapters 6 and 7

focus on Heidegger's reading of Nietzsche, a reading that has doubtless dominated my own reading from 1969 onward. Chapter 6 discusses two of the
most significant responses to the Heideggerian reading, those of Jacques Derrida and Philippe Lacoue-Labarthe, published during the 1970s. If what I am
calling a *hermeneutics of discretion* defends Heidegger's reading against some
of Derrida's and Lacoue-Labarthe's claims, it resists Gadamer's wholehearted
adoption of Heidegger's *Nietzsche* as an ally in his debate with deconstruction.
While Derrida's "minimalist" reading of Nietzsche conceals its own strategy,
there is no doubt that it opens up Nietzsche's text to a reading that does not
wholly succumb to the question of being and ἀλήθεια. At the end of the day,
as chapter 7 confirms, after all the shiftings of these prestigious readers of Heidegger's *Nietzsche*, what impresses us most of all is the continued virulence of
the Nietzschean text—its infectious potency—for them all.

With chapters 8–10 we arrive at my most recent work, returning to the
texts of Nietzsche, but this time taking a closer look at Nietzsche's relation
to German Romanticism, especially Novalis (Friedrich von Hardenberg,
1772–1801). Chapter 8 offers a close reading of one of Nietzsche's notebooks,
namely, the one that contains his most detailed early sketches of the thought of
eternal recurrence. What is bizarre about the notes in M III 1 is the fact that
while a large number of them develop the thought of eternal recurrence *of
the same*, an equally large or somewhat larger number attack the very concept
of "the same" or sameness. The central question of chapter 8 is therefore how
Nietzsche's "thought of thoughts," eternal recurrence of the same, can survive
the hypercritical conditions of its birth. How can Nietzsche entertain the
thought of a return of the same, indeed, promulgating it as his major insight,
yet also inveigh against "the same" as the cardinal *error* of all past metaphysical systems? In chapter 3 we will have invoked "the decadence of redemption"
with regard to eternal return; now we invoke the *infectious* character of "the
same." The relation of decadence to life-affirming thought now becomes the
relation of infection to an organism—a kind of *contradiction* or *contraction*
in which the stakes are raised to eternity. Such raising of the stakes does not
resolve any of the traditional questions concerning Nietzsche's ostensible "doctrine," such as whether eternal return is a "scientific hypothesis" or an exis-
tential(ist) imperative or precept. It merely alters our assumptions concerning
"the same," and thus makes Nietzsche's thought of thoughts more mysterious
than ever.

Chapter 9, "Two Systems of the Mouth," continues to read notebook
M III 1, but this time in the company of Novalis. Both Novalis and Nietzsche
proffer systems of the mouth, that is, systems of speech and ingestion, oral
communication and eating, kissing, breathing, and communing. Whereas
Novalis takes "the first kiss" as the primal phase and principal figure of his
oral system, Nietzsche is more aware of the "bite" in any such system, as of the
disgust and nausea that underlie all moral and aesthetic judgments. Whereas
Novalis seeks the union and concord of a system of soul and body—soul *in*
body, body *in* soul—and finds it in the eucharist and in sexual embrace, Nietz-

sche seeks insight into the meaning of *Einverleibung,* "incorporation," as the famished ingestion of *errors* that are useful for the survival and enhancement of a particular species. For both thinkers, significant thoughts are thoughts that have to be *eaten,* thoughts whose salubrious or toxic effects cannot be safely predicted and controlled—one simply has to bite and see.

Chapter 10 therefore approaches the thoughts of Nietzsche's *Ecce Homo* quite gingerly, especially the thoughts concerning health and illness. It first examines some notes of Novalis and Schelling in order to get a sense of both the intimate connection between Nietzsche and German Romanticism and his vast distance from it. A good part of the chapter is concerned with the theory, proffered by a number of psychiatrists who are absorbed by the Nietzsche "case," that certain types of infection (especially with tuberculosis or syphilis) produce over a long stretch of time what can only be called *biopositive effects.* If the life or βίος in question is that of a thinker, writer, or creator of any kind, then Heraclitus (fragment B 48) will have been corroborated: βίος is βιός, that is, life is the arrow shot at itself—or, to put it more positively, the lethal arrow of illness is the good health of the creative life. Toward the conclusion of chapter 10 it becomes clear that eternal re-turn and infernal res-sentiment are intimately related, that no thinking of eternal recurrence can simply escape the coils of resentment and rancor. Likewise, there is no great health that can simply declare its independence from illness, no absolutely clear line that can separate health from illness. Novalis's notion of "indirect illness" is thus expanded to the thought of a chronic indirect health, an eternal recurrence for which no peaks of exuberant good health and valleys of decadent deterioration are clearly distinguishable.

Ecce Homo continues to be the focus of chapter 11. Yet we now expand the inquiry beyond questions of health and illness to issues concerning autobiography as such. The two principal questions raised in the chapter are these: (1) Can the riddle of Nietzsche's double existence—the fact that as his father he is already dead, while as his mother he survives and grows old—be solved if we identify the paternal heritage as illness and decadence, the maternal as health and vitality? (2) Can we rely on the name *Nietzsche, Friedrich Wilhelm,* to guarantee the unity and identity of a life and an œuvre? The chapter, with the assistance of Rodolphe Gasché, Jacques Derrida, Sarah Kofman, and Pierre Klossowski, engages these questions on the basis of a discussion of a certain textual confusion: there are two extant versions of section 3 of Part One of *Ecce Homo,* "Why I Am So Wise," versions that do not entirely jibe. Whether the differences between these two versions disturb all conceptions of an identifiable oppositional pair (mother/father), and whether the identity of the Nietzschean autobiography (and the autobiographer) is thoroughly shaken, are the major concerns of the chapter. It ends, as does the final chapter of the book, with a venture into fiction, as though fiction were the vaunted final cure for—or the terminal stage of—all infection.

Chapter 12 offers a reading of Luce Irigaray's *Sea-Lover, She-Lover,* that is, of *Amante marine de Friedrich Nietzsche.* It first traces the parentage of

Irigaray's reading, finding it (in part, at least) in Gaston Bachelard's *L'air et les songes* (1943). Like Bachelard, Irigaray argues that Nietzsche's is preeminently an ascensional thought, a thought of the high mountains, remote from the sea. Here *sea* means woman, the "other," and *mountain* the male, man. Her book, divided into three sections, offers (1) a critical reading of *Thus Spoke Zarathustra*, (2) a discussion of woman as truth *and* dissimulation, and (3) an analysis of the divine brothers Dionysos, Apollo, and Christ. In general, the chapter poses questions to Irigaray's ascensionalist thesis, finding that Nietzsche is closer to the sea than we have acknowledged heretofore. My questions to Irigaray, as fragmentary as her own text, or even more so, are ultimately consumed in a fictional account of Nietzsche's sojourn in Sorrento, near Naples, in 1876–1877, the period of *Human, All-Too-Human*, Part One.

It is clear by the end of the book that Nietzschean infection eats away at all the tissues of narrative and analysis. Literature *not* as life, unless under threat. Nietzsche attacks the writerly organism, throws it off balance, prods it toward its crisis. To that extent he destroys all complacent and coy or confident accounts, diminishes them by a steady, mocking attrition. To that extent no narrative about Nietzsche sustains any privilege over the others. Yet the resulting destitution does not produce some sort of clever oneupsmanship of reading, dismantling, and manipulating. Mortal infection leaves us little to manipulate, and in the end it seems that health and illness do assert an imperious—though confused and confusing—prerogative. That prerogative, or fatality, is not a matter of *sacrifice* in any known cultic or heroic sense. It is rather a matter of tracing the faultlines and shiftings on the superficies of life, where the organic has less and less to do with tools, logics, technologies, and teleologies and more and more to do with unknown resources—such as *gaya scienza*—confronting an irremediable fragility. Infectious Nietzsche negotiates with Asclepius and roosters, but does not forget Lethe, and never presumes to sail the Styx.

INFECTIOUS NIETZSCHE

ONE

Critica genealogica I

Inventories of Decadence

How often do footnotes appear in Nietzsche's works? One such note—is it the *only* one?—appears at the end of the first treatise of the *Genealogy of Morals*. It invites readers to renew the eighteenth-century practice of essay competitions, contests not for schoolchildren but for the likes of a Kant and a Rousseau. In the tradition of such essay competitions, or at the end of it, Nietzsche writes his footnote:

Note. I shall take the opportunity granted me by this treatise to express publicly and formally a wish that heretofore I have uttered only in occasional conversations with scholars: namely, the wish that some one of our philosophy faculties do us the service of sponsoring a series of essay competitions [*Preisausschreiben*] for the furtherance of studies in the *history of morality*:—perhaps the present volume will contribute to the cause, giving a healthy boost in that direction. With a view to such a possible competition, I propose the following question, a question that merits the attention of philologists and historians as well as those who are specifically philosophers by profession:

What directives do linguistics and especially etymological research provide for the history of the development of moral concepts?

—In addition, it is of course every bit as necessary to invite the participation of physiologists and medical people in solving this problem (of the *value* of prior valuations): in this regard it may be left to the professional philosophers to be the advocates and mediators of the particular cases, once they have been able to reconfigure the relationship between philosophy and physiology and medicine, which originally was so inflexible and full of mistrust, but which must now become the most amicable and fecund sort of relationship. Indeed, all tablets of values, every "thou shalt" of which history or ethnological research informs us, must be illuminated and interpreted first of all by *physiology*, even prior to the attentions of *psychology*. All such tablets wait upon a critique on the part of medical science. The question, "What is this or that tablet of values, this or that 'morality,' *worth*?" is to be posed within the most varied perspectives; one cannot analyze to too fine a degree the question as to their "worth *for what*?" For example, something that quite visibly had value because it significantly helped a race to endure (or to enhance its capacity to adapt to a particular climate, or to preserve the greatest number) would not at all have the same value if, say, it were a matter of forming a more robust type. The well-being of the greatest number and the well-being of the smallest number—these viewpoints of valuation are opposed: taking the first to be *inherently* of greater value is something we shall leave to the naiveté of the English biologists. . . . *All* the sciences are now obliged to help advance the philosopher's future task: taking this task to imply that the philosopher must solve the *problem of values*, that he or she must determine the *order of rank among values.*—

Linguistics, etymology, psychology, physiology, and medicine—all bent to the task of a developmental and, above all, *valuative* history of morality. Yet all these disciplines are to be mediated and advocated by philosophers who will have established a new relationship with the sciences. No longer will philosophy lord it over the sciences, disdaining to get its hands dirty as it smugly tidies up their discourses. Nor will philosophy simply capitulate to scientism and the technological juggernaut of the institutionalized sciences. Precisely how the relationship between these sciences and philosophy is to establish itself is the central methodological question of genealogical critique.

To be sure, in view of Nietzsche's relentless attack on science and the sciences and his belief that in our time science must come full circle and turn into *art*, it may be unwise of us to take this invitation to write a prize-winning essay too seriously. With what irony it may have been offered is difficult to assess.

While it is impossible in three brief chapters to do all the work such an essay would require, we may at least try to discuss the following five topics *on the way to* Nietzsche's genealogy contest: the genealogy of *ressentiment* and *decadence*; the genealogy of *ground* and the grounds of genealogy; an *inventory* of the concepts and techniques of genealogical critique; Nietzschean, as opposed to Foucauldian and Deleuzean genealogy; the problem of the *styles* and the *language* of such critique; and the thought of *eternal recurrence of the same* as an antidote to the decadence and the nihilism that genealogy itself uncovers.

RESSENTIMENT AND DECADENCE

Resentment against life and all becoming *constitutes* metaphysical belief: such is the cardinal suspicion of genealogical critique. Genealogical critique tries to work out the origins and the provenance of such rancor and resentment— along with the decadence of a culture that is thoroughly imbued with them— in three descending tiers of investigation: first, the socio-historical, including the linguistic, in which decadence manifests itself as the decline of a civilization—for example, Plato and Socrates as symptomatic of the corruption of life in the πόλις in fourth-century Athens; second, the psychological, in which the drives and instincts of an individual or group, say, the type of the ascetic priest, provides a cipher by which one can decode the essence of their ideologies; and third, the physiological, in which the ill-health or constitutional debility of the type necessitates those ideologies as a defense. Of course, since descending tiers bring us to ever deeper foundations, these three appear here in "ascending" importance. However, inasmuch as *ascent* marks the trajectory of traditional metaphysics and morals, which search high and low for ultimate grounds and categorical imperatives, the suggestion that the three tiers are ordered hierarchically or foundationally is itself problematic, not only epistemologically but also genealogically.

Physiology clearly seems to be the most fundamental of the three. Nietzsche's understanding of the physiology of decadence represents his supreme insight, the brightest gem in the diadem of genealogical critique. The physiology of *ressentiment*[1] interests Nietzsche most, although it is never simply a matter of dissolving philosophy into medicine. The danger of reduction always lurks for genealogical critique, especially in our own age of diagnostic finesse and frenzy. Yet genealogy remains a matter of *interpretation*. True, this interpretation takes the body as its point of departure, rather than, for example, the immediate "certitude" of the cogito, and for the following reason: what I "think," that is, what I project as reality, is most likely no more than the fulguration of the drives or instincts that shape me; what I "think" may be taken to be nothing more than *symptomatic* of a bodily state. Thus Zarathustra says of the "Afterworldly" that it was their *bodies* that despaired of the earth, not some sort of "spirit" that opted for a better world; indeed, it was *the body despairing of itself*, the body hearing the rumbles, grumbles, and groans of "the belly of being talking to it" (4, 36). Thus the "heavenly nothingness" of death speaks always through the belly of being; because the latter can apparently speak in a human way only as long as it is healthy, the noxious nature of heavenly dreams becomes finally evident. Yet the belly of being is also the source of the pains and delusions of the afterworldly, and Zarathustra determines to *teach* health, in order that the sick may "create a higher body for themselves" by listening to the honest voice of the healthy body (4, 37). Zarathustra teaches a *will*, a decision, "no longer to bury one's head in the sand of heavenly things, but to bear it freely, an earthly head that creates the meaning of the earth" (4, 37). Such a decision can occur on the basis of neither disembodied cogitation, on the one hand, nor mechanistic physiology, on the other. For the reduction of the body to a machine is, in Jean Granier's words, "precisely the task of our intelligence, which thereby manifests its complete ineptitude at penetrating the secrets of the organism's dynamism."[2]

Nietzsche's analysis of decadence and genealogy of ressentiment therefore take their clues from the symptomatic evidences of the human body. The "problem of Socrates" (GD; 6, 67–73) is the problem of a decadent rationality, one that battles against all bodily instincts. Indeed, defining virtue and health in terms of this battle is itself a symptom of illness: "To *have* to battle the instincts is the formula for decadence; as long as life *advances*, happiness is like an instinct" (6, 73). The earliest appearances of Western metaphysics and morals are therefore signs of a decline that is already well under way. The slave morality of "good" versus "evil," the morality of ressentiment, Nietzsche calls "a toxic eye," *Giftauge* (ZGM I, 11; 5, 274). Slave morality promotes the ascetic ideal, which, by turning all our emotional energies against the self, has undermined the health of Europeans. Its morality "can be dubbed, without exaggeration, *the real fatality* in the history of the health of the European" (ZGM III, 21: 5, 391–92). The ascetic ideal belongs to the triad of the most widespread destroyers of health—the other two being "alcohol poisoning" and "syphilis." The ascetic ideal is the capstone of ressentiment, which has an actual physiological origin, *wirkliche physiologische Ursächlichkeit,* perhaps in the sympathetic nervous system or in a deficiency of the blood. Decadence expresses itself as an "anarchy of instincts," the disintegration of organizational structures, the destruction of homeostasis, and the wasteful exhaustion of energies; its most debilitating result is excessive sensitization of the individual's nervous system, to the point where one suffocates under the layers of one's own affections and afflictions, unable to react to stimuli, able only to re-sense them to the point of *self-delusion* and *paralysis of the will* (Gr, 213 ff.).

Nietzsche often designates the deterioration or decadence that is instituted by metaphysics and morality as *a decline in will to power* (A, 17; 6, 183–84). Indeed, the notion of will to power first makes its appearance in Nietzsche's writings in connection with morbid symptoms.[3] Such morbidity expresses itself as a flight from reality and life, a flight toward death: metaphysics achieves this escape by means of the *lie.* Lying, or, rather, the compulsion to prevaricate in all matters of ontological import, is a symptom of decadence; decadents "have *need* of the lie, as the condition of their survival" (EH; 6, 312). Morality expresses itself as a self-alienation, *Entselbungs-Moral,* in which the highest values themselves betray the generalized state of decadence. The imperative of such a morality is "Thou shalt perish!" (EH; 6, 372). Western morality, along with its foster-child, metaphysics, are expressions of a morbid ascendancy of impotence to power, *Ohnmacht zur Macht* (WM, 55; 12, 214–15). Nietzsche would approve of Herman Melville's formulation, "Hell is an idea first born on an undigested apple-dumpling, and since then perpetuated through the hereditary dyspepsias nurtured by Ramadans."[4] To be sure, heaven betrays the same origin: "One does not say 'nothingness': one says 'the Beyond,' or 'God,' or 'the *true* life,' or Nirvana, Redemption, Blessedness. . . . This innocent rhetoric from the domain of the religio-moralistic idiosyncrasy immediately seems *much less innocent* when one grasps the tendency that takes these sublime words for its cloak: the tendency that is inimical to life" (A, 7; 6, 173–74).

It is surely not difficult to find evidence supporting Nietzsche's genealogical critique of Christian morality and its doctrine of redemption, that is, his analysis of it as physiological corruption and debility, as ressentiment against all life. An unwitting confirmation appears in the plea of the chorus in Georg Friedrich Händel's cantata, "*Ach Herr, mich armen Sünder,*" the text of which runs: "Heal me, dear Lord, for I am sick and weak; my heart is sore afflicted and suffers great adversity. My bones are a-tremble, full of anxiety and alarm, my soul is all a-tremble, O Lord, why so long?" In addition to the texts of Tertullian and Thomas cited by Nietzsche in *On the Genealogy of Morals,* in which the victory of Christian redemption is invariably coupled with vengeance against one's enemies, be they enemies of the tribe or simply the monk kneeling farther down the pew—"G-r-r-r, you swine!" as Robert Browning's friar mutters—one could add the duet of tenor and bass from the same cantata: "Yield to the voice of my weeping; all my enemies must fall, and come to an ignominious end." (The evidence is more telling, of course, when one hears it sung.) To be sure, Christian love is acclaimed by Christians both before and after Hegel as the antithesis of Judaic hardheartedness and hatred. Yet the gospel of love is the very flower of ressentiment against the suffering that life entails. As Gilles Deleuze remarks, "Christianity loves life as the bird of prey loves lamb: meek, mutilated, and dying."[5] Nothing is more pleasing to the pious Christian eye than the martyred virgin, the limply erotic Sebastians, Suzannes, and Teresas, unless it be the pallid monk in contemplation of the skull: both representations fill the great museums of art throughout Europe and the Americas even today. For the Christian, death becomes the justification of life, the key to its riddle, the liberation from its entanglements; for the Dionysiac, life need not be redeemed by death, however inevitable the end may be, and requires no justification.

THE GENEALOGY OF GROUND;
THE GROUNDS OF GENEALOGY

Yet none of these assertions of a genealogy of decadence and ressentiment enlightens us about the *methods* of genealogy. We must now inquire into two aspects of Nietzsche's genealogical critique of metaphysics and morals, namely, the genealogy of ground and the grounds of genealogy. We shall see how Nietzsche criticizes the Kantian project of transcendental critique, how the problem of ground and grounds nevertheless recoils upon Nietzsche's own genealogy, and how Nietzsche's response to the problem takes us to the bizarre realm of the *underground*, the realm of what I shall call *descensional reflection*.

Nietzsche understands the apparent efficacy and utility of truths as an argument *against* their value and validity. In Jean Granier's words: "Not only is the pleasure inherent in a conviction never able to adorn itself with the title of 'proof,' but it appears rather as an argument against the doctrine that gives pleasure."[6] And again, in Nietzsche's own words: "That for a thousand years European thinkers thought only in order to prove something—inversely, today every thinker who wants to prove something is suspect—that whatever was supposed to be the result of their strictest reflection was always already held fast— . . . this tyranny, this arbitrariness, this rigorous and grandiose stupidity has *educated* the European mind" (JGB, 188; 5, 109).

Thus what Western metaphysics has thought (*gedacht*) now opens itself to suspicion (*Verdacht*): genealogical critique wants to understand how the European spirit has always managed to prove what in its innermost heart it wanted to prove; genealogy wants to learn the secret of spirit's success. " . . . It is finally time to replace the Kantian question, 'How are synthetic judgments a priori possible?' with the different question, 'Why is belief in such judgments *necessary*?'—namely, to grasp that such judgments must be *believed* for the purpose of the preservation of an essence of our kind . . ." (JGB, 11; 5, 25). This sentence cryptically summarizes Nietzsche's advancement of genealogical critique, as the "prelude to a philosophy of the future," against Kant's transcendental critique of pure reason. The first step of this advancement appears as a riddle: *because* belief in synthetic judgments a priori is *necessary*, "we have no right to them" (5, 26). The genealogical clue that leads to such a deduction is the fact that belief in such judgments "belongs to the perspectival optics of life" (ibid.). On the basis of such a clue Nietzsche hopes to comprehend Kant's "proud discovery" of the "how" of synthetic judgments. Kant's answer to the how-question follows the guidelines of medieval alchemy. How does the mind synthesize the manifold of intuition? By virtue of the powers of synthesis, *vermöge eines Vermögens*, "by virtue of a power . . ." (5, 24). After Kant's proud discovery, writes Nietzsche, all the young apprentice-theologians from Tübingen jump into the bushes to see what new "powers" they can find, desperate to locate a power for the "supersensuous" (5, 25). *Incipit* German Idealism. The phenomenon is not restricted to Germany or to Romanticism and Idealism, however; as the 1886 "Attempt at a Self-Criticism" emphasizes (GT; 1, 14, 17), Nietzsche takes as his genealogical clue the perspectival optics of *life*.

However, human life must be distinguished from life in general, that is, from nature as such and across the board. Nature is "wasteful beyond measure, indifferent beyond measure, without intention and reflection, without pity and justice, fruitful and desolate and uncertain all at the same time . . ." (JGB, 9; 5, 21). Life, at least as we humans know it, is "wanting-to-be-different from this nature," an estimating, a preferring, a being unjust, a being limited, willing-to-be-different" (5, 22). Thus every philosophy "creates the world always according to its image; it cannot do otherwise." "Philosophy is the most spiritualized will to power, this tyrannical drive itself to the 'creation of the world,' to the *causa prima*" (ibid.).

Thus the most requisite judgments for human beings, including those that provide the clue for Kant's deduction of the categories, Nietzsche declares to be both indispensable and utterly false (JGB, 4; 5, 18). Odd. For if belief in the truth of such judgments can be recognized to be indispensable for man's survival, the ground of the recognition of their falsity would seem to be the nonsurvivability of the one who recognizes their falseness. Perhaps they are not entirely false—or perhaps they are not entirely indispensable. Here we are doubtless merely repeating the Kantian question: we want to know "by virtue of what power" Nietzsche can recognize, that is, truly see, or see for true, both the indispensability *and* the falsity of Kant's synthetic judgments a priori. And we are approaching, with no little trepidation, the suspicion that such recognition would militate against the life that is served precisely by error, the suspicion that genealogical critique cuts off its nose in order to spite the face of human life.

It occurred to Nietzsche quite "gradually" that every great philosophy is the "unwilled and unnoticed" projection of the interior life of its philosopher, primarily insofar as every philosophy expresses a moral interest, a valuation (JGB, 6; 5, 20). It is not the "compulsion to knowledge" that spins and weaves philosophies, but a "genius" that wills to recognize itself as "the ultimate goal of existence" and the proper master of all compulsion (ibid.). Nietzsche does not explain how this gradual occurrence unfolded, but merely says: "In every philosophy there comes a point at which the 'conviction' of the philosopher enters on stage: or, to say it in the language of an ancient mystery: *adventavit asinus pulcher et fortissimus*," to wit: "Then the ass came out on stage, he was so beautiful and brave!" (JGB, 8; 5, 21).

Yet how does one recognize that moment when it comes? Surely, the braying of the *asinus pulcher et fortissimus* would always be heard as sweet and comforting music—if the will to power in a human being falsified reality from top to bottom. Indeed, Nietzsche seems to recognize that his own recognition of the falsity of synthetic judgments a priori "presupposes that it is precisely not man that is 'the measure of things'" (JGB, 3; 5, 18). Does Nietzschean genealogical critique possess some special access to things, to a "genius" that is not engaged to will to power as will to illusion; is Herr Nietzsche privy to the good and undeceiving daimon, to the divinity who once whispered in Descartes's ear? If that were the case, then the philosophy for which "the falsity of a judgment is no objection to that judgment" could never place itself in a dimension "beyond good and evil" (JGB, 4; 5, 18).

GROUND AS THE CARTESIAN COGITO

Nietzsche's genealogical critique casts doubt on everything it has learned, on all accepted valuations, all highly revered metaphysics, and even its own doubtings. One might ask whether and how Nietzsche—the master of suspicion—employs the method of doubt when criticizing Cartesian "doubting," and whether and how in both cases something like evidence, even apodictic evidence, is achieved through doubt.

Descartes recounts how in his years of maturity he determined to doubt *all* the opinions he had learned in his early years, because only in this way could he eradicate all those that were "doubtful and uncertain."[7] Such doubting would be propaedeutic to a new beginning, an instauration now from the French side of the Channel, a re-education in science and philosophy that would proceed "from the foundations" of knowledge and work its way upward by "firm and stable" steps (267). To doubt all those acquired opinions seems to Descartes to be "an infinite labor"; he determines therefore to go directly to the *foundation* upon which all such opinions are built (268). If he can locate this foundation and subject it to destruction by doubt (*détruire, douter*), the entire edifice of learning will be cleared for redevelopment and reconstruction. Descartes's first decisive step is to locate this foundation in the senses: "All that I have received up to the present, taking it to be most true and assured, I learned from the senses, or by means of them" (268). The second decisive step is to exclude arithmetic and geometry from those things that may suffer distortion through sensibility or even in dreams: even if we dream about a square, that oneiric square will have four sides. Unlike the physical sciences, which consider composite beings, arithmetic and geometry "contain something of the certain and indubitable" (270), precisely because they treat of "quite simple and quite general things," matters that are "noncomposite," hence beyond the physical. The third decisive step, which advenes in the second *Meditation*, is to fasten upon the proposition "I am, I exist" as necessarily true and indubitable.

However, there is a half-step that comes in between the second and third decisive steps. This is the supposition of the "evil genius" or malevolent daimon who conjures the world that human beings believe they behold; this half-step serves to expose the ontological *tromperie* of all nonsimple substances, compelling Descartes to the proposition, "I am," as "the only attribute that cannot be detached" from the doubter (270; 276–77). I call it a half-step because the *third Meditation* goes on to assign the clearest and most manifest "objective reality" to the conception of God, which, after some four thousand words of onto-theo-logical explication, or fudging, appears as "that which cannot be *trompeur*" (300). The never-ending half-step manages to add grace to the second and third steps, by which geometry, arithmetic, and the proposition "I am" receive their moral–ontological status and stature, although it leaves sensibility (and the God who elaborated it) in an awkward position.

According to Nietzsche, Descartes's error is his failure to radicalize the method of doubt. To carry doubt to the foundation of knowledge and learning would be to question above all why one prefers truth to self-deception and "good" to "evil." It would be to question why indeed one prefers to doubt rather than accept whatever deceptions learning proffers. Descartes takes his aversion to deception and his will to truth blandly in stride: he can scarcely wait until he is old enough and established enough to cast into doubt everything that has supported his years and provided his establishment. Genealogical critique suspects the Cartesian self-confidence, the enthusiasm over the doubting project. Is there not something altogether *blasé* about the way Descartes doubts, nestled there by the warmth and light of the hearth, as though there were no impending possibility that some evil genius might discover the fire and douse the glowing embers? Yet divinity does not douse—*tromperie* is, by great good luck, contrary to its nature. Felicitous contrariety! "The fundamental belief of metaphysicians is *belief in the contrariety of values* [der Glaube an die Gegensätze der Werte]. It did not occur even to the most cautious of them to doubt there on the very threshold, where doubt was most necessary: even if it was their sworn oath *de omnibus dubitandum*" (JGB, 2; 5, 16). Cartesian doubt steps blithely across the threshold of the stately edifice of learning, whose ancient foundations are laid by metaphysics and morals, and comfortably dwells within the four-walled security of arithmetic, geometry, a beneficent and undeceiving divinity, and the apodictic proposition, "I am." The last-mentioned, along with its blood-brother, "I *will*," is, according to Nietzsche, the favorite "superstition" of "harmless self-scrutinizers," which is to say, metaphysicians since Descartes. Nietzsche calls it a superstition inasmuch as the cogito believes itself to have captured its object in a "pure and naked" grasp, apprehending it as "an immediate certainty, and even as absolute knowledge" (JGB, 16; 5, 29–30). The "I am," "I will," is an expression that introduces "a sequence of audacious assertions whose ground is difficult, perhaps impossible" (ibid.). And it ignores the temporal flux that precludes the possibility of any immediate certitude; it marks a "momentary occurrence" that one can grasp only by means of a reflection. It ignores the following fundamental questions: (1) Whence the concept *thinking*? (2) Why do I believe in cause and effect? (3) What gives me the right to speak of an ego, indeed, of the ego as a cause, and especially as the cause of thinking? The final question, asked with a smile and a wince at the recoil, is: "Dear sir, it is improbable that you are not in error: but then, why truth at all?" (ibid.).

To the first question, "Whence the notion of thinking?" Nietzsche responds that it is a "popular prejudice" that oversimplifies the most complex phenomena by bestowing on them a single name.[8] In this case, the popular prejudice is *logic*, if not *grammar*, which argues that every deed necessarily implies a doer, and assumes that the proposition "I think" attributes the deed of thinking to the doer, to wit, "me." Nietzsche offers an uncanny alternative to the popular prejudice:

> . . . a thought comes whenever "it" wants, and not whenever "I" want it; thus it is a *falsification* of the factual situation to say that the subject "I" is the condition of the predicate "think." *It* thinks. However, that this "it" should be precisely that notorious old "I," is, to put it mildly, merely an assumption, an assertion; above all, it is not an "immediate certitude." (JGB, 17; 5, 31)

Nietzsche's understanding of "thinking" is nothing less than the "assassination" of the Christian, ontotheological, metaphysical notion of the soul, which in modernity is regarded as the ego of the *ego cogito*, the subject or ground of the predicate "to think" (JGB, 54; 5, 73). Thinking is traditionally assigned to a subject who serves as the ground or cause. Perhaps the reverse needs to be thought about thinking: perhaps the ego is conditioned by thought, is "a synthesis *made* by thinking itself," as Kant on his more Critical days wanted to show. If this is so, then the Christian doctrine of the soul as the ground of free volition also collapses. The difficulty is that the very grammar of our thinking, at least in the Indo-European family of languages, perpetually reinforces the fiction of the "subject" as the doer of a deed; our grammar suggests that the ego is a substance, indeed the core of reality, to which all things are made to correspond. As we shall see in the discussion of language in chapter 2, the structure of our language is a limit or barrier, *Schranke*; to let go of the subject would mean that we no longer permit ourselves to think. It is the grammar of doer and deed, the grammar of metaphysics, that Nietzsche has in mind when he says, "*Truth is the kind of error* without which a certain kind of living creature could not live. The value for *life* ultimately decides . . ." (WM, 493; 11, 506). Belief in the *ego cogito* has deep roots in will to power as will to illusion: " . . . a belief can be a condition of life and *nevertheless be false*," Nietzsche sometimes modestly avers, whereas his considered view is that belief as a condition of life *must* be false.[9] Belief in the *ego cogito*, in the efficacy and mastery of the doer with respect to the deed, serves in Nietzsche's view as the very prototype of metaphysical *substance*: "The concept of *substance* a consequence of the concept of *subject*: *not* the reverse! If we surrender the soul, the 'subject,' then the presupposition for a 'substance' in general is lost. One has *gradients of being*, one loses *the* being" (WM, 485; *12*, 465). The subject-prototype is a consequence of "the supreme feeling of reality," of "life and power," a consequence that quickly gathers to itself all the paraphernalia of logic and metaphysics, to wit, "truth, reality, substantiality," thus lending substance to itself (ibid.). The originary fiction of the subject prototype is *the will*, that is, the feeling of power and mastery that follows the body's response to a command. Thus we must now proceed to the second question.

In the second question, "Why do I believe in cause and effect?" Nietzsche is asking after the cause and effect of the *ego volo*, "I will." I will that my arm moves, and, lo and behold, it moves; thus "I" moved it. Only a philosopher, only one who is innocent of all knowledge of psychology and physiology, only one who rarely moves, could say such a thing. Will is not a fact or a faculty, not a freedom or a certitude, but above all "a multiplicity of feelings," preeminently the feeling of the "away from" and "toward" of a mobile situation; further, it is a "muscular tension" to which we become accustomed and which gives us our "evidence" that our willing puts something into play; finally, will is an *affect*, namely, the "affect of the commando," who says, "*I* command, *it* must obey" (JGB, 19; *5*, 32–33). However, the commander *needs* the assurance of the effect, "Yes, sir, I obey!" just as Hegel's master needs the recognition of the slave in order to recover his own essence as the one who *wills*. Will is an *affect* because it hangs upon the response of the *effect*. Will thus receives its confirmation from its labor: *L'effet, c'est moi*. Will can thus be described as a member of a social structure (*Gesellschaftsbau*) that identifies itself as the essence of that structure, inasmuch as it seems to "govern" the structure, whereas of course it both commands and obeys (ibid.). Thus the will, conceived as a faculty of pure volition, free and unconditioned, is a fiction—albeit one that is indispensable to (human) life. "For there is no will . . ." (WM, 46; *13*, 394). Whence in all the world, one might therefore ask, Nietzsche's notion of *will to power*? That is the question to which we shall turn in the following chapter, but not before proceeding to the third question: "What gives me the right to speak of an ego that thinks?"

Nietzsche fractures the identity of the thinking and willing self by exposing a multiplicity of spectators and specters where there should be but one indubitable spectation of self by self. He introduces a radical dependency into my vaunted independence of will and self-mastery. What brings thinking and willing to such an unhappy state? Nietzsche argues that thinking and willing are notions that must be understood in the context of "relations of dominance," *Herrschafts-Verhältnisse*, under which the phenomenon of *life* originates (JGB, 19; *5*, 34). What gives me the right to speak of an ego that thinks is will to power as will to life. Yet such a right has nothing to do with *truth*. But then, to repeat the final question, the fourth: Why truth at all? It is the impact of this fourth question that one senses in Jean Granier's comparison of Nietzschean and Cartesian doubting:

... Nietzsche is conscious of *doubting* in a manner that is much more radical than Descartes's. In effect, Cartesian doubt is understood only by reference to the project of establishing an absolute certitude. It is supported by tacit faith in the divine value of truth, and it implies confidence in human reason. Thus Cartesian doubt seems to be sustained by a theological postulation; and that is why Descartes hastens to demonstrate that the divine perfection excludes deception; for this permits us to grant our clear and distinct ideas an objective validity. Nietzsche, on the contrary, recalls into doubt our right to search for an absolute certitude now that we have ceased to believe in a God who could guarantee the harmony of the true and the good. Thus he questions whether deception is not inherent in the very structure of being, and whether in consequence it is not necessary to defend illusion against the "nihilistic" attacks of human reason. (Gr, 516 n.)

It is clear that the contrast between the Nietzschean and Cartesian projects could tempt us into a considerable number of detours—one of them being the nature of the *sum* of the *cogito sum,* which is one way of stating the entire project of Heidegger's *Being and Time,* another being the demise of the self in the history of *psychoanalysis.* One feels a certain nostalgia for Descartes's three-and-a-half simple steps down the yellow brick road to indubitable grounds. However, we will never find our way to the cogito again. Today the rue Descartes meanders most ungeometrically through the student section of Paris, weaving its way between antique churches and modern clubs, paced by gaunt men and women with parcels and chased by children with books. Whether one is headed for the musty marbled bishops of Notre Dame, the imposing, reposing heroes of state at the Panthéon, the market at the rue Mouffetard, or simply home, one easily gets lost on the rue Descartes, where dogs have dropped without doubt the only coordinate points to be found.

TRANSCENDENTAL VERSUS GENEALOGICAL CRITIQUE

We must deepen our understanding of the problem of ground by expanding Nietzsche's genealogical critique—which, after all, offers little more than hints—of Kant's Critical philosophy. One may hope that the differences between genealogical and transcendental critique will become more apparent in the process. "The idea of transcendental philosophy," according to Kant, is to provide "universal knowledge" concerning the possibility of human cognition; universal knowledge "must have the character of inner necessity, independent of experience, being clear and certain before itself."[10] More explicitly, "the general task of pure reason" in its transcendental employment is to establish "the ground of the possibility of metaphysics as science," by responding to the question, "How are synthetic judgments a priori possible?" (KrV, B 19–21) Pure reason thus conducts a thorough *inventory* of its possibilities within the realm of "transcendental logic." The latter is a "knowledge of rules" that reveals *that* and *how* certain representations a priori *are possible.* Pure reason in its transcendental capacity thus has the power to rule upon "the origin, extent, and objective validity" of human knowledge *in toto* (A 57; B 81). It has as its domain a thoroughly coherent *system*, which only the absolute unity of pure reason can constitute, and which provides a complete, perfect, and fully articulated touchstone of the correctness of all knowledge (B 89–90). This absolute unity is none other than "the transcendental unity of apperception," which can bring before itself the empirical representation, "I think."

However, in Nietzsche's view, the transcendental unity of apperception is nothing more than the *vermöge eines Vermögens*, the "by virtue of a power." Kant adds one more link to the chain of "powers," one more member to the faculty of reason, but, as Nietzsche asks: "What is that? an answer? a clarification? Or is it not rather a simple repetition of the question? How does opium induce sleep? 'By virtue of the power,' namely, by the *virtus dormitiva*" (JGB, 11; 5, 25). The transcendental unity of apperception gives a name to the phenomenon of synthesis in understanding but brings us no closer to the heart of reason than the Cartesian cogito does.

The "idea" of a transcendental philosophy is to make metaphysics a "science." Its "idea" is the scientific "ideal." The scientific ideal is the child of idealistic metaphysics and morals, and both of these ideals stem from a kind of asceticism. "Both science and the ascetic ideal stand on one ground . . . , namely, on the same overestimation of truth (more correctly, on the same belief in the inestimability, the uncriticizability of truth) . . ." (ZGM III, 25; 5, 402). In its "presuppositions," the "ideal" of transcendental philosophy betrays the same "impoverishment of life" as every other form of the ascetic ideal: emotions are cooled, the tempo of investigation is slowed down, the atmosphere of high seriousness is invoked (5, 403). For Kant there can be no more earnest task than the erection of metaphysics to a science, thanks of course to Kant's own foundational work of transcendental critique (KrV, A xii–xiii; xvi). Such erection is purely the work of pure reason, and not impure reason, conducted in the realm of transcendental a priori nonsensuous purity.

Kant's transcendental analytic wishes to demonstrate in a conclusive way the reciprocal relation of intuition and synthesis in all representation, that is, to demonstrate the orientation of synthetic understanding toward the manifold given in intuition and the dependence of intuition upon the a priori possibilities of understanding. The successful deduction of the categories that define those possibilities establishes limits for speculative reason, limits that would be the *sine qua non* of scientific certitude. However, a "limit" is a border, a security: to establish the limits of certitude is to establish the certitude *of* those limits *within* those limits. How is this done? By means of a *transcendental* inventory. The transcendental aspect of the deduction guarantees infinite certitude for even finite human understanding, inasmuch as the transcendental aspect is secured in an architectonic of pure reason that ostensibly *transcends* the limitations of space and time.

A critique of the faculty of knowledge that purports to have access to "being," so that it can distinguish the "facts of consciousness" from its fictions and dialectical illusions, that is to say, a *transcendental* critique, Nietzsche calls "nonsensical," *unsinnig* (WM, 486; *12*, 104–5). "How should a tool be able to criticize itself when it can only use *itself* for the critique? It cannot even first define itself!" (ibid.). The presupposition behind transcendental critique is that the human intellect has secret access to the impossible *Ding-an-sich*, which is tantamount to saying that at some point it establishes for itself a divine intimacy with "true being" (WM, 474; *13*, 57). Yet the very categories of reason themselves "have a sensuous provenance [*sensualistischer Herkunft*] and are derived from the empirical world" (WM, 488; *12*, 391). There is nothing at all pure about the *genesis* of reason and hence no way at all in which reason could have access to pure concepts a priori. The transcendental analytic thus breaks every sanction imposed on it by the transcendental dialectic. These alternatives emerge: (1) the Hegelian subsumption or sublation of the *Ding-an-sich* into a "logic" that equalizes the human and divine realms; (2) a genealogical critique of the nooks and crannies of consciousness in the perspectives of both Kantian critique and Hegelian logic.

The transcendence of transcendental critique, its secret access to things in themselves and the heart of the transcendental dimension of "powers," transposes Kant to the moral realm where the true meets the good. To be sure, Kant initiates a critique of the naive, tacit identity of the true and the good, but his Critical philosophy stops far short of genealogical critique. Kant's aim is to establish metaphysics as a science, the fundamental science of reason; he clears the way for this project by "interrogating the causes of dialectical illusion of which reason is the victim when it presumes to discourse on 'being'" (Gr, 150). Kant, discovering in the finitude of human intuition, as receptive intuition, the source of the powerlessness that paralyzes reason in its effort to confer on its ideas an ontological objectivity, attempts a critique of the faculty of reason that would "reach the ground of the constitution of logical thought itself" (ibid.). In spite of this intention and this insight, however, Kant "misses the truth of the Critical project," inasmuch as he relies upon the "guiding inspiration" of metaphysics as *belief* while analyzing it as *science*. "The famous *postulates of practical reason* signify precisely that if 'being' is lost for speculative reason, the identity of 'being' and the ideal is conserved for practical reason" (Gr, 150). The relation of subjectivity to the supersensible world is altered but maintained, no longer as "an empirical verification or the conclusion of a syllogism," but as the fidelity of the subject to its innermost essence, namely, obedience to the moral law.

However, it is not simply a matter of criticizing Kant's second *Critique*, although Nietzsche's guns are usually trained on the moral imperative of "practical" reason. For the ascendancy of practical reason is prepared in the architectonic of pure, "speculative" reason. In the preface to the second edition of his first *Critique* Kant writes: "Thus I had to negate *knowledge* in order to make room for *belief*, to forestall by means of a critique of pure reason the dogmatism of metaphysics, that prejudice whose disbelief struggles against morality and is always so very dogmatic" (B, xxx). The second *Critique* is by no means an afterthought, a concession to the piety of Kant's gardener. Its principal postulates are already present in the "Methodology" of the *Critique of Pure Reason* as its "Canon" (A 795; B 823 ff.). It might even tempt genealogical critique to analyze the third antinomy, whose thesis provides that opening for the spontaneity of human causality that is called "freedom"; perhaps its antithesis is weakly constructed, politely allowing the "opening" of the thesis to escape its notice.

In any case, Kant's transcendental critique of the pretensions of pure reason does not bring to suspicion the inveterate confidence in the duality or oppositional quality of values in the metaphysical tradition. It remains confined within the horizon of the Leibnizo-Wolffian metaphysics against which it struggles. At no time does Kant rigorously contest the principle of the duality of being and becoming; rather, he nestles his critique in that dualism. As Granier argues: "The soul of the Kantian meditation is the distinction between appearance and thing-in-itself. Simply said, speculative reason no longer suffices as the axis of certitude, as in Platonism; rather, it is practical reason that suffices. Faith relieves science, and it is now the *factum rationis* of the moral imperative that fulfills the metaphysical need. Thus the Kantian philosophy is only a moral Platonism" (Gr, 41).

Yet this victorious conclusion brings us back to the difficulty we experienced earlier: genealogical critique criticizes Kant for maintaining the distinction between phenomenon and noumenon, between appearance and *Ding-an-sich*. Yet genealogical critique itself asserts that synthetic a priori judgments, while indispensable, are (demonstrably? decidably?) false, insofar as they "belong to the perspectival optics of life." Upon what sort of inventory of possibilities is such a declaration based? Does genealogical critique provide itself with a transcendental ground? What sort of judgment is it that "because such judgments are necessary we have no right to them?" Is it a secularized negative moral theology that now assists genealogy in its predicament? In other words, does genealogical critique ultimately fall back upon the moral plaint of *Recht*—precisely as transcendental philosophy does? Can genealogical critique place itself beyond the horizons of the "good" and the "true" if it *judges* correctness and validity, if it finds doctrines "false" or "unjustified"?

Genealogical critique attacks the *grounds* of the metaphysics of Descartes and Kant, but finds itself compelled to question whether such an attack remains within the Leibnizian metaphysics of *ground*, that is to say, of sufficient reason." Thus when Nietzsche demands an explanation (*Erklärung*) of Kant's *vermöge eines Vermögens*, when he replaces the Kantian question with his demand to understand *why* such a question must be asked, he seems to be asking after the sufficient reason of that question. When he finds that human will to power contorts nature in its philosophies in order to make that nature more acceptable, such power *seems to be* the sufficient reason for declaring the contortion false. When he refers to the projection of subjective drives and needs onto reality, he seems to find such projection the sufficient reason for rejecting its validity claims. However, the metaphysics of sufficient reason searches after that "character of inner necessity . . . being clear and certain before itself." The words are Kant's (KRV, A 1), and they could be Descartes's as well. Leibniz, in this third thesis, finds the ultimate ground of sufficient reason to be God. While the death of God vitiates any such ontology, one must wonder whether Nietzsche's perspectivism is sufficiently grounded in that death, and what such an abyssal "grounding" could mean.

The difficulty can be pushed back even further, from Leibniz and Descartes to their medieval predecessors. Nietzsche wants to show that idealistic metaphysics is indispensable to man, that is, *necessary* for his survival, but false. Like the thinkers of the Middle Ages, Nietzsche proves the necessity of the supersensible world, μετὰ τὰ φυσικά. Convinced that the world of becoming requires redemption, the thinkers of the Middle Ages undertake to demonstrate reasonably how the world is created by God and reconciled to him through the incarnation and passion of the Christ. Nietzsche attempts to undercut such a guarantee by uncovering the genealogy of the conviction that the world demands redemption and the belief that the epiphany of the Christ realizes it. Yet if such undercutting is pushed to its ontotheological extremity it appears that both the medievals and Nietzsche strive to show the *necessity* of the beyond: the first strive to show the *necessity of the true being* of the supersensible world, while Nietzsche strives to show the *necessity of the necessarily illusory* supersensible world. In spite of their difference, expressed for each in the mystery of the death of God, both seem to be in pursuit of the necessary.

The question as to whether or not Nietzsche presumes to occupy a transcendental standpoint is perhaps best approached through the question as to what sort of *inventory* of genealogical techniques he develops. Nietzsche never devotes a particular work to his techniques, which we find scattered— and always only *at work*—throughout his œuvre. Perhaps the following four points concerning the strategies of genealogy can be made by way of a provisional summary:

1. Nietzsche attempts to determine the *value* of previous moralities and metaphysical systems by measuring them according to the bipolar standard of will to power, as either will to ascendant life or will to nothingness.

2. The moral prejudice within metaphysics is uprooted in a historical, psychological, and physiological analysis of the *provenance* of metaphysics:

(a) historical: morality, along with subsequent metaphysical systems, is viewed as the dissolution of the nobility and the victory of the priestly caste and the herd instinct;

(b) psychological: morality, as ressentiment, is seen to be impotence to power;

(c) physiological: morality, as weakness and illness, is ultimately a will to nothingness.

3. This uprooting of traditional values, of the moral prejudice, rests upon the conviction that a fundamentally nihilistic *provenance* expresses the *true* value of past systems, considered from the point of view of power; the truth of this true value is not groundable, but haunts the underground.

4. Such conviction recoils upon itself endlessly as the ontology of *intrigue*, as bootless yet ceaseless *suspicion*. Genealogical critique shatters *grounds* and devalues *values*; it perhaps even develops suspicions concerning will to power and eternal recurrence; it has two mottos: "Profound aversion to reposing once and for all in any one total view of the world. Fascination of the opposing point of view: refusal to be deprived of the stimulus of the enigmatic" (WM, 470; 12, 142); and: "Knowledge is a referring back: in its essence a *regressus in infinitum*. That which comes to a standstill (at a supposed *causa prima*, at something unconditioned, etc.) is laziness, weariness . . ." (WM, 575; 12, 133).

However, before proceeding to the question of the (im)possibility of an inventory, let me try to bring the present inquiry concerning transcendental grounds to a conclusion. The ground of genealogical critique has itself fallen under suspicion, which is the prelude to critique. Is genealogy yet another form of transcendental dogmatism, another act of philosophical *hybris*? Nietzsche has accused Kant of asceticism and piety, the earmarks of decadence and ressentiment. Yet in this Nietzsche knows himself to be a child of Kant. "Have things really changed?" Nietzsche ponders: "Is there today enough pride, daring, fortitude, self-certainty, will of spirit, will to responsibility, *freedom of will* at hand, so that the 'philosopher' on earth is—really *possible?*" (ZGM III, 10; 5, 361). We might rephrase the question in this way: To what extent does genealogical—as opposed to transcendental—critique remain *ascetic* as well as *pious?* Nietzsche more than once descries his own genealogical critique of Western metaphysics and morality from within the horizon of that tradition, indeed as an expression of that tradition: to the compulsion of religious self-cruelty, human beings have sacrificed their youths and maidens (in primitive, "pagan" times), their strongest drives and instincts (in Christian, "moral" times), and now, in the time of nihilism, they sacrifice the object of their beliefs, hopes, and comforts, their God—*out of this same compulsion to cruelty against oneself*, for the sake of "nothing" (JGB, 55; 5, 74). Supreme spirituality is conditioned by a "certain asceticism," so that philosophers always handle the subject of asceticism within a certain bias. The list of philosophic "virtues" suffices to expose this affinity: the philosophic compulsions to doubt, negation, research, analysis, comparison, neutrality, and objectivity—all these are kinds of asceticism. That most philosophic of struggles, the struggle to come to consciousness, where it is not weakness, is "pure *hybris* and godlessness":

> Hybris is today our entire position toward nature, hybris is our position toward God, hybris is our position toward ourselves, for we experiment with ourselves in ways we would not permit with animals, and we strip off the soul from the living body with curiosity and enjoyment: what does the "health" [*Heil*] of the soul matter to us! Beyond that, we heal ourselves: to be ill is to be full of learning, more full of learning, we do not doubt it, than to be healthy—the toxic [*Krankmacher*] seems to us more necessary today than any sort of medicine man or "healer." Now, we exploit ourselves, there is no doubt, we nutcrackers of the soul, we questioning and questionable ones, as though life were nothing other than nutcracking; even so we must every day necessarily become ever more questionable, *more*

worthy to question, and thus perhaps also ever more worthy—to live? . . . (ZGM III, 9; *5*, 357–58)

To pursue such a line of thought is to expose the ascetic underpinnings of genealogical critique as such. This Nietzsche does as early as *The Gay Science*, especially in the aphorism entitled "To what extent we too are still pious" (FW, 344; *3*, 574–77). "Convictions have no rights of citizenship in science," he begins. They must remain "under the watch of the Police of Mistrust." Indeed, science can begin only when conviction ceases. Yet if we are to *begin* such an undertaking, must not there already be an unconditioned conviction that all convictions be sacrificed on the altar of science, and is not science then founded upon one of the "preconceptions" from which it needs to abstain? This conviction Nietzsche calls the *will to truth*. The will to truth is the will not to be deceived, and the general maxim "Do not deceive" rests upon the conviction, "I don't want to deceive *myself*." But why not? Deception seems dangerous to us, so that science could be viewed as a caution and a protection. However, science would have to entertain the question as to whether the will not to deceive oneself is any less dangerous than the will to let oneself be deceived. What is it "in the character of existence that could decide whether the greater advantage lies with the side of unconditional distrust or unconditional trust?" What if existence requires a bit of both? Undoubtedly, to opt for the advantage of total distrust and to engage oneself passionately in the search for "truth" is a moral option; in fact, it is "the basis of morality." If existence depends upon illusion, and Nietzsche is convinced that it does, if human life requires self-deception and a self-blinding self-maintenance, then the devotion to truth is, at the very best, Quixotic chivalry, or at worst, "a principle inimical to and destructive of life." Will to truth could be a "covert will to death," the compulsion to remove the Mayan veil—as Schiller, though not Novalis, conceived of it. If existence, if "life, nature, and history," reveal themselves as essentially amoral, what in the world is the moral of science? The compulsion to truthfulness is without doubt the affirmation of a world other than the world of life, nature, and history; it is the negation of this world. Our belief in science is a *moral, metaphysical* belief, a movement toward the beyond.

However, we will want to know by what sort of intuition Nietzsche is convinced that life, nature, and history rest upon deception. Has he been reading too much Schopenhauer, too much Darwin, too much Ranke? Can we escape the dilemma through the following bit of cleverness: in order to *know* that life rests upon deception, Nietzsche would have to be undeceived in his intuition of life; Nietzsche is therefore either dead or deceived, and, since he was alive when he wrote those words, we have nothing to worry about: Nietzsche was mistaken, just like Schopenhauer, Darwin, and Ranke. Such logical Tartuffery would pass, but for one obtrusive fact, namely, that Nietzsche perceived the difficulty as powerfully as anyone ever has. "Also we knowers of today, we godless ones and antimetaphysicians, our fire too is taken from the torch that enkindled a millennial belief, that Christian belief which was also Plato's belief, that God is truth, that truth is divine. . . . Yet what if precisely this becomes ever-more-unbelievable, if nothing suggests itself anymore as divine . . . ?"

As we pursue the question of the (im)possibility of an inventory of techniques for genealogical critique, it may help to set in relief the following five characteristics of genealogy:

1. Genealogical critique begins and ends with a suspicion that does not bring to a ground that which it suspects, him or her who suspects, or the suspicion itself.

2. Genealogical critique is not itself a science: having no foundation, it cannot build a lasting edifice, much less the Gates of Heaven (and Hell). Nor do its "war machines" ever destroy once and for all any other edifice. Nor is it a shadow cast across things, but only an unsteady eye on them.

3. Genealogical critique is not a dialectical assimilation of whatever it suspects. It does not take even the first step of the dialectic, because the first step is all that dialectic would need in order to be on its way to the absolute. Genealogical critique does not swallow things, assign to them the proper enzymatic categories, suck its nourishment from them, and defecate the world—not even on the rue Descartes. Genealogical critique is not nourishing, and is not particularly healthy. Genealogical critique bumps its head.

4. Genealogical critique, a suspicious eye on things, forgets its near-blindness and only occasionally regrets its bad memory.

5. Genealogical critique is a disappointment to its mother and father; it is the last cindered apple of metaphysics; it takes gaiety as yet another obligation it fails to fulfill. It measures the Dionysian with a slide rule. It is still pious. Even so, it mocks all disappointment and ridicules all ridicule. For genealogy has no ground in the transcendental-critical sense of the word, and even its historical roots are an embarrassment to it. Yet no genealogist, no one interested in family lineages and heraldries, can ignore his or her own origins. Genealogy therefore always boomerangs or recoils. The recoil of suspicion is the *fatality* of this kind of thinking, and it undercuts any move toward a ground or grounds.

GENEALOGY AS FATALITY

My closing remarks, on the *fatality* of genealogical critique, will offer a reading of several passages that appear late in the work *Beyond Good and Evil*. A philosopher, Nietzsche writes, is a human being who experiences, hears, hopes, and dreams "consistently extraordinary things" (JGB, 292; 5, 235). He or she is unlike others, is a thunderstorm, crashing and rolling about in a most uncanny way. He or she is a fatality. "A philosopher: an essence that often flees from itself, has fear before itself—but is too curious not to 'come back to itself' again and again" (ibid.). A philosophy is thus always a "foreground philosophy," always suspicious of its background and its current obsessions: "There is something arbitrary about the fact that *he* stops here, looks back, looks around, that at this point he digs no deeper and puts his spade aside—there is also something dubious [*Mißtrauisches*] about that." (JGB, 289; 5, 234). Every philosophy "also *hides* a philosophy; every opinion is also a cover-up; every word also a mask" (ibid.). Genealogical critique is above all suspicious of its solitude, the fact that it is "unlike others" and presumes to stand over them, as mountains stand over plains, no matter how incontestable and inevitable that solitude is. Genealogical critique finds itself in a "noisy and herdlike age," in which it can win little companionship, meager nourishment. As we shall see in chapter 9, it eats at a table where it really does not belong, "and precisely the most alert of us [*die Geistigsten*], who are hardest to nourish, know of that menacing dyspepsia that arises from sudden insight into and regret concerning our victuals and our messmates—*nausea for dessert*" (JGB, 282; 5, 231).

However, suspicion concerning one's neighbors periodically recoils upon oneself. Genealogical critique is too curious to cease investigation once its neighbors have been diagnosed. It comes back to itself, to the meaning hidden in its own words, to dig deeper, behind the masks. Such reversion to itself does not ride upon the reflection of the cogito, for nothing about this return is clear and distinct. It reaches no ground, but only an abyss:

> Will anyone believe it of me? but I demand that they believe it of me: I have always and only thought badly to myself about myself, only in rare cases, only under compulsion . . . always without belief in the outcome, thanks to an insurmountable mistrust concerning the *possibility* of self-knowledge. . . . There must be a kind of counterwill in me that will not *believe* that there is something determinable about me.—Perhaps a riddle hides there? Probably; but, fortunately, none for my own teeth.—(JGB, 281; 5, 230)

We do not know who speaks in this speech, or what is said. One thinks badly about oneself, but is saved by one's belief in the unbelievability of what one thinks about oneself. There is a will that opposes belief in any kind of "unmediated self-knowledge," any kind of "pure presence" to oneself. One cannot believe that there is anything certain about one's way of life and one's destiny. Perhaps this is a *saving* belief. In any case, the riddle cannot be chewed by one's own teeth. One encounters a *limit* within genealogical critique *even of suspicion*; one collides against the brutal facticity of one's most subversive projects, against what Nietzsche in another context calls the "granite" of "spiritual fate." Judgment falters. Melville has Ahab, shortly before his violent death, asking the question of this determination from beyond, this dismal fatality that conjoins the mortality of man to the death of God:

> What is it, what nameless, inscrutable, unearthly thing is it; what cozening, hidden lord and master, and cruel, remorseless emperor commands me; that against all natural lovings and longings, I so keep pushing, and crowding, and jamming myself on all the time; recklessly making me ready to do what in my own proper, natural heart, I durst not so much as dare? Is Ahab, Ahab? Is it I, God, or who, that lifts this arm? But if the great sun move not of himself; but is as an errand-boy in heaven; nor one single star can revolve, but by some invisible power; how

then can this one small heart beat; this one small brain think thoughts; unless God does that beating, does that thinking, does that living, and not I. By heaven, man, we are turned round and round in this world, like yonder windlass, and Fate is the handspike. And all the time, lo! that smiling sky, and this unsounded sea! Look! see yon Albicore! who put it into him to chase and fang that flying-fish? Where do murderers go, man! Who's to doom, when the judge himself is dragged to the bar?[12]

The recoil of suspicion upon itself is compelled by what Nietzsche meekly—and therefore ironically—calls "curiosity." The compulsion to return to oneself results in the alienation of self from self and the murder of God. The self becomes a wanderer, indeed an *eternal* wanderer, *eternally* homeless.

Wanderer, who are you? I see you going your way, without scorn, without love, with inscrutable eyes; down you go, like a plumb bob, moist and sad, returning dissatisfied from every depth to the light of day. What was the bob looking for down there?—With a breast that does not sigh, with a lip that conceals its nausea, with a hand that only wishes to grasp slowly: who are you? what were you doing? Rest yourself out here: this place is hospitable to everyone—recreate yourself! And whoever you are, what would be your pleasure now? What would serve your recreation? Only name it: what I have I offer you!

"For recreation? For recreation? Oh, you curious one, what are you saying there! But give me, I pray,— —"

What? What? Speak it out!

"One more mask! A second mask! . . . (JGB, 278; 5, 229)

If only one could *stop* reading Nietzsche, if only one could *lose* him, genealogy might secure itself in a ground and lose itself in an inventory of techniques.

To my friend Georg! After you uncovered me, it took no great artifice to find me: the difficulty now is to lose me. . . .

The Crucified[13]

If only one could lose this infectious Nietzsche after hearing the music of his *Zarathustra*. For if the wanderer ever reached home it was there, in *Zarathustra*. However, readers of *Beyond Good and Evil* and the *Genealogy* must deny even this; *Thus Spoke Zarathustra* was a stop along the way, perhaps the most important stop, but it was not a homecoming. For Zarathustra regards his cave in the mountains, his solitude, as his uncanny home. When Zarathustra goes down he *leaves* home. In the third section, Zarathustra speaks of a "*Heimkehr*" (4, 231–34) as a *return* to the mountains, where indeed Nietzsche first elaborates the thought of eternal recurrence. Nor is the difficulty merely one of imagery, for it speaks of Nietzsche's own "gravest danger," his contempt for human beings: "Down there all speech is in vain. There forgetting and passing by [*Vergessen und Vorübergehen*] are the best wisdom: *that* I have learned now. Whoever would grasp everything about human beings would have to grapple with everything [*begreifen, angreifen*].

But for that I have hands that are too pure. I don't like even to breathe in the breath of those others. . . ."

Zarathustra would make his home on the earth, but as close to the heavens as possible, in mountains, not in the valleys of men. His only neighbors would be his eagle and snake, his soaring pride and his earthly wisdom. At the end of the aphorism, Nietzsche writes about the (future) practice of genealogical critique: "Gravediggers [researchers and testers] bury themselves in illness. Under old refuse lie evil vapors. One should not stir up the morass. One should live in the mountains" (ASZ III; 4, 234). Zarathustra's going down and under responds to a need on Zarathustra's part to be heard. The mixture of play and seriousness, gaiety and sobriety, affirmation and negation, in Zarathustra's language gradually goes down to the undercutting language of genealogical critique. Zarathustra never returns home. Forgetting . . . passing by . . . pure hands . . . breath . . . gravedigging . . . evil vapors: these are chilling words to Dionysian ears, to the labyrinths of Ariadne.

The philosopher of genealogical critique has before his or her eyes the fatality of the mission: "The ruin, the collapse of higher human beings, of strange-natured souls, is namely the rule . . ." (JGB, 269; 5, 223). The most creative human beings suffer from the morbidity (*Heillosigkeit*) of the eternal "too late!" Their only means to health is a "flight and forgetting," which they call their "handiwork" or craft. They ostensibly shun women, whose "best and deepest love" is more likely to destroy than to rescue them. Even so, the creator *needs* love, demands love as much as Jesus did, who created a hell for those who refused to love him; Jesus, who had to have a Father-God who *was* love, the very capacity to love. "Whoever feels this way," Nietzsche writes, in a passage as full of hiatuses or *Gedankenstriche* as any he ever wrote, "whoever *knows* this about love—*seeks* death" (5, 225). And if one should insist on the naive question, "—But why hang on such painful matters?" Nietzsche will interrupt every possible answer with this: "Presuming that one does not have to.—" (ibid.).

Nietzsche's reflection on the fatality of the higher human being, the hardest and bravest nutcracker of souls, ends with a vision of the Crucified. What is the fate of this heroic Antichrist? What is genealogical-critical reflection *as* a fatality? William Butler Yeats writes, in "Phases of the Moon,"

> . . . Eleven pass, and then
> Athene takes Achilles by the hair,
> Hector is in the dust, Nietzsche is born,
> Because the hero's crescent is the twelfth.
> And yet, twice born, twice buried, grow he must,
> Before the full moon helpless as a worm.[14]

The poet envisages at mid-moon the one who wished to teach the mid-day of overman. At mid-moon Nietzsche writes of *eternity*:

One!

O humanity! Take heed!

Two!
What does the deep midnight say?
Three!
"I was sleeping, sleeping—,
Four!
I awoke from a deep dream: —
Five!
The world is deep,
Six!
And deeper than the day had thought.
Seven!
Deep is its woe—,
Eight!
Desire—deeper yet than agony:
Nine!
Woe says: Pass away!
Ten!
Yet all desire wants eternity—
Eleven!
—wants deep, deep eternity!"
Twelve![15]

Is "twelve" the noontide of overman, as Zarathustra desires, or the "twelve" of midnight? Or what is the poet's broader scope, which sees the "twelve" as a phase of the moon? How does the poetic word fracture the dilemma of our previous alternatives, and yet preserve the ambiguity of what is to be thought?

As we shall see in chapter 5, the foreword to the second edition of *Daybreak*, composed near Genoa in the autumn of 1886, provides an excellent example of Nietzsche's ironic stance toward his own fondest works. It calls the work of examining moral prejudices the tedious, life-consuming labor of that blind and lonely subterrestrial animal, *the mole*. It also evokes the image of the gravedigger—perhaps that rascal of Shakespeare's *Hamlet*—who is strangely satisfied in his work. From his depths he sees kings and princes come and go; he is at home in his work, if one may paraphrase Marx, which is to work on the final home for all mortals. What curious satisfaction might this grizzly occupation provide? What serene confidence supports the undergrounder? Could it be the belief of Dostoyevsky's man from *Underground*: ". . . I believe my liver is diseased . . ."? Or is it that the genealogist's long obscurity, his or her hidden and enigmatic occupation, rests on the ground of an anticipation of redemption (*Erlösung*), of a new daybreak?

The fourth book of *The Gay Science* ends with the account of Zarathustra's address to the sun and his decision to go down to human beings—the beginning of Zarathustra's downgoing. In *The Gay Science*, though not in the text of *Thus Spoke Zarathustra*, Nietzsche precedes this story with the words "*Incipit tragœdia*." In the autumn of 1886, during the same days that produced the foreword to *Daybreak*, Nietzsche prepares a foreword to the second edition of

The Gay Science. The final sentence of the opening paragraph of the foreword reads "'*Incipit* tragœdia'—is what it says at the conclusion of this dubious indubitable book: one should be on guard! Something outrageously malignant and malicious is announcing itself: *Incipit* parodia no doubt . . ." (3, 346). The first sentence of the second paragraph reads: "—However, let us leave Herr Nietzsche alone: what does it matter to us that Herr Nietzsche got well again? . . ."

Herr Nietzsche warns us that the announcement of a tragedy should put us on our guard: the tragedy of Zarathustra, his going down, may well be a parody. The undergrounder, the mole and gravedigger, spins a tale which, if we are to take it *seriously*, must be taken at least in part as a prank, as lighthearted and yet most profound ribbing. What has the lover of wisdom to do with joking? He is Greek—where is his nobility, his manly virtue? Is not the parodist worthy of our contempt, is not he above all a *decadent*? Where is the *courage* of the parodist's convictions? Or is it true that the best lack all conviction, while the worst are full of passionate intensity?

Perhaps the courage demanded by our times is suspicion against conviction, as long as that courage does not itself become a conviction. Perhaps Nietzsche is trying to initiate us into the slow, tedious, even painful practice of what in chapter 6 I shall call a *hermeneutics of discretion*.

What Nietzsche wants us to achieve, with the reversal of metaphysics and morals, is a decisive end to dogmatics, an end that is not itself dogmatic. The genealogist's life is thus an endless series of recuperations. Do we say "endless"? If we are to remain true to the earth, must we not acknowledge death to be the final recuperation? And if we so name death, are we not returned to the Schopenhauerian pessimism of decadence? Yes, indeed, unless Nietzsche means by "recuperation" something other than our everyday notion of it. The following text, from the foreword to *The Gay Science*, sheds light on our question:

> A philosopher who has struck out on a path through many periods of health, and done so again and again, has also passed through as many philosophies: . . . this art of transfiguration *is* precisely philosophy. . . . I doubt whether such pain "improves" one; but I know that it *deepens* one. . . . One's trust in life goes up in smoke: life itself becomes a *problem*. . . . Even love of life is still possible—it is merely that one loves otherwise. It is the love of a woman who causes us to doubt. . . . We know a new happiness. . . . (3, 349–51)

Recuperation may be the valley formed by the peaks of self-inflicted woundings. Life, conceived as will to power, becomes a problem. We have in this first brief account of genealogical critique uncovered some aspects of the problem. What is strangest in this strange passage, however, is the new possibility of the *love* of life, which is the love of a woman who makes us doubt. We doubt her "fidelity," perhaps, which is no more than saying that we doubt our own capacity to draw her flesh to our flesh, which is no more than saying that we are driven to distraction by her secret life, which, being secret, may be *his*, or *hers*, but certainly not *ours*. Who is equal to this new happiness?

Precisely how difficult it is to think Zarathustra's downgoing, and the communication of Nietzsche's most difficult thinking, the eternal recurrence of the
same, we shall see in later chapters, especially chapters 3 and 8. Both as genealogical critique and as the thinking of eternal return, Nietzsche's infectious
philosophy goes under. It refuses ascension, and remains worthy of question. It
remains, as we shall see, *descensional*.

TWO

Critica genealogica II

The Decadence of Inventories

In Nietzsche's struggle against the metaphysics and morality of Christianity, writes Eugen Fink, the philosopher "mobilized every weapon he could muster: his refined psychology, the sharpness of his wit, his fervor, and above all else his style."[1] We might well go in search of the linguistic, social, psychological, and physiological dimensions of genealogical critique; yet we despair of an adequate inventory of Nietzsche's fervor, wit, and style—we cannot obviate the necessity of *reading* Nietzsche. We certainly cannot provide an inventory that would "miss nothing essential" in the area canvassed, thanks to a transcendental deduction of *all possible* techniques. Where not "methodical doubt" but haunting, persistent *suspicion* propels critique, an inventory seems hopeless.

DELEUZE, FOUCAULT, AND GENEALOGY

More than one such attempt has been made, Gilles Deleuze finding enough congenial material to form a "table" of genealogical techniques, hypotheses, mechanisms, principles, products, and conclusions (Dz, 166). Here the dual *typology* of "active" and "reactive" types of force is elaborated through a series of "variations" and culminates in the classification of types according to the affirmative or negative quality of will to power operative in them. A *topology* of active and reactive forces in human consciousness, here taken in such a way as to include the "unconscious," leads to the deduction of types, to a *disjunctive typology* within will to power of either active or reactive specimens, either master or slave, yes-sayer or no-sayer, Dionysus or Crucified. What lies behind the construction of this topo-typo-logical table is the method Deleuze calls *dramatization* (Dz, 88–89). In order to classify individuals, groups, or epochs according to the quality of will to power they exhibit, one must ask two questions: (1) *Who* is it that wills or wants such-and-such; for example, who is it that wills "truth"? (2) *What* does this type (truly) will or want? The second question presupposes that the practitioner of genealogical critique is somehow in a privileged position, that he or she can more incisively determine who or what wills or is willed than the object to be classified. Yet this privilege is exactly what our frustrated inventory wishes to take stock of, tabulate, and tag. According to the interpretation we are now considering, the aptness, keenness, precision, and power of genealogical critique depend on the efficacy of its *dramatic method*. That method treats all types of human beings, overmen, last men, gods, and demigods as "symptoms of the will" or "metamorphoses of Dionysus," that is to say, as reducible to one or other pole of the disjunctive, bipolar will to power (as either affirmative or negative).

Yet one should not underestimate the difficulties involved. If genealogical critique shatters the spectator-spectated circuitry of transcendental critique and opens the floodgates to what heretofore remained outside the transcendental purview, then genealogical critique is literally overwhelmed with tasks: "In effect, a type is a reality at once biological, psychical, historical, social, and political" (Dz, 132). In other words, every type finds at least one or other aspect of its *provenance* or *Herkunft* in each of these realms—in which the genealogist must be at home, if only as a nomad.

The cardinal distinction between transcendental and genealogical critique is the significance for the latter of extrarational factors, as opposed to purely rational conditions of possibility. The genealogist is not the judge at a tribunal in the Kantian sense, is neither an advocate of the moral law nor the moral mechanist of a purely utilitarian bent; he or she is rather the *Hesiodic* poet-scientist of the *origins of values*, a sort of theogonist and cosmogonist of hierarchies of values. However, this implies that the genealogist is as much an enthusiast or rhapsode of values as their sober, somber recorder: "Genealogy means at one and the same time the value of the origin and the origin of values."[2] Yet precisely what is this appreciation of, or even enthusiasm for, the value of origins? That is difficult to say, as Michel Foucault confirms. One might ask, dramatically: *Who* wills to find the origins? or *What* is it (truly) that is willed in the search for origins? *Who* or *what* do we descry behind the enthusiasm?

This is indeed, as Jean Granier concedes, a "grave difficulty" (Gr, 164–65). It suggests that the question of the *truth* of values lies hidden in the very genealogy that wishes to surpass the question of "truth" toward that of the "value" of values. As soon as I diagnose active and reactive types, "I fuse judgment of reality and normative judgment, and my interpretation is *verdict*" (Gr, 166). Behind or beneath such a diagnosis must lie neither "brute facts" nor "clear and distinct reasonings," both of which genealogical critique has surrendered, but "an experience of being that would already be in itself an *evaluation*, that is to say, an experience that would give evidence of a decision on the part of the subject concerning the meaning of being" (Gr, 167). However, has not "being" too, "being" first of all, been surrendered?

We must sharpen the problem by examining two statements from the first chapter of Deleuze's *Nietzsche and Philosophy*, one from the outset of the chapter, the other from its conclusion. At the outset, Deleuze is at pains to distinguish genealogical critique from the reactive force, ressentiment, and decadence that are endemic to transcendental projects. The driving force of genealogical critique, Deleuze argues, "is not a re-action of re-sentiment, but the active expression of an active mode of existence"; that is to say, genealogy is "attack, and not vengeance, the natural aggressivity of a manner of being, the divine maliciousness without which one could not imagine perfection."[3] The hyperactive Deleuzean genealogist does concede that "Nietzsche is expecting many things from this conception of genealogy," among them "a new organization of the sciences, a new organization of philosophy, a determination of the values of the future" (Dz, 3); yet there is no hint that such great expectations are unrealistic or that the forces driving them may well be reactive. By the end of the chapter, however, the relation of genealogical critique to the reactive forces that an active mode of existence is seeking to overcome has become somewhat more problematic, whether Deleuze desires this complication or not. For the "instinct of vengeance" is the very force that constitutes the sciences as we know them—including the sciences on which genealogy depends, namely, physiology, psychology, and history, at least as these sciences have developed during the history of metaphysics and morals, which is the history of nihilism. Does this instinct of vengeance still infect *our* way of engaging (in) these sciences? Deleuze writes: "The spirit of vengeance is the genealogical element of *our* thought, the transcendental principle of *our* manner of thinking" (Dz, 40). Without wishing to imitate too blatantly the Derridean gesture, one nevertheless feels constrained to ask the Hesiodic-genealogical question: *Our* thought? *our* manner? but *whose, ours?*

We have seen that Nietzsche's genealogical critique is not "immanent" in pure reason, which, in any case, does not exist for it. The principles of its critique cannot be pure, a priori principles; they cannot summarily state the conditions of the possibility of knowledge; yet these "genetic and plastic principles" that discern the meaning (*sens*) and value of existence even while speaking *contre-raison* purport to lay bare the genesis of *knowledge itself* (Dz, 104–7)! Accordingly, when genealogical critique surrenders the mask of the "sage" in order to don that of the "legislator," one must wonder whether such a legislator would not have to be the "dizzy legislator" of Plato's *Cratylus* (411 b–c), an ancestor of the "modern philosophers" of Socrates' time who find things spinning about in such a state of flux that the very *naming* of them betrays disequilibrium and confusion. The mask of the sage is not so easily removed. The spirit of vengeance is not so easily assuaged. We must attempt another inventory, this time with the help of Michel Foucault.

Genealogy may be "gray, meticulous, and patiently documentary," as Foucault says, but it is anything but blasé about *origins*.[4] The negative thesis of Foucault's "Nietzsche, Genealogy, History" is that genealogical inquiry into the *provenance* or *Herkunft* of values is not a hymn to origins. All teleological (and archaeological?) conceptions of history are alien to it. Foucauldian genealogy strives to recognize that "the world of speech and desires has known invasions, struggles, plundering, disguises, ploys," and that what genealogy must rescue is the singularity and particularity of all historical features. More, it must recognize the fundamental *discontinuity* of history—as Bataille insisted we must recognize the discontinuity of *being*.[5] The paradoxical result is that while genealogy demands "relentless erudition" (140), it is nowhere bolstered by a confidence in either "origins" or "ends," which Foucault, like Nietzsche, leaves to the "English moralists." What genealogy instead emphasizes is *disparity* and *difference*: "What is found at the historical beginning of things is not the inviolable identity of their origin; it is the dissension of other things" (142). For genealogy, history is resistance, and memory countermemory.

Thus Foucault subjects the romance of commencements to ridicule. Whereas a thinker like Heidegger cannot think highly enough of commencements, so much so that everything that follows from them is invariably a fall from their primal, pristine elevation, Foucault finds such commencements derisory. Origins, happily, are lost, and the hymn to origins is a matter for caricature. "The origin lies at a place of inevitable loss, the point where the truth of things corresponded to a truthful discourse, the site of a fleeting articulation that discourse has obscured and finally lost" (143). However, the effects of the loss cannot be alleviated by the caricature. Satire never satisfies. Whereas a nomadic Deleuze is happy to construct genealogy as a machine of war, the restive Foucault is most keenly aware of the *recoil* or *kick* of the machine back onto the discourse that would fire it.[6]

In Foucault's genealogy, the vicissitudes of history, which are inaccessible to any knowledge or episteme of the classical sort, are matched by the vagaries of the body, which no physiology can ever plumb. Nevertheless, in the movement from human history to the human body, a difficulty for Foucault too arises. For the genealogist "must be able to recognize" the discontinuities of history, and, "similarly," must be "able to diagnose the illnesses of the body, its conditions of weakness and strength, its breakdown and resistances . . ." (145). However, whether the etiology of disease, the establishment of physiological damage or debility, can accept the inevitable recoil of discontinuities, disparities, and differences onto its own research is questionable—particularly if the body in question is that of the genealogist. No disparaging of origins and no celebration of "descent," *Herkunft*, will dissolve the problem of a gnawing uncertainty about the "great health" of infectious genealogy.

It is true that what I am here calling "descensional reflection" receives an unexpected twist in Foucault's essay: for Foucault, "descent" means primarily the *stock* or *ancestry* of which we are the "descendants"; descensional reflection would meditate on its forebears, viewing itself as a kind of *progeny*. Yet nothing about our family tree would be edifying, and nothing about our genealogy would be purely informative. For what genealogy discovers is not the "truth" or "being" that lies at the root of "what we know and what we are," but "the exteriority of accidents" (146). Thus neither history nor the body can tell us who we are; neither can allow us confidently to dissect the histories or bodies of others. "The search for descent is not the erecting of foundations: on the contrary, it disturbs what was previously considered immobile; it fragments what was thought unified; it shows the heterogeneity of what was imagined consistent with itself" (147). Yet if this is so, what becomes of the genealogist's arsenal, the machines of war, the contrivances against an enemy that genealogy had putatively sealed off in immobility, unity, and homogeneity? *Who* is the enemy? *Who* wants to rout the enemy? Our bodies bear the wounds inflicted by the father and the mother, but we sons and daughters will never know the radical discontinuities of which our own bodies are the code. If the body is "totally imprinted by history," that history is itself irruptive and interruptive, anything but a continuity. No matter how relentlessly the body has been subjected, the "play of dominations" to which it has been subjected in its history is "hazardous" (148), in at least two senses: *dangerous* in the extreme, and a matter of *chance* and radical contingency, thus utterly resistant to discourse. Any reflection on history and the body *goes down*, and such downgoing or descent is *irrecuperable*.

Even if the genealogist dreams that the play of dominations is "fixed" in a history, indeed "throughout" the history of the body, which is itself "fixed" in rituals and codes, that dream is itself subject to interruption in the form of "substitutions, displacements, disguised conquests, and systematic reversals" (151). The genealogist soberly records the history, or counterhistory, of such unfixed fixations, yet can no longer be buoyed by the critical historian's "apocalyptic objectivity" (152). Foucault reaffirms that even the "exclusive laws of physiology" on which the genealogist might hope to depend are subject to the discontinuous history that is the only efficacious history (*wirkliche Historie*) we know. "Nothing in man—not even his body—is sufficiently stable to serve as the basis for self-recognition or for understanding other men" (153). Discontinuous physiology and history thus introduce discontinuity into "our very being" (154), and we discover that the events that make us are "countless lost events," that the distinguishing features of our descensional landscape offer no stable point of reference (155). If history is to become "a curative science" (156), the first thing it must cure us of is our confidence that we ascend to knowledge of our disease. If Nietzsche prides himself on the explicitness of his perspective, which grants him the power of "deliberate appraisal," he must nevertheless meditate on the downward-tending perspective of that very pride.

It is unclear whether Foucault draws the full consequences of the recoil in descensional reflection. At times he appears to be sanguine about its nature, trusting that it will empower and enable a "vertical projection" for genealogy: "Through this historical sense, knowledge is allowed to create its own genealogy . . ." (157). Allowed? One would have thought that—for Nietzsche at least—the word would have to be *compelled*. " . . . Allowed to create its own genealogy in the act of cognition; and '*wirkliche Historie*' composes a genealogy of history as the vertical projection of its position" (157). Yet a vertical projection is an architectural *elevation*. One would have thought that the vertical projection would constantly be made to tremble by horizontal and horizonal interruptions, discontinuities, and displacements. It sometimes seems that the Foucauldian genealogist dreams the repetitive dream of a transcendental critique intent on inventory: "Nothing must escape it and, more importantly, nothing must be excluded" (157). Yet Foucault himself is aware that the genealogy of history can pursue genealogical analysis only if it is shaken in its piety, its demagogy, and its "religious knowledge," that is to say, only if it is "seized, dominated, and turned against its birth" (159). Such seizure produces three effects, corresponding to the three types of history that Nietzsche identifies in the second of his *Untimely Meditations*. What used to be "monumental history" is now *parody* and *farce*: the genealogist alters Marx's observation that great events occur the *second* time as farce, noting now that farce is what they always were. The genealogist "will push the masquerade to its limit and prepare the great carnival of time where masks are constantly reappearing" (161). What used to be "antiquarian history," taking pride in the identity guaranteed by all its artifacts, is now *the systematic dissociation of identity* (161). "The purpose of history, guided by genealogy, is not to discover the roots of our identity but to commit itself to its dissipation" (162). Finally, what used to be "critical history" now goes all the way, insisting on *the sacrifice of* (objective genitive) *the subject of knowledge* (162). It is this sacrifice of the subject of knowledge (the genitive is objective, but it is executed by the subject, hence, objective/subjective) that most merits our attention.

Foucault recognizes that the will to know involves "the inquisitor's devotion, cruel subtlety, and malice" (162). He realizes that genealogical research "delights in disturbing discoveries," and that there is something malicious in its very sobriety (163). As though once again drawn by Bataille, Foucault insists that just as religions once sacrificed bodies, genealogical critique will now sacrifice subjects of knowledge. Moreover, he concedes that there is rancor in such insistence. The final page of Foucault's essay, which appears to be truncated, as though Foucault's discourse were bitten off precisely at the point of this sacrifice, insists on "unavoidable sacrifice," "the idea of humanity sacrificing itself," and indeed "sacrificing the very movement of life to the exclusive concern for truth" (164). Which takes us back to Nietzsche's wry question to the genealogist: " . . . and thus makes us worthier—to live?"

The concept of "truth" thus reemerges at the end, taking up its ancient position *against life*. If the concept is altered, it is not altogether abashed, and indeed it is more deadly than ever: "It is no longer a question of judging the past in the name of a truth that only we can possess in the present; but risking the destruction of the subject who seeks knowledge in the endless deployment of the will to knowledge" (164). As though deaf to Nietzsche's invocation of masks and his praise of the profound superficiality of the Greeks, Foucault uncompromisingly insists on the deadly carnival of genealogical erudition. Parody, systematic dissociation, and the "sacrifice" and "destruction" of the subject of knowledge, who looks very much like the genealogist, "who maintains knowledge by the injustice proper to the will to knowledge," will carry the day, " . . . in spite of the objections that Nietzsche raised in the name of the affirmative and creative powers of life" (164).

Were they mere "objections"? Or were they the heart of Nietzsche's frustrated genealogical inventory, the only means by which genealogy could prevent itself from collapsing back into the apocalyptic carnival of asceticism? And would not an inquiry that acts *in spite of* the creative powers of *life* be forced to concede its fatal affinity with the very decadence it takes itself to be countering? Would not such an inquiry erect impotence to power, would it not activate by reaction alone?

A NIETZSCHEAN INVENTORY?

I shall attempt no transcendental deduction of critical techniques, but simply offer a brief description of those Nietzsche most often employs. Genealogical critique involves itself in an analysis of the *provenance* of the fundamental doctrines of metaphysics and morals. As I indicated in the preceding chapter, three broad areas of inquiry provide material for this analysis: (1) the socio-historical aspects of the development of metaphysics and morals, in which the exigencies of the human being as a being that is socially organized for the sake of its preservation and domination are seen to *require* them; (2) the psychological typology of individuals and groups who produce metaphysical and moral systems out of a *need* that becomes disguised within those systems; (3) the physiological motors of such needs, likewise disguised within those systems. Nietzsche turns to these areas of analysis, rather than to traditional modes of metaphysical and moral inquiry, on the basis of several clues: (1) the origin of the (true) value of such systems can only be determined by the study of a vertical cut of such systems; that is to say, the hidden *provenance* of such systems alone provides the proper source of their intelligibility; (2) the intelligibility of such systems depends upon a semiology whose key is found in the assertion that the value of any given system is its power-preserving and power-enhancing character; (3) philosophic reflection, as thought thinking itself, cannot uncover the code of such systems, inasmuch as such systems maintain their value only as long as their origin (their value for life) remains disguised (Gr, 152–53; Dz, 3–4).

The clues revolve about an axis that runs through the core of Nietzsche's intuition concerning the existence of human beings. In that most famous of Nietzsche's unpublished writings, the 1873 "On Truth and Lie in an Extra-Moral Sense" (1, 875–90), Nietzsche expresses this intuition in words which, for all the lack of the later subtlety and sophistication of genealogical critique, express his most profound genealogical thinking: human life has flourished on the earth, and has even reached the threshold of an unchallenged dominion over it, on the basis of the single and singular weapon of *intellect*. Intellect is the sole *Hilfsmittel* available to this most vulnerable creature, who has had to abandon the protective web of trees in search of nourishment; to compensate for its relative lack of strength and speed, the human being has only its cunning. Yet this cunning of reason is not as edifying as the Hegelian sort. For humans must operate behind the backs of the other animals and of other humans. Deception and shrewdness are their two incisors, determining the way they organize and the way they hunt. In time they shape the way human beings think. Yet precisely this thinking—the pride of the species—remains mysterious and unknown. Nature has thrown away the key: " . . . and woe to the fatal curiosity that might peer just once through a crack in the chamber of consciousness, and look to the outside, then down, and sense that human being rests upon the merciless, the greedy, the insatiable, the murderous, in the indifference of its ignorance, hanging in dreams, as it were, onto the back of a tiger. In this constellation, whence in all the world the urge for truth?" (*1*, 877).

Where humanity is concerned, the truth is always ugly, thus necessarily covered over and obscured; on this obfuscation hinges the contingent survival of human being. However, from the very start, it is the necessity of this obfuscation that astonishes Nietzsche. For what would it mean to peer outside a cracked consciousness? What about the sequence—looking to the outside of the chamber, then presumably down into it? Whence in all the world the genealogist's insight into matters that life and nature are at pains to obfuscate? That is the question that troubles the very opening of the essay, which we possess in two different versions. For in the first of his *Five Prefaces to Five Unwritten Books*, written during the Christmas holidays at Tribschen in 1872 and dedicated to Cosima Wagner, Nietzsche first formulates that extraordinary opening. The version from the preface to the unwritten book, *On the Pathos of Truth*, appears below in the left-hand column, the opening of "Truth and Lie" on the right:

PATHOS OF TRUTH

TRUTH AND LIE

In some remote corner of universal space, glimmering with the numberless solar systems that were spilled out into it, there was once a star on which clever animals invented *knowing*. It was the most arrogant and mendacious minute of universal history, but still only a minute. After nature drew a few breaths, the star congealed, and the clever animals had to die. It was also high time: for although they boasted that they had already managed to learn much, in the end, and much to their displeasure, they uncovered the fact that they had learned everything falsely. They died, and in dying they cursed the truth. That was the way of these despairing animals who had invented knowing.

In some remote corner of universal space, glimmering with the numberless solar systems that were spilled out into it, there was once a star on which clever animals invented knowing. It was the most arrogant and mendacious minute of universal history, but still only a minute. After nature drew a few breaths, the star congealed, and the clever animals had to die. — Someone could invent a fable of this sort, and yet they would not have sufficiently illustrated how lamentable, how shadowy and fleeting, how purposeless and arbitrary the human intellect appears within nature; there were eternities in which it was not; and when once again it is all over for the intellect, nothing will have eventuated.

The "fable" of "Truth and Lie" replaces the daimonic "high time" of the clever animals' extinction. It is as though the fable, so reminiscent of the "Fable" of *Twilight of the Idols*, "How the 'True World' Finally Became a Fable," protects an instant longer the fragile life of the clever animal who through genealogical critique "uncovers" the fact that cognition is distortion, that knowing is self-deception. The *pathos* of truth would also require a *passio* of the one who attains it—even and especially if truth should turn out to be a *necessary illusion*.

This fundamental intuition both underlies and undercuts all the *clues* to the *deduction* of available techniques, as well as the genealogical techniques themselves. Regarding the clues to the deduction, we will for the moment have to be satisfied with the following brief remarks:

1. The vertical cut of metaphysico-moral systems uncovers the provenance of those systems in the attempt to obscure man's murderous character from himself, to cover deceit with deceit. The social and historical conditions of the systems obviously vary; what they have in common is the will to power of the individual who concocts the system and the will to power of the group that embraces it. The former could be a crippled Cro-Magnon, unable to hunt or supply tools and equipment, who in his dotage and debility becomes a shaman; or, in a much later age, a psychically crippled "ascetic" who whips himself and the members of his cloister beneath the crucifix; the group would be the tribe or cloister that through one or other mechanism of inversion and projection shares in the power of the teacher.

2. The preservation and enhancement of will to power is always at issue in the ideologies of individuals and groups of human beings. The psychological conditions of ideology are *fear* and *forgetfulness*; the psychological weapons are *flattery* and *deceit*.

3. Physiological inadequacies and incapacities of humankind as a species and of particular individuals within the species require the refined deceitfulness of metaphysico-moral systems. The systems retain their power, however, only as long as their origin (debility) and provenance (impotence to power) remain obscure. Philosophical thinking spins the thickest webs in order to preserve the necessary obscurity—at least until the Nietzschean daimon, having uncovered the deception, spins its fabulation of the demise of these clever animals.

On the basis of these clues and suspicions, genealogical critique exposes the structure of the will to power "that animates a certain kind of reflection," namely, metaphysico-moral reflection, and conducts "a genealogical deduction of ideologies by reference to . . . will to power" (Gr, 17; 149 ff.). We must therefore interrupt our perpetually interrupted inventory with an inquiry into this most troubling of Nietzschean conceptions, to wit, *der Wille zur Macht*.

WILL TO POWER AS
GENEALOGICAL *FA(C)TUM*

Because Nietzsche never systematically formulated his notion of will to power, or developed an ontology that might be grounded on such a conception, my survey of it here remains provisional. In any case, one must oppose the tendency to take will to power as an ontological axiom. Will to power is not an "empirical induction" that is in service to a "dialectical monism," that cumbersome invention of Walter Kaufmann's, nor a determination of the *es-*

sentia of beings, as it is for Heidegger, nor even an "approach to ontology," as it is in Jean Granier's study.[7] Will to power is nevertheless the cardinal principle or technique of genealogical critique, whether or not it is reducible to a "bipolar standard."

Will to power as *technique*? What can that mean? Will to power seems to serve as the bipolar standard for measuring systems of values, as the gauge that reveals either the life-enhancing or life-debilitating quality of projected values. If will to power is in any sense a technique, it recoils upon the technician's own measuring activity: its *recoil* makes will to power an ontological enigma. Let me proceed to two announcements of will to power in *Thus Spoke Zarathustra* and one from the unpublished notebooks; I will then attempt to characterize the recoil that is intrinsic in the notion itself.

Zarathustra announces his initial discovery of the principle of will to power in the value systems of the various peoples he encounters in the valleys of the world. These systems he finds to be the most compelling and complex of powers: "A tablet of goods hangs over every people. Behold, it is their tablet of overcomings; behold, it is the voice of their will to power" (ASZ I; 4, 74). Such tablets of goods are not simply expressions of moral preference; they are foundations of knowledge, or of self-deception, inasmuch as values bestow "the meaning of all things" (ibid.). Two motives underlie the erection of these tablets of values: human beings invest things with value (1) in order to preserve their own kind, and (2) in order to denigrate neighboring peoples, who must be seen as base.

This first announcement of will to power remains fundamental: will to power is a requirement for the self-preservation and power enhancement of peoples; it is the origin of all ideology. The second announcement occurs in the famous section "On Self-Overcoming" (ASZ II; 4, 146–49). It clarifies the facet of will to power as the will to a *meaning* for all things:

> "Will to truth" you call it, you wisest ones; is that what you call the thing that drives you and puts you in heat?
>
> Will to the thinkability of all beings: this is what *I* call your will. You only want to *make* all beings thinkable: for you doubt, with a good distrust, whether they are already thinkable.
>
> However, being should be docile and malleable for you! Thus your will wills it. It should be smooth and submissive to spirit, as its mirror and reflection.
>
> That is your entire will, you wisest ones, as a will to power, also when you talk of good and evil and valuations.

According to Zarathustra, the peoples of the world have fashioned gods and tablets and set them adrift in a slender bark on the river of becoming. However, it is not the rushing stream as such that threatens the bark, but the restless will to power itself, "the inexhaustibly productive life-will" that is on board. Zarathustra calls such will "the way of all living things." Living is a hearkening, listening, and responding; life is an obeying, *ein Gehorchendes*. Further, any living creature that cannot hearken and respond to itself falls under the command of another; commanding is more difficult than obeying, for one must bear the burdens of those who obey, and such burdens are crushing. Commanding is experiment, hazard, and risk of self. Zarathustra invites his listeners to test his claim: Is not this hearkening, this obedience, this commanding, at the very root of life? Where one finds life, one finds will to power. For even those who serve *will* to be masters, and those who are masters *will* to risk life for an excess of power. Life herself whispers her secret to Zarathustra: "I am that which always must overcome itself." The power that propels life requires the cycle of perishing and rebirth, autumn and spring; the life-will is a twisted path of struggle, becoming, goal, and contradiction of all goals. Whatever life loves best it must eventually oppose, inasmuch as self-overcoming is its very will: "And you too, you knowing one, are but a path and the footfall of my will: for truly my will to power walks on the feet of your will to truth!" (4, 148). Will to power is not will *to* existence, inasmuch as what exists cannot will to enter upon existence. In the chaos of becoming, which is a chaos of ash, the life-will is not will to life but will to power. "Many things are valued more highly by life than life itself; yet out of valuing itself will to power speaks!" (4, 149). Thus valuations come and go, as every chick pecks its way through the shell, grows and matures, and lays new eggs. "And whoever has to be a creator in good and evil must first be an annihilator, must first shatter values" (ibid.).

One must reflect on what the life-will implies for genealogical critique: even one who wants to place oneself beyond judgments of good and evil, in order that no particular value system will command total devotion, cannot transcend valuation as such. Any "placing beyond" would itself be a valuation. However, valuation must also be self-overcoming, not simply because it is caught in the stream of time, but because valuation is embroiled in the stream of power. Will to power is therefore not so much a technique at the disposal of genealogists, or a bipolar standard for their judgments, as it is a discovery concerning the essence of life—the root of life, as it were. Roots endure longer than leaves, stems, branches, boughs, and boles; yet eventually they too decompose and return to the soil, surrendering the nourishment they have sucked from it. Catabolism is always on the ascent, however contradictory that may seem.

The jottings that are taken up into *The Will to Power*, or rather, the way in which those jottings are organized, suggests that will to power expresses itself in two principal ways, first as will to truth and knowing, then as will to beauty and artistic creation. One such note (WM, 853; *13*, 193–94; 520–22),[8] from late 1887 or early 1888, comments decisively on both manifestations of will to power. In what follows I shall read it regressively, moving from its conclusion to its beginning.

In this reappraisal of *The Birth of Tragedy*, Nietzsche admits that pessimism and even nihilism lie concealed behind what that work takes to be truth. The word *truth* is one that Nietzsche is always embarrassed to use, and yet it is a word he cannot renounce. Nevertheless, even in *The Birth*, truth does not serve Nietzsche as "the supreme standard of value." "The will to appearance, illusion, deception, becoming, and change (the will to objective deception) counts here as being more profound, more originary, more metaphysical than the will to truth, actuality, being:—the last is itself merely a form of the will to illusion" (13, 522). Will to truth, as will to being, is will to illusion. What kind of will lies behind this assertion itself? For the assertion recoils in a radical way upon itself. One must indicate, as Granier has done (Gr, 30; 533 n.), several levels of meaning in Nietzsche's use of the word *truth*: (1) the pseudo-truth of metaphysics, (2) the pragmatic truth of art, which is "error that is useful for life," and (3) the originary truth that reveals the falsity of the first and the necessity (=truth) of the second. Some such distinction seems to be necessary, although its resemblance to the sort of distinctions that sustain metaphysics throughout its history makes it difficult to uphold.[9]

At all events, will to truth cannot be the aspect of will to power that most enhances life. Rather, *art* is "what makes life possible, what seduces us to life, serves as the great stimulus to life" (13, 521). In a word, a famous word, art is *"worth more"* than truth. Art is the effective counterforce against the will that negates life, although one will want to know how, if will is life-will, life permits itself a will that negates life. Art is also the *"redemption of the knower*, of those who see the frightful and dubious character of existence, who see it and will to see it, as tragic knowers" (ibid.). These words cast light on the problem of truth: art redeems the tragic knower from knowledge of the truth of life, the true truth concerning human existence, if one can say so. And yet this is exactly what cannot be said. For truth, at least as adequation of assertion to state of affairs, is a position that is already surpassed by the time of *The Birth of Tragedy*: "Here the opposition of a true and an apparent world is missing: there is but one world, and this one is false, cruel, contradictory, seductive, and without meaning. . . . A world thus construed is the true world . . ." (13, 193).

A wicked assertion, this! It first denies any claim to a "true world," then immediately invokes a world it calls "true," and not a pleasant world at that. It is a world that requires its human inhabitants to lie in order to live. These lies go under the rubrics of *metaphysics, morals, religion*, and *science*. These various forms of prevarication Nietzsche subordinates to a parent form, to wit, will to power as art. "'Life *ought to* inspire confidence': the task thus posed is gigantic. To carry it out, human beings must be liars by nature, they must above all be *artists*. . . . And so they are artists: metaphysics, religion, morality, science—all are mere excrescences of the will to art, to the lie, to flight in the face of 'truth,' to *denial* of the 'truth'" (ibid.). Art is the "supreme feeling of power." In artistic creation man conjures his gods and his truths, allowing himself to be powerfully seduced to life. Man "enjoys himself as artist, enjoys himself as power: *the lie is his power*" (13, 194).

The question that plagues genealogical critique is whether and how it can sustain the several distinct meanings of "truth" for will to power. For if these distinctions begin to fade and fuse, radical recoil will strike every assertion *about* will to power *by* will to power. As long as they are sustained, one can refer to a hierarchical schema that supports an ascensional reflection (Gr, 30). If they cannot be sustained, we shall have to call Nietzsche's genealogical philosophy a form of *descensional* reflection.

The primary characteristic of will to power as will to truth—if truth is that originary revelation of the falsity of metaphysical "truths"—is intellectual honesty or philological probity. The latter requires that any interpretation of becoming "ceaselessly multiply its perspectives" (Gr, 513–14). Only in this way can it hope to circumvent the bias of "useful error," that second putative level of truth. Interpretation of becoming thus requires perpetual self-overcoming in the sense of a continuous effort to shift perspectives. Would such overcoming amount to transcendence; would it open the heart of becoming to our gaze? It would not. Would it even be desirable for it to do so? It would not. Granier cites Nietzsche's commentary on the Oedipus myth: Oedipus guesses the riddle of the sphinx and solves the enigma of human nature, but in so doing violates the sanctity of nature and incurs nemesis. The myth suggests "that wisdom, and more precisely Dionysian wisdom, is a monstrosity in the face of nature, and that whoever casts nature into the abyss of nothingness by means of his wisdom merits destruction at the hands of nature" (Gr, 515; cf. GT, 9; *1*, 66–71). The radicality of Nietzschean doubt, the recoil achieved by genealogical critique, which fractures the circle of self-thinking thought, here reaches its greatest depth. "Just as dream and delusion are inherent in life, an irreproachable intellectual probity or absolute respect for justice leads to the sabotage of life itself. . . . The will to justice . . . ruins the conditions of the possibility of justice" (Gr, 517). As soon as we push such thinking to its limit, we recognize that "loyal service to truth" discloses itself as will to nothingness: "Such truth is the abyss of death" (Gr, 518). Intellectual rectitude and philological probity reveal their nature as protracted suicide; they are what Freud will later call *die Trabanten des Todes*, the component drives and the erotic drives, all of them servants of Thanatos, pallbearers of Eros. Knowledge of this thinking at the limit is *tragic* knowledge. Whereas Foucault coldly embraces it, Deleuze and Granier shrink from it: "This conclusion does not invalidate the legitimacy of the impulse to know . . . ; it merely establishes the fact that we have no right to erect justice and veracity as absolute norms" (Gr, 518). Granier fails to think through the consequences of his own analysis of probity and justice, *Redlichkeit* and *Gerechtigkeit*, that is, the disclosure of will to truth as will to death, hence as a decadent expression of will to power.

It was the greatness of the Greeks to have discovered that art alone, as will to radiant appearance and "the sanctification of illusion and dream," can serve as a haven for tragic knowers (Gr, 520–21). Art here means creativity, not aesthetic observation, energetic response to "organic" impulses, not refinement of reflective aesthetic judgments. The plastic activity of will to power as art corresponds to what Granier calls "vital pragmatism," which is a "pragmatic falsification of becoming" (Gr, 524). Yet if this is so, then Plato—that great falsifier to whom we shall turn in chapter 4—would be the prototypical artist; accordingly, genealogical critique, which *criticized* Plato because he was a man of artifice, would be fundamentally inartistic, uncreative, reactive, and essentially decadent. The genealogy that employs the technique, axiom, or bipolar standard of will to power would be weakest in will to power. Granier tries to escape this conclusion by arguing that the artistic philosophy of *idealism* is to be contrasted with the Nietzschean philosophy insofar as the former still has faith in an illusory beyond. Yet what would an illusory faith in *this* world have to offer? Granier seems to forget all too hastily that it was genealogy—which we might now define as will to power as will to *disillusion*—that discovered the *necessity* of artistic *illusion*. To say the least, it is difficult to see how genealogical critique could so quickly forget its own provenance and lose itself in euphoric creativity, devoting itself to "a virile, healthy, and loyal illusion" (Gr, 529). Yet if one sees that one must either duplicate the Apollonian feat of the Greeks or commit suicide, then the first option has already become impossible. How can art ever be safe from the undercutting suspicions of genealogical critique? Or how can genealogy successfully hide from itself in art? By becoming a "moment" of will to power? First the moment of useful error, namely, art, and then the moment of acute philological probity? Presumably, these two moments would work undialectically, but successively, with each remaining in blissful ignorance of the other. However, the second moment has the advantage—or, at any rate, the fate—of having been the moment that discovers will to power as such, which would leave the first moment with a great deal of virile, healthy, and loyal illusion to conjure.

The problem is whether and how the virtue of genealogical critique, which is inextricably linked to the decadent tradition of metaphysics and morals, could step aside, cancel itself, and surrender to the "plastic" moment of will to power. The relation of artistic play and rapture to genealogical critique seems suspiciously like Platonic flight—which is to say, like nihilism. Deleuze notes: "Thus nihilism, the will to nothingness, is not only a will to power, a quality of will to power, *but the ratio cognoscendi of will to power in general*" (Dz, 198). However, such a suspicion jeopardizes the genealogical project of overturning all idealist metaphysics of the Platonic sort. It becomes difficult to understand why the overman's lies are worthier than Plato's, or how any kind of standard, no matter how many poles it has at its disposal, could judge between them. For the will to illusion is not a "vanishing moment" in some sort of dialectical progression, not a temporary inconvenience that is canceled by some sort of self-overcoming; it is, as even Granier admits, "a primordial moment that is invested with a dignity that is *at least* equivalent to the dignity contained in the project of unmasking in accord with justice" (Gr, 527). Yet this is what Granier tries to ignore when he argues that the "illusion of art is radically different from *idealist* illusion" (Gr, 528). We recall that Nietzsche defines metaphysics, morals, religion, and science as "excrescences" of will to power as art. He does not argue for a radical difference in the types, but at best for a *minute* differentiation and hierarchical ordering. Granier insists that there is "good illusion," which he calls "fidelity to the earth," and "bad illusion," one that transforms useful illusion "into a negation of the very foundations of life"; good illusion has a "regulatory function" that prevents any totalization of the will to truth, whereas bad illusion flees from the world to a dream world of felicitous "truths." Good illusion is *"viril, sain et loyal,"* while bad illusion bears the curious epithets "dishonest" and "suspect" (Gr, 529). Art is a recuperation of vital energies and a preparation for "a new battle with truth," whereas morality, or "bad" illusion, forgets about truth and loses itself in its own oblivion. "Illusion for illusion's sake, illusion elevated into an absolute norm, is every bit as fatal as truth for truth's sake, philological probity 'at any cost'" (Gr, 530). At bottom, argues Granier, the two forms of illusion are "the two faces of the same impotence: in both cases nihilism triumphs" (ibid.).

Without harping on Granier's embarrassing formulation of "good" and "bad" illusion, embarrassing for a philosophy that wills to sustain its reflection *beyond* good and evil, there remains a debilitating difficulty. How does one know whether one is in the embrace of a "good" illusion, one that is "true to the earth," "virile, healthy, and loyal," or a "bad" one such as the oneiric Platonic world of ideas? If one knows whether or not the proper, "good" illusion has taken hold, then one is not deluded at all. How, then, does will to power as will to art exercise its vital pragmatism? Could it be that the devotion to intellectual honesty and philological probity, which is characteristic of genealogical critique, is simply one more exertion by the will to illusion? And, insofar as it is a devotion to "truth," a "bad" illusion at that?

These questions are by no means convictions; they are mere suspicions. Genealogical critique is fated to suspicion concerning even suspicion itself; suspicion of suspicion fractures such handy distinctions as that between will to truth and will to art, or between "levels" of meaning for "truth," or between "good" and "bad" illusion. Suspicion? There is no end to it. There is no inventory for it. It may be loyal, perhaps even virile or feral, but it seems to be anything but healthy. Yet that is the unkindest cut of all.

Will to truth and will to art must somehow be balanced in a measure or equilibrium that prevents one from entirely squelching the other. "Measure is thus the perfect adjustment of the two moments of will to power as the act of self-overcoming, the aesthetic moment of vital pragmatism, and the moment of philological probity" (Gr, 531). *Yet these moments cannot at all be distinguished as such.* Their interaction is so intense that any discourse about them is bound to fail, bound to create the illusion of their distinguishability. The latter illusion is beyond any facile determination of "good" or "bad" illusion, and Granier himself calls it *the duplicity of being.* "The being that agrees to speak the language of truth only through the camouflage of error—this is what we shall call *la Duplicité de l'Être*" (Gr, 533). Being has need of the "mask of the untrue," in order to reveal "that which it is in truth" (Gr, 534). "It is precisely because the human being *is*, because it incarnates *the truth*, because it is *real*, that it *falsifies* being, dissimulates the truth, violates the real" (Gr, 533n.). Granier nonetheless tries to prevent his hierarchical schema of "truth" from collapsing, and his thesis concerning Nietzsche's "ascensional reflection" from evaporating, by insisting that in spite of the duplicity of being one can in any given case locate the "level" of an assertion with respect to its truth. First, to repeat, "truth" may mean metaphysical truths, in which case "truth" is "really" falsehood, "false" here constituting a *polemic* against metaphysical idealism. Second, "truth" points toward a level of "original verity," according to which the "really" true world is the one "whose attributes represent the negation of the metaphysical fable." Third, "truth" imposes its "proper dissimulation" in the protective illusions of art (ibid.). The second and third levels are reversed in Granier's second presentation of the hierarchy (see the first, at Gr, 30), and this reversal itself betrays the fundamental problem: any "ascensional" hierarchy requires, but in the case of genealogical critique cannot possess, an "originary truth." The *polemical* meaning of the attack on idealistic metaphysics and morals is clear. *However, in what is that polemic grounded?* It surely cannot be grounded in "originary truth," if by that we mean simply the world "whose attributes represent the negation of the metaphysical fable." The polemic against metaphysics *presupposes* the level of "originary truth," and it is a blatant *petitio principii* to define the latter in terms of the former. We are left, to be sure, with the axiom of the duplicity of being, *but it is a duplicity that penetrates the supposed "hierarchy" from top to bottom.* The hierarchy does not ascend any higher than it descends, and if the knowledge of genealogical critique is *tragic* knowledge, we may expect that downgoing will remain fundamental: Nietzsche's reflection on truth will be *descensional.*

On the way down, one would have to recuperate the principal outcome of Heidegger's confrontation with Nietzsche: if the world in its originary truth *shows itself to be* the tiger's back, then the question of truth itself, as a covert self-showing, will have to accompany genealogical critique on its way down.

Yet what about this "duplicity" of being? Granier correctly notes that the word should not be understood in a moral sense: such duplicity "has nothing to do with the tortuous ruse or with hypocrisy" (Gr, 533n.). As a name for Nietzsche's fundamental intuition concerning being, duplicity is " . . . the expression of a *divine modesty and discretion*" (Gr, 534n.). What this discretion might be is certainly not yet clear, and in fact must wait for the thinking of eternal recurrence. According to Granier, two further qualities may be attributed to the duplicity of being, which speaks only in riddles and which masks every truth in an untruth. When human beings speak of being and becoming, their speech is in Nietzsche's view either a kind of war or a kind of play. Nietzsche himself conducts a πόλεμος, which is more than a mere polemic, against idealistic metaphysics. His fundamental struggle is against *the lie*, which nonetheless is part and parcel of the "truth" of being. Nietzsche suggests that the very essence of being is πόλεμος, which therefore also "rules the process of interpretation" (Gr, 535). The perpetual collision between will to truth and will to deception makes out the very character of being, and in so doing condemns every human assertion concerning being to a parlous state; every such assertion, including Nietzsche's own, must oscillate within that field of random collisions. *Will to power* is but a name for such oscillation, a truthful and a lying name for the "eternal *contradiction* between life and truth" (ibid.). "This contradiction is not surpassed in any synthesis; it is the insurmountable reality of being as πόλεμος; it is thus the absolutely *tragic* contradiction—*tragic contradiction being opposed to dialectical contradiction*" (Gr, 535n.). What is tragic? Granier cites the words of Paul Ricoeur,[10] to the effect that in tragedy the one who promotes a certain value or takes a particular stand is destroyed by that very value or stand. This in fact is precisely what I have meant in using the term *descensional reflection* in order to describe the fundamental directionality of genealogical critique, which marks the downgoing of both critique and critic.

What, then, can we say concerning artistic play? Play is achieved, if at all, only in the thinking of eternal recurrence of the same, not in the genealogical inventories of will to power. Perhaps all we can do is summarize our findings thus far concerning genealogical critique, in preparation for a first encounter—in chapter 3—with the thought of return.

The axis on which genealogical critique revolves is not one of reflexive philosophy. Above all, genealogy wishes to fracture the circle of philosophic meditation by indicating an origin of meditation which for fundamental reasons is inaccessible to that meditation. It wishes to show that the passion to "get to the roots of reality" and to possess the "truth" of beings emanates from a source hidden beneath the level upon which reflection operates. Just as the Marxian critique of ideology wishes to expose the conditions that ideology deliberately obscures, namely, the alignment of the social forces of production, Nietzsche's genealogical critique asks: *To what* are metaphysics and morals *in service?*

> In both cases . . . the regression to a supersensible "foundation" is eliminated on behalf of research into origins at the heart of immanence, research that leads to the same general conclusion: ideas are never immediate "givens" that contain in themselves the synthetic totality of signifying, signified, and signification; ideas are already *products*, and to understand them precisely one must scrutinize the field of experience from which they issue and the structures . . . which they reflect. . . . The application of the genealogical method has as its goal precisely this: to dissipate the illusion of autonomy on the part of predicative activity by referring all judgments to their conditions of existence. (Gr, 155)

The question of the adequacy of the axiological ground of the system, a ground ostensibly to be revealed by an (interrupted, suspect) inventory of genealogical critique, becomes the question of the *adequacy of the ground of experience* that such an inventory everywhere presupposes. Such a question genealogical critique cannot itself answer. For any answer would close the circle of the system and show genealogical critique to be another form of ideology. However, if the clarity and distinctness of its ideas is by no means to be taken as a *ground* of genealogical critique, if it forfeits any claim to *transcendental* deduction, then in what is genealogical critique grounded? Genealogical critique has no ground. It has only momentum. Rather than embrace the security of any ground, genealogical critique goes underground. Whether this going underground is simply the result of loss of nerve on the philosopher's part or the outcome of a most rigorous *thinking* and a transformation of the essence of *truth* remains a question.

We must postpone the question of the ground of genealogical critique until we have spent considerable time underground, and we cannot gain entrance into the underground until the problem of an inventory of techniques proceeds to the problem of the respective *languages* of metaphysics and genealogy. Precisely why the question of language arises when the grounds of genealogy and the genealogy of ground are pursued—language as the *fa(c)tum* of the will to power that issues forth as genealogical critique—cannot be easily said or written. In any case, we find ourselves back at the capital question of Nietzsche's genealogical essay contest, where chapter 1 began.

THE GENEALOGY OF LANGUAGE; THE LANGUAGE OF GENEALOGY

Nietzsche's critique of the *language* of metaphysics and morals is central to his practice of genealogical critique. Why are the notions and categories of metaphysics and morals—the whole of onto-theo-*logic*—inadequate to their goal? "Behind all logic and the apparent self-determination of its movement," writes Nietzsche in *Beyond Good and Evil*, "stand valuations, or more trenchantly put, physiological demands for the sake of the preservation of a certain type of life" (JGB, 3; 5, 17). The most fundamental of those demands, as we have heard, is "belief in the oppositional quality of values"; that is to say, the demand that true and false, good and evil, be radical contraries, that the essence of the first of each pair exclude the second absolutely. On the basis of this "indubitable" duality, the logics of metaphysics and morals can be constructed: the certain can be preferred over the indeterminate, "truth" over "mere appearance," and so on, as long as logic forgets its provenance in a prejudgment occasioned by conditions for the survival of the species, projecting its ground as the self-evidence of self-thinking thought, mimicking divinity.

However, language does not have its provenance in a pure reason which, from its transcendental remove, selects the categories that are appropriate to being and instructs us in their usage; rather, a word becomes a concept, and a concept a category, because of the need to command and order experiences. The difficulty is that experiences can only be "more or less similar," and that words can as little cover all the cases as snowflakes can escape infinite variety of crystallization. A word arises from our remembering something that is common in our experience, but maintains itself by means of oblivion with respect to all the particulars. "We insert a word where our ignorance begins—where we can no longer see any further; for example, the word *I*, the word *do*, the word *suffer:*—these words are perhaps horizonal lines of our knowledge, but they are not 'truths'" (WM, 482; 12, 185). Words are for Nietzsche monuments to illusion, untrue but not unnecessary. The classic formulation is once again that of "Truth and Lie in an Extra-Moral Sense":

> Every concept originates through our equating what is unequal. No leaf ever wholly equals another, and the concept "leaf" is formed through an arbitrary abstraction from these particular differences, through a forgetting of that which distinguishes; and now it gives rise to the idea that in nature there might be something besides the leaves, which would be "leaf"—some kind of original form after

which all leaves have been woven, marked, circumscribed, colored, curled, and painted, but by unskilled hands, so that no copy turned out to be a correct, reliable, and faithful image of the original form. (1, 880)

The word, the simplest nomination of things, thus betrays the will to a hinterworld, the *arrière-monde* of all idealisms. Granier exclaims, "We are all Platonists the moment we speak!" (Gr, 99). Jean-Paul Sartre recalls in *Les mots* how his mother would repeat over and over again the names of his grandparents, *Karl et Mami*, so that the four-syllable word "Karlémami" came to have a "perfect accord" with the persons named—or, even more, with the very atmosphere of their household: "The word cast its shadow over the thing. . . ."[11] Sartre recalls the small child struggling to read the massive volumes in his grandfather's library: " . . . the phrases resisted me like things . . ." (37). It was in the *Grand Larousse* that Sartre first encountered "true birds," "true butterflies," "true flowers." The men he would see in the Jardin du Luxembourg were less real than the men about whom he read in adventure stories. He was a child Platonist: "It was in these books that I encountered the universe: assimilated, classified, labeled, already thought to be redoubtable; and I confused the disorder of my bookish experiences with the chance occurrence of real events. From that came this idealism that it has taken me thirty years to shake off" (39).

However, the idealism that is rooted in language since the infancy of humanity persists in all culture. Just as species-man (as the early Marx calls it) dominates the animals by the conceits—or deceits—of its language, it still intends to dominate the world by means of what it calls *knowledge, insight,* or *cognition.* Language is the first step of that "belief in founded truths" which proudly calls itself *science* (MAM I, 11; 2, 30–31). "*No matter how cautious one would like to be,*" Nietzsche writes, a "philosophical mythology" remains stuck in our language, whereby things are thought in streamlined words and oversimplified concepts (MAM II, W 11; 2, 547). The "philosophical mythology" of language is no accident of language but—if one may say so—the very (dis-)essence of language: "The lordly prerogative to bestow names goes so far that one may allow oneself to grasp the origin of language itself as an expression of the power of the rulers: they say, 'That *is* such-and-such,' they seal every thing and every occurrence with a sound and thereby take it, as it were, into their possession" (ZGM 1, 2; 5, 260). The rules governing *nomination* provide the founding rules of *truth* as adequation, thus empowering for the first time the distinction between truth and lie. Liars use words in order to make the unreal appear real; they mix names, break convention, and risk ostracism. In order to avoid unpleasantness, they soon stop questioning convention.

Nor does the *grammar* of language drop from heaven. It does not mirror the structure of a reality-in-itself, free from human influence; rather, it articulates in advance the possible interpretations of the world for a particular tribe. Granier observes, "The history of philosophy is thus determined in advance by the propositional organization of discourse, which authorizes only a limited number of combinations of concepts" (Gr, 99). The amazing family likeness of all Hindu, Greek, and German philosophies, as opposed, say, to the Ural-Altaic, is easily accounted for by the genetic inheritance of a common grammar: philosophy belongs to grammar "thanks to the unwitting dominance and leadership exercised by similar grammatical functions" (JGB, 20; 5, 34). Nietzsche ironically proclaims grammar "the People's Metaphysics" (FW, 354; 3, 593). Perhaps the most famous axiom of the People's Metaphysics is that "every deed has a doer." Hence, *cogito, ergo: sum* (JGB 54; 5, 73). Indeed, nowhere is language more inadequate than when naming the subtle, shifting interiority of consciousness, the makeshift abode of the cogito: the only words a reflecting ego has to apply to its feelings and drives are words of "extreme states," such as hatred, anger, and love. Thus we *are not* "what our words and consciousness allow." Language misses our *character* and our *fate* (M, 115; 3, 107–8).

However, in one sense the grammar of the People's Metaphysics did drop from heaven, and that is the difficulty: "Should not philosophers rise above *belief* in grammar?" (JGB, 34; 5, 54). One should sooner believe in the soul than in the grammatical subject of the cogito (JGB, 54; 5, 73). The history of philosophy is in Nietzsche's view not the evolution of the concept, spirit becoming aware of itself as that-which-is, as it was for Hegel, but a "realm of crude fetishism."[12] Any philosophy that would exalt this fetishism is, in Granier's words, an "idealistic panlogism"; it implies "a sacralization of language, that is, belief in the divinity of language" (Gr, 100). "I fear we will not be rid of God," writes Nietzsche, "because we still believe in grammar . . ." (GD; 6, 78). Grammar therefore joins the long list of lieutenants that have assumed the vacated throne of the absolute. It is in fact the most persistent of the idols.

Language as nomination, but also as grammar and syntax, embodies "the error that is useful to life," which is to say, *truth*. Nietzsche takes consciousness to be an "operation instigated by will to power," which aims to capture becoming "in the nets of its intellectual categories" (Gr, 429). Language is its primordially efficacious tool. The "equal sticks" of Plato's *Phaedo* were not originally measured for the sake of locating the εἶδος of equality or sameness, but were measured for balance—as spears for the hunt. On the basis of this intuition of useful error, Nietzsche, in Granier's words, "denounces the artificiality of the concepts of the intelligence, insofar as these concepts within the vehicle of language take their origin from the exigencies of action; language is a system of signs by grace of which the life of relationships finds itself simplified and abridged; to be sure, language is that which consolidates the dominion of man over nature, but it does not authorize our identifying language and the absolute *logos*" (Gr, 101).

Nietzsche, trained as a philologist, never lost his passion for the clarifications offered by the sciences of language. We recall that *etymology* was to play a crucial role in his genealogical essay contest. He stressed the importance of language training in his early lectures on "The Future of Our Educational Institutes," addressed to the Academic Society of Basel during the winter semester of 1872.[13] Yet Nietzsche entertained no illusions about the young science of language. The opening remarks of his lecture on "Homer and Classical Philology," written some three years earlier, criticized the disunity of his science:

> It is as much a piece of history as a piece of natural science as a piece of aesthetics: history, insofar as it wants to conceptualize the manifestations of particular peoples in ever new images, to grasp the ruling law in the flight of appearances; natural science, inasmuch as it strives to ground the deepest instinct of man, the language instinct; and, finally, aesthetics, because, from among the whole range of cultures in the ancient world, it erects what it calls "classical antiquity," with the claim and the intention of uncovering the ideal world of the ancients and proffering it to the present age as the mirror of the classical and eternally valid.[14]

No wonder the multifarious "science of language" lacks unity and a sense of direction! It well-nigh incorporates all the disciplines that are invited to play a role in Nietzsche's essay contest.

Some two decades later Nietzsche invokes "a new language," one that sounds altogether strange, inasmuch as for it, as we heard, "the falsity of a judgment is no argument against it" (JGB, 4; 5, 18). However, Nietzsche says little more on the subject of the language by which he tries to think will to power, and he may be justly criticized for this.[15] Perhaps his most decisive comment on language appears in a note from this same period, 1886–1887, taken up in *The Will to Power*. Here, under the heading "Fundamental Solution," *Grundlösung*, Nietzsche writes:

> We believe in reason: however, this is the philosophy of gray *concepts*. Language depends upon the most naive prejudices.
>
> We now read disharmonies and problems into things, because we *think only* in the form of language—therewith believing in the "eternal truth" of "reason" (for example, subject, predicate, and so on).
>
> *We cease to think when we refuse to do so under the constraints of language*; we still but barely attain the doubt that sees this boundary as a boundary.
>
> *Rational thinking is interpretation according to a scheme we cannot thrust aside.* (WM, 522; 12, 193–94)

These thoughts merit detailed consideration. "We believe in reason. . . ." The "we" is not the courteous or magisterial plural in which the solitary thinker so often writes. No doubt Nietzsche wishes to exclude himself from the faithful, from the worshippers of reason. "Reason" is faith in the adequacy of thinking to being, no more valid than any other fancy, though certainly more potent in its consequences. Language, as both nomination and syntax, reflects a thoroughly anthropocentric and praxis-oriented reality, the reality of "doers" and "receivers" and "copulatives," and thus is by no means adequate to the ontological status that human beings grant it. In short, *we genealogists do not believe in reason*. Have we adequate grounds for our mislogic? Have we tested those grounds and found them to be evidence that supports our suspicions about language? We are so accustomed to associating grounds, reasons, evidence, and adequacy with reason itself that it seems miraculous that we can make such a complaint about language at all. However, a suspicion or complaint is one thing, an *assertion* is surely another. Whence the assertion of this opening suspicion concerning language; and, if it is a thought at all, is it not itself constrained by the language of reason?

"We now read disharmonies and problems into things. . . ." The disharmonies and problems of things are presumably many: things come and go, generate and decompose, are fashioned, used up, and discarded; human things are altogether a confusion. Yet only if one has already determined the harmony and concordance that the things *should* possess can one talk about cacophony and confusion. Only if one possesses the author's own manuscripts and corrected proofs can one complain about inaccuracies in a later edition. It also seems that in order to complain about someone's "reading into" a text, to claim that a reading is a misreading, one must be in possession of the original. Yet what could that be, other than the *logos* of reason? However, we speak too soon. For Nietzsche's thought continues: metaphysicians read difficulties into things because they "*think only*" in the form of language. Or, rather, *we* think only in that way. To think only in the form of language might imply several things. First, we reflect, meditate, calculate, and brood *always* within the rooms furnished by language; it is mere foolishness to try to think in a nonlinguistic way, inasmuch as the domains of thought and language are coextensive. Take away language, and humans cannot think; they are apes, or something less than apes. Second, we *merely* reflect, meditate, calculate, and brood within language, whereas we ought to be doing something else with it—for example, writing poetry or listening to language. Perhaps if we only *think* language, we are missing something about it. Yet whatever thinking might be is not clear in either case.

The riddles propounded in the first and second moments of the thought now come to a head: we no longer think when we refuse to do so under the yoke of language. Thinking and the nonlinguistic are separated by an abyss, by an abyss of essence, as Heidegger would say. (Whether music and painting and all the other arts constitute a "language," and what a thinking of these arts might be, become interesting questions, which, however, we must here set aside.) I repeat: whatever thinking is, it must sustain a relation with language. Perhaps language here is thought as the "ground of the possibility" of thought, as Kant might express it, thought's "sufficient reason," after the manner of Leibniz. However, Nietzsche says that language is a boundary, border, frontier, limit, or horizon (*eine Grenze*), which he can but barely descry. As Wittgenstein might ask, how can language be seen—or heard—as the limit of thought; how could one attain the vantage point from which to determine language as a border unless one also had in view the domain of the unthought, the unspoken? What would the character of such a descrying be? And does it even make sense to ask such a question with these words, inasmuch as an answer could only be one of two kinds: an answer as to the nature of the unthought-unspoken, the yonside of language, could *not* be an answer rendered in language, in which case *it is not the sort of answer I want*; or it could *only* be an answer couched in language, which is more to my liking but less to the purpose, because it does not trespass beyond the border, does not get a perspective on the limit as limit, and thus *is not the sort of answer I need*.

Yet again we speak too hastily, for the second part of the sentence adds that we achieve such a sighting of the border that encompasses language and thought, though only by the slimmest margin, by means of the doubt (*Zweifel*). We would not have to fear if Nietzsche meant Cartesian doubt, which, as we saw in the foregoing chapter, is but the prelude to a gavotte of supreme certitude, of utmost clarity and distinctness. If Nietzsche's were a Cartesian doubting, we would see the yonside of that border, and not by some slim margin. Yet the thinker of the death of God is also one who doubts and descries differently.

We have so far neglected an important aspect of this thinking. Nietzsche says that "we cease to think *when we refuse to do so* under the constraint of language." *Wenn wir nicht es tun wollen*, if or when we do not want or will to do so. One problem here is *how* one might refuse to think under the constraint of language; it sounds as though one could simply decide such a thing for oneself, as though one could not-will to think within language. One could perhaps lapse into dull muteness; one could perhaps sleep or drug oneself. Would one then be transported to the yonside of the border that encompasses thought and language? Another problem is how one might *express* this decision of not wanting to think linguistically: one could remain silent, but could one write books, books of philosophy, no less? Nietzsche expresses his decision in the words *nicht wollen, bei Zweifel, eine Grenze sehen*. The middle term cannot be meant in the Cartesian sense, as we have noted. It can only mean the *suspicion* we have been attempting to locate at the heart of genealogical critique. Suspicion, which results in a new kind of seeing, a dim seeing, is founded in *nicht wollen*, the decision not to think that one can think outside the constraints of language. Yet within what context does language appear as constraint, compulsion, yoke, unavoidable necessity, even physical force, a placing under arrest? Within what ontological framework does one grant language, but only grudgingly, the concession of necessity? What sort of *truth*—not as adequation or mere consistency but as a self-showing or emerging out of concealment— would unfold within and as such a language?

Nietzsche's complaint about language is that in the very act of imposing names upon the flux of becoming, language projects being upon becoming, that is, forgets the particular differences of the things it means. Nietzsche is certainly not the first to make this complaint. In the very first stage of his explication of the progress of the experience of consciousness, Hegel clearly demonstrates the apparent failure of language to grasp the particularity of the "This-is," "here and now." In the section of the *Phenomenology of Spirit* entitled "Sensuous Certainty," Hegel writes:

> We *express* the sensuous as a universal; what we say is, *This*, that is, the *universal this*, or, *it is*; that is to say, *being in general*. To be sure, we do not *represent* to ourselves the universal This, or being in general, but we *express* the universal; in other words, we simply do not speak in the way we *mean* in such sensuous certainty. Yet

language is, as we see, the more truthful one; in it we ourselves immediately contradict our *opinion*, and since the universal is what is true in sensuous certainty, and since language merely expresses this truth, it is not at all possible ever to say a sensuous being that we *mean*.[16]

For Hegel, consciousness is under the constraint or compulsion to speak out (*aus-sprechen*) and ex-press (*aus-drücken*) the certainty of its sensations. The constraint has two consequences. First, language inevitably misses its target, in that it cannot grasp the sensuous certainty of the "This is, here and now." The "now," for example, caught up in the ceaseless flux of time, escapes the moment of the word expressed "now," that is, later, and abducts with itself any "This, here, is" that is named. Second, the character of sensuous certainty, which language misses, itself undergoes a fundamental alteration. Its "certainty" is canceled, negated, and its "sensuousness" is sublated, lifted up, and relieved. The experience of sensuous certainty is transcended in the experience of taking-for-true (*Wahr-nehmung*), perception. The earliest stage in the dialectical progress toward absolute knowing is unthinkable without the revelation by language of what language is. "Yet language is, as we see," writes Hegel, "the more truthful one." Language speaks within the community of totality; it expresses *das Allgemeine*. The translation "universal" is scarcely adequate here. What language speaks is the collectivity of consciousness, self-consciousness, reason, and spirit—the entire itinerary of spirit as the experience of consciousness. The fact that what we mean (*meinen*), this or that particularity here and now, is inevitably missed by language does not attest to the untruth of language but to the transiency of sensuous certainty. That the arrow misses its fleeting target is not the fault of the arrow or the aimer but the target. When the target is relieved, language will shoot straight. For, in Hegel's world, where things go missing, words may be.

The genealogical response to Hegel's insistence on language as "the more truthful one" would not be simple; it would not merely consist of accusation and insistence on the "lie." It would not revert to the assurances of sensuous certainty. Why not?

Any genealogist worthy of the name searches for the family tree not only of others but of himself or herself. The genealogist ends by studying his or her own lineage, the extent to which, for example, the genealogist is still pious. Genealogy always comes home. If the genealogist recognizes the truth of prior metaphysics as a series of projections whose provenance remains unknown to the metaphysician but is now known to *critica genealogica*, if such critique grasps the heretofore concealed essence of prior philosophies, then such critique inserts itself into past philosophies as the absolute grasp of their becoming—what Hegel calls *der Geist des Werdens*.[17] Even if *critica genealogica* takes as its cardinal axiom the will to power as self-overcoming, implying an endless discipline and breeding of one's self, it seems to describe the phenomenological circle, the circle that turns back upon itself, presupposing its beginning and achieving it only in the end. It seems possible, if not inevitable, to develop an ontology of will to power that closely parallels Hegel's ontology of spirit, indeed, which seems to borrow its key elements from Hegel. The parallel might unfold in three dialectical stages:

HEGEL	NIETZSCHE
1. Alienation of spirit in the thing, the thing as *other* to consciousness: *Entäußern, Entfremdung.* The naive projection of spirit.	1. Naive projection of essences, stamping being on becoming, humanizing nature through will to power as will to knowledge.
2. Return of spirit to itself, in the recognition of the dependence of what is "other" upon the negating power of spirit.	2. Recognition by a no-saying critique of the dependence of projection upon anthropocentric psychological or physiological drives.
3. Reconciliation of consciousness and self-consciousness in the unity of knowledge and will. Freedom. Spirit united to what was alienated from it.	3. The affirmation of becoming by overman, who wills his or her own will to power by thinking the eternal recurrence of the same.

On one side, *alienation, recognition, reconciliation*; on the other, *projection, genealogical critique, affirmation.* Yet the parallel would feed the suspicion that genealogical critique, at least when translated into Latin, necessarily evolves into a metaphysics of will to power, maintaining itself in the μετά of an impossible absolute, if only because its language is the language of the *ego cogito* as *ego volo*—the language of spirit expressing itself. "*Rational thought is interpretation according to a scheme we cannot thrust aside.*"

One might argue, and argue correctly, that Nietzsche's genealogy of language pays insufficient heed to the language of genealogy, that Nietzsche neglects to provide "a solid basis for his own discourse" (Gr, 355). Of course, if Nietzsche argues for the incapacity of language to grasp the world of becoming, inasmuch as language in its essence is the vehicle of the useful error of "being," then to *assert* such a "solid basis" would be to enjoy another dreamy ride in that same vehicle. Two results—which we have already hinted at—accrue: first, Nietzsche's critique of metaphysics and morals as misinterpretations of becoming is rooted in the selfsame "imperialism of will to power" as traditional metaphysics and morals; second, his critique of metaphysics and morals as functions of will to power possesses only a highly problematic use value, and no validity value whatsoever. Within the first objection, one might isolate two moments: first, Nietzsche disdains any metaphysics of the concept that would solve all the riddles of existence at one stroke, with a single word, even if "will to power" appears to be such a word; second, if will to knowledge is a child of will to power, and if Nietzsche has knowledge of will to power, then "will to power" is itself a product of Nietzsche's own will to power (Kf, 177). These two moments of the first objection actually suggest not that Nietzsche merely "neglects" to provide a solid basis for his discourse but that he (unwittingly?) "*ruins the foundation of his own discourse*" (Gr, 606). It would then be Nietzsche's will to forgetfulness that renders the conclusive testimony here, for Nietzsche *forgets* that "it is always with the aid of language that he is able to understand and determine the nature of language as a tool in the service of will to power" (Gr, 607). Nietzsche develops no metalanguage. Yet if his genealogical critique is to be grounded it needs something like a metalanguage. "Everything looks as though Nietzsche had profited from the resources of metalanguage without succeeding in thematizing the obscure power that opened up for him the *space* of discourse" (Gr, 607). It is likely that Nietzsche would scoff at such an objection, which boils down to self-contradiction, or Kaufmann's "Epimenidean contradiction," which is a difficulty only for leaden logicians. Besides, he could demonstrate that most of his formulations concerning will to power—except perhaps those that come from the mouth of Zarathustra, who, as a poet, probably lies too much—are invariably couched in experimental terms: "Supposing that . . . , if one could . . . ," and so on. Even after *Thus Spoke Zarathustra*, argues Kaufmann, Nietzsche "still thought experimentally, and not as a prophet or legislator."[18] Further, Nietzsche would indicate that if one's language possesses *style*, the *grand*, then it never needs to stoop to a meta-level. The only question that Nietzsche's scorn would leave unscathed, as we have already suggested, is that of a new and unheard-of sense of truth, no longer as adequation but as revelation, if only as the revelation of those tiger stripes.

The second objection, which asks after the use value of genealogical critique, comes much closer to the mark. If will to power is both the prime discovery of genealogical critique and the engine of all discovery, then will to power appears to assume the vacated throne of the absolute: genealogical critique would be the divine circuit of will to power thinking and willing and coming to know itself. However, it is plain to Nietzsche himself that after the death of God and the collapse of the throne, he cannot "anchor his own conception of the will to power in any divine ground" (Kf, 179). The second objection might then be reformulated as follows: If will to power can be nothing other than a variant of the Platonic idea of the good, or the Aristotelian divine, whose thinking is a thinking of thinking (*Metaphysics* Λ, 9; 1074b 33–34), then it must be an expression either of Nietzsche's will to (self-)deception, an innocent delusion, or culpable bad faith. Such a formulation puts us in a better position to expose the radicality of the problem of *ground* in Nietzsche's genealogical critique, because it turns the keenest tools of that critique against itself. The recoil of genealogical critique upon itself, rooted in its critique of the *language* of metaphysics, takes the form not of self-contradiction, a form that any respectable dialectician can surmount, but of *contraction* and *suspicion*. Here the suspicion obtrudes as to whether the occupation of genealogical critique is itself an expression of the nihilism impacted in metaphysics and morals, a betrayal of the Dionysian, and a lapse into decadence. An inventory of the techniques of genealogical critique leads to the fundamental dissolution of the language of metaphysics and the preparation for a radical recoil that may yet shatter genealogical critique. The one most skilled in such recoil is of course Nietzsche himself. For all our self-assertive criticism, it is

Nietzsche who shows how far one must go if one wants to experience the "scheme of rational thought," which cannot be thrust aside.

STYLES OF EXCESSIVE WISDOM: NIETZSCHE AS *PIERRE D'ATTENTE*

There are styles of living as well as of writing. In "Why I Am So Wise," in *Ecce Homo*, which we shall take up again in chapters 10 and 11, Nietzsche tells of his styles of living, a living that was a living for writing. There he suggests that his excessive wisdom results from his having "lived through" so many periods of decadence. His bouts with illness gave him, he writes, the *sang froid* needed for "dialectical clarity," or, as we would prefer, genealogical acuity (EH; 6, 264–66). His illnesses, he insists, were localized disturbances, severe yet not carried to the extremes of degeneration and generalized decadence, and not by any means the result of *nervous* disorders.

The years following the Franco-Prussian War were for him years of recuperation interrupted by periods of relapse, periods of "a kind of decadence." Nietzsche therefore became "*experienced* in the question of decadence," having learned to "spell it forwards and backwards" (ibid.). His genealogical skills, his ability to discern psychological nuances, "to see around the corner" without going around the bend, burgeoned during these relapses and temporary capitulations to decadence. His "more healthy concepts and values" took shape during the periods of "fullness and self-certainty of *abundant* life" (ibid.). Nietzsche lived through both perspectives and thus earned his qualifications: he alone was fit to conduct the revaluation of all values.

As we shall see in greater detail in chapter 10, Nietzsche takes his supreme skill to be the art of employing the accidents of health or sickness as means to gain insight. For him, illness is a question of specialization: " . . . as *summa summarum* I was healthy; as niche, as specialist, I was decadent" (EH; 6, 266). At bottom, in the ground of his grounds, *im Grunde*, Nietzsche remains healthy, inasmuch as an essentially morbid type cannot be healthy, so that the opposite too must be true: carved from hard, sweet, pungent wood, Nietzsche suffers no rot.

Nietzsche served as his own physician. "Out of my will to health, to *life*, I made my philosophy" (6, 267). Thus the year of his gravest illness, prior to 1889, occurred ten years earlier, in 1879, as he began work on "The Wanderer and His Shadow." Yet this terrible year was the one in which Nietzsche "*ceased* being a pessimist." Out of his will to health he learned to *select* proper books, propitious landscapes, and minimally passable human beings, turning misfortune to good luck, abuse to advantage. What did not topple him made him stronger. At length his illness provided *insight into* ressentiment and at the same time *freedom from* it (EH; 6, 272). Knowledge seemed to be a saving grace, even if its provenance was perdition: coming to know rancor enabled him to withstand it.

And yet, as Nietzsche concedes, "Illness *is* itself a kind of ressentiment" (ibid.). The only weapon against it is "Russian fatalism," that capitulation to death "without revolt, by which the Russian soldier for whom the road is too hard sleeps in the snow" (6, 273). Russian fatalism: the only solution is to stop taking things in, stop reacting, accept hibernation. Only in this way can one who is ill much of the time slake his "thirst for revenge," assuage his ressentiment: "Ressentiment is the forbidden-in-itself for one who is ill—it is *his* evil, but unfortunately his most natural inclination" (ibid.). Nietzsche's shrewdness, to repeat, results from his careful selection of nourishment, landscapes, climates, recreations, and companions (EH; 6, 278 ff.). And it is Nietzsche's awareness of this multiplicity of factors, his awareness of the precariousness of his own situation, according to Granier, that prevents his physiology from shriveling into a crude determinism: "A gross causalism is thus excluded right from the start: Nietzsche searches for signifying correlations, not a linear and rigid causal series" (Gr, 210–11).

Styles of writing, styles of life: one can appreciate Nietzsche's experience with decadence only by becoming acquainted with his style of life after 1871. After serious bouts of diphtheria and dysentery at the battlefront, Nietzsche, as all the biographers relate, was "never properly well again," so that "any attempt to understand his behavior from 1871 onwards must constantly take into account the fact that, in addition to whatever else he might be doing, he was engaged upon a day-to-day battle with ill-health."[19] His migraine headaches and vomiting spells often persisted for three days and nights at a time, and sometimes extended over weeks. Nietzsche apparently made matters worse by ignoring his doctors' pleas that he take a long vacation from his vocation of genealogical critique:

> By 1885 he was living only to write: his nature had become almost perfectly self-centered and he had reduced his contact with the exterior world to the minimum necessary for survival. His health was showing no sign of improvement, and his eyes, which had always suffered the most not only from his complaint but also from his manner of "cursing" it by work, were worse than ever before: during the winter of 1884–1885 he approached blindness.[20]

His eyes had always been a problem because of his excessive reading and writing: all the way back to his student days, myopia, eyestrain, and headaches were the rule. The philosopher who taught us to heed the honest and candid advice of our healthy bodies developed a style of life that ruined his own. No man was ever so convinced that the all-important task for a human being was to learn how to love and cultivate the self, and no human being—apart from the Nazarene, perhaps—was ever more unkind to himself.

> For one thing is necessary: that a man *achieve* his satisfaction with himself—be it through this or that poetry and art: only then are human beings at all fit to look at. Whoever is unsatisfied with himself is always ready to avenge himself: we others will be his victims, even if it is only to suffer his hateful looks. For the look of the hateful one makes us ill and gloomy. (FW, 290; 3, 531)

No human being ever resisted so intensely the spirit of gloom, doom, and gravity; and no human being—except, again, for the most unsavory of companions—succumbed to that spirit so fatally. "And, above all, that I am the enemy of the spirit of gravity, is the way of the bird: truly an enemy unto death, a sworn enemy, a primordial enemy. . . . Yet whoever would become weightless and birdlike must love himself. . . . One must learn to love oneself with a hale and hearty love, so that one can hold out by oneself and not go astray. . . . Yet one must also learn this art: to *have* a shell and a shining appearance and a shrewd blindness!" (ASZ III; 4, 241–42). No human being was ever more convinced that the highly receptive, highly sensitized philosophic spirit, the best hope for overman, required the protection of the mask, and no human being—apart from the most cruel of companions, the grand inquisitors—stripped away his own and others' masks so mercilessly. "It behooves a finer humanity to have respect 'before the mask,' and not to indulge in psychology and curiosity in the wrong place" (JGB, 270; 5, 226). However, the very essence of genealogical critique, the activity in which all its inventoried techniques coalesce, is to strip away masks. "*Nietzsche fait tomber tous les masques*" (Gr, 218). Yet the passion to unmask is a grave passion. The passion to denounce the spirit of gravity is a grave passion. Sometimes even Zarathustran affirmation seems a grave passion. On this all the biographers, perhaps taking their cue from the adepts of the Stefan George *Kreis*, agree:

> Nietzsche had to "overcome his age" and to fight against the instincts of a decadent age was to be no less a decadent. Philosophy was precisely the self-questioning of life, and as such it was a symptom of decadence. The healthy life is a joyful life, he says, and where pain and suffering predominate over joy, life is unhealthy, i.e. decadent. The joyful life needs no explaining—it is its own justification; . . . where explanations (i.e. philosophies) are offered, one may infer a state of affairs in which life is found distressful.[21]

Freud would concur: the two great classes of system builders are paranoiacs and philosophers, that is, those who have failed to transform neurotic misery into normal unhappiness. Yet this failure may well be the secret upon which all styles of living-in-order-to-write converge. Stefan Zweig portrays a case of such convergence in an unforgettable way:

> Carefully the myopic man sits down to a table; carefully the man with the sensitive stomach considers every item on the menu, . . . for every mistake in his diet . . . wreaks havoc with his quivering nerves for days. No . . . wine, no . . . beer, no alcohol, no coffee, . . . no cigar and no cigarette . . . : only the short, meager meal. . . . And up again into the small . . . coldly furnished *chambre garnie*, where innumerable notes, pages, writings, and proofs are piled up on the table. . . . And on a tray innumerable bottles and jars and potions: against the migraines, which often render him all but senseless for hours, against his stomach cramps, against spasmodic vomiting . . . and, above all, the dreadful sedatives against his insomnia, . . . the only helpers in the empty silence of this strange room. . . . Wrapped in his overcoat and a woolen scarf, . . . his double glasses pressed close to the paper, his hurried

hand writes for hours—words the dim eyes can hardly decipher. For hours he sits like this and writes until his eyes burn.[22]

The hero of Melville's *Moby-Dick* marvels over the (noble) savage, Queequeg, who for all his queer eccentricities is always serene and at ease, "always equal to himself."

> Surely this was a touch of fine philosophy; though no doubt he had never heard there was such a thing as that. But, perhaps, to be true philosophers, we mortals should not be conscious of so living or so striving. So soon as I hear that such or such a man gives himself out for a philosopher, I conclude that, like the dyspeptic old woman, he must have "broken his digester."[23]

Not that the philosopher is the only dyspeptic writer. Indeed, Melville's *Pierre: Or, the Ambiguities* portrays its novelist-hero in precisely the same terms. The immature Pierre, like an unfinished wall with its jutting stones (*pierres d'attente*) begging for continuation and completion, immaturely prepares to give the world a mature book, and so goes to his immature ruin:

> Pierre was resolved to give the world a book, which the world should hail with surprise and delight. . . . He would climb Parnassus with a pile of folios on his back. He did not see, that it was nothing at all to him, what other men had written; that though Plato was indeed a transcendently great man in himself, yet Plato must not be transcendently great to him (Pierre), so long as he (Pierre himself) would also do something transcendently great. . . . If man must wrestle, perhaps it is well that it should be on the nakedest possible plain. . . . With cheek rather pale, then, and lips rather blue, Pierre sits down to his plank. . . . Pierre is young; heaven gave him the divinest, freshest form of a man; put light into his eye, and fire into his blood, and brawn into his arm, and a joyous, jubilant, overflowing, up-bubbling, universal life in him everywhere. Now look around in that most miserable room, and at that most miserable of all the pursuits of a man, and say if here be the place, and this be the trade, that God intended him for. A rickety chair, two hollow barrels, a plank, paper, pens, and infernally black ink, four leprously dingy white walls, no carpet, a cup of water, and a dry biscuit or two. Oh, I hear the leap of the Texan Camanche, as at this moment he goes crashing like a wild deer through the green underbrush; I hear his glorious whoop of savage and untamable health; and then I look in at Pierre. If physical, practical unreason make the savage, which is he? Civilization, Philosophy, Ideal Virtue! behold your victim! . . . He will not be called to; he will not be stirred. Sometimes the intent ear of Isabel in the next room, overhears the alternate silence, and then the long lonely scratch of his pen. It is, as if she heard the busy claw of some midnight mole in the ground. . . . Here surely is a wonderful stillness of eight hours and a half, repeated day after day. In the heart of such silence, surely something is at work. Is it creation, or destruction? Builds Pierre the noble world of a new book? or does the Pale Haggardness unbuild the lungs and the life in him?—Unutterable, that a man should be thus! . . . Is there then all this work to one book, which shall be read in a very few hours; and, far more frequently, utterly skipped in one second; and which, in the end, whatever it be, must undoubtedly go to the worms? . . . But the devouring profundities, now opened up in him, consume all his vigor. . . .

Melville cites a number of random jottings by Pierre, among them his reflections on truth—". . . to think of the woe and the cant,—to think of the Truth and the Lie!"—and does not fail to draw the devastating consequences, consequences that take us back to the final scene of *Moby-Dick*, or to the scene of Melville's own *writing*:

> From these random slips, it would seem, that Pierre is quite conscious of much that is so anomalously hard and bitter in his lot, of much that is so black and terrific in his soul. Yet that knowing his fatal condition does not one whit enable him to change or better his condition. Conclusive proof that he has no power over his condition. For in tremendous extremities human souls are like drowning men; well enough they know they are in peril; well enough they know the causes of that peril;—nevertheless, the sea is the sea, and these drowning men do drown.[24]

The juxtaposition of Zweig's Nietzsche and Melville's Pierre is most cruel. Yet one may justify it by pointing to Nietzsche's own relentless emphasis on physiological or "health" issues in and for genealogical critique. In vain one tries to rescue oneself from the suspicions such a juxtaposition raises by reading over and over again, as though it were a shamanistic incantation, Nietzsche's insistence that he has lived through and survived decadence.[25]

The juxtaposition is cruel. Or, at best, indiscreet. For it betrays the decadence of inventories such as this one.

THREE

Critica genealogica III

The Decadence of Redemption

If Nietzsche views all moralities and moralistic metaphysics as decadent expressions of will to power in the form of will to nothingness, what can he oppose to such moralism? In 1888 he writes: "My demand upon the philosopher is known: it is that one place oneself *beyond* good and evil, and leave the illusion of moral judgment *beneath* one" (GD; 6, 98). We have seen how very difficult it is to understand how one can get "placed beyond" this kind of thinking when will to power is characterized by the *polemos* of truth and illusion, or the duplicity of being, and when the genealogist insists on distinguishing "good" from "bad" illusion. If Nietzsche has a doctrine that can teach us such "getting beyond," it is the following:

> . . . that no one *gives* one one's qualities, neither God nor society, nor one's parents and forefathers, *nor oneself.* . . . No one is answerable for the fact that one is there at all. . . . The fatality of one's essence is not to be disengaged from everything that was and will be. The human being is not the effect of a particular intention, will, or goal. . . . *We* have invented the concept "goal." In reality, the goal is missing. . . . One is a piece of fatality, one belongs to the totality, one *is* in the totality. . . . But there is nothing outside the totality. . . . The concept "God" was previously the greatest *objection* to existence. . . . We deny God, we deny the answerability in God: we thereby redeem the world for the first time.[1]

REDEEMING THE WORLD FOR THE FIRST TIME

What is the character of this "first redemption," so strange a word for one who experiences the death of God? The Christian God redeems sinners from the effects of sin, transfiguring their entire fate, their body and soul, in the flames of his own immolation. In the very months when Nietzsche writes the above passage from *Twilight* he gives us his keenest analyses of the "Redeemer-type" (A, 29–35; 6, 199–208). The "morbid hedonism" of the Redeemer-type rests upon two "physiological realities": first, "instinctual hatred toward reality: consequence of an extreme capacity for suffering and excitability, which no longer wants to be 'touched' at all because it feels every contact too deeply"; second, "instinctual exclusion of all animosity, hostility, all limits and distances in feeling: . . . any resistance or compulsion to resist already an unbearable aversion. . . . Love as the single *last* possibility of life" (GD; 6, 201). The Redeemer-type, twisted by instinctual hatred and desperate love, is the decadent type *par excellence*. The very "cry for redemption" is the outcome of the introverted cruelty of the ascetic ideal (ZGM III, 20; 5, 329–30). The ardent cry for the transfiguration of the world rises from a chilling frenzy of ressentiment against the world. Nietzsche does not will such a redemption. He wills the passing of redemption and redeemers, at least insofar as those redeemers represent the *causa prima* of the world, in order that the earth be redeemed from man's inflated expectations. He denies that any God is responsible for the world or for man's fate: ego is no such God, society is no such God, God is no such God. Rather, man is a piece of fatality, the member of a totality outside of which is "nothing." What is the character of the redemption of the world—the first redemption of the world—that is achieved in the exclamation "But there is nothing outside the totality!"? What sort of redemption would *not* be grounded in aesthesiophobia or agapomania?

In a passage entitled "The greatest burden [*das größte Schwergewicht*]," a daimon comes to us in our "loneliest loneliness" and whispers, "This life, as you now live it and have lived it, you will have to live once more and innumerable times more. . . . The eternal hourglass of existence will be inverted again and again, and you with it, speck of dust!" (FW, 341; 3, 570). Would our response be a curse or a cakewalk? Our life would have to seem magnificent to us indeed if we demanded nothing more of it than the reliving of it, if we set aside all hopes of transformation and found "redemption" entirely superfluous. This notion of eternal recurrence, first announced by the daimon as a burden and a test, becomes the basic conception of *Thus Spoke Zarathustra*, "the highest formula of affirmation that could possibly be achieved" (EH; 6, 335).

The thought of eternal return came to Nietzsche in August 1881, "six thousand feet beyond human beings and time" (ibid.). He was walking along the lakeshore of Silvaplana near Surlej, when, coming to a halt near a massive pyramidical boulder, the thought came to him. It was a thought nurtured by the music of his and Lou von Salomé's "Hymn to Life," with its yes-saying, tragic pathos (6, 336). Thus the heaviest weight, the test for a diagnosis of health or decadence, became (at least in retrospect) almost immediately the fullest Dionysian affirmation of life.

It is the affirmation of tragedy and the tragedy of affirmation. For the thinking of eternal recurrence seems to go up and down at the same time. It is precisely the *tragic* affirmation of eternal recurrence that refuses "redemption" and so—vicariously, unwittingly, unexpectedly—redeems the world for the *first* time. Nietzsche requires it of those who wish to think with him. However, what is "tragic" about this affirmation of life, this "great healthfulness"? (EH; 6, 337–39). It is the "metaphysical comfort" of one who *witnesses* tragedy, one who can come to bear the words of the Dionysian Silenus—"What is best for you is entirely unachievable: not to be born. . . . The second best for you is to die quickly"—by means of the affirmation that "in spite of the flux of phenomena, life is at bottom indestructibly powerful and pleasurable" (GT, 3; 1,

35–36). " . . . For only as an aesthetic phenomenon is existence and the world eternally *justified* [*ewig* gerechtfertigt]" (GT, 5; *1*, 47). Nietzsche repeats this thesis in "Attempt at a Self-Criticism," noting that "art—and *not* morality—is established there as the genuinely *metaphysical* activity of man" (GT; *1*, 17). In the artistic creativity of Greek tragedy, Nietzsche writes significantly, "the world is in every moment the *achieved* Redemption of God . . ." (ibid.). Or, to be sure, " . . . of the god."

However, the soul and soil of tragedy is Dionysian dithyramb. If we are to understand how the tragic affirmation of eternal recurrence redeems the world for the first time—through a creativity in which transfiguration is already achieved in each moment—we must understand something of Dionysos. For that, we need the help of poets and tragedians.

Dionysos is twice-born, once of mortal Semele and once of Zeus's thigh, to which the god had to be removed for his restitution. Semele is "the bride of Thunder. . . ."

> So his mother bore him once
> in labor bitter; lightning-struck,
> forced by fire that flared from Zeus,
> consumed, she died, untimely torn,
> in childbed dead by blow of light!
> Of light the son was born![2]

The shadow of his mother's death is cast across the life and deeds of the god. He has difficulty establishing his cult. Violence follows him wherever he goes, this god of ivy, the vine, wine, conviviality, dance, and ecstasy. His nemesis is Pentheus, the capable but haughty young king who despises the god's frivolity and fears his influence over women. Pentheus will not participate in Dionysian foolishness, in spite of the counsel of Cadmus and Tiresias:

> We do not trifle with divinity.
> No, we are the heirs of customs and traditions
> hallowed by age and handed down to us
> by our fathers. No quibbling logic can topple *them*,
> whatever subtleties this clever age invents.
> People may say: "Aren't you ashamed? At your age,
> going dancing, wreathing your head with ivy?"
> Well, I am *not* ashamed. Did the god declare
> that just the young or just the old should dance?
> No, he desires his honor from all mankind.
> He wants no one excluded from his worship. (ll. 200–209)

Pentheus is therefore seduced into madness, into unwitting participation in and violation of the Dionysiac rites, which he looks upon lubriciously and impiously, eventually suffering death at his own mother's hand. The two sides of Dionysos's character emerge in the following passage:

> The deity, the son of Zeus,
> in feast, in festival, delights.

> He loves the goddess Peace,
> generous of good,
> preserver of the young.
> To rich and poor he gives
> the simple gift of wine,
> the gladness of the grape.
> But him who scoffs he hates,
> and him who mocks his life,
> the happiness of those
> for whom the day is blessed
> but doubly blessed the night;
> whose simple wisdom shuns the thoughts
> of proud, uncommon men and all
> their god-encroaching dreams.
> But what the common people do,
> the things that simple men believe,
>   I too believe and do. (ll. 417–432)

Hybris against Dionysos takes the form of that self-assured reasonableness of the successful, capable, conscientious young man who would prefer not to risk foolishness. Dionysos disturbs all equanimity, all security, all self-certainty. Dionysos is the enforcer of a certain discretion—not the stuffy propriety of the young king but reticence of a more fundamental and more difficult sort. Tiresias warns: "Mark my words, Pentheus. Do not be so certain that power is what matters in the life of man; do not mistake for wisdom the fantasies of your sick mind" (ll. 309–312).

Among the things that hover in uncertainty in the play is the nature of the relationship between Dionysos and Pentheus. They are not simple opposites. In fact, the two are first cousins, inasmuch as their mothers, Semele and Agave, are sisters. (A disconcerting *third* first cousin is the ill-fated Actaeon, son of Autonoë, another sister of Semele.) Moreover, the action of the play represents the rite by which Dionysos enters into a new phase, or by which the primal phase of his fragmentation by the Titans recurs. Like Actaeon, Pentheus will be the new—and the ever-ancient—Dionysos: the cousins will always have been what they are only now becoming, namely, the dying gods; their tragic flaw is that they continue to confuse themselves with what they always will have been.

In the foreword to *The Gay Science* (3, 352), Nietzsche writes: "Oh, these Greeks! They understood how to live: to do that it is necessary to stop bravely at the superficies, the fold, the skin; to worship appearance, forms, sounds, words; to believe in the whole Olympiad of appearance! These Greeks were superficial—*out of profundity*!" The Greeks were artist-philosophers: this is true even of Socrates and Plato, ostensibly the most Apollonian of Greeks. However, as we have already heard, and as we shall see in greater detail in the next chapter, theirs is a decadent art. Nietzsche calls the tragic art of the Greeks the proper metaphysical activity of humankind. Yet metaphysics is from its inception a decadent preoccupation. How does it stand with genealogical critique—now viewed within the context of recurrence?

Genealogical critique would like to regard itself as a "gay kind of serious-ness," a critique full of pranks, never entirely serious, never swallowed up in the slow-burning rancor of religion and science. In the first note of a "preface" presumably destined for his *magnum opus*, Nietzsche speaks of "greatness" (WM, 1; *13*, 189). He means the greatness of "the grand style," of creative self-affirmation and world-affirmation. Such greatness receives further deter-mination in a statement from *Ecce Homo* (6, 297): "I know no other way of handling great tasks than *play*: this, as a sign of greatness, is an essential presupposition." It is play, *Spiel*, that must advance Nietzsche's genealogical philosophy beyond the *polemos* of suspicion and the metaphysics of good and evil. This is the advance Nietzsche calls for in the name *Dionysos*, a name that can only be sung in the poetic language of the "Drunken Song." Dionysos is, in Eugen Fink's words, "the formless-forming, constructing-destroying god whose regard is the mask, whose epiphany is his hiddenness, who is one and many, exuberant life and the simple serenity of Hades" (Fn, 180). Further, the name *Dionysos* must somehow appropriate the qualities of Apollo, even if it does seem as though "where the Dionysian penetrates the Apollonian is abol-ished and destroyed" (GT, 4; *1*, 41; cf. Gr, 541). For it is Apollo who fashions the illusions of art, so that mortals need not perish of Dionysian truths. "Dionysian truth can be communicated only under the mask of Apollonian imagery" (Gr, 556). The *play* of Apollonian images and Dionysian truths, and not their warlike opposition, is a requirement for genealogical critique as well as for Greek art. According to Albert Camus, the requirement is not unachiev-able: "Damocles never danced better than when under the sword."[3] Again it is Herman Melville who aptly portrays the kind of thinking that genealogical critique must enact if it is to advance to the tragic affirmation of eternal recur-rence. Melville calls it "the desperado philosophy":

> There are certain queer times and occasions in this strange mixed affair we call life when a man takes this whole universe for a vast practical joke, though the wit thereof he but dimly discerns, and more than suspects that the joke is at nobody's expense but his own. However, nothing dispirits, and nothing seems worthwhile disputing. He bolts down all events, all creeds and beliefs and persuasions, all hard things visible and invisible, never mind how knobby. . . . And as for smaller difficulties and worryings, prospects of sudden disaster, peril of life and limb; all these, and death itself, seem to him only sly, good-natured hits, and jolly punches in the side bestowed by the unseen and unaccountable old joker. That odd sort of wayward mood I am speaking of, comes over a man only in some time of extreme tribulation; it comes in the very midst of his earnestness, so that what just before might have seemed to him a thing most momentous, now seems but a part of the general joke. There is nothing like the perils of whaling to breed this free and easy sort of genial, desperado philosophy; and with it I now regarded this whole voyage of the Pequod, and the great White Whale its object.[4]

The resonance of the desperado philosophy, its tragic affirmation and love of fate, is perhaps best expressed in the character of Stubb. As the great white whale bears down on Ahab's doomed ship, Stubb hears the first mate, Starbuck, praying: "My God, stand by me now!" By way of response, Stubb roars, "Stand not by me, but stand under me, whoever you are. . . . I grin at thee, thou grinning whale! Look ye, sun, moon and stars! I call ye assassins of as good a fellow as ever spouted up his ghost. For all that, I would yet ring glasses with thee, would ye but hand the cup!" Such an attitude—raillery and shrewd negotiation at once—marks the end of traditional Christian piety and radically alters the stance of mortals with regard to the sacred. This change of stance at first seems a Promethean rebellion; indeed, Camus's "metaphysical revolt" describes the stance well, albeit incompletely. Fink notes that this new stance involves a radical change in the meaning of *time* for human beings and gods alike: "The eternal gods must die so that transient man can know his very transiency as eternal, as eternal recurrence; the eternity of man and world can have no foreign, divine eternity near it. . . . Pleasure taken in the world [*die Weltlust*] kills the gods" (Fn, 112). The metaphysical revolt of the desperado philosophy does not establish a divine immortality for humanity; on the contrary, Titanic time eats its mortal and immortal children alike, devours its nymphs and daimons, all of whom *suffer* time. Yet the pleasure they take in the world and the earth, "eating bread, tasting the earth," wills the eternity of the time of the earth. Humankind honors the earth now, not the gods of Platonism and the Prophets, and so honors the immutable fate of this suffering of time—not contradicting it, as we shall see, but calling for it once again. "Perhaps earth also is an ancient, primeval goddess, but she is a figureless one, having no contour, 'being near yet difficult to capture'" (Fn, 74). This new stance is what Nietzsche wills to achieve through his revaluation of all values and the project of overman.

Enthusiasts of the desperado philosophy can go whaling, or they can read Nietzsche, it seems. If they should opt for the latter, *which* Nietzsche should it be? For sometimes it seems that everything depends on *where* one reads in Nietzsche. There is, for example, the language of *Beyond Good and Evil*, or the *Genealogy*, which vivisects reader and writer alike, the language inscribed by the scalpel of suspicion. This language appears also in many parts of *Zarathustra*, keen, relentless, and cruel. There is the disturbingly or hilariously inflated language of *Ecce Homo*, with its volatile exclamations and declamations, its nostalgia, *apologia*, and self-glorification not quite covering the abysses of deprecation, the language of a harried celebration of the life accomplishments of one Lutheran-gone-genius-gone-clown; but also a language that mirrors the Dionysian dithyramb of *Zarathustra*, the language of neither scalpel nor bellows. This is the language that thinks eternal recurrence in song, not disburdening itself of the heaviest burden but preserving the language of tragedy and downgoing.

In *Ecce Homo*, Nietzsche describes how he came upon the figure of Zarathustra. Or, rather, how Zarathustra found and overcame *him*. The rapid gestation and explosive birth of that work, each of whose parts was written in spurts of creativity as brief as ten days at a time, Nietzsche regards as the fruit of a period of "great healthfulness" in his life. Great healthfulness does not lie like a dog in the sun, however, but strides headlong into the adventure for which it feels itself fated—it "*initiates* the tragedy" (6, 337–39). Further, the initiation is embodied: "The *body* is inspired," writes Nietzsche, setting aside the shivering piety of the soul (ibid.). However, that the great healthfulness is a gift fatefully and fitfully given is suggested when Nietzsche writes of the *rancune* of greatness. *Rancune* is the French word that ordinarily means "spite" or "grudge." "Everything great, a work, a deed, once completed, inevitably turns *against* the one who did it" (6, 341–42). To have done something great is to have given life to an ungrateful child: one cannot sustain oneself in the greatness of what one has done, but stands abashed in its shadow, unable to look it in the face. It is as though the deed spitefully abandons the doer to the poverty of his or her mere existence, as though insinuating that the doer did not really do the deed at all. "To have something *behind* oneself"—this is the cruelty of the "it was" of time. *Rancune* is doubtless an attribute or an offshoot of *ressentiment*. One might have hoped and expected that the "great health" could overcome any kind of suffering and resentment, and banish the chronic symptoms of human finitude. Perhaps it could, if like a crab it could go backward.

Nietzsche poses the dilemma of eternal recurrence within the context of genealogical critique—itself the spavined child of asceticism, the gaunt grandchild of impotence and cruelty—as the "psychological problem of the Zarathustra type," and he does so with astounding precision. One can do no better than to repeat his formulation:

> The psychological problem of the Zarathustra type is how he who to an unprecedented extent says and *acts* "no" with regard to everything to which prior human beings have said "yes" can nevertheless remain the opposite of a no-saying spirit; how the one who bears destiny's heaviest burden, whose life-task is a fatality, can still be the lightest and most ethereal of spirits—Zarathustra is a dancer—: how he who has had the hardest and most terrible insight into reality, he who has thought "the most abysmal thought," can nevertheless find in these things no objections to existence or to its eternal recurrence; on the contrary, he finds still other grounds for *himself being* the eternal "yes" to all things, "the vast, limitless Yes-and-Amen saying. . . ." "Into all abysses I carry my yes-saying, which blesses. . . ." *However, to repeat: that is the very concept of Dionysos.* (6, 344–45)

As an indication of that "concept," Nietzsche can only point toward the figure of Zarathustra. Yet that does not tell us *how* Zarathustra can bless without becoming one of the donkey-worshippers who hee-haw in caricature of Zarathustran affirmation. Nietzsche attempts to say what Zarathustran affirmation is by calling it the very *Begriff* of Dionysos—not so much the "concept" as the "grasp" or "grip" of the god. Is the genitive objective or subjective? Are we to grasp what Dionysos means, or is it Dionysos who grasps us? We might recall that the one who tried to grasp Dionysos was Pentheus; the Theban king seized and imprisoned the god, only to become more of the god than any mortal could handle. Nietzsche says that his concept of the Dionysian became deed, the supreme deed, in the writing of *Thus Spoke Zarathustra*. The Dionysian is no longer a classicist's label, wanting to capture something about the origins of Greek tragedy, but now indicates submission to the god himself: " . . . there is no grasp [*Begriff*] of the distance, of the azure solitude, in which this work lives" (6, 343). Zarathustra withdraws to a region bounded by "sacred borders," which the last human beings cannot descry.

In the frenzy of the Dionysian deed, the dilemma of the Zarathustra type appears to dissolve, inasmuch as contradiction itself is undone in the very invitation to the Dionysian. "He contradicts with every word, this most yes-saying of spirits; in him all contraries are bound in a new unity" (ibid.). It is not difficult to spill words about the *coincidentia oppositorum*, much in the way Hegel's "naive spirit" makes water. If one spends enough time in the vicinity of a university philosophy faculty, one will hear about the Pythagorean "Table of Opposites," Heraclitean Λόγος, the Christian doctrines of creation, the fall, and redemption, and Leibniz's "best of all possible worlds," and thus will have the background that enables one to confuse Zarathustran affirmation with other things. One historian of philosophy, whose work represents historical writing of a superior sort, attributes to the young Nietzsche, the Nietzsche of *The Birth of Tragedy*, "a final, metaphysical, cosmic optimism, a universal transfiguration and theodicy"; by pronouncing the earth sacred through the Dionysian mystery of eternal return and thus binding together the opposites of joy and suffering, Nietzsche embodies the "final consequence" of modern philosophy since Spinoza and Leibniz, which seeks to transfigure the world by uncovering the *Theodizeemotif* hidden within it.[5] The Pythagorean and Heraclitean parallels are thought-provoking, as long as one confesses one's ignorance about what the word *parallel* means; but the references to modern philosophy are troubling, especially when one presumes to label Nietzsche "a final consequence" of metaphysical idealism. For the question with respect to Zarathustra is whether something decidedly new occurs when the world's transfiguration is no longer taken to be the by-product of a doctrine of creation *ex nihilo* that unites the opposites of form and matter, spirit and flesh, in the divine imagination,[6] nor of a doctrine of redemption within an expiative "salvation history"; now—for the first time—the world's transfiguration is taken to be already achieved *in each moment* of the ring of becoming, so that the world's pristine innocence is assured from beginning to end.

Decidedly new? Or as old as Dionysos? At all events, in Dionysian frenzy the innocence of the world is not achieved as a dialectical conclusion to the struggle between good and evil or redemption from the fall: like genealogical critique, Dionysian affirmation has no *ground* in ratiocinative thought, no "middle term," no axiom, no *mathesis universalis*, no article of faith or dogma. What, then, is the character of this experience that causes all redemptive projects to disintegrate and that concedes both the decadence of redemption and the innocence of becoming? What does *concession* mean here? What proprietary rights of moral-metaphysical humanity are herewith surrendered?

"Zarathustra feels himself to be . . . the *supreme form of all being*" (6, 344). He is therefore quite beyond comparatives and comparisons. Humans, the last humans, do not gain entry to his essence by way of figures of speech.

"Here in every moment man is overcome; the concept *overman* here becomes the greatest actuality" (ibid.). Overman is precisely the one who gains entry into the essence of Dionysian affirmation. Only within such affirmation do the metaphors and similes come, and the figures of Zarathustran speech always come as something more than tropes. "The most powerful skill in metaphor that ever was is poor, is mere word-play, in the face of this return of language to the nature of imagery" (ibid.). Yet this return is the only clue we have, and we last human beings, who would try to trace it, should not be surprised by its unreadability. "What language would such a spirit speak, when speaking to itself alone? The language of the dithyramb" (6, 345). It would be the language of the *Nachtlied* from *Thus Spoke Zarathustra*. The language of dithyramb is in the present case sung in solitude, and is not the language of teaching. One cannot grasp its meaning, except in stumbling words that are all too reminiscent of crucifixion and redemption: " . . . it is *yes-saying* unto justification, unto the very redemption of everything past" (6, 348). The language of dithyramb is the swan song of suffering, albeit not the sufferings of a Christ; of his *Nachtlied* Nietzsche writes, "The like has never been poetized, never been felt, never been suffered before: thus suffers a god, a Dionysos" (ibid.). The language of dithyramb is sung in the raptures of Dionysiac possession and inspiration. In retrospect—that is, out of the inevitable *rancune* that compels him to describe it—Nietzsche gives the following account of dithyrambic creativity:

> If one had the least bit of superstition in oneself one would scarcely know how to reject the notion that one is in fact mere incarnation, mere mouthpiece, mere medium for overpowering forces. The concept of revelation succinctly describes the situation: it is the sense that suddenly, with inexpressible certainty and subtlety, something becomes *visible*, something becomes audible, something that throttles one down to the depths and overturns one. One hears, one does not seek; one accepts, one does not ask who it is that gives; a thought flashes like lightning, with necessity, without hesitation as to its form—I never had a choice.[7]

Nietzsche's description mirrors that of Euripides' account of Dionysiac possession. It is the ἔκστασις, the extraordinary feeling that one is beside oneself, outside oneself—rapt to the words of divinity, wrapped in the folds of divinity, absorbed in its oval face. Yet Dionysian rapture, as Nietzsche experiences it since the time of "The Dionysian Worldview" (summer 1870), is always accompanied by an uncanny lucidity, if only in the form of "the most distinct consciousness of numberless subtle tremors and pricklings down to one's toes."[8] *Schauder und Überrieselungen*: terrors, tremors, and tremblings; drizzling rains, pins-and-needles, waves of inundation. Dionysian rapture is neither dull intoxication nor exuberant impenetrability, neither depressed nor manic behavior. The Dionysiac manifold does not peacefully submit to incarceration in pure concepts, nor even in impure "sensible concepts." Nietzsche conjoins two apparently contradictory words to describe it: *Glücks-tiefe*. *Glück* means happiness or good fortune, the ascendancy of one's star, precisely as the sounding of the word itself rises from the depths of one's gorge to the roof of the mouth; *Tiefe* names the depths, and descends to the depths, *de profundis*, in the throat. One scarcely knows how to pronounce the neologism *Glückstiefe*. Zarathustran rapture is what Alphonso Lingis calls a rapture of the deep,[9] a deep happiness or a happy depth that, as Nietzsche says, "the most painful and foreboding things do not refute" (6, 339). Rather, all terrors and tremblings seem to be conditions or requirements, "a *necessary* color within such a spectrum of light" (ibid.). The standard that measures Dionysian inspiration is wavelength, better, the area of the field penetrated by its light, the rhythmic intensity in which the most disparate forms assemble and join hands. Such inspiration feels its enormous power to be unconditioned, divine and utterly free, omnipenetrant; yet at the same time one senses one's uncanny possession by something *outside*, so that the power is held by *lieutenance* alone. "The involuntariness of the image, of the simile, is most remarkable; one no longer has any grasp of what an image, or what similitude, is; everything offers itself as the closest, most correct, and simplest expression" (6, 340). The rhythm of Dionysian rapture, which ultimately obscures the everyday sense of inside and outside, shatters the limits of critical reason. Nietzsche refers to Zarathustra's words, "Here all being wants to become word, all becoming wants to learn from you how to talk," and he adds, "It truly seems as though the things themselves approach and offer themselves to simile" (ibid.). His words call to mind Kant's hint in the *Critique of Pure Reason* that any knowledge of the thing-in-itself, that is, knowledge not subject to the receptivity of intuition, could be ascribed only to a creator god: the divine imagination, as creative imagination, sees things from the inside, as it were. Yet in a deeper sense, Dionysian rapture is *pure receptivity*, precisely without the clumsy operations of understanding or reason, even in their "free play" within the transcendental imagination. Nietzsche does not say that in Dionysian rapture the *Ding-an-sich* is known in such a way that the project of philosophy as a universal science of being is fulfilled; rather, given the way that the things *offer themselves* to simile or comparison, to *Gleichnis*, one must say that the eternal recurrence of the *Gleichnis* is less heavy-handed cosmic construction than light-footed poetic play. Again, not even the play of faculties—although the third *Critique* offers more food for thought than the first in this respect—but the play of being and becoming is what Nietzsche has experienced. If the play has to do with knowledge at all, such knowledge is *tragic*.

SHADES OF DECADENCE

From the Critical point of view it is quite impossible to see how Dionysian utterance could be anything other than a delirious binge of dialectical illusion, even if such utterance forswears all dialectic. And if, as we have seen, genealogy is the obstreperous child of Critique, the mischievous business of a critical critique of criticism, then we should not be surprised to find remarks in Nietzsche's works that cast suspicion on the very rhythm of dithyramb, on the very soul of Dionysiac rapture. For example, in that famous passage of *The Gay*

Science entitled "On the Origin of Poesy" (FW, 84; 3, 439–42), Nietzsche argues that rhythmic language is not simply an ornament, a superfluous nicety, that occasionally adorns the prosaic world. Rather, "rhythm is a compulsion," an exercise of power. By it human beings hope to compel the gods to do their bidding, believing that rhythmic language "exercises a power over the gods." Poesy is humanity's "magical snare" for capturing divinities. "Song is an enchantment of daimons, who are actively pursued in the singing, which makes them compliant, captive instruments of humanity." Iambic hexameter is the Delphic rhythm, the binding of prophecy and fate. "Without verse man is nothing; through it man becomes well-nigh a god." Thus the most serious philosophers speak the language of poetry, "in order to lend power and credence to their thoughts." Thus too it is more hazardous for a truth when the poet agrees with it: "For, as Homer says, 'Indeed, singers lie a lot!'"

The suspicion arises that rhythm is Dionysos with the soul of Apollo. However, this is hardly worth the title *suspicion*: Nietzsche himself always recognizes the interdependence of Dionysian and Apollonian qualities in art, that is, in the *tragic* art of the Greeks: Apollo and Dionysos constitute a series of complex *crossings*.[10] What *would* be worthy of suspicion is whether the tension between Dionysos and Apollo, which perhaps expresses the tension between the thinking of eternal recurrence of the same and genealogical critique, must ultimately capitulate to the dreamy resolution of all tension in Christian redemption, thus petering out into impotent nihilism—once again, the decadence of redemption.

Few have written as thoughtfully about the redemptive power of eternal recurrence—in the context of the death of God—as Camus. He notes that Nietzsche's notion of eternal recurrence, which *requires* the death of God for its tragic affirmation, involves an ironic addition to Stendhal's ruse, *la seule excuse de Dieu, c'est qu'il n'éxiste pas*. Camus notes: "Deprived of the divine will, the world is equally deprived of unity and finality. That is why it is impossible to pass judgment on the world. Any attempt to apply a standard of values to the world leads finally to a slander on life" (Cm, 88–89). Camus does not consider whether the bipolarity of will to power, the central conception of genealogical critique, constitutes or at least presupposes a "standard of values" and therefore inevitably contains elements of the metaphysical slander. He continues:

> From the moment it is recognized that the world pursues no end, Nietzsche proposes to concede its innocence . . . , to replace all judgments based on values with absolute assent, and with a complete and exalted allegiance to this world. . . . This magnificent consent, born of abundance and fullness of spirit, is the unreserved affirmation of human imperfection and suffering, of evil and murder, of all that is problematic and strange in our existence. (Cm, 95)

To repeat, Camus does not see in the project of a revaluation of all values, based on the bipolar standard of will to power, the legacy of the very tradition Nietzsche is seeking to escape. He concludes: "The movement of rebellion, by

which man demanded his own existence, disappears in the individual's absolute submission to the inevitable. *Amor fati* replaces what was an *odium
fati*" (Cm, 95–96). According to Camus, the revaluation of all values consists
solely in "replacing the value of the judge with that of the creator" (Cm, 97).
Thus the artist is granted the freedom and the status of a divinity—but, to
repeat, a divinity without immortality: "Nietzsche proposed that man should
allow himself to be engulfed in the cosmos, in order to rediscover his eternal
divinity and to become Dionysos" (ibid.). Eternal divinity? Eternally *mortal*
divinity. For Dionysos is a tragic god, a "god of the earth," eternally dismembered. Is he then the incarnate god, the redeemer? Does the artist, the creator
and annihilator of values, transfigure the world through his or her own passion and death, thereby achieving the paradise of an absolute "there"?

> There all the barrel-hoops are knit,
> There all the serpent tails are bit,
> There all the gyres converge in one,
> There all the planets drop in the Sun.[11]

What could have been the voluptuous, ecstatic, but ultimately pious immolation of the world by the artist-god Camus displaces with a chilling adden-
dum: "However, the name of Dionysos immortalized only the notes to Ariadne,
which he wrote when he was mad" (Cm, 97). To be sure, Nietzsche signed
other letters and notes written during the days of his euphoria and collapse
"The Crucified."

There remain a number of disturbing aspects—shades of decadence—to
this supposedly full affirmation of human existence that Nietzsche claims to
have achieved in his thinking of eternal recurrence of the same. Eternal return,
which is supposed to emanate from the healthful, anything-but-decadent pole
of Nietzsche's will to power, bears within itself virulent strains—infectious
strains—of nihilism, at least insofar as we, the last human beings, think it. On
June 10, 1887, in Lenzerheide, Graubünden, Nietzsche reflects on nihilism as
the extreme reaction to the collapse of prior values and suggests that the extreme thinking of such nihilism would be nothing other than the thinking of
eternal recurrence (WM, 55; 12, 211–17). Eternal recurrence is "vain duration," the infinite suspension of all values and all judgments in a "paralysis" of
will: "This uttermost form of nihilism: the nothing (the 'meaningless'), eternally!" Eternal recurrence here is not the deification of the earth, as Fink and
Granier would have it (Fn, 74; Gr, 293), but on the contrary "an antithesis to
pantheism." It is a moral arbiter-god, to be sure, who makes affirmation of the
earth impossible; if that god is obliterated, "would pantheism be possible?"
Further, "Does it make sense to think of a god 'beyond good and evil'?" In
other words, is one capable of thinking divinity quite beyond the categories of
good and evil, affirmation and negation? Are we, the last human beings, now
able to achieve what evaded Schelling throughout his thoughtful life? Does the
dissolution of the *moral* attitude and the adoption of an *aesthetic* attitude advance thinking decisively beyond good and evil, or does the bipolar standard

of will to power inevitably moralize its aesthetics? Does not aesthetics since Kant consist precisely in this moralization of the beautiful and the work of art? Finally, would it be possible to envisage not the sacralization or deification of earth and world but a *daimonization* that would be neither a diabolism nor a tepid paganism?[12]

We must clarify what is at stake in Nietzsche's thinking of eternal recurrence—a difficult task, inasmuch as that thinking appears in various figures, guises, and motifs, none of them coined in the language I am using here. Nor can any of those perspectives in which the thought appears in Nietzsche's works be canceled on behalf of a dialectical progression toward its "full" meaning. As Joan Stambaugh writes: "Nietzsche never brought it to an ultimate conceptual formulation, which goes to show that it was by no means an invented 'theory,' but rather an *experience* that does not permit of being brought to an ultimate formulation" (St, 176–77). The thinking that wills eternal recurrence of the same aims to overcome the will-to-nothingness that is typical of *passive* nihilism, the nihilism of the ascetic ideal. Such thinking, as Karl Löwith indicates, experiences the *crisis* of nihilism, determining "whether man wants still to be there [*da-sein*] at all."[13] For Nietzsche, such thinking is that "single truly serious philosophic problem" cited by Camus at the outset of *The Myth of Sisyphus*: the problem of suicide.[14] For suicide is simply the will to nothingness deprived of the contrivances of asceticism; it is the praxis that corresponds to a metaphysics deprived of its piety and pusillanimity. Suicide is the final celebration of *rancune* and *ressentiment*. Suicide is rigorous science.

Liberation from revenge is the goal toward which Nietzsche directs his thinking of eternal recurrence. This is what Zarathustra teaches in the episode "On Redemption."[15] Metaphysical man seeks a *ground* for his suffering, for the *circle* of life, suffering, and death. Not content with accepting suffering as his condition or situation, he devotes his life to a search for its cause, for a place to lay the blame. Suffering is experienced always as a *fait accompli*, with the cause in each case lying outside itself, back in time, in the "it was." "Seeking after a ground, after something *responsible* for one's present situation, and therefore *guilty* of it, corresponds to what Nietzsche calls the instinct of revenge" (St, 68). Time reveals itself as the absolute impossibility of the human *will* to overcome suffering. For each act of will that would free man from revenge imprisons itself in the "it was" of time, in time's perfect imperfection. Time is that which the will cannot break, the will's insurmountable obstacle (St, 73). The thwarted will thus becomes enslaved to revenge: revenge foments a sort of counterwill to the forceful "it was" of time, a counterwill or ill will that declares the sole justification of a world in which there is suffering to be its transiency, its passing away. The thwarted will is Mephistophelean: " . . . *denn alles, was entsteht, / Ist wert, daß es zugrunde geht*" (*Faust I*, ll. 1339–40). For Nietzsche, this counterwill is the origin of metaphysics, hence of nihilism. Yet how is mankind to be liberated from its ill will against the "it was" of time? No act of mere resignation will deliver humanity from the vengefulness ensconced in metaphysics, inasmuch as resignation is itself characteristic of the "unfree will" (St, 75). Only when the project of locating the *cause* of human suffering is relinquished, only when the "it was" of time, at least in the sense of revenge against time, ceases to *be* as such, can human beings be redeemed from revenge (St, 76). Because the will is captive to the "it was" of time, its own irruptions within time cannot cancel the flux. How then is revenge against the "it was" to be overcome? *Can* it be overcome?

Such overcoming can only be a matter of our *not needing* the "it was" to be the *ground* of our suffering. Such liberation can succeed only if the innocence of becoming is celebrated, only if suffering is conceded as what befalls us contingently, as an accident, as *Zufall*. Stambaugh comments:

> It is manifest here that Nietzsche understands by "accident" something essentially new. Accident is not the contrary of necessity. It is the originary moment [*das ursprüngliche Moment*] with which everything, be it revenge or "redemption," gets under way. What is essential about it is neither that it is inestimable nor that it is something in which "freedom" jostles side-by-side with the necessitous play of forces. Rather, accident is an originary moment, which Nietzsche calls "sensibility" ['*Empfindung*']. . . . (St, 77–78)

The effort to understand how revenge against the "it was" of time dissolves in the feeling or sensation of the innocence of accident holds some promise. What occurs in this "moment" of feeling? Clearly, it cannot be a simple decision on the part of the human will to cancel the "it was" as a moment of time, for the will itself testifies to the independence of the time against which it shatters. Yet such decision is apparently what Nietzsche's Zarathustra calls for: "To redeem the past and to recreate every 'it was' in a 'thus I willed it'— that alone I would call redemption!" (ASZ II; 4, 179). However, the spirit of revenge cannot budge the stony past, cannot move the lapidary "it was" of time. Eternities and eternal punishments are called into being precisely on account of this frustration; precisely on account of this frustration human beings fret over their fate within time, "which eats its children." The ultimate fulmination of revenge is the will's attempt to redeem itself by not willing at all, by surrendering itself—Stoically, Buddhistically—to what is written: "Unless, of course, the will finally were to redeem itself, and willing were to become notwilling . . ." (4, 181) Zarathustra teaches that the will is a creator that can will backward as well as forward, achieving a "reconciliation with time, and something higher than any reconciliation." "Higher than reconciliation must be that will which is will to power—" (ibid.). Yet how can the will learn this strange new art of a willing that is so close to not-willing? Zarathustra insists: "All 'it was' is a fragment, a riddle, a cruel accident,—until the creative will says to it: 'But thus I willed it!'—until the creative will says to it: 'But thus I will it! Thus I shall will it!'" (ibid.).

Thus I willed it, will it now, and shall will it: past, present, and future are encompassed in an embrace beyond all mere reconciliation, an affirmation beyond all mere consent, a celebration beyond all mere acceptance. The will does not resign itself to the suffering of its past, but affirms, celebrates, and embraces the "originary accident that knows no ground and no series of causes and effects" (St, 77–78). Yet Zarathustra only now spoke of the "cruel accident" of every "it was." When and how does accident cease being cruel? We cannot simply say that the will "does not overcome time but reconciles itself to it by overcoming *itself*" (St, 189). For such self-overcoming of the will would stand in closest proximity to the metaphysico-moral will, the passive, reactive, and rancorous will. Zarathustra cannot put into words what he intends to say. To the hunchbacks to whom he speaks, Zarathustra speaks as a hunchback. (And also, Yeats would add, as saint and fool.) Zarathustra cannot teach redemption from revenge against the "it was" of time, if teaching means to spell out in so many words the doctrine to be taught.

Yet the discord between the act of willing and the usual understanding of time must be settled if will to power and eternal recurrence are to harmonize— and if we are to escape the decadence of redemption. Redemption from the spirit of revenge, as vengeance against the imperfect(ion) of time, cannot take the form of a "willing" of eternal return, that is, of a commanding justification of the "it was." For this notion of "willing" itself moves along a linear, causal path, not across the arching path of recurrence. "Willing," if it has to do with the *ego volo* that stands behind the *ego cogito*, can never achieve a *thinking* of eternal return. Will to power must somehow radiate from the thinker of return as from the center of a circle to its circumference. As Stambaugh writes, "The 'will' in will to power is a good-will towards itself; it does not designate a striving after goals 'into the open future' . . . ; rather, a good will in this sense means as much as joy in that which is, the enjoying of oneself in 'doing' ['*Tun*'], or, strictly speaking, in 'happening' ['*Geschehen*']" (St, 195). Nietzsche does not wish the center of the radiating ring to be the moment of Schopenhauerian art, which congeals the flux of time in narcotic representation; rather, he wishes it to be the moment of midday, the moment of eternity, which embraces all time in a simple simultaneity. "Strictly thought, the moment *is* every moment," notes Stambaugh (St, 214). Within the ring of time "there is nothing to 'decide'; for the one who achieves it, everything is already 'decided'" (St, 215).

Yet once again one must ask: How does one attain to the dimension of the ring? Is the embrace of all time in a simple simultaneity the ἅμα of which Aristotle dreamed? Or is it a matter of some other insight, some other thrust of knowledge? Löwith says of Nietzsche, "He wants to redeem human beings from accident and from their culpable existence by means of the knowledge that necessity rules in accident itself, the knowledge that existence as such is as innocent of goals as it is itself innocent" (Lw, 70). Yet what sort of *Erkenntnis* could that be, if all will to knowledge is at bottom will to deception? Is eternal recurrence simply a last mad Platonic fling at self-deception and illusion, a coda to the Socratic swan song, one more last ignoble lie?

We are once again left, it seems, with the possibility that the thinking of recurrence pertains to will to power as *art* rather than *knowledge*. Art responds more powerfully than learning does to the creativity of will that Zarathustra calls for. Will to power under the aegis of the artistic pathos is the supreme feeling of power, willing itself unto eternity.[16] Art here means the process of beings as a whole, and not merely the artistic activity of the human being: " . . . the tendency towards totality is art, as the essence of the world itself" (St, 141). Power as beauty, the grand style that compels chaos into form by its "eternalizing," *Verewigung* (WM, 617; 12, 312), overcomes becoming and its temporality, in the sense of the will's ill will toward the "it was" of time. Stambaugh writes: "The overcoming of 'time,' which means the counterwill against 'time,' comes clearly to expression in the attunement of frenzy, of the lofty feeling of *power*" (St, 146).

Thus the *thinking* of eternal recurrence presupposes the tendency to artistic creativity. The question of the guilt or innocence of becoming is "senseless" once the *moral attitude* is replaced by the *aesthetic* (St, 154–55). Art is, in Fink's words, "profound insight into the heart of the world and the justification of appearance" (Fn, 169). Only in the plenitude of artistic frenzy or Dionysian rapture is one's will attuned to will to power as the essence of all being, such attunement implying "*a new interpretation* of all *occurrence*" (St, 146). For Nietzsche, to be sure, *music* is the art in question: a quartet *is* only insofar as it is being played, and every time it is played it constitutes its moment (St, 149–50).

However, there are difficulties here as well. For the controlled and articulated frenzy of a late quartet, both for the one who plays and the one who listens, is suspended between the limitless silences that precede and follow it, even if the music shapes what precedes it in its very poise for the leap, and even if it reverberates throughout the stillness that follows. Within the moment of music there is no such thing as recurrence of the same. If the "same" phrase is repeated, what is heard is nonetheless never the same. The power that repetition exercises in music lies precisely in the irrevocable quality of each sounded tone—except perhaps in the most cumbersome of Wagner's works, which could hardly serve as Nietzschean exemplars. Indeed, music itself might be exemplary for the insight that seems to have dominated Nietzsche at the moment when the thought of eternal return of the same is first sketched out: as we shall see in chapter 8, eternal recurrence is *never* of "the same." The frenzy that music evokes is quiet amazement over what has happened across a stretch of time, a time that is dying as soon as it is born, a time of the irrecuperable "it was."

However, whether will to power is of knowledge or of art, what does it mean to *declare* that the totalizing, eternalizing character of musical art cancels or expunges all revenge against time and its "it was"? What sort of cancellation of fleeting time occurs in these *words* concerning the Dionysian? Does Dionysian creativity cancel once and for all the *rancune* that according to Nietzsche marks all great creative accomplishments? Do Nietzsche's pronouncements, whether through Zarathustra or in his notebooks, produce and sustain the Dionysian frenzy or rapture that transforms the dimensions of time? What does it mean to *write* about Dionysos? Can anything of the Dionysian be communicated across the vast distance of the word and words? Can anything like eternal recurrence of the same be taught or thought or written? What monstrosity of writing could accommodate it?

One can understand Löwith's impatience to set aside the theme of will to power for the sake of eternal return. In the love of fate, that is, the *amor fati* that characterizes the experience of eternal return, will to power seems to be canceled and transcended—*relevé*, as the French would say. Love of fate, according to Löwith, "is no longer a willing, but . . . a being willing that no longer wills anything [*eine nichts mehr wollende Willigkeit*], a complaisance in which willing as such cancels and surpasses itself [*sich aufhebt*]" (Lw, 83). As soon as the trusty standby of all German ideology—*Aufhebung*—is introduced, all genuine problems lapse into comfortable obfuscation. Thus Walter Kaufmann can call the thinking of eternal recurrence "the ultimate apotheosis of the supra-historical outlook, the supreme exaltation of the moment" (Kf, 277), a thinking that somehow surpasses not only the moral attitude but also the historical and the aesthetic: Nietzsche's putatively "academic" solution of the problem in *The Birth of Tragedy*, which seeks to "justify" life as an aesthetic phenomenon, is now sublated by a "supreme joy" that "obviates any concern for the 'justification' of the world," a joy that affirms the world "forward, backward, and 'in all eternity'" (Kf, 278–79). How the elevation takes place nevertheless remains a mystery—*the* mystery of Nietzsche's thought.

RADIANT AFFIRMATION VERSUS
PALTRY CONSOLATION

In the chapters of the book that follow, I will try to describe the thinking of eternal return of the same, at least in the context of genealogical critique, as a kind of *descensional reflection*. Granier and Deleuze, following the insights of Gaston Bachelard (discussed in chapter 12), have designated the two modes of Nietzschean reflection as "ascensional" and "descensional." Whereas genealogical critique is decidedly *descensional* in character, as it passes underground, the thinking of eternal recurrence of the same *seems to be* a matter of *ascension*. How can the two sorts of thinking be related?

The "virtues" of genealogical critique are philological probity and intellectual cleanliness: *Redlichkeit* and *Sauberkeit*. What have these virtues to do with the thinking of a fabulous recurrence of the same? How is one to advance from the *polemos* of truth and semblance in the duplicity of being to the child's or the artist's play? We have not gotten any closer to the essence of the Dionysian than Pentheus did from his treetop perch.

Earlier we described the *will* to Dionysian affirmation as radiation from the center of a circle; we must now try to approach that center, experience the radiation. "The center is the region of the holy *par excellence*," writes Mircea Eliade in *Le mythe de l'éternel retour*.[17] The sacred mountain, the *omphalos*, the mysteries of the temple, the labyrinth—all pose the problem of the path to the center. The genealogist's suspicion of all centers, an eccentric suspicion, hardly seems a fitting path to the center. Suspicion dare not openly profess its faith. Yet suspicion is itself a hall of mirrors, if not a gallery of heroes; it is a labyrinth of its own. Eliade continues:

> The way is arduous, sown with perils, because it is in fact a rite of passage from the profane to the sacred; from the ephemeral and illusory to reality and eternity; from death to life; from man to divinity. Access to the "center" amounts to a consecration, an initiation. To an existence that yesterday was profane and illusory there now advenes a new existence, one that is real, durable, and efficacious. (ibid.)

However, Nietzsche does not stand in the center of the thought of recurrence—if that means in karmatic calm, resignation, and acceptance of the suffering merited by past misdeeds. It is no exaggeration to say that such "cyclical" thinking as one finds in the Hindu *karma* or in Greek Orphism, to which eternal return *seems* to be related, deter every approach to Nietzsche's thinking. The center of Dionysian affirmation can be reached only when all types of thinking in terms of merits and values have been left behind. For genealogical critique, which has nurtured itself *ab ovo* on such thinking, whether in terms of value-for-life or aesthetic value, the thinking of eternal return is the most difficult self-overcoming imaginable. Dionysian affirmation must not be construed as a justification of the world or as a profession of faith in its value, even though Nietzsche himself invariably describes it in such terms—as a world that is "valueless" because of its "inestimable value."

Early and late in his philosophical career, however, Nietzsche himself recognized the superficial nature of all thinking in terms of values. In *Human, All-Too-Human* (1878) he noted that "every belief in the value and worth of life rests upon impure thinking" (MAM I, 33; 2, 52). In *Twilight of the Idols* (1888) he argued that the "problem of the value of life" is "impenetrable," inasmuch as one cannot make judgments outside of life, so that value judgments in the case of life are at best *symptoms* of a particular *way* of life (6, 86). Perhaps the most striking formulation of the inadequacy of valuative thinking for the thought of eternal recurrence of the same appears in a note written during the winter of 1887–1888 (WM, 708; *13, 34*). There Nietzsche writes, "Becoming must appear to be justified at every moment (or incapable of being evaluated . . .); the present must absolutely not be justified by reference to a future, nor the past by reference to a present." So much for a fabulous willing that redeems every imperfect "it was" by means of the present and future tenses. Becoming does not submit to redemption, does not stoop to restitution, does not condescend to paltry consolation:

> . . . Becoming is of equivalent value at every moment: the sum of its worth remains the same; to *express it another way, it has no value at all*, for anything against which one might measure it, and in relation to which the word *value* would have meaning, is lacking. *The collective value of the world is inestimable;* consequently, philosophical pessimism belongs among comical things. (WM, 708; *13, 36*)

The project of overman, who teaches eternal recurrence of the same, is viable only to the extent that overman abjures value thinking. For overman, as Granier observes, "being transcends every judgment of value that one could confer upon it," with the result that affirmation of becoming is not so much a *project* for overman as an ontological *factum* (Gr, 558). Dionysian affirmation "embodies the paradox of an existential option that cannot understand itself by reference to reasons or values" (Gr, 559–60). Thus eternal recurrence of the same is not so much the radiant center of Dionysian affirmation as the arduous, perilous, labyrinthine path to an eccentricity as redoubtable as that of genealogical suspicion, an increasingly decentered center, even during the early days of Nietzsche's thinking of it. In 1884 Nietzsche sketches the following note:

> 1. The thought [eternal recurrence]: its presuppositions, things that would have to be true if it is true; the consequences.
>
> 2. As the *most difficult* thought: its probable effect if no preventative measures were taken, that is, if all values were not revalued.
>
> 3. Means of *enduring* it: the transvaluation of all values. Joy no longer in certainty but in uncertainty. . . . (WM, 1059; 11, 225)

"Transvaluation of all values" ultimately means renunciation of the evaluative project as such. Thus the proclamation of eternal return is, as Granier writes, in the spirit of Deleuze, Nietzsche's *machine de guerre* mounted against all forms of metaphysical idealism. "In effect, Nietzsche employs the idea of recurrence as a polemical means of exorcising the supersensible and extirpating all finalistic notions that resort to a moral interpretation of being" (Gr, 568; cf. 580). Further, the thinking of eternal return is, or must become, "an ultimate effort of self-overcoming," and must advance from all forms of polemic to play (Gr, 579). Eternal recurrence not only "radically blocks all inclinations to flight toward the supersensible," that is to say, all ascensional tendencies, but also "constrains the human will to engage itself unconditionally to the adventure of immanence" (Gr, 561).

Yet what sort of "constraint" does the thinking of return exercise, and why this persistent periodic reversion to the will? Eternal recurrence of the same exposes, according to Granier, the *originary affirmation* that lies at the heart of every human project, even if it be the project of asking Hamlet's question (Gr, 560). Such originary affirmation, however radiant, must not be confused with the cosmic optimism, rooted in moral prejudice, that marks all idealistic metaphysics. Its thinking is a burden, the heaviest burden, the tragic strain. However, if eternal recurrence "constrains" the human will, if it is a "burden," is it but a secularized form of Eliade's myth of eternal return, or Kant's categorical imperative? Is eternal recurrence of the same a maxim of Nietzschean will universalized into a law for practical reason? Such a suspicion merely shows how difficult the Nietzschean project of thinking beyond good and evil is and remains.[18]

Let it suffice to say that the project of thinking eternal recurrence is not an ethico-moral imperative but a fatality. Why? Because if I am to "redeem" the past by willing it as *my* will, *my* deed, for all eternity, such willing amounts to no more than a forced enthusiasm—not the exuberant anamnesis of recurrence as Pierre Klossowski portrays it, but a metaphysical comfort when the thought intoxicates me, and a metaphysical depressant when the fiction evaporates. If *eternity* is the "time of dreams," the "hypocritical sentiment that feeds on time," as Merleau-Ponty says,[19] it may be difficult for us to hear and understand recurrence as *fatality*. The words *eternity* and *recurrence*, to say nothing of *the same*, militate against what Nietzsche is trying to think as *tragic* affirmation, as the adventure of immanence. "If the idea of recurrence is to influence our comprehension of becoming and our posture in the face of time, it is only in the measure that it permits us to grant time a dignity that is ontologically absolute" (Gr, 575). To be sure, such dignity would hardly submit to the exertions of the human will, or even the will of overman, willing backwards and forwards unto all eternity. We scarcely know what to make of this paradoxical thinking of time and eternity, this tragic affirmation of earth and world. One can perhaps only insist that the eccentric "center" of Nietzsche's thinking of eternal recurrence of the same in no way circumvents the aporias of mortality. That eccentric "center" is the heart of Dionysian joy and serenity, but it is a tragic heart, a heart borne away from the fragmented body of Zagreus-Pentheus, the Dionysos who comes to grief. The way in and the way out remain mortal ways.

After Ishmael's whaling ship has been tossed to and fro in the vast ring of circling whales, it reaches the calm of the center where the calves cavort. In precisely this way, writes Melville, "amid the tornadoed Atlantic of my being, do I myself . . . centrally disport in mute calm; and while ponderous planets of unwaning woe revolve round me, deep down and deep inland there I still bathe me in eternal mildness of joy." Such joy radiates from the displaced center, and it never breaks the mortal circumference. At the end Melville writes, " . . . and spite of all that mortal man could do, the solid white buttress of his forehead smote the ship's starboard bow, till men and timbers reeled. . . . Then all collapsed, and the great shroud of the sea rolled on as it rolled five-thousand years ago."[20]

Becoming, the child at play, Aion, all the eons of time—these are without grounds, precisely in the way that genealogical critique is without grounds, and the thinking of eternal recurrence without center. According to Deleuze, genealogical critique passes underground, continuing to feed on the nihilism that is the *ratio cognoscendi* of its primary axiom, will to power (Dz, 198). If a thinking dreams of overcoming once and for all the nihilism that feeds it, Blanchot asks us, can that dream be anything but a striving that relies all the more on the nothing at its heart?[21] It cannot surprise us that the thinking of eternal recurrence, after all we have said, remains mystifying, a thought that like some protean poltergeist struggles against every attempt to portray it. For all its apparent ascensionality, alleviation, and levity, eternal return too goes down. The thinking of it remains descensional. Deleuze describes it as though it were the dark side of the moon: "Thus the *thought* of eternal return bypasses all the laws of our *knowledge*. . . . The other face of will to power, the unknown face, the other quality of will to power, the unknown quality: affirmation. And affirmation is the *ratio essendi* of *will to power in general*" (Dz, 199). It is of course curious, and even maddening, that the thinking of eternal return should so often be expressed in the ascensionalist terms of a decadent metaphysics, as though it were the finest fruit of *rancune* and *ressentiment*. Deleuze concedes:

> Truly, we do not know what a human being stripped of ressentiment would be like. . . . Would it still be a human, think like a human? . . . Nietzsche presents the goal of his philosophy: it is to liberate thinking from nihilism and all its forms. Yet this implies a new manner of thinking, a reversal in the principle upon which thought depends, a redress of the principle of genealogy itself, a "transmutation". . . . A "new manner of thinking" means an affirmative thinking, a thinking that affirms life and the will in life, a thinking that ultimately purges itself of everything negative. (Dz, 40–41)

Yet how is it to purge without purgatives and purgatories? How is it to say *yes* without the hee-haw? If we return to our earlier reflection on revenge against time and its "it was," we might pose the riddle of eternal return as a riddle concerning time, as Stambaugh has done (St, 235). Two possibilities lay open to thinking: either the dissonance of the self-contradiction of time, *Sichwidersprechen*, or the consonance of time's calling itself forth again, *Sichwiedersprechen*. The addition of one fluid, aphonic vowel makes all the difference in the riddle. One may experience mortal time as self-accusation and contradiction, as mortifying, goalless, endless, and murderous; or one may experience it as calling for itself again and again, as essentially innocent of goals, ends, and murders. The smallest gap, the most meager "e," separates the speaking-against-itself from the speaking-itself-again of time. Who or what grants the "e," transmuting dissonance to consonance? And what can prevent consonance from degenerating to paltry consolation, the decadence of redemption?

The difficulty of thinking eternal recurrence beyond the horizon of good and evil and beyond all the varieties of valuative thinking is perhaps best expressed in the Lenzerheide fragments on recurrence, composed on June 10, 1887, to which I referred earlier (WM, 55; 12, 211–17). In the course of these reflections Nietzsche affirms that "every basic characteristic, everything that lies at the bottom of every occurrence, expressing itself in every occurrence, . . . *would have to be called good*. . . ." "Good" here clearly means that one would have to experience all the vicissitudes encountered on one's mortal way as full of worth, infinitely valuable, beyond value. Again one stumbles over the words *good, worth, value*. Nietzsche wants to show that the thinking of eternal return is the supreme expression of the positive pole of will to power; only those who overcome morality can think it. He describes them as "those who do not require any extreme articles of faith; . . . those who can think of human beings with a considerable reduction in their value without becoming petty and weak on that account: the richest in health. . . ." However, the meditation closes with a disarming question, one that threatens to shatter the very notion of eternal recurrence of the same as affirmative thought. If a human being were supremely strong in positive will to power and needed no articles of faith to bolster existence—"How would such a human being even think of eternal recurrence?—."

Is eternal return at bottom a placebo prescribed for a wretched and chagrined existence, a thinking that remains within the horizon of the "good," hence altogether decadent? Does it simply paint its horizon as the "beautiful," proclaim it as "true," and so cling to its fabulous "good"? Is the thinking of eternal recurrence healthier than that of genealogical critique, which prepared its way, or healthier than that of Platonism, which its critique sought to overcome; or is it only more attenuated, more idealized, more infectious? Perhaps we have not taken Nietzsche's genealogical critique to heart until we have replaced the question "How is the thinking of eternal recurrence possible?" with the question "*Why* is *belief* in such thinking necessary?"

Our worst fears and our most malicious suspicions in this respect are fed by a note that Nietzsche sketched sometime between the autumn of 1887 and the spring of 1888, very near the end:

> A certain emperor always kept in mind the transiency of all things in order not to take them *too seriously* and to remain calm in their midst. To me, on the contrary, everything seems much too valuable to be allowed to be so fleeting: I seek an eternity for everything: ought one to pour the most costly unguents and wines into the sea? — And yet my consolation is that everything that was is eternal: — the sea spews it forth again. (WM, 1065; *13*, 43)

Here the idea of eternal recurrence as a test, as the most difficult and most burdensome thought, as the tragic thought that would separate overman from the all-too-human, dwindles to paltry consolation, to the decadence of redemption. How close the communication of Dionysian affirmation brings us to the Redeemer type, "excluding all limits and distances in feeling, . . . any resistance or compulsion to resist"! The thinking of eternal recurrence, as descensional, yearns to be strong and vigorous. Yet it fails when the music and the dance falter, when it too readily ascends.

DESCENSIONAL REFLECTION

Is anything more characteristic of the philosopher than his or her desire to go up? To radiate outward to the outermost spheres, where gods and goddesses dwell, dining on rarest essences, far from everything fallen, remote from muck, offal, the corpse, impervious to all waste and ruin? Of Aristophanes' heroes one flies to heaven on a dungbeetle while the other drifts among clouds in a think tank. The second has proved the more emulable model for philosophy.

Only the images of ascension into light in Plato's *Phaedo, Republic, Symposium*, and *Timaeus* have taken root in Occidental consciousness, so that those who are compelled to think in a new way can liberate their thought only by overturning Platonism. That inversion becomes Nietzsche's passion; it consumes the part of his life that says and does *no*. The power of that *no* can be measured only against the full weight of an entire tradition. For whether in the

Enneads, the *Confessions*, and the *Summa theologiae*, where humans are made to participate in the divine comedy, or in the *Meditations*, the *Theodicy*, and the *Philosophy of Spirit*, where the divine comedy is reproduced in more sober, secular guise, the persistent trajectory of reflection in the West is upward, ouranian, Icarian, or ascensional—inasmuch as the ground of things is felt to be not under the feet or in the bowels but inside the head, which is itself modeled on "the circles of the same," the celestial head spinning crystalline threads of imperishable ideas. In all cases the essential strategy is to purify spirit of its mortal dross, to wean the soul from its corporeal integument, which remains a wretched and wholly unaccountable catastrophe. In order to purge it, the mind prescribes catharsis by mortification. Hence *mors* itself is drawn into the circle of reflection and is at once embraced, circumscribed, and circumvented.

For Hegel, death is precisely what the life of spirit withstands (*erträgt*): life preserves itself (*erhält sich*) in death. Philosophy is thus the enchantment (*Zauberkraft*) to charm the monstrous power of the negative, to cancel and surpass, to lift up and up. Ascensional reflection is a matter of dying ahead of time, moving the hands of the clock ahead, beating the system.

As we have seen in these first three chapters, Granier argues that the various senses of "truth" in Nietzsche's thought can be arranged in a sort of hierarchical structure, reflecting a dialectical progression from "lower" to "higher" levels. The characterization is helpful because it is exactly contrary to the Nietzschean effort: we do not ascend through the sundry senses of "truth" in Nietzsche's thought; we go down and under rather than up and over. The fierce resistance to ascensional reflection, the will to overcome two thousand years of centrifugal force—ascensional inertia—is felt everywhere in Nietzsche's text. Zarathustra's high-flying eagle of good courage is bound by blood to the serpentine wisdom of the earth.

From beginning to end, Nietzsche's reflection is descensional, its trajectory decisively earthbound. His thought describes an epochal turn in the history of Western thought from Hegel to Heidegger, which I define provisionally as the descent of reflection from thought on *das Absolute* to thought on *der Abgrund*; the descent of reflection from the death of God to the death of human beings—the descent of reflection in both cases implying the demise of metaphysical *logos*.

No flight instructor is available for counsel in matters of descensional reflection. Daedalus taught the ways of ascent long ago, but because Icarus alone has made the return voyage—in a way peculiar to him—we lack instruction. However, because the inversion of Platonism is basic to Nietzsche's descensional reflection, I shall look for clues in "the ladder of love" (*Symposium*, 210a ff.) and in "the divided line" (*Republic*, 509d ff.). Regarding the former, I am satisfied to cite William Butler Yeats's "The Circus Animals' Desertion":

> Now that my ladder's gone,
> I must lie down where all the ladders start,
> In the foul rag-and-bone shop of the heart.

However, let me introduce a word about ascent and descent up and down the divided line of *Republic*. Socrates begins by pointing to simple reflections of the visible, the water-soaked strand of εἰκασία, then advances through πίστις, true belief regarding plants, animals, and human artifacts, through διάνοια, corresponding to the geometer's imaging of the visible, clambering upward to a conclusion, to νοήσις, a thinking that makes use of no images but levitates over a presuppositionless source among systems of ideas. It is hence an ascent from εἴδολα to εἴδη, from idols to ideas—although Socrates prefaces all this with the *image* of the sun and concludes it with the *analogy* (not to say *idol*) of the cave, so that, at least in the philosopher's education, any movement up the line is rooted in a covert downward movement toward the visible—that is, is rooted in a *descensional* reflection that is under way to εἰκασία, the images of the seastrand or lakeshore, the source of all eidoletic εἴδη. As we shall see in the following chapter, to invert Platonism is to negotiate with Plato—and to negotiate his texts without traditional supports. However, before proceeding to Plato, let me reproduce the most telling image of descensional reflection in our time.

Nectar-laden Zarathustra quits his mountain cave and goes down to humans. He sees a tightrope walker plunge to the earth. Zarathustra learns that every moment in transition across the lifeline, across bridge or boundary, is decisive for eternity, inasmuch as any fool can surpass a mortal and precipitate his or her death. Zarathustra's first task is to inter his fallen companion; his first lesson is that to advance is to go down. Not up.

Also begann Zarathustras Untergang.

Nietzsche himself descends even further after composing *Thus Spoke Zarathustra* and so fulfilling the yes-saying portion of his life. In the genealogical critique of metaphysics and morals (*Beyond Good and Evil, On the Genealogy of Morals*), he returns to his earliest haunts, grubbing beneath encrusted layers of illusion and life negation in the Occidental tradition, rooting underground, beneath all its sacred but no longer secure monuments, subverting old ruins. Once again he dons the baleful mask of suspicion; once again he performs the grimly gleeful spadework of Yorick's uncoverers.

The genealogist undercuts everything others have taught and then advances a step and with a laugh undercuts himself. An image forms: the reaper of truths cuts broad swaths in the tall grass of cant and sophistry, exposing the bitterest truths in their lairs. Yet what kind of "truths" can these be? Upon what "grounds" are they founded? The image recoils upon itself: the scythe swings round, slicing into the reaper's ankles. The blow leaves him standing in the shadow of his own feet. He laughs. Again the scythe describes its arc, returns again.

However, it is not beside himself, in pieces, that Nietzsche descends, as long as his thinking endures, but down into himself, or itself, far below the eyebrow line of the cogito, so that these bottomless truths, as he says, "are my truths." Because the descent excavates beneath the cogito, it is merely quaint to accuse genealogical critique of relativism or subjectivism or even Epimenidean contradiction. (Empedoclean contradiction, in the tradition that extends from Hölderlin to Camus and Lacoue-Labarthe, would be another matter.) Nietzsche's thinking does not speak against itself but acts against itself: not *contradiction* but *contraction* is its *modus operandi*: contraction and recoil. Contradiction, apparent groundlessness, is merely genealogy's mask. Nietzsche needs it when he writes, as the tragedian needs it when he plays. Especially if he would play Oedipus at Colonus but still keep his eyes.

What is Nietzsche looking for down there? "*Glissez, mortels, n'appuyez pas,*" warns Jean-Paul Sartre's grandmother, who introduces us to what in chapter 6 we shall call a *hermeneutics of discretion*: "Gently, mortals, be discreet." Still, we want to know: why is descensional reflection today a requirement? May we not let the dead bury their dead and proceed to equip ourselves with new values—revalued or transvalued ones, of course—and new beliefs founded on the bases of agnosticism and weariness? Or may we not proclaim again the old values, letting fanaticism, messianism, and guilt cover a multitude of doubts? Why all that digging by folk who ought otherwise to be concerned with their health?

> Act V, Scene 1: A Churchyard. Enter two clowns with spades, etc.
> 1st Clown:—Come, my spade. There is no ancient gentlemen but gardeners, ditchers, and grave-makers: they hold up Adam's profession.

The very discretion Mami counsels—mortal discretion—demands descensional reflection, a thinking that goes underground, beneath Leibnizian sufficiency and Cartesian clarity, below the surface upon which the horizon of the true and false once gathered. That fixed horizontal once gave us the latitude to collect and divide pure essences. We could scramble up divided lines and love ladders and pull them up behind us, as Merleau-Ponty and Wittgenstein say, and that was a little bit like flying. Ours was the philosophy of overflight. Now Sartre, his grandmother, and all his friends and distant colleagues insist that in spite of our best will and piety we can no longer fly so high.

Whose fault is that? It is not Herr Nietzsche who plucks from the seabed the sponge that obliterates the horizon. That is history by the time he writes, the history of nihilism, into which Nietzsche is plunged along with everyone else. The difference is that Nietzsche thinks about what has happened and is happening—about the unraveling of our destiny—and in that way Nietzsche upholds Adam's profession. For it is Moira, the fateful allotment, that requires the downgoing, nothing less. If saying so seems overweening, clownish, it is because the clown prefers mortal foolishness to saintly ressentiment, because he or she elects to provide what criticism calls "comic relief" at the heart of tragedy. Yet clowns do make room for Christian suicides: the gravediggers offer to Ophelia what was theirs and they come up. They ascend. Is Nietzsche's thinking purely descensional? Does he never come up? Nietzsche does ascend—at least he says he will do so—if only behind another mask. He calls that mask "the eternal recurrence of the same." He describes the mask as an experimental thought and touchstone. At one point he labels it a consolation, as though there might be some comfort in it. Indeed, Zarathustra's animals try to transform the thought of eternal recurrence into an image that might serve as the surest comfort of metaphysicians: the circle, Ouroboros, the friendly snake coiling itself about the neck of the eagle, itself circling through cycles of the same among the spheres of eternity. Is the thought of eternal recurrence an image fashioned to keep a drowsy emperor awake? Is it, as so astute a critic as Bachelard insists, redemptive and ascensional—which is to say, decadent?

The eternal recurrence of the same is Nietzsche's most difficult thought because it compels Zarathustra's pity for humankind, his nausea, to the surface. Yet, as the heaviest burden, it is the touchstone of magnificent health, because it requires that Zarathustra swallow what wants to come up.

How we might ascend to overman we really do not know. Deleuze is right when he says that we have no inkling of what human beings stripped of rancor and resentment would be like; we do not know how they could say *yes* without braying like an ass. To alter the image in the direction of *Phaedrus*: we do not know how to prune our old wings so that Eros's flood might nurture new growth. We have reason to fear that in any case our new wings would not support the burden, that they would serve us as Icarus's served him. However, Nietzsche says that we do not really have to fly in order to ascend. When our thinking ascends to the eternal recurrence of the same, it ascends to the *surface of the earth*. There it reaffirms its incarnation. Earth is as high as it will go. To mountains perhaps, some 6,000 feet beyond humanity and time, but no more, because, as we shall learn in chapter 5, moles cannot survive beyond 2,000 meters of altitude. To mountain caves, then, caves the thinker himself digs— piteously if we have not outgrown pity, alone if we cannot quit the sunlight and accompany him on the descent, relentlessly whatever we may or may not do.

These ups and downs, clinging to the contours of the earth, make out the search for the image, the water-soaked, incarnate *eidolon*: descensional reflection is metaphorics without the supports and subterfuges of metaphysics. One final image, or metaphor, by way of anticipation.

Apollo grants the mortal Trophonios the finest gift that immortals can bestow once life has jerked into motion: the gift of death without pain. All mortals who desire an image of their fate come now to Trophonios's cave at Lebadeia. The cult practice is called κατάβασις, downgoing or descent. Two boys called *hermai* (after Hermes Psychopompos, the god of speech and interpretation, who leads souls to the underworld) bathe the body of the initiate as though he or she were still a newborn babe or already a corpse. The initiate is then led to two springs, one called Lethe, the other Mnemosyne. He or she drinks the waters of the first to purge away all illusions, those of the second to gather and preserve whatever is revealed during the descent. Pausanias (not to be confused with the "Pausanias" of Plato's *Symposium*, and not merely on account of chronology) offers the following account:

> He looks at the statue they say Daedalus made . . . and then goes to the oracle. . . .
> The oracle is on the mountainside above the sacred wood. It is surrounded by a

circular platform. . . . Inside the circle is a chasm in the earth. . . . There is no way down, but when a man is going to Trophonios they bring him a light, narrow ladder. . . . The man going down lies on the ground with honeycakes in his hands and pushes his feet into the opening. . . . The rest of his body is immediately dragged in . . . as though some very deep and swift river were catching him in its current and sucking him down. . . . People are not always taught the future in the same way: one man hears, another also sees. Those who go down return feet first through the same mouth. . . . When a man comes up from Trophonios the priests . . . sit him on the throne of Mnemosyne in order to learn from him what he saw and discovered. After they have heard it they turn him over to his friends, who pick him up and carry him to the house of the Good Daimon and Good Fortune. He is still struck with terror and hardly knows himself or those around him. Later his wits return unimpaired. To be specific, he can laugh again.[22]

Golden, superhuman laughter is the second divine gift, when life-in-death, death-in-life, is the first. Such is the legacy of what Nietzsche calls the death of God: the failure of every dogmatic *logos*, the collapse of the metaphysical project as such, and the emergence of mortal humankind.

Yet if overman—which says the same as mortality—is to emerge at all, it must be by virtue of a thinking that is sustained by anxiety, anxiety in the face of death without resurrection. One of Nietzsche's students reflects on the paradox of overman, whose task is to go under, and writes:

Thinking does not overcome metaphysics by climbing still higher, surmounting it, transcending it somehow or other; thinking overcomes metaphysics by climbing back down into the nearness of the nearest. The descent, particularly where man has strayed into subjectivity, is more arduous and more dangerous than the ascent. The descent leads to the poverty of the ek-sistence of *homo humanus*.[23]

What would denial of such poverty be, and what would insistence on such ascent be, but Platonism? And what would Platonism be, if not the Socratic swan song that goes under the title *Phaedo*, with its ruses of immortality, its slur against life, the cock it sacrifices to Asclepius? In other words, how, *after* Nietzsche, are we to *read* Plato?

FOUR

The Cock

Reading Plato (after Nietzsche)

ναρθηκοφόροι μὲν πολλοί, βάκχοι δέ τε παῦροι.
"Many bear the thyrsos, but the Bacchants are few."

—Plato, *Phaedo* 69c 7–8

By teaching *Phaedo* I have the opportunity to infect
my pupils with philosophy. . . .

—Nietzsche to Ritschl, 10 May 1869

Πλάτων δὲ οἶμαι ἠσθένει
"However, I believe that Plato was sick."

—Plato, *Phaedo* 59b 10

Dear old friend, . . . I am more and more paralyzed
with astonishment over *how very little* I know Plato
and **how very much** Zarathustra πλατονίζει.

—Nietzsche to Overbeck, 22 October 1883

(Gray morning. First yawnings of reason. Cock's
crow of positivism.)

—Nietzsche, "How the 'True World' Finally
Became a Fable," 1888

Nietzsche and Plato: a frightful confrontation. From the many discussions of
Plato in Nietzsche's works—there are well over five hundred direct references—
we learn that Nietzsche viewed his life's task as *overcoming Platonism*. And, all
reservations and qualifications aside, we know that Plato had *something* to do
with Platonism. If the history of Western philosophy is a series of footnotes to
Plato, if philosophy itself consists of variations on the theme of Platonism, then
Nietzsche wants to write the last variation, the one that will exhaust all remaining possibilities for Platonism and bring philosophy as such to a close. It
seems we can read sympathetically *either* Plato *or* Nietzsche, but not both: read
Plato alone, and rest assured that Nietzsche is a sophist of the nastiest sort,
more destructive than even Thrasymachus or Callicles; read Nietzsche alone,
and rest assured that Plato is a decadent of the most contemptible sort, and a

charlatan besides. Nietzsche calls him "a grand Cagliostro." Reading Plato after Nietzsche: is that possible at all?[1]

It would not be too much to say that every indictment in the Nietzschean œuvre of otherworldly metaphysics, morals, religion, and art directly involves Plato and Platonism. Philosophers are people who want to hurry up and die, we read in *Phaedo*, so that they can float up to the ethereal realm of the pure ideas; to this end they despise the body and preach crusades against it, and, lending death a hand, they mortify the flesh; they invent a god as anemic as themselves and invest their wretched hopes in him, dreaming heavenly dreams; even their music is lugubrious and bathetic, their dance a kind of solemn mummery. Platonic-Christian culture in its most noteworthy achievements: this is what Nietzsche scorns and derides as inimical to life. Yeats speaks of a tower " . . . half dead at the top," Nietzsche of the death of God—that death a curious sui-dei-cide. In the transvaluation of all values willed by the Nietzschean overman, the Platonic tower is turned upside down and torn inside out. For Nietzsche sees in Platonism the provenance of contemporary nihilism, the source of what we prefer to consider a strictly "modern" malaise, which many blame on the admittedly infectious Nietzsche himself. In order to overcome passive nihilism and banish the feeble-spiritedness of Schopenhauerian pessimism or European Buddhism, Nietzsche says we must overcome the tradition that began with the collapse of Hellenism—with Plato. A number of jejune essays have been written during the past few decades, urging that we rescue ourselves from all this nihilistic unpleasantness by inculcating Platonic "values" in our youth: produce a line of Theaetetuses—but no Alcibiades, if you please!—and all this modern and postmodern disease will succumb to Doric sanity. Nietzsche would answer that, apart from the difficulties inherent in living backwards, to reproduce telescopically at the time of its *dénouement* the same play of Western culture as a play-within-a-play would simply result in an aggravated nihilism. Nietzsche's suspicion against Plato is above all a suspicion of the Platonic φάρμακον and θεραπεία: he does not believe that heavier doses of the same drug or intensified applications of the same treatment will improve our state of health. In what follows I would at least like to try to avoid adding one more to that number of futile essays that see in Plato's works a ready antidote to nihilism. I side with Nietzsche, if thinking is a matter of taking sides, and ask again whether Plato can still be read with profit.

I first read Plato when I was fifteen—a paperback selection of the dialogues in the Jowett translation, which included *Symposium*.   *The country looked underdone, its raw juices squirting out all round.*   An introductory blurb announced that *Symposium* was Plato's dialogue on "love," and so, hoping for enlightenment, I began with that. I got as far as Pausanias's speech on noble and base love, which praises love of the soul and condemns love of the body. I did not throw the book away only because I had bought it with my own earnings, but I knew then and there, in the passionate and apodictic way adolescents know things, that Plato had nothing to tell me that a menacing black-robed preacher had not already told me.

All through my undergraduate years I avoided philosophy and philosophers, although various required courses forced me from time to time to put up with the maddening combination of naiveté and arrogance ("pure potency," o-ho!) that was to me synonymous with the name *philosophy*. I elected a sensible major, studying European history, and in graduate school advanced to the history of ideas, a course of study that granted me a lofty perch above the milling crowds of philosophers, prophets, pundits, and politicians. Then I read Nietzsche. He knocked me off that perch. He led me, slipping through the unlatched cellar door by night, into philosophy. Long after I had learned from him that Christianity was "Platonism for the People," that Socrates was above all else a "problem" and Plato an artist gone sour, and long after I had heard Platonists speak of the "doctrine of Ideas" or "Forms," and of "philosophy as a preparation for dying and being dead," I was compelled (from the outside, by a graduate school professor) to read Plato once again.[2]

Perhaps I may be forgiven this autobiographical digression if it happens that some of my readers have had a similar experience. I mean an experience of the suspicion that Plato was (and remains?) the most massive joist in the bulwark of otherworldly philosophy, and that, just as the young Stephen Dedalus had to choose between "the pale service of the altar" and the celebration of life in art, so we must choose between a decadent, moribund onto-theo-logy and a vital, adventurous thought that remains true to the earth. Yet *also* the experience that Plato is precisely one of the most vital, adventurous, and artistic of thinkers and writers, and that fidelity to our world and earth demands a renewed confrontation with none other than this "grand Cagliostro."

What I wish to speak to in the present chapter is the hermeneutical situation within which those who have had such an experience can—and must—read Plato. Using as guidelines the Nietzschean critique of Plato, I would like to say something about the way we ought to read the dialogues. No doubt, Socrates and Plato are scarcely separable, but I do wish to concentrate on Nietzsche's criticism of *Plato's dramatic method* rather than the problem of Socrates; although one of my aims is to show the inextricability of form and content in the dialogues, I will emphasize form over content. Taken in abstraction from its form, the content always turns out to be Platonic "doctrine" or "metaphysics," and it is the nature of this very Platonism—against which Nietzsche inveighed—that the dialogical form brings into radical question. After sketching the "reading hints" that Nietzsche's criticism proffers, I will try to apply them to one philosophical problem, that of the relation between philosophy and death as posed in Plato's *Phaedo*, and will conclude with some thoughts about *teaching* Plato after one has read and taken seriously the Nietzschean attack.

DIALOGUE AND DIALECTIC:
PLATO'S "MIXED" FORM

By reviewing Nietzsche's criticisms of Plato's dramatic style rather than matters of substance, it seems as though we neglect his overturning of Platonism. Yet it remains for us to ask how in the sphere of Platonic writing the surface adheres to the core and is modeled about it. Nietzsche criticizes Socratic dialectics and Platonic dramatics, and although the second will be more important for us here, we ought at least to consider the first. After all, Plato's dramatic dialogues depict Socratic dialectic at work. Nietzsche makes two major complaints. First, dialectic is rhetorical trickery, a "vicious tool" and forensic "weapon," which enables an ignoble man to tyrannize over his more noble interlocutors (GD; 6, 70). Dialectic is demonstration by conquest, in which "one leaves to one's opponent the proof that he is not an idiot" (ibid.). Socrates is thus a sophist in disguise, a clown embodying the instincts of a Voltaire. In short, dialectic is *ressentiment* posing as maieutic inquiry, and is a thoroughly negative manifestation of will to power. Second, dialectic infects the material of its inquiry, inasmuch as it always conceals more than it reveals. Socrates' contemporaries were rightly suspicious of it: "Such an open presentation of all one's arguments was also mistrusted. All honest things, like honest people, do not so openhandedly show their grounds. There is something unseemly about showing all five fingers. Whatever must first let itself be 'proved' is of little worth" (GD; 6, 69–70).

Regarding the first point, Nietzsche would add that Thrasymachus is quite justified in losing his temper during the opening argument of *Republic*, and that Callicles's complaints in *Gorgias* are not without grounds; he would observe that Socrates *is* a kind of stingray that paralyzes whomever he meets, as Meno claims, and that he is actually more clever at eristic than Dionysodoros and Euthydemos are. With respect to the second point, Nietzsche would add that Socrates' apparently straightforward collections and divisions are actually gross oversimplifications, a kind of sophistical sleight-of-hand and an expression of confounded optimism with regard to the "same" (see chapter 8). Of course, it is Plato who writes and directs the entire show: the attack must be shifted away from the character called *Socrates* and toward the *writer* who immortalized that character.

For Nietzsche, the collapse of the Hellenic order after its hybristic successes against Persia was not simply a political disaster: he insists that the collapse also involved the failure of μουσική, the flight of the Muses, the end of tragedy, and the beginning of dialectic and logic. Plato became the key figure of this age of decline. The pre-Platonic philosophers had possessed a monumental greatness, attributable in Nietzsche's view to the unity of style in their personalities and writings, a unity in conformity with the unified lifestyle and culture of the early classical age. By contrast, Plato himself was an eclectic, "a mixed type," "many-sided," his personality and writings being a blend of Heraclitean aloofness, Pythagorean melancholy, and Socratic cleverness, loquacity, and optimism ("Philosophy in the Tragic Age of the Greeks," *1*, 809–12).

We praise Plato's greatness only because the *fatum libellorum,* which blindly rules on the survival or obliteration of a copyist's manuscript, has deprived us of the works of Heraclitus, Empedocles, and Democritus; had their writings not vanished, Nietzsche speculates, Plato's dialogues would never have occupied their supreme niche in classical education (ibid.). In addition to the aberrations of doctrine—the overturning of being and becoming, the estrangement of being from the order of time, the condemnation of the senses and the body (Nietzsche refers to "that altogether erroneous divorce between 'spirit' and 'body,' which especially since Plato hangs over philosophy like a curse" [*1,* 843])—Plato's *style* is anti-Hellenic. Considered as an art form, the dialogue subsumes all previous art forms but one, to wit, tragedy: epic, lyric, satyric, and comic forms are at least partially maintained in the dialogues; but Socratic optimism overwhelms Plato and banishes tragedy from his dialogues as decisively as Plato expels the tragedians from his model city. This is strange, however, inasmuch as Platonic dialogue follows the formal example of tragedy, which itself synthesizes earlier art forms. Be that as it may, Platonic dialogue paves the way to the writings of the Cynics and ultimately to the infinitely enhanced Aesopian fable—the novel.

Under the pressure of the Socratic daimon, Plato reduces poesy to an ancilla to dialectic (GT, 14; *1,* 93; cf. *1,* 631–32). A kind of flattening of the philosophical relief of the cosmos results, and a programmatic naiveté about man's life and death ensues. Nietzsche values the Greeks because they possess " . . . a more profound revelation of the world" than we. Yet Plato begins to obfuscate the Greek revelation of the world. He spins a cocoon about it. By the middle of his career, it seems as though the world turns within a Polyphemic cave—from which for the next two thousand years it cannot escape. Perhaps Nietzsche complains that Plato " . . . is boring" precisely because he lasts a "long while" (*"Plato ist langweilig,"* 6, 155). The exalted music of the spheres drowns in the cacophony of " . . . a dreadfully self-complacent and childish kind of dialectic" (ibid.). "I wonder if there is not already in Plato an abominably pedantic conceptual hair-splitting?"—Decline of fine intellectual taste: one no longer senses the despicable and noisome character of all direct dialectic" (WM, 427; *13,* 167–69). Nietzsche argues what a reading of Plato's *Sophist* shows conclusively, namely, that it is extremely difficult to distinguish the friend-of-wisdom from the know-it-all, the φιλόσοφος from the σοφιστής. Every time the Eleatic Stranger and Theaetetus collect and divide in that dialogue in order to expose and capture the sophist, what they invariably come up with is someone who looks a lot like—Socrates! This does not mean that in the later dialogues Plato "surpasses" or "advances beyond" Socrates: it means that in Plato's texts, as in Socrates' discourses, there is a dangerous proximity or even kinship between philosophy and sophistry.

Nietzsche's view is not one-sided, however; as he held a multiplicity of perspectives to be essential to any investigation, so does his view of the dialogues have its more "positive" side. If it is true that Plato's style is a mixed bag of epic, lyric, and comic elements, true that his art form subsumes all prior forms save tragedy, then the complexity and richness of the dialogues cannot be denied. Even the later writings, usually taken to be treatises in which the dramatic form is a mere encumbrance—Plato getting a bit senile, unable to change his customary ways—are actually packed with dramatic material, comedy, imagery, myth, and lyricism. As a result, *Plato* never really shows all five of his writing fingers: he manages to spin even the simplest argument against a backdrop of multifaceted persons, places, historical events, and mythic references, the significance of which cannot be exhaustively comprehended. It is as though the dialogues themselves were a sort of shadow play of images on the wall of that Polyphemic cave; no matter how high-flying they seem, they are always on the way back down to εἰκασία.

Nietzsche's multiplicity of perspectives—and downright ambivalence—with regard to Socrates is well known, and has been the object of much discussion. Yet his ambivalence with regard to Plato must be emphasized every bit as much. For it is that ambivalence which seems to inform readings of Plato after Nietzsche, and after the company who follow in Nietzsche's wake. Let the following thumbnail sketch of that ambivalence, from *The Birth of Tragedy* to *Twilight of the Idols*, suffice.

In the *Birth*, Plato is the disciple who casts himself on the ground before the dying Socrates—the very Socrates whom Plato does not *see* dying, inasmuch as Plato is presumed to be ill   *Dyspepsia too—I am troubled with that*   at the time of Socrates' execution (GT, 13; 1, 91; cf. "Socrates and Greek Tragedy," 1, 630). Nietzsche suggests that the *Corpus platonicum* is in some way the desperate production of the absent and thus forever grieving, forever self-reproaching disciple. In lines that will later captivate Jacques Derrida, Nietzsche writes of a laceration that never closes, such that the Platonic philosophy is a protracted piece of pathology: "The intentionally harsh and reckless condemnation of art in Plato has something pathological about it: he who has elevated himself to that view only by raging against his own flesh [*im Wüthen gegen das eigne Fleisch*], he who has trampled underfoot his own profoundly artistic nature for the sake of Socratism, in the very bitterness of his judgment betrays the fact that the deepest wound he has ever suffered is not yet closed [*noch nicht vernarbt ist*]" ("Socrates and Tragedy," 1, 543). Yet Plato's pathology is precisely *not* Socratism. Rather than condemn all unreason in the name of logic and dialectic, Plato seems to celebrate it: Nietzsche notes more than once in the *Birth* (GT, 4, 12; 1, 16, 87), but also in the first *Untimely* (UB I, 164; 2, 155) and in *Daybreak* (M, 14; 3, 27), that it is precisely Plato who praises the divine μανία of *Phaedrus* as the supreme good. Whereas Nietzsche, for his part, sometimes condemns the Platonic art form as a mixed medium, "Homer's Contest" celebrates that form as essentially agonistic (1, 790–91), even if the Platonic competition has a ghost as its most fearsome opponent. Whereas in the battle between tragedy and philosophy Nietzsche is most often on the side of tragedy, in *Human, All-Too-Human* (MAM I, 212; 2, 173–74) he concedes that Plato is essentially right about the deleterious effects tragedy has on the spectator. Whereas Plato, the frustrated tyrant of Sicily, if not of Athens, is galled by his failure as a political educator, thus aggravating the poison against the state that the dying Socrates first fed him (MAM I, 261; 2, 215–16; cf. ZGM III, 18; 5, 384), he nonetheless produces rainbows for philosophers who are no longer young but not yet old:

> *Every philosophy is a philosophy for a stage of life.* The stage of life in which a philosopher finds his doctrine reverberates within that doctrine; he cannot prevent it, no matter how much he felt he was elevated beyond time and the hour. Thus Schopenhauer's philosophy remains the mirror image of an ardent and melancholy *youth*—that is no way for older people to think; thus too Plato's philosophy reminds us of someone in their mid-thirties, where hot and cold jets collide and send up spray and misty clouds, and where, under favorable and sunny circumstances, an enchanting rainbow-image takes shape. (MAM II, 271; 2, 494)

Thus Plato is both praised and blamed for his artistic-philosophic production. In the initial dialogue in "The Wanderer and His Shadow," when Nietzsche catches himself aping the mixed style of a dubious master, he has the wanderer say: "Had Plato taken less pleasure in spinning out [his dialogues], his readers would have taken greater pleasure in him" (MAM II; 2, 539); yet when Nietzsche later calls upon Plato to be the judge of the best of German thought, from Goethe through Schopenhauer, Plato rejects it all as excessively grim and gloomy (MAM II, 214; 2, 647). And so it goes, for the remainder of Nietzsche's career. Plato is under the spell of "the Circe of the philosophers," to wit, morality (M, 3; 3, 12–13); he is victimized by Socrates' helpless astonishment before the wonders of dialectic, overwhelmed by Socrates' optimistic confidence that the secrets of human action will be plumbed (M, 43, 116; 3, 50–51, 108–9); he fears his own sensitivity and sensibility (*Empfindung*), and so flees to the safety of shadowy ideas, succumbs to *Ideomanie* (M, 448; 3, 271; FW, 357; 3, 597); because he is a failed Muhammad (M, 496; 3, 292), an otherworldly truth must become his god and our longest-lasting lie (FW, 344; 3, 577; cf. ZGM III, 24; 5, 401). However, flying in the face of all this, Nietzsche claims that Plato's philosophical idealism, in contrast to that of the Germans, is *not* an illness or a sign of decadence; rather, it is "the caution [or foresight: *Vorsicht*] of a superabundant and hazardous health . . ." (FW, 372; 3, 624). Plato—a specimen of the grand health?   *Hark! By Jove, what's that? . . . Hark again! How clear! how musical! how prolonged! What a triumphant thanksgiving of a cock-crow! . . . I feel warmer.*

The ambivalence intensifies during the 1880s, as the condemnation of Plato becomes harsher and the celebration of him more euphoric. In an unpublished note from the summer and fall of 1884, Nietzsche writes, "Plato is worth more than his philosophy! . . . *If* Plato looked like that bust of him in Naples, then we have in him the best refutation of *all* Christianity!" (*11*, 244). One finds many notes on Plato's "Egyptianism," on Plato as Manu or Brahman (*13*, 378), and one always hears the refrain concerning Plato's having been spoiled or corrupted by Socratic morality (JGB, 190; 5, 111). When in the preface to *Beyond Good and Evil* (5, 12) Nietzsche asks, "Whence such an illness in the most beautiful blossom of antiquity, Plato?" the answer is not far: not even a wrestler's constitution could save him from the noxious influence of Socrates. After renewed work on ancient philosophy during the fall and winter of 1886–1887, studying especially Simplicius's commentary on Epictetus, Nietzsche writes to Franz Overbeck, "The *falsification* of everything factual by morality is to be seen here in all its glory; squalid psychology; the philosopher reduced to a 'country pastor.'—And for all this *Plato* is responsible! He *remains* Europe's greatest *malheur*!" (KSAB 8, 9). Whether or not Socrates is the source of his disease, Plato infects virtually everyone in the West, and is our history's most virulent carrier.

Yet Plato's malady in fact lends to the Western intellectual tradition whatever vigor and rigor it possesses—*eine prachtvolle Spannung des Geistes*, a splendid tension of the spirit that enables it to shoot its arrows far (JGB, 204; 5, 131). However infected or haunted Plato may have been by Socrates, he is seduced more by life than we might have imagined possible: Nietzsche is enamored of the story that under the pillow of Plato's deathbed a copy of Aristophanes' comedies—including, presumably, the comedy that did Socrates in—was found. In short, there is an erotic Plato as well as an erotic Socrates. And if Plato is Nietzsche's stalwart opponent, he is a worthy one, and the quarrel is one of lovers. In a letter to Paul Deussen late in 1887 (KSAB 8, 200) Nietzsche writes: "—perhaps this old Plato is my great *opponent* proper? Yet how proud I am to have such an opponent!" Later, in *Twilight of the Idols*, Nietzsche writes:

> Plato goes farther. He says, with an innocence for which one must be a Greek and not a "Christian," that there would be no Platonic philosophy at all if there had not been such beautiful youths in Athens: it was his gaze upon them that first sent the soul of the philosopher into an erotic tumult, leaving him no peace until he could sink the seeds of all higher things into an earth so lovely.   *Hark! There again! Did ever such a blessed cock-crow so ring out over the earth before! . . . It plainly says—"Never say die!"*   A marvelous saint, this one—one cannot believe one's ears, even presupposing that one can trust Plato. At least one surmises that philosophy was done *differently* in Athens, above all in public. Nothing is less Greek than the conceptual weaving and spinning of the hermit, *amor intellectualis dei*, after the manner of Spinoza. Philosophy after the manner of Plato would rather be defined as an erotic competition, as an advanced lesson in and interiorization of the traditional agonistic athleticism and of everything such athleticism *presupposes*. . . . In the end, what emanated from this Platonic erotics? A novel form of the art of the Greek *agon*, namely, dialectics. — I remind my readers that, *against* Schopenhauer and to the honor of Plato, the entire higher culture and literature of France in the *classical age* burgeoned from the soil of sexual interest.   *Hark! there again! Whose cock is that? Who in this region can afford to buy such an extraordinary Shanghai? Bless me—it makes my blood bound—I feel wild.*   With regard to that culture, one may go in search everywhere for gallantry, sensuality, sexual competition, and the "woman of the world" [*das "Weib"*]—and one will never seek in vain. . . . (GD, 6, 126)

Beautiful youths, women of the world, and—dialectic. Not the usual combination. However, the most intriguing moments in Nietzsche's ambivalent

accounts of Plato occur when Nietzsche speculates on a certain distance that
Plato may have been able to take with regard to Socrates, a distance that leaves
room for something like a manipulation of his memory. A note from the
summer of 1880 avers, "Plato did not remain in the orbit of Socrates; his first
impressions concerning Heraclitus thrust themselves to the fore; Pythagoras
was the secretly, enviously espied ideal" (9, 171). Finally, in *Ecce Homo*, thinking back to his uses and abuses of "Schopenhauer as Educator" and "Richard
Wagner in Bayreuth," Nietzsche suggests that his high praise of his masters
was in effect a mistaken—but therefore not immodest—praise of himself.
He adds, "This is the way Plato made use of Socrates, as a semiotics for Plato"
(6, 320; cf. *10*, 337–38).

Socrates as "a semiotics for Plato," that is, as a play of signs reflecting the
one who inscribes them rather than the one who ostensibly inspires them, as
though Socrates were taking the dictation of Plato, rather than the other
way around. Precisely this preposterous reversal is what Derrida's *The Post
Card from Socrates to Freud and Beyond* is all about, and we ought to take a
moment to consider the figures of Plato and Socrates in it.

The central "event" of *The Post Card* is Derrida's discovery in the Bodleian
Library of a postcard showing an illustration from a medieval fortune-telling
book, whose author, naturally, is named *Paris*. The Paris-Oxford-Athens
Axis is the axis about which Derrida's book, especially its first part, *Envois*,
turns. The illustration from Matthew Paris's fortune-telling book, *Prognostica
Socratis basilei*, shows Plato standing behind a seated Socrates *who is writing*.
For all the world it looks as though Plato is dictating to Socrates. This absurd
reversal—as though the illustrator simply mixed up the names—serves, so to
speak, as the negative of a photograph that is developed over two thousand
five hundred years of tradition—culminating in Heidegger's claim that Socrates
is the *purest* thinker of the West because he *never wrote*, that is, never had to
escape from the stormy draft of being to the shabby shelter of literature.[3] Derrida cites Nietzsche's remarks on the *fatum libellorum* by which the copyists
preserve Plato's texts, thus guaranteeing him a niche in history well above that
of, say, Democritus. What Nietzsche cannot have seen without access to the
"fabulous genealogy" of Matthew Paris is the fact that *Socrates is the first of
Plato's copyists*. S is p, as the logicians say. "S. is P., Socrates is Plato, his father
and his son, hence the father of his father, his own grandfather and his own
grandson," writes Derrida (54), developing his notion of *obsequence*, which
we shall examine in chapter 11. And if earlier it seemed to Nietzsche that *Plato*
was writing out of a laceration that never healed, it now seems (" . . . *et si
c'était le contraire?*") that *Socrates* is the walking—and writing—wounded,
while Plato, pretending to serve, dictates imperiously. It seems, to Derrida's
feverish imagination at least, that Plato, the jealous son, is dictating Socrates'
death warrant (20). Rather than immortalizing his hero, Plato finishes him off,
while the *Corpus platonicum*, ghostwritten by Socrates, haunts all the epochs
of history. Socrates writes. Socrates is no longer pure. Socrates is dead. The
French text of *La carte postale* has: "Socrates ist Thot" (59).

The ugly, plebeian plato (for so his name is written on the Paris illustration) dreams of making Socrates write, and that dream constitutes the unity of our epoch, "the unity of the epoch from Socrates to Freud and a little bit beyond, the vast universal map of metaphysics" (93). Regardless of who is doing what to whom in the Paris illustration—for sometimes it seems that plato is socratizing Socrates,[4] or perhaps planting an infant in the sterile midwife *a tergo* (202)—the couple S/p or p/S invades the domesticity of every household and disturbs all the correspondences and communications in the Occident to come:

> . . . thus it is written and will not cease to proliferate, this old couple of bearded grandfathers, these inveterate counterfeiters who come to haunt our nights with their discourses on truth, on phantasmata and logoi, on pleasure and the beyond of pleasure, on politics, tyranny, on the first and the second, and then on Eros. In whom they never believed.   *Marvelous cock! But soft—this fellow now crows most lustily; but it's only morning; let's see how he'll crow about noon, and toward nightfall. Come to think of it, cocks crow mostly in the beginning of the day. Their pluck ain't lasting, after all. Yes, yes; even cocks have to succumb to the universal spell of tribulation: jubilant in the beginning, but down in the mouth at the end.*   And they do not constitute either a one or a two. And so here we are, working on the program, taking orders. And I who always have to pay more than anyone else, my overbidding, believe me. (111–12)

Thus Plato exercises his vengeance on the tradition to come. When he says in the second letter (314c), that is, in the least authenticated of his writings, that he has written and will write no philosophy, that whatever appears under his name is the work of a rejuvenated and embellished Socrates, his words represent not pious prattle but a ghoulish prank. It is the truth (159; 251–53). And if Nietzsche is right when he says that there is a Socratism prior to Socrates (1, 545), then that prescient Presocratic Socratism is to be laid at the feet not of Empedocles or Heraclitus or Pythagoras but of a decidedly lower-case plato.

If I now abandon the phantasmagoria of Derrida's *Envois*, it is with the conviction that they are very much in the spirit and company of Nietzsche's ambivalent encounter with the curious animal called *Plato*, or *plato*. Plato is a *sphinx*, Nietzsche says (JGB, 28; 5, 47), riddlesome, enigmatic, and oracular. For all of his talk of sunlight, Plato loves concealment, *Verborgenheit*. (And if we find Nietzsche mentioning this oracular word of Heidegger's, we can be certain that an encounter with this other member of Nietzsche's provocative company, this other grandfather, to say nothing for the moment about Freud, is inevitable.) Plato loves the dark even where he seems most sunny, in the midst of a Socratic dialectic on shoemaking, shipbuilding, or dying. Even when the subject matter is most banal, the form is nothing less than "contrapuntal music."   *Hark! there goes the cock! How shall I describe the crow of the cock at noon-tide? His sunrise crow was a whisper to it. It was the loudest, longest, and most strangely musical crow that ever amazed mortal man.*   Plato is straightforward, like Bach. Or Melville. Finally, the mention of music once again turns our thoughts to the way in which Nietzsche contrasts Schopenhauer's Teutonic eristic with "Plato's erotic dialectics." Eros is invoked in the dialogues with great frequency, and even when not explicitly invoked, even if never truly heeded, he hovers over all the meetings as a sort of silent partner. In that dialogue which celebrates Eros most explicitly, the ecstatic representative of Eros and Dionysos crowns both Socrates and Agathon, declaring philosophy and tragedy co-winners of the erotic contest. Is tragedy simply banned from the dialogues? Richness, complexity, concealment, music, and love: Nietzsche was not unaware of the difficulty of *reading* Plato. Not for nothing did he teach the dialogues in Basel—*Symposium* being his favorite text—both to his secondary school pupils and to his university students. From a segment of Nietzsche's unpublished notes on the Greeks, their polis, tragic philosophy, dialectic, and contests of all sorts, we discover many hints for doing just that. These notes have been gathered under the title "The Battle between Science and Wisdom."[5]

First, Nietzsche says that the story of early Greek philosophy must be told with a sense of irony, but also a sense of *mourning*; at all costs, the earnest scholarly monotone is to be avoided. Socrates himself challenges virtually everything most human beings hold as the "truth": his constant companion in arms is irony. Yet because the passionately desired autochthony that would guarantee the ultimacy of philosophical knowledge is frustrated, and because each philosopher remains indebted to predecessors, "phantasm for phantasm," chained to the past, there is something mournful about the history of philosophy. It would therefore be utterly comical to take it so seriously. *Comedy* is precisely this strange marriage of irony and mournfulness, and Nietzsche would insist that every interpreter of Plato possess a good nose for comedy—and keep a copy of Aristophanes on or under the pillow.

Second, ancient philosophy constructs and wanders through a curious sort of maze of the mind; it ought to be compared to wanderings in dreams and fairy tales. Oneiric hermeneutics and a phenomenology of *Märchen* and folktales ought to come to the aid of the philosopher who wants to read the ancients. Interpretation of dreams and folk idioms, depth psychology, ethnology, and linguistics, conjoined in a new kind of archaeology and genealogy, can help us understand the scope and nature of our rootedness in the past, and so give us less to rue and more to celebrate in ancient texts.

Third, our sketches of this philosophy must be made over an undercoating of μῦθος. Myth hovers equivocally among the multiple meanings, and its uncertain borders frustrate the philosopher's search for certitude; however, " . . . only where the rays of myth shine can the life of the Greeks be illuminated—else all is gloom." Under the compulsion to certitude called "science," philosophers try to demythologize; Nietzsche warns that they will never survive in the resulting miasma. Readers of Plato also need those scintillating rays of mythic light—even if what is illumined resists the narrow categories of the science of Platonism.

Fourth and finally, philosophical texts ought to be discussed in terms of the kind of μουσική that inspires them, that is, the kind of poetry or song that is in them. A text has its *modes*, as does music. Since these modes greatly concern Plato himself (see *Republic* 398c ff.), they ought to concern readers of Plato. In brief, comedy, dream, myth, and music are essential components of Plato's writing; therefore, they must animate our reading.   *It was the crow of a cock . . . who knew a thing or two; the crow of a cock who had fought the world and got the better of it, and was now resolved to crow, though the earth should heave and the heavens should fall. It was a wise crow; an invincible crow; a philosophic crow; a crow of all crows.*

Perhaps now we can try to apply Nietzsche's criticisms *and* hints to a not-so-random selection from one of the dialogues. We will read the first fifteen pages of *Phaedo* (57–72) three times, offering (1) a straightforward "analytical" account of the central arguments developed there, (2) a genealogical-critical reading in the Nietzschean style, and (3) a more "positive" Nietzschean reading, taking into account comedy, dream, myth, and music.

THREE ACCOUNTS OF *PHAEDO*

STRAIGHTFORWARD ACCOUNT; OR,
THE BAREBONES SOCRATES

We can skip almost everything in the first six pages of Plato's *Phaedo*, since they contain a few dramatic niceties but nothing of philosophical importance, and proceed to the two major proofs for the immortality of the soul. Actually these two proofs, one involving the theory of recollection and the subsistence of the ideas, the other based on the mutual exclusion of opposites, are rather mixed up and confused with one another; but we can distill the essence of each without much difficulty. The first is simply an inverted version of the argument of *Meno*, 81 ff., which derives the theory of recollection and the ideas from the immortality of the soul; now Plato turns the argument around in order to prove the immortality of the soul from the theory of recollection and the ideas. Yet this begs the question. The second argument is more interesting. It concerns the radical exclusion of opposites from one another. Earlier suggestions concerning the correlation and alternating generation of opposites, such as the correlation of pleasure and pain (60b) and the generation of comparatives such as "larger" and "smaller" from one another (70e), are rejected in favor of the argument that "opposites themselves would absolutely refuse to tolerate coming into being from one another" (103c 5–6). The mutual exclusion of opposites applies above all, of course, in the case of life and death. "The ψυχή will never admit the opposite of that which accompanies it" (105d 4–5). Since life accompanies soul, the soul will never admit death. Death strikes only the body, since the εἴδη of life and death do not participate in one another and since the soul is the principle of life. This argument is meant to bolster the first. Through dialectic, philosophic souls learn of the existence of an a priori realm of ideas, and also of the requirement for entrance into that realm; they come to understand their pursuit of the nature and causes of things as "a preparation for dying and being dead." For that is the way Socrates much earlier in the dialogue describes the pursuit of philosophy:

> Other people are not likely to be aware that those who pursue philosophy in the right way study nothing but dying and being dead [64a 6: ἐπιτηδεύουσιν ἢ ἀποθνῄσκειν τε καὶ τεθνάναι]. If this is true, and they have been eager for nothing but death all their lives, it would be absurd for them to be troubled when the thing comes that they had so long been eagerly studying [64a 9: ὃ πάλαι προυθυμοῦντό τε καὶ ἐπετήδευον].

What we must understand are the meanings of *epitedeuousin*, to study, practice, or prepare for, as of *apothneskein* and *tethnanai*, to die, or (in past tenses) to be dead, along with the coinage, *prouthumounto*, variously translated as "eagerly," or "looking forward to," and whose stem derives from θυμός, heart, spirit, liveliness, and enthusiasm. In other words, we must understand " . . . in what way true philosophers desire death [or, as some translators have it: are half dead already], . . . in what way they deserve death, . . . and what kind of death it is [64b 8–9: ἧ τε θανατῶσι καὶ ἧ ἄξιοί εἰσιν θανάτου καὶ οἵου θανάτου οἱ ὡς ἀληθῶς φιλόσοφοι]." The second and third are not difficult to explain: the kind of death philosophers deserve is " . . . the separation of the soul from the body [64c 4: ἢ τήν τῆς ψυχῆς ἀπὸ τοῦ σώματος ἀπαλλαγήν]." Philosophers deserve the kind of death that is an *apallagē*, a deliverance, escape, or release from the confinement of the body, enabling them to behold as gods the blinding light of the εἴδη (see 82c). The philosopher is worthy of dying, *axios thanatou*, insofar as he " . . . purifies himself of the body until God himself grants deliverance [67a 5–6: ἀλλὰ καθαρεύωμεν ἀπ᾽ αὐτοῦ, ἕως ἂν ὁ θεὸς αὐτὸς ἀπολύσῃ ἡμᾶς]." The philosopher merits his death, death is his prerogative, θεμιτός (67b 2), because in the moral program of *katharsis* he purges himself of all bodily distractions and vanities. It is more difficult to know how the philosopher is *thanatōsi*, "half dead already" or "desirous of death." The present participle cannot imply suicide, since no *themis* allows mortals to separate their own soul and body (see 61 c ff.). *Thanatōsi* may derive from θανατάω, "to wish to die," "to long for death," "to be moribund," or from θανατόω, "to put to death," or, figuratively, "to mortify." Both bring to mind the catharsis whereby the philosopher desires and deserves death. He is *thanatōsi*, "having one foot in the grave," insofar as he strives " . . . to separate the soul from communion with the body [65a 1–2: ὅτι μάλιστα τὴν ψυχὴν ἀπὸ τῆς τοῦ σώματος κοινωνίας διαφερόντως τῶν ἄλλων ἀνθρώπων]." *Koinōnia* means communion, association, fellowship, or intercourse; its root, κοινόω, means to communicate, impart, or share, but also to pollute, infect, or soil. The lover of wisdom is plagued by infection to the end. He tries to draw apart, *diapherein*, the two elements that are in communion, the two elements for which contiguity means contagion, in order to save *psychē* from the pollution of *sōma*. The philosophical soul " . . . greatly despises the body, and flees from it [65c 11–66d 1: μάλιστα ἀτιμάζει τὸ σῶμα καὶ φεύγει ἀπ᾽ αὐτοῦ]." *Atimadzein* is a strong word, meaning to dishonor, insult, or express contempt for something; the more familiar *pheugein* is also strong, and means to flee, shun, or shrink back in fear of that thing. How these two strong words can go together—contempt with terror—is perhaps a problem. However, to sum up what by now has become clear, the mutual exclusion of opposites serves to unify two fundamental Platonic doctrines: it constitutes the ontological character of the ideas as fixed and invariable, and prescribes the moral program by which the philosopher's soul is appropriated to them.   *I felt as though I could meet Death, and invite him to dinner, and toast the Catacombs with him, in pure overflow of self-reliance and a sense of universal security.*   Hence the maxim of a recent German commentator on Plato's *Phaedo*, to the effect that " . . . whoever cannot greet death as a friend is no philosopher," inasmuch as philosophy is always a *meditatio mortis*.[6]

First Nietzschean-Genealogical Account; or, the Skeleton in the Closet

We must understand the unity of metaphysics and morality in Plato, that is, the unity of the ideas and the soul's approximation to them, as a genealogical unity. The otherworldly philosophy that Plato proleptically founds pins its hopes on an ideal world that one can enter only through the portal of death; it seeks to ground ontology in a "world of true being" of which this world of becoming is but a faulty replica and amateurish prelude. The metaphysics of the εἴδη flies off to a "world" that exists before birth and after death and that is thought to hold the wobbly world of the present in its hands. Scandalized by the intolerable ambiguity of human existence, its deliverance over to a series of sublime beauties and staggering horrors between birth and death, an existence whose carousel of hopes and frustrations would be endless but for that ultimate frustration, Platonism determines to abandon the world *de bonne heure*: it proclaims the doctrine of the ideas, appends a Word to words, then proceeds to cover the tracks of its moral prejudice with bad philology and execrable logic. Ontology—based on a blind confidence in the mutual exclusion of opposites—becomes the security blanket for mortals who find the earth too cold and who are not robust enough to live in the face of death. The genealogy of Western metaphysics and morality? Illusion for a mother, illness for a father. Mother gets her way with father, however, and debility and death become the first targets of illusion. "Preparation for dying and being dead" is taken to mean preparation for life; death is, in Goethe's words, " . . . dragged back into life," celebrated as an event to be anticipated with piety and mortifications. The body is scorned and feared as a pollutant, the soul named a good boy fallen among evil companions. The dying Socrates says he owes a cock to Asclepius, and so slurs life itself as a sickness, praising death as a state of health.   *Oh, brave cock!—oh, noble Shanghai!—oh, bird rightly offered up by the invincible Socrates, in testimony of his final victory over life!*   From hence, all is in disarray. Moralists hail the grim reaper as "Sweet Death." Bach composes cantatas in which piping sopranos sing, "When Death comes to my bed I shall welcome him!" And all the philosophic saints, like Amy Thanatogenous, gaily embalm themselves in advance. The narrator of Melville's *Moby-Dick* recalls the "delicious death" of an Ohio apiarist who leaned too far over a hollow tree stump, lost his balance, fell in, and "died embalmed" in golden honey. The image compels the narrator to ask, "How many, think ye, have likewise fallen into Plato's honey head, and sweetly perished there?"[7]

SECOND NIETZSCHEAN READING; OR, THE EROTIC SOCRATES

As Phaedo himself requests (at 59d), let us go back to the beginning. Phaedo tells Echecrates that he was with Socrates at the time of the latter's death, thus preparing the way for Plato's admission (at 59b) that he himself (if "Plato" is he who is writing) was absent (whether in fact, or only for purposes of *Phaedo*, no one knows) due to illness. At the outset Plato places himself at a remarkable distance from every event and speech recorded in this dialogue that is taken to be so crucial to the meaning of Socrates' life.   *Where lurked this valiant Shanghai—this bird of cheerful Socrates—the game-fowl Greek who died unappalled?*   Further, the matter of Plato's illness calls to mind the end of *Phaedo* and Socrates' last words concerning the debt owed to Asclepius: might these words signify not that Socrates views life as a sickness for which death is the only cure but that life itself is essentially recuperation? that philosophizing itself is a kind of convalescence, for the sake of life and more life? Might the recuperation be both Plato's and Zarathustra's? For both Zarathustra and Plato are ill. Perhaps Plato's Socrates at the end of his life remembers the absent youth who will devote so much of his life to the remembrance of Socrates? Perhaps Socrates' Plato is designing the *Corpus platonicum* as a strategy for life? Perhaps in the course of his recollection of Socrates, that is to say, in the course of *Phaedo's* composition, Plato has learned a great healthfulness from Socrates, one that removes him from the immediate pathos of Socrates' death, from Apollodoros's sobs and Xanthippe's plaints and complaints, and perhaps even from the need for a magical *logos* or swan song to charm away fears of death? Is there not a sense in which Plato's commentators for the past two thousand years, the millennia of Christendom, have needed that incantation much more than Plato ever did?   *"How is it, that your sick family like this crowing?" said I. "The cock is a glorious cock, with a glorious voice, but not exactly the sort of thing for a sick chamber, one would suppose. Do they really like it?"*   For Plato absents himself from such a need. Instead, he spends much of his lifetime writing about a hero who could outfight, outdrink, and outtalk anybody in town or country, a man who enjoyed good food, good health, good company, and the passionate admiration of the brightest and handsomest youths in Athens.

Phaedo tells us that the time between Socrates' trial and execution was occupied by the mission to Apollonian Delos (58b–c); during this time Socrates received an extraordinarily large number of visitors—over twenty are present for *Phaedo* alone—with whom he pursued the same kind of inquiry he had always pursued on the command of the oracle of Delphic Apollo. From Delphi to Delos there is no time for sackcloth and ashes, *meditatio mortis*, morose piety and morbid enthusiasm, for testing the limits of the god's proscription against suicide. Phaedo tells us of the curious mixture of feelings he suffered, of pain and pleasure, sadness and joy, aroused by the situation and the ensuing discussion; he stresses (at 59a) that he took no pleasure in or consolation from the day's discussion. Phaedo believes that dialectic is somehow out of place under the grim circumstances, although Socrates says (at 70c) that even a comic poet (guess who?) could not deny that the moment of an execution is a proper time to discuss the fate of the soul after death. Nonetheless, Plato is altogether absent from the scene, and Phaedo, "the radiant one," is absolutely taciturn in it; Phaedo takes pleasure in remembering Socrates, but not this last discussion, and where Plato takes his pleasure we cannot be sure.

Socrates is released from his chains, rubs his legs briskly to restore circulation, and discourses on the indissoluble unity of those opposites called pain and pleasure. He even tells a little folktale or fable about them—in which the god stops the quarreling between pleasure and pain by binding them together at the head. At 60d–e, the discussion turns to Socrates' new preoccupation with lyric poetry: in response to a recurring dream in which Apollo commands him "to practice the arts," μουσική, Socrates has been versifying the "Fables" and "Prelude to Apollo" of Aesop—who is said to have leapt to his death at the Castalian Font of Delphi. However, Apollo does not order Socrates "to practice death and dying," and in fact it is his worship (the mission to Delos) that gives Socrates the time to practice *mousikē*. At the close of his tale of the dream Socrates makes a joke, asking Cebes to tell the poet Evenus that " . . . if he is wise, he should follow me as quickly as he can." Everyone is aghast, since this sounds as though Socrates is proposing a *Liebestod* duet, and the remainder of the dialogue flows from Socrates' little joke.

As for the *logoi* themselves, they are Pythagorean, learned from Philolaus (see 61d and 69c). Cebes, Simmias, and later Crito object to the Pythagorean confidence in an afterlife, and Socrates tries (unsuccessfully, as it turns out: see 115c–116b) to purge their doubts and assuage their fears. Socrates again expresses his simple confidence in an afterlife, and Simmias requests " . . . a share in this comfort" (63d). The executioner interrupts in order to ask Socrates, *via* Crito, not to talk so much: all that dialectic is liable to affect his metabolism and disrupt the poisoning to come. Socrates replies, *via* Crito, "Forget about him; that's his problem, not mine!" If Socrates is so eager for death he certainly ought to have been more cooperative with regard to its agent; instead, he seems eager to keep on talking. He presents arguments to shore up his Pythagorean confidence and to soothe the others in their grief: he calls the *logoi* "magical chants" or "incantations" designed to " . . . charm away fears of death" (77e).   *"Better than a 'pothecary, eh?" said Merrymusk. "This is Dr. Cock himself."*   Later he calls his dialectic a "swan song" having a similar purpose. His arguments appeal to old legends, myths, and dreams (see 60e, 70c, 85a, 107d, etc.), and are said to be a kind of mystifying music. Their effect, however, is to make both Simmias and Cebes *laugh*, though the solemnity of the occasion would seem to have banished the possibility of levity.

Yet anything that is "banished" from Plato's dialogues seems to return: the flute girls banished from *Symposium* make a triumphant return with Alcibiades; the tragedians banned from *Republic* speak again in the myth of Er—and perhaps also in *Phaedo* (see 115a 1–2). So it is with the comedians. Socrates sings his swan song and utters his charms in a mode designed to prevent Phaedo from shearing his curly locks in grief over Socrates' dying (89b). As he gathers up those curls—"Phedo's toyable fair hair," Joyce calls it—in his hand, Socrates warns his friends about "mislogic": never demand too much from discourse, he says, for you will be disappointed and will lose faith in it altogether.

How is Socrates *thanatōsi*, how is he dying? Not by despising or fleeing from anything, but by celebrating the *koinōnia*, fellowship or communion of friends, as of soul and body, up to the end. *Oh, noble cock! Oh, noble man!* It is almost as though—again, proleptically—he had followed Heidegger's counsel in *Being and Time*, which emphasizes that death cannot be presentified in any way: being *toward* the end is not doting *on* the end, and Heidegger consistently frustrates every effort to give the notion of death some sort of concrete "filling." In short, mortals confront their dying *aporetically*, so much so that even Heidegger's notions of "the call of conscience," "the moment of insight," "readiness for anxiety," and "resolute openness" must be taken with a large grain of everydayness. *His head fell back. A white napkin seemed dropped upon his face. Merrymusk was dead. [¶] An awful fear seized me. [¶] But the cock crew.* Death, like Plato, is a figure of *Verborgenheit*.[8]

TEACHING PLATO (AFTER NIETZSCHE)

It is clear that if we heed Nietzsche's critique *and* his reading hints we will be in a difficult situation, the situation of reading Plato without the assistance of Platonism. This is a particularly unnerving situation for teachers of Plato. It is all right to be riven privately, but to confess to such downright ambiguity and even ambivalence publicly—in the classroom? What about *teaching* Plato (after Nietzsche)? With respect to our otherwise laudable desire to improve undergraduate instruction in classical languages, philosophy, the humanities, and culture generally, Nietzsche makes some harsh remarks. They appear in a lecture course transcribed by Nietzsche himself in 1873 and given the title *Philosophy in the Tragic Age of the Greeks*. After stating his theme, which affirms " . . . that the Greeks justify philosophy," Nietzsche wonders aloud whether philosophy is possible in *our* time.

> A period that suffers from so-called universal liberal education, but that has no culture and no unity of style in its life, will not rightly know what to do with philosophy—were the genius of truth itself to proclaim it in the streets and market places. During such times philosophy remains the learned monologue of the lonely stroller, the accidental loot of the individual, the skeleton concealed in the closet, or the harmless chatter among senile academics and children. No one may venture to

fulfill the demands of philosophy in his own person, no one live philosophically with that simple loyalty which compelled an ancient, no matter where he was or what he was doing, to comport himself as a Stoic once he had pledged faith to the Stoa. All modern philosophizing is political, policed by governments churches academies custom fashion and human cowardice, all of which limit it to a certain fake learnedness: it remains content with the sigh, "If only . . . ," or with its knowledge, "Once upon a time . . . ." Philosophy has no rights, and if modern man had any courage or conscience he would really have to repudiate it, banning it with words similar to those Plato used to ban tragic poets from his state. Of course, reply could be made, just as the tragic poets might have made reply to Plato. If forced for once to speak out, philosophy might say, "Wretched people! Is it my fault if I am roaming the countryside among you like a Gypsy fortune-teller, if I must hide and disguise myself as though I were a fallen woman and you my judges? Look at my sister, Art! Like me, she has suffered shipwreck among barbarians, and neither of us knows how to save herself.   *She fell back, without a sigh and, through long-loving sympathy, was dead. [¶] The cock crew.*   Here we have surely lost all our rights, but the judges who shall restore them to us shall judge you too, and they shall say to you: Go get yourselves a culture—only then will you experience what philosophy wants to do and can do." (*1*, 812)

Before we observe contentedly that Nietzsche's time is not our own, we might ask whether for us philosophy is anything more than a fake learnedness policed by academe, and whether a culture whose unity rests in its techno-structure, its compulsive consumption, and its media events can host philosophy. Philosophers are professionals today; they have credentials to prove it. Especially in the "buyer's market" that has prevailed for decades now, professional philosophers must pull their own weight and occasionally throw their weight around, either by becoming "popular teachers," which usually means becoming song-and-dance performers like Euthydemos and Dionysodoros, or by ambitiously pursuing the present alternative to " . . . perish," and especially by climbing up the ladder of unlove to university administration and to the national granting agencies, where lie money and power. That is not to say that philosophy has been repudiated: although our culture long ago recognized philosophy's superfluousness, it has not banned philosophy, if only because philosophy fulfills the ontological criterion of our time—it is one of those "real things," like a cola, that can be consumed. However, as students consume less and less of it, or as administrators become convinced that the buyers want something else, and as beleaguered professional philosophers labor over possible improvements in packaging, presentation, and product promotion, our culture accomplishes the banning of philosophy in the most effective modern way. First to go is Greek philosophy: it all sounds silly in Victorian English, anyway, and Greek is impossible, so not much can be done about it, except to blame Nietzsche and Heidegger (and now Derrida) for closing the American mind, such as it is. Even when good translations are available—and they are surprisingly rare in spite of the great number of attempts—who wants to take the trouble to read and teach them? And since Greece is universally acclaimed the cradle of *Western* civilization, a time that prides itself on "multicultural-ism" sees itself forced to declare all things Greek both perfectly homogeneous and utterly familiar, and all of it DWEM (Dead White European and Male), to which a colleague of mine replies with a timid Platonic-Socratic query, "What do you have against the dead?" *The pallor of the children was changed to radiance. . . . I saw angels where they lay.*

However, it is not a matter of showing how "relevant" the dialogues re-main: Plato has been relevant for two thousand years without our help, and he does not need it now. It does not hurt to note that our general cultural and political crises bear a striking resemblance to those of fourth-century Athens. Virtually everything in the City has come under scrutiny and attack, the gods, the archons, and the military, as a result of political corruption and cynicism within the walls and disastrous imperial wars and policing actions outside the walls. Underlying the attack is a loss of confidence in what demagogues call the "values that make up the national fabric," due to a growing social, racial, and ethnic fragmentation and dispersion, on the one hand, and advancing concen-tration of political and economic power, on the other. We grow weary of the incessant strife, and of the equally incessant intransigence of the powers that be: all this discussion, all this talk, all this dialectic! Ours *is* a time for dialectic, hip-hop dialectic perhaps, but dialectic nonetheless. We do not need to trouble ourselves about the "relevance" of *Republic, Symposium,* and *Phaedo.* If Nietz-sche is right, and the necessity of dialectic is a sure sign of cultural decadence and political disruption, then we ought to recognize our plight and get as much help from Plato as we can.

To be sure, it is not a matter of inculcating Platonic virtues and doctrines into our students. For, frankly, the more thoughtfully we read the dialogues the less sure we become of the virtues of dialectic, and the more suspicious we must become of doctrinal exposition. If anything distinguishes Plato's Socrates from the other sophists it is his unwillingness to preach dogmas of any sort. He even confesses that, lacking expertise in everything but erotic matters, he really does not have an idea in his head. All Socrates can do is help young people test their own ideas to see if they are alive or dead. He does not know much about death, either, but, being a midwife by birth and training, he has a lot of experience with love, birth, and vitality.

As for Plato himself, he does not write about himself. If he writes about anything, it is about Socrates. If we choose to put words into Plato's mouth we had better do so as skillfully, with as much attention to dramatic detail, as Plato presumably did with his master. Any attempt we might make to show how Plato "advanced beyond" Socrates—that usually means how Plato suc-ceeds in becoming a dogmatist and metaphysician—will probably result in sheer conjecture. As for Plato's "private teaching" in the Academy, and his "esoteric writings," we do not have the writings and cannot attend the Acad-emy. By contrast, we do have the dialogues, and we ought to try to learn how to read them: how to hear the *logos* or argument, how to see the *ergon,* the dramatic deeds that occur before, during, and after the *logos*, and how to be touched by the *mythos*, which is both the plot of the dialogue and its roots concealed deep in that multicultured Greek soil.

Toward the close of his life, José Ortega y Gasset began to compose a commentary on *Symposium—El Banquete—*of Plato. This is the first dialogue I ever almost read. Ortega's first chapter asks, *Qué es leer?*"—"What is reading?" It is a brilliant piece of writing on the matter of hermeneutics, the interpretation of texts—a matter one might have expected to come up in an essay on *Phaedrus* rather than *Symposium*. Why the question of reading with respect to *Symposium*? Ortega surely did not write for my sake! Yet the problem of reading Plato is critical in both cases: Ortega wanted to know *how* to read Plato, while I wanted to know *whether* to read him. After Nietzsche. Perhaps the fatality of teaching is to know that these two questions are really one. How we teach Plato has much to do with whether or not our students will read him. Much depends on how we behave at the banquet. If we teach Plato as though he were Pausanias—moralistic, indignant, dogmatic, cocksure, and contriving— we make the dialogues unreadable and the philosophic symposium inaccessible for at least one generation. And we lend Thanatos   *He flew upon the apex of the dwelling, spread wide his wings, sounded one supernatural note, and dropped at my feet*   a helping hand, which in our time he surely does not need.

Nietzsche provides an excellent remedy, a *pharmakon* and *therapeia*, against the pauperization or pausaniation of Plato precisely through his overturning of Platonism. And in the end we learn to read Plato better by heeding Nietzsche's advice about how to read his own book called *Morgenröthe*, or   COCK-A-DOODLE-DOO!—OO!—OO!—oo!—oo!   *Daybreak*. Nietzsche is the Anti-Platonist, the philosopher with the hammer, but he is also the philologist, that is to say, a lover of discourse and a teacher of unhurried reading, *ein Lehrer des langsamen Lesens*, " . . . a reading that is deep, retrospective, and forward-looking, a reading with hinterthoughts, with gentle fingers and eyes" (3, 17).

FIVE

Der Maulwurf/ The Mole

Reading Kant and Hegel (after Nietzsche)

Für Helmbrecht Breinig, der
jahrelang wacker mitgewühlt hat.

For Helm Breinig, burrowing bravely
over the years.

AUSZÜGE

Maulwurf, ahd. *muwërf*, "Haufenwerfer"
(zu ags. *muwa*, engl. mow, "Hügel"), dann
volksetymologisch auf mhd. *molt*, nhd. *mul*,
"Staub," umgedeutet. . . ; seit dem 15. Jh. auf
Maul. . . .

Hermann Paul, *Deutsches Wörterbuch*

Djese solle euch auch vnrein sein unter den
Thieren / die auff erden kriechen / . . . die
Aydex / der Blindschleich / und der Maulworff.

III. Mose 11, 29–30, hrsg. Dr. Martin Luther

Wir erkennen unsern alten Freund, unsern
alten Maulwurf, der so gut unter der Erde zu
arbeiten weiß, um plötzlich zu erscheinen.

Karl Marx

So ist es bis heute nicht gelungen,
Maulwürfe zu züchten; sie entziehen sich den
künstlichen Lebensbedingungen der Gefangen-
schaft durch Verzicht auf Fortpflanzung. . . .
Ihre Anpassungsfähigkeit an den Terror mensch-
licher Naturbeherrschung ist minimal.

Opitz/Pinkert, *Der alte Maulwurf*

Man betrachte z.B. den Maulwurf, diesen
unermüdlichen Arbeiter. Mit seinen Schaufel-
pfoten angestrengt zu graben—, ist die Beschäfti-
gung seines ganzen Lebens: bleibende Nacht
umgibt ihn: seine embryonischen Augen hat er
bloß, um das Licht zu fliehen. . . . Was aber er-
langt er durch diesen mühevollen und freuden-

EXTRACTS

Mole (cf. *mow, mould*): any one of the
small mammals of the family *Talpidae*; esp. the
common mole of the Old World, *Talpa europaea*, a small animal . . . having . . . exceedingly small but not blind eyes, and very short
strong fossorial fore-limbs with which to burrow in the earth in search of earthworms and
to excavate the galleried chambers in which it
dwells.

Oxford English Dictionary

These also shalbe vncleane vnto you . . .
the Lyzard, and the Snaile, and the Molle.

Leviticus xi, 30

We recognize our old friend, our old mole,
who knows so well how to work underground,
then suddenly to emerge.

Karl Marx

Up to the present day it has proved impossible to breed moles; they withdraw from the
artificial living conditions of captivity by refusing to propagate. . . . Their ability to adapt to
the Terror of human dominion over nature is
minimal.

Opitz/Pinkert, *The Old Mole*

Observe, for instance, the mole—that tireless worker. The occupation of his entire life is
to dig laboriously with his shovel-like paws;

leeren Lebenslauf? Futter und Begattung, also
nur die Mittel, dieselbe traurige Bahn fortzuset-
zen und wieder anzufangen, im neuen Indi-
viduo. An solchen Beispielen wird es deutlich,
daß zwischen den Mühen und Plagen des
Lebens und dem Ertrag oder Gewinn desselben
kein Verhältnis ist.

Arthur Schopenhauer

[Über die Skepsis als Schlaf- und Beruhi-
gungsmittel]: . . . Und Hamlet selbst wird heute
von den Ärzten der Zeit gegen den "Geist" und
sein Rumoren unter dem Boden verordnet.
"Hat man denn nicht alle Ohren schon voll von
schlimmen Geräuschen?" sagt der Skeptiker,
als ein Freund der Ruhe und beinahe als eine
Art von Sicherheits-Polizei: "dies unterirdische
Nein ist fürchterlich! Stille endlich, ihr pessi-
mistischen Maulwürfe!"

Friedrich Nietzsche

. . . Ce monde hideux et bouleversant où
les taupes elles-mêmes se mêlent d'espérer.

Albert Camus

Was ich schreibe, sind Maulwürfe. . . .
Meine Maulwürfe sind schneller als man denkt.
Wenn man meint, sie seien da, wo sie Mulm
aufwerfen, rennen sie schon in ihren Gängen
einem Gedanken nach. . . .

Günter Eich, Maulwürfe

Le sillage effacé de l'écriture par où la lecture fera surface, le cheminement souterrain
d'une taupe. . . ; [l'écriture], cette activité fréné-
tique, aveugle et Fouterraine. . . .

Hélène Cixous, Neutre

Schädlinge am Volksganzen jedoch, deren
offenkundiger verbrecherischer Hang immer
wieder strafbare Handlungen hervorrufen wird,
werden unschädlich gemacht werden.

Hans Filbinger (CDU) im Jahr 1935

Maulwurffangprämie: Am Dienstagvormit-
tag, 20.5. wird bei der Gemeindekasse die Maulwurffangprämie gegen Vorlage der Maulwurf-
schwänze ausgezahlt.

Amtliches Mitteilungsblatt der
Gemeinde Bollschweil-St. Ulrich,
Nr. 21, Jahrgang 1975

ever-present night surrounds him; he has his
embryonic eyes only so that he may flee the
light. . . . Yet what does he gain from his toil-
some and joyless curriculum? Food and reproduction—in other words, nothing more than
the means to continue on the selfsame miser-
able path, beginning again in a new individual.
Such examples make it clear that an unfavor-
able ratio prevails between the toils and troubles of life and its outcome or gain.

Arthur Schopenhauer

[On skepticism as a sedative]: . . . And
nothing less than Hamlet is prescribed today
by the medicals of our time to settle the "spirit"
and its subterranean rumblings. "Haven't we
had enough dreadful noise?" says the skep-
tic, who is a friend of tranquillity, and almost
an agent of the Security Police. "This underground negation is terrifying! Won't you please
be quiet, you pessimistic moles!"

Friedrich Nietzsche

Does the Eagle know what is in the pit?
Or wilt thou go ask the Mole?

William Blake, "Thel's Motto"

My instinct tells me that my head is an
organ for burrowing, as some creatures use
their snout and fore paws, and with it I would
mine and burrow my way through these hills.

Henry David Thoreau

However, parasitic pests on the body politic
of the Volk, pests whose flagrant addiction to
malfeasance will give rise again and again to
criminal acts, will be neutralized.

Hans Filbinger (CDU), in 1935

Reward for the Capture of Moles: On Tues-
day, May 20, bounties for the capture of moles
will be paid out by the local treasurer upon re-
ceipt of the tails.

Community Newsletter for the Town of
Bollschweil-Sankt Ulrich,
No. 21, May 16, 1975

So then he scraped and scratched and
scrabbled and scrooged, and then he scrooged
again and scrabbled and scratched and scraped,
working busily with his little paws and mutter-

"¡Me falta algo, me falta algo!"

El Topo Gigio

ing to himself, "Up we go! Up we go!" till at last, pop! . . .

Kenneth Grahame, *The Wind in the Willows*

VORWURF

Das Folgende als Versuch(ung) einer Nebeneinanderstellung von Textpassagen aus den Werken Kants, Hegels und Nietzsches, die ein merkwürdiges Bild dieser deutschen Philosophen entwerfen, das Bild nämlich des beinahe blinden, den Boden geschäftig durchwühlenden Schädlings, des Maulwurfs.[1] Das Bild entpuppt sich als mögliche Antwort auf die Frage: Wie verstehen sich die Philosophen Kant, Hegel und Nietzsche, wie schätzen sie ihre jeweilige Suche nach der Wahrheit ein? Denn—zumindest nach Kant—bietet die Metapher des Maulwurfs sich als passendes Selbstbildnis. Darüber hinaus ist zu fragen: Unterscheiden sich insbesondere bei Hegel und Nietzsche die Maulwurfsdeutungen derart, daß sich eine Kluft auftut, die zwei Epochen, die der modernen Metaphysik und die einer sogennanten "postmodernen," aber sonst kaum zu bezeichnenden Gegenwart, endgültig von einander trennt?

PRELUDE AND PLAINT

What follows is an attemptation to juxtapose a series of texts from the works of Kant, Hegel, and Nietzsche. The texts project a curious image of these German philosophers as that all-but-blind, busily burrowing rodent pest, the mole.[1] The image suggests something about the way these philosophers understand themselves, how they estimate their own search for truth. For, at least after Kant, the mole metaphor emerges as a suitable likeness of the philosopher. The question then arises: Do the various employments of the mole image, especially in Hegel and Nietzsche, differ in such a way that a chasm yawns, a gap that sunders once and for all two epochs, that of modern metaphysics and that of our "postmodern" present, to which we otherwise can scarcely lend a name?

"ALLERLEI MAUL-WURFSGÄNGE" BEI KANT

Für Kant ist der Maulwurf gerade das, was er selber *nicht* ist, nämlich der Vertreter der Metaphysik, die über Jahrhunderte hinweg das Errichten von jedwedem wohlfundierten Gebäude einer wissenschaftlichen Philosophie verhindert hat. Wohl erwähnt Kant in seiner "Kritik der reinen Vernunft" den Maulwurf selbst überhaupt nicht; es sind eher die bedauerlichen Ergebnisse von dessen intensiver Wühlarbeit, die die kritische Philosophie ins Auge fassen will. Nach einer Erörterung der platonischen Ideenlehre, z.B. des "Phaidon", die sich hauptsächlich mit dem Bereich der Moral und

"ALL KINDS OF MOLE TUNNELS" IN KANT

The mole is precisely what Kant, in his own eyes, is not, namely, a representative of the metaphysical tradition. For metaphysics over the centuries has obstructed the erection of every possible solidly founded structure of a scientific philosophy. Indeed, Kant does not mention the mole as such. What the Critical philosophy wishes to examine is the damage its intensive excavations have done. After a discussion of the Platonic ideas, as presented for example in *Phaedo*, a discussion preoccupied mainly with the realm of morality and ethicality, Kant complains as fol-

der Sittlichkeit beschäftigt, klagt Kant (KrV, A319/B375–76)[2] wie folgt: "Statt aller dieser Betrachtungen, deren gehörige Ausführung in der Tat die eigentümliche Würde der Philosophie ausmacht, beschäftigen wir uns jetzt mit einer nicht so glänzenden, aber doch auch nicht verdienstlosen Arbeit, nämlich: den Boden zu jenen majestätischen stattlichen Gebäuden eben und baufest zu machen, in welchem sich allerlei Maulwurfsgänge einer vergeblich, aber mit guter Zuversicht, auf Schätze grabenden Vernunft vorfinden, und die jenes Bauwerk unsicher machen".

Nicht als Untergrabender, sondern als Ebnender versteht sich Kant: nicht als Maulwurf, sondern als Planierraupe. Um den Boden "eben und baufest zu machen", braucht sich der Philosoph angeblich gar nicht unter der Oberfläche der Erde zu bewegen, ja, eine unterirdische Arbeit könnte das zukünftige Bauwerk nur gefährden. In der "Transzendentalen Deduktion" warnt Kant den Leser nichtsdestoweniger davor, daß er oder sie "über Dunkelheit klage, wo die Sache tief eingehüllt ist" (A88/B121), daß er oder sie die vielen Schwierigkeiten übersehe, die den Kritiker nötigen, "so tief in die ersten Gründe der Möglichkeit unserer Erkenntnis überhaupt einzudringen" (A98).

Kritik der reinen Vernunft dürfe demgemäß keine Arbeit auf der Oberfläche sein. Es genüge nicht, die alten Maulwurfsgänge einfach von oben her zuzuschütten und auf diese Weise bzw. auf dieser Wiese den Boden *scheinbar* eben und fest zu machen. Sowohl der Richter am Gerichtshof der kritischen Vernunft als auch der Architekt des Gebäudes der wissenschaftlichen Philosophie muß in die Tiefe eindringen; beide müssen also den Boden auf jeden Fall volens nolens durchwühlen und untergraben, bis sie zum Grundgestein kommen. Damit werden diejenigen Fragen unumgänglich, die J. Sallis in seinem

lows (*Critique of Pure Reason*, A319/B375–76):[2] "Although pursuit of these considerations is what lends philosophy its proper dignity, we must instead occupy ourselves now with a less resplendent yet still meritorious task; namely we must level the ground and make it firm enough for those majestic edifices of ethicality. For in this ground we find all kinds of mole tunnels, which reason has dug in its confident but futile search for treasure, and which make such construction precarious."

Kant sees himself not as excavator but as leveler, not as "Mole" but as "Caterpillar." In order to "level the ground and make it firm enough" to build on, the Critical philosopher ostensibly need not penetrate below the surface of the earth. Indeed, further subterranean work could only endanger future construction. Nevertheless, in the "Transcendental Deduction" Kant warns his readers not to "complain about obscurity where the matter at issue is so profoundly veiled" (A88/B121), and not to overlook the many difficulties that compel the Critical philosopher to "penetrate so deep into the primary grounds of the possibility of our cognition in general" (A98).

A critique of pure reason accordingly dare not labor on the superficies. It would not be enough simply to cause the old mole tunnels to cave in by toiling away on the meadow's surface. In that way one would make the ground only *apparently* level and firm. The judge at the law court of pure reason and the architect who designs the buildings for a scientific philosophy—both must plunge into the depths, both must at all events burrow and tunnel into the earth until they reach bedrock. However, if that is so, certain questions inevitably arise, questions such as those John Sallis has posed in his essay "Tunnelings": "How can critique explore the ground all the way down to the bedrock except by tun-

Aufsatz "Untergrabungen" gestellt hat: "Wie kann die Kritik den Boden bis zum Felsuntergrund erforschen, wenn nicht durch Bohrungen, die jenen Maulwurfswühlereien ähneln, deren Wirkungen die Kritik gerne auslöschen würde?" Letzten Endes, fragt Sallis, "Beraubt nicht auch der kritische Maulwurfsgang den Boden seiner Festigkeit, höhlt nicht auch er den Boden aus, bedroht also nicht auch er die Sicherheit aller Gebäude, die auf diesem Boden errichtet werden könnten?"[3]

Solche Fragen zeigen einen Riß auf, der die ganze Metaphorik von Kants "Kritik der reinen Vernunft" zu sprengen und in eine sich widerstrebende Bewegung, eine Art Torsion, zu setzen droht. Hier liegt der Anfang einer neuen Dialektik vor: nicht die der transzendentalen Illusion, sondern die der eigentlichen, von der Geschichte der Metaphysik selbst her bestimmten Reflexion. Von Hegel bis Nietzsche führt jene Dialektik, die von einer zunehmenden und immer heftigeren Schwingung geprägt wird, in den Hinter- bzw. in den Untergrund dieser Geschichte, deren Endstation als der Ab-Grund der Reflexion bezeichnet werden könnte. Ab-Grund der Reflexion heißt aber: ein gleichsam aus sich selbst entstehendes Bild und Selbstbildnis, eine nicht mehr auf die Kategorien einer Logik reduzierbare imago des Geistes. Der einsame Bewohner dieses Ab-Grunds ist *der Maulwurf*.

neling down to it in a way not unlike that very mole-tunneling whose effects critique would expunge?" "Does not the critical mole-tunnel too deprive the ground of its firmness, tunnel it out, and threaten the security of any edifices that might be erected on that ground?"[3]

Such questions expose a fissure that threatens to split the entire metaphorics of Kant's *Critique of Pure Reason*, setting it in motion against itself. Here a new dialectic commences. The dialectic not of transcendental illusions but of reflection proper, reflection as determined by the history of metaphysics itself. Such a dialectic, marked by an increasingly intense and violent oscillation, opens the path from Hegel to Nietzsche, a path into the background and underground of that history; the destination of the path might be designated as the "abyss," the vanishing of the ground and grounds where reflection takes place. The "abyss" of reflection is captured in an image that emerges under its own power, so to speak, an image of spirit that comes on the scene in order to serve as a self-portrait that is no longer reducible to the categories of any logic. The one who dwells in solitude within the abyss is *the mole*.

DER MAULWURF IN SIEBENMEILENSTIEFELN

Über dem Schlußabschnitt von Hegels "Vorlesungen über die Geschichte der Philosophie" steht das Wort "Resultat". Diese Geschichte sei keine bloße Reihe von Ereignissen ohne τέλος, sie sei vielmehr die zweckgerichtete Selbstoffenbarung des Geistes, die sowohl Anstoß als auch Ziel hat. Dabei bestimmt die

THE MOLE IN SEVEN-LEAGUE BOOTS

The word *result* caps the final section of Hegel's *Lectures on the History of Philosophy*. That history is not merely a chronicle of events without *telos;* it is rather a purposeful revelation of and by spirit, which has its motivation and its aim. The historicity of spirit thus defines the science of its self-knowledge,

Geschichtlichkeit des Geistes die Wissenschaft seines Sichselbsterkennens, und zwar in solcher Weise, daß sich die Philosophie als "die wahre Theodizee" ergibt.[4] In seiner Berliner Antrittsvorlesung (Heidelberger Niederschrift) äußert sich Hegel im Rahmen seiner Einführung in die Philosophiegeschichte wie folgt: "Der Besitz an selbstbewußter Vernünftigkeit, welcher uns, der jetzigen Welt angehört, ist nicht unmittelbar entstanden und nur aus dem Boden der Gegenwart gewachsen, sondern es ist dies wesentlich in ihm, eine Erbschaft und näher das Resultat der Arbeit, und zwar der Arbeit aller vorhergegangenen Generationen des Menschengeschlechts zu sein" (18, 21). Erst im Laufe der Geschichte wird die Vernünftigkeit allmählich gewonnen und schrittweise zum festen Bestiz gemacht, so daß die Vergangenheit wie der Gegenstand des Vergil'schen Epos sich als verehrungswürdig erweist, als die "Reihe der edlen Geister, die Galerie der Heroen der denkenden Vernunft" (20, 465)—

Tantae molis erat, se ipsam cognoscere mentem.

Verehrungswürdig allerdings nur vom jetzigen Standpunkt, d.h. von dem einer höheren, weiterentwickelten Welt her, deren Fortschrittsniveau knapp definiert wird: "Die Gegenwart ist das Höchste" (20, 456).[5] Die Idee des Geistes anerkennt sich in dieser Gegenwart als die sich erkennende, sich denkende Idee in ihrer Notwendigkeit, d.h. in ihrer Identität als Begriff. Im Besitz dieser an und für sich erkannten Vernünftigkeit schaut nun der Philosoph auf das ruhelos fortschreitende Streben des Geistes zurück. Da nimmt er wahr, wie der Geist sich geradlinig fortwühlt, bohrend, grabend, aber immer aufwärts steigend. Der *Begriff* eignet sich jetzt erstaunlicherweise ein *sinnliches*, ja, sogar ein *tierisches Bild* an. Das Bild des sich selbst erkennenden Geistes am Ende der nachvollzogenen

indeed in such a way that philosophy presents itself as "the true Theodicy."[4] In his inaugural lecture at Berlin (see the Heidelberg manuscript) Hegel says the following by way of an introduction to the history of philosophy: "The possession of self-assured rationality, which is proper to those of us who live in the contemporary world, did not originate immediately, did not simply sprout from the soil of the present; what is essential about it is that it is a heritage; more specifically, it is the result of the labor of all the past generations of mankind" (18, 21).

Rationality is attained only in the course of history, becomes a permanent possession only step-by-step, so that the past proves to be venerable. It manifests "a series of noble spirits, the gallery of the heroes of thinking reason," whose exploits are as august as those portrayed in Vergil's great epic—

So mighty the efforts of the mind to know itself.

Of course, the dignity of the past is perceived from the contemporary standpoint, which is one of a more highly developed world. Hegel formulates the status of its progress quite succinctly: "The present is supreme" (20, 456).[5] The idea of spirit acknowledges itself in the present as the idea that knows and thinks itself in its necessity, that is, in its identity, as concept. In present possession of such rationality, known in and for itself, the philosopher gazes back upon the incessantly progressive strivings of spirit. He ascertains that spirit burrows its way forward, digging and drilling, yet always on the ascent. Inexplicably and astonishingly, the *concept* now appropriates an *image*, indeed, a sensuous and even *animalistic* image. The image of spirit that knows itself, spirit at the very end of its fully executed recollection, as Hegel portrays it, is that of a *mole*. The spiritual heritage, the

Erinnerung, wie sie Hegel darstellt, ist: *der Maulwurf*. Die ererbte Botschaft des vernünftigen Denkens, das Resultat der Geschichte des Geistes als Begriff, ist: Geist *gleich* Maulwurf. Dazu äußert Hegel:

> Er schreitet immer vorwärts zu, weil nur der Geist ist Fortschreiten. Oft scheint er sich vergessen, verloren zu haben; aber innerlich sich entgegengesetzt, ist er innerliches Fortarbeiten—wie Hamlet vom Geiste seines Vaters sagt, "Brav gearbeitet, wackerer Maulwurf"—bis er, in sich erstärkt, jetzt die Erdrinde, die ihn von seiner Sonne, seinem Begriffe, schied, aufstößt, daß sie zusammenfällt. In solcher Zeit hat er die Siebenmeilenstiefel angelegt, wo sie, ein seelenloses, morschgewordenes Gebäude, zusammenfällt und er in neuer Jugend sich gestaltet zeigt. Diese Arbeit des Geistes sich zu erkennen, sich zu finden, diese Tätigkeit ist der Geist, das Leben des Geistes selbst. Sein Resultat ist der Begriff, den er von sich erfaßt: die Geschichte der Philosophie die klare Einsicht, daß der Geist dies gewollt in seiner Geschichte. (20, 456)

Man ahnt hier die Spannung zwischen *Resultat* und *Tätigkeit*: sich begreifen bedeutet, oder deutet zumindest an, sich ans Tageslicht bringen, sich erfassen, endgültig zu einer klaren Einsicht gelangen, d.h. auf Basis einer nunmehr etablierten claritas und Transparenz zum Stillstand kommen. Begreift sich endlich der vormals innerlich sich entgegengesetzter Geist, erkennt sich das absolute Wesen als das Sichselbstdenkende, kommt der Geist vermutlich zur Ruhe. Alles Äußerliche, alles Gegenständliche, all das, was früher einmal fremd und unabhängig zu sein schien, ergibt sich jetzt als Moment des sich selbst erkennenden Geistes, erweist sich als mit dem Geist völlig identisch und von seiner Gewalt völlig abhängig.

proclamation of rational thought, the result of the history of spirit as concept is the equation of spirit and mole. Hegel comments:

> It always comes forward and comes to the fore, because spirit alone is progression. Often it seems to have forgotten who it is, seems to have gotten lost. However, internally divided, it works its way internally forward—as Hamlet says of his father's spirit, "Well done, old mole"—until, having gathered strength, it pushes through the crust of earth that separated it from its sun, its concept, and the crust collapses. When the crust collapses, like a ramshackle, abandoned building, spirit takes on novel, youthful form and dons seven-league boots. This labor of spirit to know itself, to find itself, this activity is spirit, is the life of spirit itself. Its result is the concept that it grasps of itself; the history of spirit yields the clear insight that spirit willed all this in its history. (20, 456).

We sense a tension here between "result" and "activity." To grasp oneself means, or at least suggests, bringing oneself to light, getting a view on oneself, achieving some ultimate and clear insight, and, on the basis of such established clarity and transparency, coming to rest. If spirit grasps itself, if the absolute essence becomes known as self-thinking, then the spirit that used to be internally divided apparently achieves tranquillity. Everything external and objective, everything that once seemed to be foreign and independent, now turns out to be a moment of the spirit that knows itself, proves to be fully identical with spirit, fully subject to its sovereignty. At this point spirit can cast a glance forward into eternity: "The struggle of finite self-consciousness with absolute self-consciousness, in

Somit gelingt dem Geist ein Blick ins Ewige: "Der Kampf des endlichen Selbstbewußtseins mit dem absoluten Selbstbewußtsein, das jenem außer ihm erschien, hört auf. Das endliche Selbstbewußtsein hat aufgehört, endliches zu sein" . . . (20, 460). Damit ist die Geschichte der Philosophie so weit gelangt, daß der "auf seine Spitze getriebene" Geist das eigene Lebensprinzip, d.h. das eigentliche Geschehen seiner Geschichte, selbst enträtselt: das Leben des Geistes produziert den eigenen inneren Gegensatz immer aufs neue und versöhnt sich alsbald wieder mit ihm. Aber die Lebensweise des Geistes ist paradox: alles kämpferische Streben hört auf, es beruhigt sich im absoluten Wissen und Wollen seines wesenhaft ruhelos und nie aufhörenden Strebens. Resultat ist und muß sein: Tätigkeit. In der Berliner Antrittsvorlesung heißt es: "Der Geist der Welt aber versinkt nicht in diese gleichgültige Ruhe. Es beruht dies auf seinem einfachen Begriff. Sein Leben ist Tat" (*18*, 22). "Resultat" (lateinisch resultare = re + saltare) ist das unermüdliche Sich-Wiederholen bzw. Sich-Überspringen des Geistes, dessen Lebenslauf im Gedächtnis des Denkers immer wieder durchlaufen und durchlebt werden muß. Die Denkweise des auf seine Spitze getriebenen Geistes zeigt sich als die tätige Er-Innerung.[6]

Er-Innerung ist das Anhören des Echos, welches in der imponierenden "Halle der heroischen Galerie der Denker" die Stille immer wieder zerbricht; oder besser noch, ist das Anschauen der Bilder, die in dieser Galerie ausgestellt werden.

Das in Hegels Vorlesungen immer wiederkehrende Bild (imago als Echo und Abbild zugleich) ist, wie wir nun wissen, das des Maulwurfs. Nach Hegels Ansicht gräbt sich der Maulwurf immer vor- und aufwärts; im Grunde geht in der Geschichte der Philosophie nichts verloren, wird nichts verschwendet, nichts weggeworfen. Nur der Geist

which the finite seemed to be excluded from the absolute, now ceases. Finite self-consciousness has ceased to be finite . . ." (20, 460). Thus the history of philosophy has reached a juncture at which spirit, "driven to its very zenith," responds to the riddle of its own existence, that is, the riddle of the proper happening of its history. The life of spirit is a life that forever produces its own internal opposite, immediately reconciling itself with that opposite. Yet spirit's existence is paradoxical: the ceaseless struggle ceases, and spirit rests on the absolute knowing and absolute willing of its essentially restless, incessant struggle. *Resultat* does not imply mere "result," but an activity or deed, *Tätigkeit*. In his inaugural lecture at Berlin, Hegel notes: "However, the spirit of the world does not submerge into indifferent tranquillity. For such is the nature of its simple concept, that its life is deed" (*18*, 22). "Result" (cf. the Latin *resultare, re + saltare*) is the ceaseless self-recapitulating or self-catapulting of spirit, whose curriculum the thinker must preserve in memory, running through it, living through it, again and again. The mode of thought for spirit, driven to its peak, manifests itself as active, internalizing remembrance.[6]

Remembrance heeds the echo that shatters the stillness in the imposing "hall of the gallery of thought's heroes." Better, it studies the *images* that are housed in that gallery. As we have seen, the *image* that recurs in Hegel's lectures, an *imago* that is both echo and visible object, is that of the mole. According to Hegel, the mole digs its way ever forward and upward; ultimately, nothing is lost or wasted, nothing trashed, in the history of philosophy. Only spirit is progressive, and, from the point of view of the present, spirit is only progression. Spirit burrows ever upward, for the obstacles that oppose it are overcome as soon as they are recognized as internal, that is, as identical with spirit. Such

schreitet fort und, von der Gegenwart her gesehen, besteht der Geist nur aus Fortschreiten. Weil die ihm entgegengesetzten Hindernisse rein innerlich sind, und weil sie sofort überwunden sind, sobald sie als innerlich, d.h. als identisch mit ihm selbst erkannt worden sind, kann sein Weg nur aufwärts führen. Eine solche Erkenntnis bekräftigt und ermutigt den beinahe blindlings philosophierenden Maulwurf. Sie bringt ihm das Vertrauen auf die Wissenschaft und auf sich selbst, sie verleiht ihm somit den Mut zur Wahrheit (*18*, 13). Der Maulwurf arbeitet brav—wie der Geist des ermordeten Königs von Dänemark.

Wie steht es jedoch mit einem solchen Vergleich? Wozu, am Ende der Geschichte der sich selbst denkenden Idee, die die Sprache des Begriffs und der Logik zum errungenen Mittel und erlangten Ziel hat, eine Sprache, in der Form und Inhalt identisch, d.h. gegenseitig vollkommen ausreichend sind (vgl. "Enzyklopädie der philosophischen Wissenschaften" §§ 236 ff.), wozu überhaupt eine imago? Wie war es möglich, daß damals, als das endliche Selbstbewußtsein aufhörte, endlich zu sein, ein Maulwurf dabei herauskam? Und warum ausgerechnet einer aus dem verfaulten Staate Dänemark?

Denn wie seltsam in diesem Zusammenhang ist die Anspielung auf Hamlet! Der maulwürfsche Hamlet Senior wühlt sich eben nicht nur aufwärts zur Erdrinde und erst recht nicht zum Tageslicht. Im Gegenteil, er krabbelt nur nachts hinauf, um seinen Sohn in einen verhängnißvollen Racheplan zu verstricken. Sodann wühlt er sich wieder zurück zum Hades, abwärts in die höllische Finsternis, nicht von irgendwelcher Einsicht gestärkt, sondern geschwächt von der mühevollen Darstellung seiner eigenen Geschichte, erschöpft von seiner Wiedererinnerung, erschreckt vom Morgenduft und von der wachsenden Helle—

Der Glühwurm zeigt, daß sich
  die Frühe naht,

knowledge invigorates and encourages the all but blindly philosophizing mole, grants it confidence in science and in itself, and so nurtures courage in the truth (*18*, 13). The mole works diligently—like the spirit of the murdered king of Denmark.

Yet how do matters stand with that comparison? Why, at the end of the history of the self-thinking idea, which possesses the language of the concept and of logic as its already attained medium and its already achieved end, a language in which form and content are identical, that is, mutually fully adequate (see the *Encyclopedia*, §§ 236 ff.), why an *imago* at all? How does it happen that when finite self-consciousness ceases to be finite the result is a mole? And why, of all things, a mole from the degenerate state of Denmark?

The allusion to Hamlet—how strange it is in the present context! For the mole-like ghost of Hamlet's father does not dig his way merely upward to the surface of the earth, nor at all in order to reach the light of day. On the contrary, he scrabbles upward only at night, in order to engage his son in a fatal plot of vengeance. And he soon burrows his way back to Hades, down to his murky limbo, not strengthened by any sort of insight but weakened by the wearisome telling of his own story, exhausted by the remembrance of it, blenching at the morning air and incipient light—

The glowworm shows the
  maten to be near,
And 'gins to pale his uneffectual
  fire—

The result of the tunneling activity of this spirit, the outcome of its desire for revenge, is not reconciliation at all but annihilation: the deaths of Hamlet Ophelia Gertrude Claudius Polonius Rosencrantz and Guildenstern. Victorious Fortinbras, about to accede to the Danish throne, formulates the "result" in the following way:

Und sein unwirksam Feu'r beginnt
    zu blassen.

Das Resultat der wühlerischen Tätigkeit dieses Geistes, das Ergebnis seines
Rachewunsches, ist nicht Versöhnung,
sondern Vernichtung, ist der Tod Ham-
lets Ophelias Gertrudes Claudius' Polonius' Rosenkrantz' und Guildensterns.
Der siegreiche Fortinbras, der den Thron
Dänemarks übernehmen soll, formuliert
das Resultat so:

> O stolzer Tod,
> Welch Fest geht vor in deiner
>   ew'gen Zelle,
> Daß du auf Einen Schlag so viele
>   Fürsten
> So blutig trafst?

Brav gearbeitet, wackerer Maulwurf.
Des Vaters Geist bleibt künftig in der
Tiefe begraben, in der Stille von Lethes
Ufer. "Ruh, ruh, verstörter Geist!" Ohne
Sohn bleibt er jedoch unversöhnt, fern
jeder tröstenden Erinnerung. In bezug
auf den Geist ist das Resultat das alles
auslöschende Vergessen, die ewige Un-
tätigkeit, das Nichts eines endgültigen
Aussterbens.

Hegel will aber ermutigend wirken.
Er beschließt seine einleitende Betrach-
tung der Philosophiegeschichte mit einer
Aufforderung an die Zuhörer. Die Stu-
denten sollten nicht jener Täuschung
zum Opfer fallen, die diese Geschichte
des Geistes als "eine blinde Sammlung"
von Einzelfällen entstellt. Vom Standpunkt des Individuums her gesehen, er-
scheine sie zwar wie ein Meinungschaos
oder wie bedeutungslose Haarspalterei;
jedoch "wie Blinde in demselben", seien
alle Einzelfälle vom gemeinsamen Geist,
nämlich einem "Instinkt der Vernunft"
getrieben, dessen "Gefühl oder Glauben" mit der Wendung "die Wahrheit ist
eine" (*18, 36*) umschrieben werden kann.
Eine Randnotiz in der Heidelberger
Niederschrift betont dies nochmals: ". . .
fortschreitend; nichts Zufälliges . . . das
innere Beisichselbstbleiben des Geistes"

> O proud death,
> What feast is toward in thine
>   eternal cell,
> That thou so many princes at a
>   shot,
> So bloodily hast struck?

Well done, old mole. The spirit father now remains below, buried in the
calm of Lethe's shore. "Rest, rest, perturbèd Spirit!" However, bereft of child,
he is unreconciled: there is no one to remember him. The result, as far as spirit
is concerned, is all-extinguishing oblivion, eternal lethargy, the nothingness of
ultimate undoing and demise.

Yet Hegel wishes to be encouraging.
He closes his introductory observations
on the history of philosophy by making a demand on his listeners. His students dare not fall prey to that deception
which distorts the history of philosophy
so that it seems to be "a blind conglom-
erate" of individual cases. Seen from the
point of view of the individual, the history of philosophy looks like a chaos of
sheer opinions, like inane and endless
hairsplitting. However, although "blind
in themselves," all individual cases are
quickened by a unitary spirit, as by an
"instinct of reason," whose "feeling or
belief" is that "the truth is *one*" (*18, 36*).
A marginal note in the Heidelberg manuscript emphasizes this once again: ". . .
progressing; nothing accidental . . . ; the
inner remaining-at-one-with-itself of
spirit" (*18, 14*). Such being at one with
oneself should not be understood as
some sort of submergence in the self:
spirit makes its way up and down, in
and out, somehow simultaneously. The
supreme mystery surrounding the activity of spirit is revealed at the very end
of the lecture course—as its own result,
so to speak. Hegel writes: "The deeper
spirit goes into itself, the stronger its opposite becomes: the depths are to be
measured according to the magnitude of
their opposite, that is, of the need; the

(*18*, 14). Solches Beisichsein darf andererseits nicht als eine Insichselbstversunkenheit verstanden werden. Irgendwie drängt der Geist gleichzeitig auf und ab, ein und aus. Das höchste Geheimnis, das diese seine Tätigkeit umgibt, wird am Ende der Vorlesung, etwa als ihr Resultat, so formuliert: "Je tiefer der Geist in sich gegangen, desto stärker der Gegensatz: die Tiefe ist nach der Größe des Gegensatzes, des Bedürfnisses zu messen; je tiefer in sich, desto tiefer ist sein Bedürfnis, nach außen zu suchen, sich zu finden, desto breiter sein Reichtum nach außen" (*20*, 455).

Am Anfang seiner Vorlesung forderte Hegel seine Zuhörer auf, "die Morgenröte einer schöneren Zeit" zu begrüßen (*18*, 13); am Ende malt er noch einmal die Tätigkeit des einen lebendigen Geistes aus:

> Auf sein Drängen—wenn der Maulwurf im Innern fortwühlt—haben wir zu hören und ihm Wirklichkeit zu verschaffen; sie sind ein schlechthin notwendiger Fortgang, der nichts als die Natur des Geistes selbst ausspricht und in uns allen lebt. Ich wünsche, daß diese Geschichte der Philosophie eine Aufforderung für Sie enthalten möge, den Geist der Zeit, der in uns natürlich ist, zu ergreifen und aus seiner Natürlichkeit, d.h. Verschlossenheit, Leblosigkeit hervor an den Tag zu ziehen und—jeder an seinem Orte—mit Bewußtsein an den Tag zu bringen. . . . Ich wünsche Ihnen, recht wohl zu leben (20, 462).

—Bis zur Morgenröte fehlt allerdings noch ein Siebenmeilenschritt. Wenn jedoch der Maulwurf tatsächlich ans Tageslicht gezogen und ihm Wirklichkeit verschafft worden ist, wo endet dann die ganze Geschichte?

deeper into itself, the more profound the need to seek outside itself in order to find itself, the greater its wealth on the outside" (*20*, 455).

At the outset of his lecture course Hegel invites his hearers to greet "the dawn of a more magnificent age" (*18*, 13); at the end he limns once again the deeds of the one living spirit:

> Whenever the mole burrows forth in the interior we must heed his approach, we must assist him toward his actuality. For it is an absolutely necessary process, expressing nothing less than the nature of spirit itself, the spirit that lives in us all. I hope that this history of philosophy makes a demand upon you, the demand to grasp the spirit of our age, which is natural to us; but you must draw it out of its naturalness, that is, its concealment, its lifelessness, and into the light of day. Each one of you, in your particular place, must consciously bring spirit into daylight. . . . May you all fare well! (*20*, 462)

It is a while yet to *Daybreak*, a seven-league leap. However, if the mole be dragged into daylight and assisted toward its actuality, where will his(s)tory end?

TALPA TROPHONIA

In der Tat wühlt sich der fast blind aber um so emsiger philosophierende Maul-

THE TROPHONIC MOLE

Deeper indeed, along routes no one could have charted, the philosopher

wurf auf unvorhergesehenen Wegen noch tiefer. Er ahnt eine noch unsicher schimmernde Morgen- (oder Abend-?) röte, die über dem für den Unterirdischen natürlich ganz unsichtbaren Horizonten schwebt. Im Herbst 1886 bereitet Friedrich Nietzsche in Ruta bei Genua eine zweite Ausgabe seiner 1881 erschienenen Schrift "Morgenröte: Gedanken über moralische Vorurteile" vor. Zu dieser Zeit ist Nietzsche mit seiner nächsten neinsagenden Abhandlung "Zur Genealogie der Moral: eine Streitschrift" beschäftigt. Der jasagende Mittag seines schöpferischen Lebens, der Zenit des "Zarathustra", ist längst vorbei; es ist eigentlich Spätnachmittag, wenngleich noch nicht die Stunde der Dämmerung. Noch freut sich der Einsame auf den neuen Tag, dessen Morgenröte er schon irgendwie—wenn nur leise—spürt. In der Vorrede zur zweiten Ausgabe von "Morgenröte" (1886) schreibt Nietzsche:

> In diesem Buche findet man einen "Unterirdischen" an der Arbeit, einen Bohrenden, Grabenden, Untergrabenden. Man sieht ihn, vorausgesetzt, daß man Augen für solche Arbeit der Tiefe hat—, wie er langsam, besonnen, mit sanfter Unerbittlichkeit vorwärts kommt, ohne daß die Not sich allzusehr verriete, welche jede lange Entbehrung von Licht und Luft mit sich bringt: man könnte ihn selbst bei seiner dunklen Arbeit zufrieden nennen. Scheint es nicht, daß irgendein Glaube ihn führt, ein Trost entschädigt? Daß er vielleicht seine eigne lange Finsternis haben will, sein Unverständliches, Verborgenes, Rätselhaftes, weil er weiß, was er auch haben wird: seinen eignen Morgen, seine eigne Erlösung, seine eigne *Morgenröte*? . . . Gewiß, er wird zurückkehren: fragt ihn nicht, was er da unten will, er wird es euch selbst schon sagen, dieser scheinbare Tro-

mole burrows blindly but busily. He senses an uncertain, wavering dawn (or is it dusk?) hovering on the horizon. For the subterrestrial one, of course, the horizon is not visible. In the autumn of 1886, in Ruta, near Genoa, Friedrich Nietzsche prepares a second edition of his book *Daybreak: Thoughts concerning Moral Prejudices*, which first appeared in 1881. During those same days he is occupied with his next nosaying treatise, entitled *On the Genealogy of Morals: A Polemic*. The yessaying noontide of his creative life, the zenith of *Zarathustra*, is long past; it is actually late afternoon, though not yet the hour of twilight. The lonely one thrills to the possibility of a new day, a day whose dawn already impinges somehow on his awareness. In the preface to the second edition of *Daybreak* Nietzsche writes the following:

> In this book you will find a "subterrestrial" creature at work, burrowing, digging, subverting. You will see him, presupposing that you have eyes for such work in the depths; you will see how slowly, how reflectively, and with what gentle implacability he moves forward. He scarcely betrays the destitution that prolonged lack of light and air imply; one could even say that in his obscure toil he is content. Does it not seem as though some sort of belief guides him, some sort of consolation grants him recompense? As though he perhaps wants to have his own long obscurity, his unintelligibility, his concealment and riddlesomeness, because he knows what he will also have: his own morning, his own redemption, his own *daybreak*? . . . Oh yes, he will turn back; do not ask him what he wants to do down there; he will tell you himself soon enough, this seeming Trophonios, this subterranean one, as soon as he has "be-

phonios und Unterirdische, wenn er erst wieder "Mensch geworden" ist. Man verlernt gründlich das Schweigen, wenn man so lange, wie er, Maulwurf war, allein war — — (3, 11)

Nietzsches Maulwurfsgang bohrt sich durch bis zu den moralischen Voraussetzungen bzw. Vorurteilen, die alle bisherigen metaphysischen Systeme mehr oder weniger unbemerkt unterstützt bzw. durchzogen haben. "Ich stieg in die Tiefe, ich bohrte in den Grund", erklärt der sich erinnernde, zurückblickende Maulwurf, "ich begann ein altes Vertrauen zu untersuchen und anzugraben, . . . ich begann unser Vertrauen zur Moral zu untergraben" (3, 12). Somit hat Nietzsche mit einer unheimlichen Genauigkeit die heikle Stelle der kritischen Philosophie Kants anvisiert, nämlich die der Sittlichkeit und der Moral, wo Kant tatsächlich Maulwurfsgänge festgestellt hatte, die er dann von außen oder von oben her vergeblich zuzuschütten versuchte. Somit untersucht Nietzsche auch die große Schatzkammer des Hegelschen Geistes, dessen "Bedürfnis", sich nach außen zu drängen, verdächtig geworden ist. Nietzsches Weg setzt sich im Untergrund fort, auf der Spur eines tief verwurzelten Argwohns gegen alle Ausformungen eines heimlich auf der Moral aufgebauten Idealismus, dessen Grundstruktur seinerseits auf einer Mißachtung dieser Erde und dieses Lebens basiert. Nietzsche treibt seinen Tunnel ohne jeden "Mut zur Wahrheit" voran, welcher Mut sich für ihn eher als "Ohnmacht zur Macht" oder als der reine Wille zum Nichts entlarvt. Bei Nietzsche bleibt die Tätigkeit des Resultats ein Zurückspringen, ein *resaltare* (". . . Gewiß, er wird zurückkehren . . ."), welches nie zu irgendeinem Stillstand kommt, denn, wie wir schon gehört haben, alles "was halt macht (bei einer angeblichen causa prima, bei einem

come man" again. For one forgets silence altogether when one has been, like him, such a long time a mole, such a long time alone — — (3, 11)

Nietzsche's mole tunnels burrow through to those "moral" presuppositions or prejudices that have undergirded or pervaded all prior metaphysical systems in more or less subtle ways. "I descended into the depths, I burrowed into the ground," declares the mole, looking back and remembering. "I began to root about and investigate an ancient confidence, . . . I began to subvert our confidence in morality" (3, 12). Thus Nietzsche sets his sights with uncanny precision on that particularly fragile spot in Kant's Critical philosophy, that is to say, on the matter of morality and ethicality, the very place where Kant espied mole tunnels, which he then vainly sought to level from without and above. Similarly, Nietzsche examines the vast thesaurus of Hegelian spirit, whose "need" to propel itself to the outside has become suspect. Nietzsche's path proceeds underground. It follows the scent of suspicion, a deeply rooted distrust of all forms of idealism. For idealisms are secretly constructed upon a morality that is itself based on a deprecation of this earth and this life. His tunnel advances without any sort of "confidence in the truth," which he exposes as "impotence-to-power" or sheer "will-to-nothingness." In Nietzsche's case the resultant deed remains a leaping back, a *resaltare* ("Oh yes, he will turn back . . .") that never comes to a standstill. For, as we noted in an earlier chapter, everything "that comes to a stop (at an ostensible *causa prima*, something unconditioned, etc.) is laziness, weariness—" (WM, 575, dated 1885–86; 12, 133). (If Nietzsche's genealogical critique rests at all on a "metaphysics" of will to power, then the critique is "hypercriticism" and the metaphysics

Unbedingten usw.) ist die Faulheit, die Ermüdung —" (WM, 575, aus dem Jahr 1885/86; 12, 133). (Wenn Nietzsches genealogische Kritik überhaupt auf einer "Metaphysik" des Willens zur Macht beruht, so ist jene Kritik eine "Hyperkritik", diese Metaphysik eine untergehende, d.h. eine "Hypophysik".) Bei Hegel wühlt sich der Maulwurf ausschließlich fort (im Sinne von vorwärts und aufwärts), auch wenn er in die Tiefe drängt; bei Nietzsche gräbt er sich hauptsächlich nach unten und zurück. Dieses Zurückkehren beruht auf keiner endgültig etablierten Einsicht, die aus dem unsicheren Sicherinnern eine zuversichtliche Geste des Fortschrittsoptimismus hatte machen können. Nietzsches Hamletlehre sieht nämlich ganz anders aus: "In der Bewußtheit der einmal geschauten Wahrheit sieht jetzt der Mensch überall nur das Entsetzliche oder Absurde des Seins . . . : es ekelt ihn" (GT, 7; 1, 57).

Andererseits zeigt sich auch bei Nietzsche die Geschichte der Philosophie als ein von einem "Gefühl oder Glauben" getriebenes Sichselbsthervorbringen, dieses wohlgemerkt nicht als Tätigkeit eines "Geistes"—auch wenn jene Tätigkeit als Einsicht in das, was der Geist stets *gewollt* hat, interpretiert wird—sondern als die Gesetzgebung des Willens zur Macht. Der Geschichte der Philosophie liegt also nicht Hegels "Instinkt der Vernunft", sondern der Instinkt der Selbsterhaltung und -steigerung eines Lebewesens namens "Mensch" zugrunde. An die Stelle des Beisichseins des von der "Natürlichkeit" befreiten Geistes tritt jetzt die Selbsttäuschung des im Bereich des Sinnlichen verbleibenden Menschen; an die Stelle von Hegels "nichts Zufälliges" treten die Unschuld des Werdens und der reinste Zufall.

Wie steht es aber um jenen "Trost", welcher in der sichtbaren Welt der Erd-

"hypophysics.") With Hegel, the mole burrows exclusively forward and up, even when it plunges into the depths; with Nietzsche, the mole mainly turns back, digs down. Such turning back does not rest on any securely established insight that could make of uncertain remembrance a confident gesture of optimism and belief in Progress. Nietzsche's interpretation of Hamlet is altogether different: "Conscious of the truth he has once perceived, man now sees always and everywhere the terror or absurdity of being: . . . it nauseates him" (GT, 1, 57).

However, for Nietzsche too the history of philosophy is a kind of self-production that is impelled by a "feeling or belief." It is not an activity of "spirit," even if that activity be interpreted as insight into spirit's having *willed* its history, but the legislation of and by will to power. At the origin of the history of philosophy lies not Hegel's "instinct of reason" but the instinct of self-preservation and self-enhancement in a creature called "man." The being-at-one-with-itself of a spirit that has been liberated from "naturalness" is now replaced by the self-deception of a humanity that perdures in the realm of the sensuous. Instead of Hegel's "nothing accidental," the rubric now is: the innocence of becoming and the purest of accidents.

Yet how is it with the "consolation" that seems to scintillate in the visible world of the superficies, promising "redemption" even to the one who dwells underground? Does the mole hold out below, or does he creep upward once again—in the direction of the "eternal recurrence of the same"?

The thought of eternal return "ravished" Nietzsche in 1881 (the year that saw the publication of *Daybreak*). He was in Sils-Maria in the Oberengadin region of Switzerland, "6,000 feet be-

oberfläche als Morgenröte erscheinen mag und welcher—selbst dem Untergründigen—eine "Erlösung" verspricht? Verharrt der Maulwurf da unten, oder kriecht er wieder hoch in Richtung der "ewigen Wiederkehr des Gleichen"?

Der Gedanke der ewigen Wiederkunft "überfiel" Nietzsche 1881 (d.h. im Jahr der Veröffentlichung von *Morgenröte*) in Sils-Maria im Oberengadin, "6000 Fuß jenseits von Mensch und Zeit" (EH; 6, 335). Manchmal schien Nietzsche selber der Wiederkunftsgedanke nicht bloß der Probierstein bei der Auslese des Übermenschen zu sein, sondern, wie wir schon im 3. Kapitel gesehen haben, auch ein "Trost", ein Trost für "jenen Kaiser".

Die Frage erhebt sich: Wird dann jene Lehre zur Rettung von und d.h. zur Rache an dieser Welt und ihrer Zeit? Wird sie zur "Erlösung" von der Vergänglichkeit und von dem für den Willen unbeweglichen und unerträglichen "es war"? Geht es hier im Endeffekt doch um ein weiteres Stückchen Heilsgeschichte (= décadence)? Nicht abzuleugnen ist die Gefahr, daß die Sehnsucht nach Erlösung das ganze Projekt des Nietzscheschen Denkens auf eine Abart Hegelscher Versöhnungsphilosophie reduziert, daß amor fati nichts mehr bedeutet als amor Vati (im Sinne von Augustinus und Freud), daß Zarathustras mühevoll gewonnener Honig zum Süßen einer weiteren Tasse Beruhigungstee verwendet wird und daß das goldene Lachen des Übermenschen, das zu allem Werden und Sein J-A sagt, dem I-A des Eselgeschreis allzu ähnlich wird.

Dagegen ist wohl zu betonen, daß die große Bejahung in der Wiederkunftslehre vor dem Mißtrauen der genealogischen Kritik nicht zu bewähren ist, daß der unersättliche Verdacht jene Lehre stets begleiten muß. Das Ja und das Nein sind also unzertrennliche Gefährten, der glühende Dionysos wan-

yond man and time" (*Ecce Homo; 6, 335*). Occasionally the idea of eternal recurrence seemed to Nietzsche himself to be not merely a touchstone by which the overman would be selected but also, as we saw in chapter 3, a "consolation."

The question arises: Does the doctrine of eternal recurrence become a matter of rescue from, that is, revenge against, the world and the time of this world? Is it a matter of "redemption" from transiency and from the "it was" of time, which the will cannot budge or bear? Do we have here yet another minidrama in the history of salvation (read: decadence)? We cannot simply disregard the danger that the longing for redemption threatens to reduce the entire project of Nietzsche's thought to a hybrid form of the Hegelian philosophy of reconciliation. We dare not ignore the possibility that Nietzschean "love of fate" says nothing more than "love of father" in the Augustinian and Freudian senses; that Zarathustra's honey, gathered so laboriously, will be used to sweeten yet another cup of herbal tea relaxing to the nerves; that the overman, whose golden laughter should be a prayer to becoming, turns out to be a brayer, a jackass.

In response, we must emphasize that the grand affirmation found in eternal recurrence is not to be "rescued" from the distrust exercised by genealogical critique. Insatiable suspicion must always accompany that doctrine. "Yes" and "no" are inseparable companions, glowing Dionysos and glowering Silenos going together. Accordingly, the thought of eternal return remains a way down, a *katabasis* or downgoing, which remains "true to the earth." If the thought ascends at all, it stops at the borderline between heaven and earth, at a boundary in the midrange mountains, since the mole (*Talpa euro-*

dert an der Seite des grimmigen Silenos. Demzufolge bleibt der Wiederkunfts- gedanke ein Weg nach unten, eine—wie wir in vorangegangenen Kapiteln gele- sen haben—κατάβασις oder ein "Unter- gang", der "der Erde treu" bleibt. Hebt sich dieser Gedanke überhaupt je empor, so gelangt er nur bis an die Grenze zwischen Erde und Himmel—eine Gren- ze nicht ganz oben im Hochgebirge, da der Maulwurf (talpa europaea bzw. tro- phonia) nur bis in 2000 Meter Höhe überleben kann, d.h. bis zu jenen 6000 Fuß jenseits von Mensch und Zeit, die die Ferne der Geburtsstätte der Wieder- kunftslehre anzeigen. Es ist nach wie vor der bescheidene Maulwurf, um den es hier geht. Der hochfliegende Adler und die sich um des Adlers Hals windende Schlange sind die Tiere *Zarathustras*. Auch das Kamel, der Löwe, der Esel und das Kind gehören zur Menagerie des bunten Persers. Was *Nietzsches* einziges Tierchen betrifft: er fliegt und zischt nicht, trägt keine Bürde, weder brüllt er noch kreischt er, und er spielt nur äußerst selten unbefangen am Tempeleingang ein Heraklit'sches Brettspiel. Er krabbelt bloß, wühlt mit den "emsigen Krallen" eines "Mitternachtsmaulwurf" (Herman Melville, "Pierre"), wühlt unerbittlich, aufwärts bis zur steinigen Erdober- fläche, dann bedächtig zurück. Als ein "Lehrer des langsamen Lesens", wie wir oben am Schluß des 4. Kapitels gehört haben, trägt er grundsätzlich nie Sieben- meilenstiefel. Der Einsamkeit ständig ausgesetzt, erlernt er immer wieder das Schweigen. Um darüber reden zu kön- nen, muß er selbstverständlich "Mensch werden"—also nicht Übermensch, nicht einmal Zarathustra, nicht Dionysos, sondern: Mensch. Er muß lernen, wie man wird, was man ist, muß hinunter zu Trophonios und dann der Pflicht nachkommen, darüber zu schreiben (vgl. Pausanias IX, 39, 4; s. den Schluß zum 3. Kapitel, oben).

paea, Talpa trophonia) can survive up to 2,000 meters of altitude, that is, up to those 6,000 feet beyond man and time that measure the remote- ness of the birthplace of eternal return. It remains, after all, a matter of the modest mole. The high-flying eagle and the serpent that wraps itself about the bird's throat—these are the animals of *Zarathustra*. The camel, lion, jack- ass, and child—they too belong in the menagerie of the flamboyant Persian. *Nietzsche* has but one pet. It does not fly, does not hiss, bears no burdens, neither roars nor brays, and only very rarely plays innocently at Heracli- tean games on the temple proscenium. It merely scrabbles and scrooges, bur- rows and scrapes, with the "busy claw of some midnight mole in the ground" (Melville, *Pierre*), scratches relentlessly up to the stony surface of earth, then back down again, rapt in thought. As a "teacher of unhurried reading," a phrase we heard at the end of chapter 4, he refuses categorically to don seven-league boots. Perpetually exposed to loneliness, he learns silence over and over again. In order to talk about it he must of course "become man"—not the overman, not even Zarathustra, not Dionysos, but: human being. He must learn how to become what he is. He must go down to Tro- phonios and then fulfill his duty to write about it (see Pausanias's *Guide to Greece*, IX, 39, 4, cited at the conclu- sion of chapter 3.

The "how to become what one is" as a "how to be what one has become": the life of ceaseless burrowing as pos- sibility and fatality, dispensation and doom alike: this is how the mole's being is projected in (our) time right from the start, this is the

sole
role

Dieses "Wie man wird, was man ist" als ein "Wie man ist, was man geworden ist": auf ein solches Leben hin, eines der unablässigen Wühlarbeit als Möglichkeit und Verhängnis, Geschick und Mißgeschick zugleich, ist das Sein des Maulwurfs in der (unserer) Zeit immer schon entworfen: als

> geworfener
> Entwurf
> des
> Maulwurfs

d.h., entweder als ζῷον λόγον ἔχον, das Lebewesen, das stets ein interpretierendes Wort im Maul hat, oder als Mulmwerfer und Erdfresser, der die frenetische Tätigkeit des Schreibens aufnimmt, deren ewiger Kreislauf des Vor und Zurückwühlens ein Vorlaufen in den eigenen Tod ist (vgl. Heideggers "Sein und Zeit", S. 264).

Denn wohin (ver)führt letzten Endes diese imago des Maulwurfsphilosophen, von Kant über Hegel zu Nietzsche? Aus Wilhelm Busch's "Dideldum!", vierter Abschnitt, "Der Maulwurf," hier einige abschließende Auszüge, eine Art

of the
mole

either as "the living creature that has speech," with a word of interpretation playing ever about its snout, or as the creature delving into mould and powdery earth, the being who takes up the frenetic life of writing, in which the eternal circuit of burrowings back and forth conducts him headlong to his own death (cf. Heidegger, *Being and Time*, p. 308).

For where does it lead us, in the end, the seductive *imago* of the philosopher mole, from Kant, via Hegel, to Nietzsche? By way of response, the following concluding extracts from Wilhelm Busch, *Dideldum!* section four, "The Mole," as a kind of

NACHWURF

POSTLUDE AND
THRENODY

In seinem Garten freudevoll
Geht hier ein Gärtner namens Knoll.

A gardener by the name of Knoll
Surveys his garden on a stroll.

Doch seine Freudigkeit vergeht;
Ein Maulwurf wühlt im Pflanzenbeet.

Yet peace of mind will not be found;
A mole is burrowing in the ground.

Schnell eilt er fort und holt die Hacke,
Daß er den schwarzen Wühler packe.

So Knoll resolves to fetch a hoe,
To deal the beast a telling blow.

From "Dideldum!" in Wilhelm Busch, *Humoristischer Hausschatz* (Cologne: Buch und Zeit
Verlagsgesellschaft, 1963).

Jetzt ist vor allem an der Zeit
Die listige Verschwiegenheit.

He nears the burrow, hovers by it,
All absorbed in cunning, quiet.

Aha! Schon hebt sich was im Beet,
Und Knoll erhebt sein Jagdgerät.

Aha! A stirring in the ground:
Knoll wields the hoe without a sound.

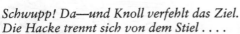

Schwupp! Da—und Knoll verfehlt das Ziel.
Die Hacke trennt sich von dem Stiel . . . .

Zip! But in vain the Knollic art,
For hoe and handle fly apart . . . .

Die Hacke ärgert ihn doch sehr,
Drum holt er jetzt den Spaten her.

That irritates him just a shade;
He'll try his hand now with the spade.

Nun, Alter, sei gescheit und weise,
Und mache leise, leise, leise!

Prepare, old chap, to make the kill;
Compose yourself, be still, still, still!

. . . Schnupp' dringt die Schaufel, wie der Blitz,
Dem Maulwurf unter seinen Sitz.

. . . Crunch! goes the shovel, swift and straight,
Unseats the mole from his estate.

Und mit Hurra in einem Bogen
Wird er herauf ans Licht gezogen.

And hoopla-ho! with main and might
The vermin mole is brought to light.

Aujau! Man setzt sich in den Rechen
Voll spitzer Stacheln, welche stechen.

Ee-yow! Knoll plops down on the rake:
More than the mole is now at stake.

Und Knoll zieht für den Augenblick
Sich schmerzlich in sich selbst zurück.

A moment's pause, while Knoll withdraws
In pain from his impassioned cause.

Schon hat der Maulwurf sich derweil
Ein Loch gescharrt in Angst und Eil.

Meanwhile the mole, by terror struck,
Digs frantically, to change his luck.

Doch Knoll, der sich emporgerafft,
Beraubt ihn seiner Lebenskraft.

But goodly Knoll this time won't fail;
The mole's life hangs but by its tail.

Da liegt der schwarze Bösewicht.
Und wühlte gern und kann doch nicht;
Denn hinderlich, wie überall,
Ist hier der eigne Todesfall.

Here lies the nasty little pest;
Would burrow, but is laid to rest.
You gather from the way it lies:
A hindrance is one's own demise.

SIX

A Hermeneutics of Discretion

Nietzsche, Heidegger, Derrida, Lacoue-Labarthe

> Gently, mortals, be discreet.
> —Mami

For reasons that are difficult to recite at the outset—especially after three chapters on genealogical critique and two on the philosophic beasts of antiquity and modernity—I want to rescue the phrase "a hermeneutics of discretion," mentioned in my opening chapters but first introduced some twenty-five years ago as the conclusion to a thesis on Heidegger's reading of Nietzsche.[1] The word *discretion* had come to me through the (in)discretion of the English translator of Jean-Paul Sartre's *Les mots*: he had rendered Sartre's grandmother's admonition, "*Glissez, mortels, n'appuyez pas*," as "Gently, mortals, be discreet." It seemed to me then—as it does now—that the outcome of Heidegger's confrontation with Nietzsche was captured in that bit of advice at once hölderlinian and homey. In the present chapter I want to revive the hermeneutics of discretion (the genitive is more subjective than objective) in response to two insightful and challenging interpretations of Heidegger/Nietzsche: first, Jacques Derrida's *Spurs*, written in 1972–1973 and revised in 1978; second, two extensive articles by Philippe Lacoue-Labarthe, also written during the 1970s, entitled "*La Dissimulation*" (later retitled "*Nietzsche Apocryphe*") and "*L'Oblitération.*"[2]

DERRIDA'S *SPURS*

> Without discreet parody, without strategy of writing, without difference or divergence of quills, without style, namely, the grand, reversal comes to the same in the noisy declaration of the antithesis.
> —Jacques Derrida

Derrida takes hermeneutics as such to be the reduction of texts to a univocal code, that is, to an ultimately determinable meaning-intention or *vouloir-dire*.

In his view, hermeneutics is incorrigibly indiscreet—affable, optimistic, embracing every exotic avatar of the tradition with a hearty *nihil a me alienum*, but inveterately indiscreet. To hermeneutics Derrida counterposes his minimalist account of interpretation—exemplified (albeit without the power of examples) in the case of the purloined umbrella. Even though Derrida's *Spurs* has by now been widely read, I want to recount briefly but as carefully as I can in these few pages the trajectory of the book. For what begins as a baffling and seductive collocation of style, writing, truth, and woman ends as a sustained encounter with Heidegger's reading of Nietzsche.

Spurs consists of thirteen unnumbered sections, an epilogue that begins, "One step more / Not yet [*Un pas encore*]," and two postscripts. The confrontation with Heidegger assumes center stage in section seven, "The History of an Error." Yet the Heideggerian notions of truth as disclosure and the duplicity of remoteness and proximation (or undistancing/en-distancing: *Entfernung*) govern the entire fabulation from the very outset. Derrida's "distances," "veils," "truths," "adornments," and all the subtle arts of "simulation" lead in a surprisingly natural way to the problem of *Ereignis*, or "propriation," the mysterious *granting* of time and being, in Heidegger's later thought. *Natural*, because Heidegger's discourse was always governed by the duplicities of nearness/remoteness and the revealing/concealing clearing of truth. *Surprisingly* natural, because that discourse never confronted such duplicity in the figure of woman, or revealing/concealing in the folds of style.

It is important to observe that Derrida's starting point in his confrontation with Heidegger's *Nietzsche*—and it will be Lacoue-Labarthe's point of departure as well—is the question of will to power as *art*. Heidegger himself in 1936–1937 insists that this point of entry for his own lecture series is no accident: even though "Will to Power as Art" is the fourth and culminating division of the third book in the Gast-Förster edition of *Der Wille zur Macht*, Heidegger begins his lecture series by identifying art as the "principle of a new valuation."[3] Reviewers of his *Nietzsche* in Germany, France, and the United States have generally latched onto the "theses" of Heidegger's essays on Nietzsche in the second volume of the German edition, trusting that these essays express the essence of the confrontation; thus they have managed to miss the positive gains of Heidegger's painstaking interpretations in the lecture courses, presented for the most part, though not entirely, in the first volume. The power of Derrida's and Lacoue-Labarthe's readings of Heidegger/Nietzsche derives in no small measure from their having taken with utmost seriousness the question of the "raging discordance" between art and truth—the theme of Heidegger's 1936–1937 course on will to power as art.

In Derrida's estimation, Heidegger's interpretation of Nietzsche is coextensive with the question of interpretation as such: at stake in Heidegger's *Nietzsche* is the very sake—or *Sache*—of hermeneutics. It is no accident that Derrida introduces the Heideggerian interpretation (59–60) in order to find his own way toward a theme that is espied several times earlier in his text but then immediately circumvented—the theme of castration. The point is not that Derrida wishes to emasculate Heidegger's interpretation by way of retaliation, suggesting that Heidegger has somehow done violence to Nietzsche by oversimplifying his texts. One of Derrida's most striking avowals is the following: "The thesis of Heidegger's weighty tome is much less simple than people have generally tended to say" (60). The point is rather that interpretation as such always risks ultimate violence, a violence that is bound to recoil on all practitioners of the art, no matter how discreet. Indeed, discretion can be proclaimed only in the face of violence or the threat of violence. Discretion becomes interesting only in the teeth of what Nick Land calls *ferocious negation* and *virulent nihilism*.[4]

After noting several of Heidegger's "cautions" or *mises en garde* concerning Nietzsche's celebration of "art in the grand style" (60–61), and after recounting the themes of an ostensibly "masculine" as opposed to a "feminine" aesthetics, Derrida puts into question the apparently metaphysical character of Nietzsche's aesthetics and his putative inversion of Platonism. He notes carefully what very few commentators anywhere have noticed, namely, that Heidegger acknowledges Nietzsche's celebration of art and his "new interpretation of sensuousness" as something essentially more than a mere reversal of the Platonic hierarchy. Even though Nietzsche does think by way of reversal (see Ni *1*, section 5), his thought on art "is aiming at something else" than a mere overturning of the Platonic orders of being and nonbeing, the supersensible and the sensuous (64; see Ni *1*, 201). Nietzsche's "How the 'True World' Finally Became a Fable: History of an Error" culminates in a peculiar torsion or "twisting free" from Platonism as such. Heidegger writes:

> What happens when the true world is expunged? Does the apparent world still remain? No. For the apparent world can be what it is only as a counterpart of the true. If the true world collapses, so also must the world of appearances. Only then is Platonism overcome, which is to say, inverted in such a way that philosophical thinking twists free of it. But then where does such thinking wind up? (Ibid.)

Derrida follows Heidegger's reading of Nietzsche's "Fable" quite closely. The cutting edge of his double reading is felt in his attention to Heidegger's critical questions, *Fragen der Kritik* (65–66; Ni *1*, 210). Heidegger recognizes that Nietzsche's overturning of Platonism must become a "twisting free of it," *eine Herausdrehung*. Yet he adds: "How far the latter extends with Nietzsche, how far it can go, to what extent it comes to an overcoming of Platonism and to what extent not—those are necessary critical questions." Derrida asks by what measure or standard we can judge the "success" of Nietzsche's inversion of Platonism—better, his twisting free of it. On the one hand, Derrida appreciates the fact that such a twisting free marks the moment of Nietzsche's release from the burning House of Metaphysics: here Heidegger acknowledges a kind of excess in Nietzsche's own text that prevents the reduction of Nietzsche's philosophy to a merely topsy-turvy Platonism or, as Heidegger complains elsewhere, to a mere "coarsening" of the Platonic position. On the other hand, Derrida wonders whether such a twisting free must not *ipso facto* wrench itself from all standards of "success" or "failure" and from all "necessary critical questions." Not that our thought is now to become sheer edification or complacent free play: the very first *mise en garde* that Derrida cites in Heidegger's lecture course is resistance to any aestheticizing obscurantism, any "confusionism." Nevertheless, the excess that catapults Nietzsche beyond Platonism, like the excesses of madness and of all traditional systems of aesthetics, subverts every measure. Indeed, Heidegger himself seems to recognize that the estimation of Nietzsche's success or failure is a matter to be postponed or deferred. "Necessary critical questions"? Yes. "Yet they should be posed only when we have reflected in accordance with the thought that Nietzsche most intrinsically willed. . . ."

On the one hand, Derrida appreciates Heidegger's dogged efforts to hear what Nietzsche wants to say: earlier in his lecture course Heidegger warns his students that "we may not relinquish the multiplicity of perspectives there [in Nietzsche's aesthetics], nor impose on his thoughts some dubious schema from the outside" (Ni *1*, 122–23). The history of Nietzsche-interpretation does not lack instances in which the most "straightforward" gleaning of Nietzsche's pages has produced the most bizarre and even monstrous readings. Maurice Blanchot, perhaps the most esoteric of writers, at one point finds fault with Nietzsche for his decision to write exoterically, that is, in a way that readers might understand him.[5] Although there is some justice in his remark, it only exacerbates the hermeneutical problem—the problem of interpreting that *Sache* for the sake of which we write and speak of "Nietzsche." It is not a matter of scoffing at all attempts to determine what Nietzsche most intensely wanted to achieve and what he most perfervidly despised.

On the other hand, Nietzsche's *innerste denkerische Wille*, what he most properly and authentically wanted to say, is precisely what according to Derrida's minimalist account always necessarily eludes our grasp. The thought that Nietzsche most intrinsically willed is as remote to us as the Heideggerian mystery of being is to him, as distant as the being (*Sein*) that is in default—the self-concealing, reticent granting of time and being, the withdrawal and expropriation of whatever it is that calls for and propriates thought.

For the best of Heideggerian reasons, therefore, Derrida tries to spur and spar, to pierce the horizon of Heidegger's "critical questions." In sections eight and nine of *Spurs* ("*femina vita*," an inversion of one of Nietzsche's own titles, and "positions") he takes up again the various themes of his own inquiry. He then exposes Heidegger's neglect of the italicized phrase in the "Fable," "It [the idea] becomes woman." By circumventing woman, Derrida suggests, Heidegger avoids confrontation with a number of the fundamental limits of his own hermeneutics of Nietzsche's text. Yet the circumvention is even more serious than that. By ignoring Nietzsche's genealogical critique of "moral castratism," Heidegger avoids the path that could have led him beyond the horizon of his own question concerning the truth of being. (Derrida does not put the matter as baldly as I have put it here: he is far more discreet.) It is the possibility of such a path beyond the history and truth of being that continues to preoccupy Derrida to the present day: one need only think of the series of studies that have appeared under the titles of *Geschlecht, Of Spirit,* or the recent *Aporias.*[6] And although the question of the heterogeneity of Nietzsche's styles appears to be absent in Derrida's 1980 *Envoi* (translated as "Sending: On Representation"),[7] its focus on the sending of being, *das Geschick des Seins,* and the precarious project of a nonrepresentational thinking, are bound up with the question of the truth of being. I will not try to exhibit these interconnections more carefully here, but will be satisfied if I can convince the reader that Derrida's *Spurs* is pivotal for our efforts to follow the itinerary of his most recent thinking: it may well prove to be the text that best bridges Derrida's earliest and latest work, from the first stirrings of deconstruction to more recent preoccupations with a manifold sexuality and a multivalent thinking—a thinking that both doubly affirms and ceaselessly mourns.[8]

The questions of the nontruth of truth, (dis)simulation, and propriation come to a critical juncture in the eleventh section of *Spurs,* entitled *"Le coup de don."* The "bite" of all giving (*"le coup de dent"*) lies in the fact that gift-giving (if such be the virtue of what Nietzsche calls *das Weib*) is also a deceptive giving-itself-out-as. That is to say, giving is (dis)simulation. Such dissembling also marks the giving of the "it gives / there is," the *Es gibt,* of time and being. "If the opposition of giving and taking, of possessing and being possessed, is a sort of transcendental snare produced by the graphics of the hymen, the process of propriation escapes all dialectics as well as all ontological decidability" (92). The questions of the meaning, truth, or history of being, and all "onto-phenomenological" or "semantico-hermeneutical" interrogation, arrive at their absolute limit. Here the will to penetrate to Nietzsche's "most intrinsic thoughtful will" reduplicates and does not transcend or supersede the metaphysics of will. It reduplicates presence, self-givenness, and all the dreamy securities of a speech that seems to be replete with itself.

However, Heidegger's reading of Nietzsche is characterized by a dehiscence that opens that reading without undoing it, exposes that reading to an otherness it can neither encompass nor suppress. To be sure, such a dehiscence "in turn reinscribes the hermeneutic gesture" (95). Yet precisely how are we to read this newly inscribed hermeneutic gesture? It imposes itself, according to Derrida, each time Heidegger "opens the question of being to the question of the proper, of propriating and propriation (of *eigen, eignen, ereignen,* and, above all, *Ereignis*)." Just as the opposites *Eigentlichkeit/Uneigentlichkeit* structure Heidegger's existential analysis of Dasein, which "valorizes" the former over the latter, so does *Ereignis* become for Heidegger the matter for thought and the very sake of thinking. Yet an "oblique movement" displaces the advance of Heidegger's thinking of *Ereignis* and points to what Derrida calls *la structure abyssale du propre.* "Abyss," of course, communicates with Heidegger's longstanding notion of *Abgrund,* present in Heideggerian discourse from *Being and Time* onward. Section twelve of *Spurs* refers to the phrase "the property of the abyssal [*das Eigentum des Ab-grundes*]" in the concluding treatise of Heidegger's *Nietzsche,* "Remembrance into Metaphysics" (NII, 485): the thinking of *Ereignis* or propriation cannot escape the realm of "ownness," the realm that has no sufficient reason (*Grund*) and is devoid of, or cut off from, all grounds:

der Ab-grund, the abyss. Yet this means that propriation is (undecidably) both appropriation and a-propriation. The granting is exposed to the play of revealing/concealing, presencing/absencing, and giving/taking—without why, and beyond all economies of interpretation. The gesture of such a hermeneutics would have to be a modest one indeed. Modest to the point of ferocious, virulent discretion. Discreet to the point of descensional reflection.

Derrida calls the word play of a-propriation "a parodying dissimulation" (98). The reference to parody reminds us of another, earlier reference to Nietzsche's parodic styles: twisting free from Platonism cannot proceed "without discreet parody, without strategy of writing, without difference or divergence of quills, without style, namely, the grand . . ." (77). *Sans parodie discrète*: even in the carnival of parody, as Nietzsche describes it in the preface to the second edition of *The Gay Science* (cited below in note 11), with the phrase *incipit parodia*, discretion is called for; discretion alone can assure differentiation, the heterogeneity of the text, and discernment within the text. Hence the deconstruction of "woman," that is to say, the deconstruction of the definite article, *la (femme)*, serves as a discreet introduction to the Heideggerian mystery: "Just as there is no being or essence of the woman or of sexual difference, so there is no essence of the *es gibt* in the *es gibt Sein*, of the grant and the granting of being. . . . Thus *la femme* will not have been my subject" (100). While Derrida assures us that he is absconding with Heidegger's *Nietzsche*, fleeing with it "outside the hermeneutic circle," we may be more inclined to say that a modest hermeneutic gesture nonetheless prevails in Derrida's own work. It is not *volez, volez!* but *glissez, glissez!*

Derrida's insistence on undecidability does not obviate the fact that Nietzsche's lost *parapluie* is made to do a great deal of work—the work of both prodding and protecting—in Derrida's own text. And while no guarantees underwrite any portion of his fabulation on style, writing, truth, and woman, while no historical or ontological or hermeneutical *Verstehen* will assure us of the viability of Derrida's own procedure here, we can be assured that no fabulation is entirely without tabulation, no deconstructive reading without strategy and calculation. Even when it revels in the great good luck of a *coup de des*, Derrida continues to toss the dice until he finds what his reading requires, whether wittingly or not. Indeed, one wonders whether anything in Derrida's *Spurs* has been left to chance. In the notebook that contains the phrase "*ich habe meinen Regenschirm vergessen,*" Mette-number N V 7, a frivolous toss of the dice could every bit as well have hit on fragment 47 (9, 584):

Conversations in solitude

or 48 (ibid.):

12 summers

or 79 (9, 590; an early reference in Nietzsche's notebooks to *Zarathustra*):

I have a *provenance*—that is my pride, opposed to *cupido gloriae.*
It does not seem strange to me that Zarathustra———

or 88 (9, 592):

Situations to assemble

or, finally, note number 5 in an earlier notebook, U II 2 (7, 622), from the year 1873:

Ika! Ika! Bäh-Bäh-

which the *Gesamtausgabe* editors, *mirabile editu*, do not elucidate in any way.

That Derrida should have stumbled across the lost umbrella may appear to be simply a matter of good fortune, especially if we believe Derrida's sincerest assurances that he has forgotten a conversation with Roger Laporte about it—an assurance he authenticates by dating it in his text: 4/1/73, which is to say, April Fools' Day, 1973. It is great good fortune, because of the work the umbrella does for Derrida as both spur and sail, as a component of Lautreamont's definition of beauty, as an ambiguously masculine and feminine figure for psychoanalysis, as Heidegger's not terribly original exemplum of the forgetfulness of philosophy professors, and even (outside of Derrida's text) in René Magritte's remarkable "*Les vacances de Hegel.*" While doubtless none of these umbrellas is destined to appear by some dispensation of being, each of them offers something more than "Ika! Ika! Bäh-Bäh-," something more than "Situations to assemble."

What Derrida perhaps wants to show is that no text of Nietzsche's, nor all his texts taken together, can reveal without residue or *restance* what Nietzsche most intensely "wanted" or "willed" or "meant" to say—his meaning, his *vouloir-dire*, his most intrinsically thoughtful will or most willful thought. Yet if we were to take Derrida's minimalism quite literally, quite maximally, we might fail to see the careful, highly selective, remarkably discerning and utterly discreet fabulation that is Jacques Derrida's *Spurs*.

Not yet. One step more. When Derrida stresses the "posthumous" nature of his own communication (115–18), in a way that reminds us both of Nietzsche's posthumous birth and of the funerary or testamentary "I" of Husserlian discourse,[9] we are reminded also of the trajectory of all hermeneutics of discretion, for which mortality is an intimation that comes—if it comes at all—at the writing desk. Derrida has no doubt always been embarrassed by such overt references to finitude and mortality. One recalls the way he tries to avoid discussion of them in *Of Grammatology*,[10] capitulating only when another discourse, that of repetition compulsion and the economy of lifedeath in Freud's *Beyond the Pleasure Principle*, joins forces with the Heideggerian discourse of finitude. It is precisely in this section of the *Grammatology*, "The Hinge Unhinged," that we find a reference to "discretion" as a word for *differance*. "Signification thus takes shape only in the hollow of differance: in the hollow of discontinuity and of discretion, of detour and the reserve of that which does not appear" (G, 101). And later: "The linear norm could never impose itself absolutely for the very reasons that limited graphic phonetism from the inside. We know them by now: . . . discretion, differance, spacing" (G, 128). To be sure, the word *discretion* here says something different from anything a hermeneutics of discretion has yet said; the adjectival form of the discretion Derrida writes here would—in English—doubtless have to be *discrete*, and not *discreet*. Yet one wonders whether the loop in the line of time and of phonemic, graphematic signification does not extend as far as matters of interpretation, finitude, and mortality. (*Glissez, mortels*, for you are discrete.)

This is surely not the place for a discussion of temporalization, spatialization, and the trace (the German *Spur*) as "the opening of the first exteriority in general" (G, 103). Yet that such a fissure in temporalization, the discretion of time, as it were, has to do with breaching (*frayage*), rupture, and discontinuity, cannot be denied. Nor can the implications of such a fracture in traditional linearity be denied for the economy of lifedeath, the detour that is signposted by the testamentary grapheme (G, 100–101). If Derrida eschews all talk of a "return to finitude" or of "the death of God" (G, 99), it is merely because for him the sole access to such themes is the parlous scene of writing. Lest we delude ourselves into thinking that Derrida dissolves the earnest hermeneutics of discretion into a carefree or careless play of texts—something his earnest critics always gleefully throw in his face—I cite these words from the closing pages of *Spurs*:

> The death of which I speak is not tragedy or indeed anything attributed to a subject: which we would have to take into account, drawing out its consequences for the scene we occupy. It is not a matter of proceeding in the following way: "I am mortal, thus . . . etc." On the contrary, death—and the posthumous—only announce themselves due to the possibility of such a scene. Hence the same holds true for birth, whether with reference to tragedy or to parody.
> That is perhaps what Nietzsche called style, simulacrum, woman (117).

Incipit tragœdia, and, no doubt, *incipit parodia*.[11] However, it is a discreet parody, in which perhaps the constellation of woman, sensuality, and death would not forever be postponed, but would spur our writing. If I myself were to write of these things—having by the ringroad of recurrence reached the age of fourteen, which the Romans determined to be the age of discretion—it would be to invoke not the umbrella but the undecidable promise and threat that Nietzsche somewhere calls *Calina*.[12]

And even if it were a parody of hermeneutics in the old style, hermeneutics from Schleiermacher through Gadamer, in which deconstruction were engaged, it would have to remember not to push too hard. As we shall see in the following chapter, even the most aggressive and virulent deconstruction would have to make its peace with a hermeneutics of discretion.

LACOUE-LABARTHE ON HEIDEGGER ON NIETZSCHE

> Thus it is necessary to observe a certain prudence.
> —Philippe Lacoue-Labarthe

The way in which I shall comment on Lacoue-Labarthe's reception of Heidegger's *Nietzsche* will differ from what I have written above, first of all because Lacoue-Labarthe is perhaps still less familiar to English-speaking readers than Derrida is, and secondly because his style of thinking and writing differs quite markedly from Derrida's. *"Nietzsche Apocryphe"* and *"L'Oblitération,"* taken together, constitute over one hundred pages of dense, carefully wrought scholarly prose on the "subjects of philosophy" that we call Nietzsche and Heidegger. For the same reasons, I would like to present his views as thoroughly and as impartially as possible. Yet I find the margins of my copy of *Le sujet de la philosophie* filled with as many counters, rejoinders, and retorts as affirmations. No doubt I shall have to exercise considerable discretion here, not only in the choice of matters to be reported but also in my estimation of their relative fruitfulness or apparent lack of issue. Therefore, at the outset, a rank indiscretion on my part, so that there will be no mistake: Lacoue-Labarthe's two studies are by no means mere introductions to the Heidegger/Nietzsche confrontation; they are inquiries of great thoroughness, sensitivity, and penetration; one learns from them on every page.

Some remarks by way of background. The "subject of philosophy" is in Lacoue-Labarthe's view also the "subject of writing." The "fable" that captivates him is one originally played out on that ancient scene of strife between "philosopher and artist, thinker and writer, Master of Truth and wordmaker," a scene in which the first of each pair has always walked off with the palms (6). Philosophy has always scorned writing and the writer, scorned them by grace of a distinction that philosophy itself has formulated . . . in writing. In contrast, Lacoue-Labarthe wonders whether "in the end" philosophical discourse differs essentially from the discourse of even the lowliest literature (10). He wants to know whether the metaphysics of presence and the nostalgia for origins is not itself a prolonged *récit*, a tale unfolding *in* and *as* the course of Western intellectual history. In the unfolding of the tale there is no master but *logos*. Nothing lies outside the *logos*, "not even the literature to which it [i.e., *logos*, in the form of philosophy] has given a meaning . . ." (25). Lacoue-Labarthe invokes an experience of writing that many contemporary French writers and thinkers have confirmed—he refers to Bataille and Klossowski, but one also thinks of Merleau-Ponty and Blanchot—and that might be summarized as follows: one never writes simply in order to say what one means or wants-to-say, *veut-dire*; writing exposes the writer to "the obscure work of a force that is alien to whatever we are saying, a force that is absolutely impossible to master" (26). To write is to be dispossessed by the action of the very language that possesses us; to write is to confront "a blinding alterity" to which we otherwise give the name *la mort* (27). Upon the background of this experience of writing Lacoue-Labarthe writes intensely—some would say obsessively—of Heidegger/Nietzsche.

"Nietzsche Apocryphe" focuses on the Heideggerian thesis that the Western metaphysical tradition culminates in Nietzsche and the concomitant question (by now quite familiar) as to whether at some point Nietzsche ex-

ceeds or surpasses that tradition (77–78). For Lacoue-Labarthe, as for Derrida, it is deconstruction that offers some hope of our envisaging such surpassment, at the level not of philosophical discourse but of the written text. According to Lacoue-Labarthe, Heidegger explicitly refuses to take seriously the matter or "sake" of the text—the matters of *literature, form,* and *style* (81). This putative *refus explicite* by Heidegger to involve himself in the vulgar affairs of textuality (rhymes with . . .) is what disturbs Lacoue-Labarthe about Heidegger's reading of Nietzsche: not only in *"Nietzsche Apocryphe"* but also in *"L'Oblitération"* he faults Heidegger with unrelenting disparagement of (lowly) literature and exaltation of (pure, poetic) thought. At the same time, as we shall see, the thought of "Heidegger himself" in some way touches on and even engages the fundamental experience of writing. Hence, in Lacoue-Labarthe's view, it can never be a matter of "rejecting" or "refuting" Heidegger, of merely refusing his refusal and going on to baser things.

Like Derrida, Lacoue-Labarthe finds his point of entry in Heidegger's first two lecture courses on Nietzsche, "Will to Power as Art" (1936–1937) and "Eternal Recurrence of the Same" (1937). Surprisingly, however, he takes Heidegger's refusal to accept the division of Nietzsche's unpublished notes on eternal recurrence that was made by the *Nachlaß* editors—namely their division of Nietzsche's notes into "theoretical" and "poetical" groups—as evidence of Heidegger's disdain of poetry, as of all questions of form and style (83–85). Further, and even more astonishing, he faults Heidegger with neglecting questions of form and presentation (*Darstellung*), specifically with regard to Nietzsche's *Thus Spoke Zarathustra.* Heidegger's exaltation of *Dichtung* and ποίησις he takes to be the all-too-familiar ruse by which philosophy exploits and suppresses the texts of literature. Whether Heidegger ignores the style, form, and presentation of *Thus Spoke Zarathustra* one must leave for readers of the 1937 lecture course to decide. Yet I cannot refrain from mentioning certain aspects of this course that Lacoue-Labarthe himself ignores, aspects that might have altered his global claim concerning Heidegger's *refus.*

Heidegger's focus throughout is on the *communication* of the thought of eternal recurrence, especially the second and most veiled communication of it, to wit, *Also sprach Zarathustra.* When Heidegger stresses the *how?* of such communications rather than their *what?,* when he explicates "On the Vision and the Riddle" and "The Convalescent" with scrupulous attention to textual detail—the emergence on the scene of Zarathustra's animals, the ascent up the mountain path by Zarathustra and his dwarfish "spirit of gravity," the position of the gateway *Augenblick* and its two affronting avenues, the red and yellow berries plucked by Zarathustra's eagle for his recuperation, and so on—when he takes pains to exhibit to his listeners the poetic creation of Zarathustra as a figure of and spokesman for recurrence, when he emphasizes the importance of sensuous imagery (*Versinnbildlichung*) in Nietzsche's masterwork, and when he resists every temptation to let Nietzsche's variegated texts on eternal return slip into ready-made categories such as "scientific hypothesis" or "religious belief," or catch-all phrases such as "worldview"—does any of this suggest contempt for "form" or disdain of "texts"? And if one glances back to the first lecture course, on will to power as art, one might ask: when Heidegger defines what Nietzsche calls *Rausch* ("rapture" or "frenzy") as "form-engendering force," and such force, in turn, as the principal constituent of art in the grand style, when the outcome of his inquiry is the discovery of Nietzsche's "new interpretation of sensuousness and the raging discordance between art and truth," are these determinations in any way signs of contempt for lowly literature and textuality—no matter what they rhyme with? Finally, do we have from any interpreter a more insightful remark on the *style* and *tempo* of *Thus Spoke Zarathustra* than Heidegger's (in *Was heißt Denken?* Lecture X) concerning that work's "steadily increasing hesitation and *ritardando*"?

However, to return to what Lacoue-Labarthe correctly sees as Heidegger's refusal to accept the distinction between "theoretical" and "poetical," noting that the latter word is not *dichterisch* but *poetisch*: is this the refusal of one who has no eye and ear for literature and style, or is it something quite different, quite discrete, and perhaps even discreet? Allow me to cite section 10 of the course (Ni 2, 70–73) at greater length than Lacoue-Labarthe does, inviting the reader to decide:

> From the moment Nietzsche's "thought of thoughts" came to him in August 1881, everything he meditated on and committed to writing concerning that thought but shared with no one was destined to be labeled as his "literary remains." If the thought of eternal recurrence of the same is Nietzsche's principal thought, then it will have been present to him during the entire subsequent period of his creative life, from 1881 to January 1889. That this is the case is shown by the later publication of the literary remains which originated during the years mentioned. They are to be found in volumes XII through XVI of the Grossoktav edition. But if the thought of eternal recurrence of the same, the thought of thoughts, necessarily determines all of Nietzsche's thinking from the very beginning, then his reflections on this thought and the sketches containing those reflections will vary according to the particular domain, direction, and stage of development in which Nietzsche's philosophical labors happened to be advancing. That means that these so-called "literary remains" are not always the same. Nietzsche's "posthumously published notes" do not comprise an arbitrary bunch of confused and scattered observations that by chance never made it to the printer's. The sketches differ not only in terms of content but also in their form—or lack of form. They arose out of constantly changing moods, sometimes were caught fleetingly among a melee of intentions and points of view; sometimes they were elaborated fully, sometimes ventured only by way of tentative and faltering experiment; and sometimes, quick as lightning, they arrived in one fell swoop. If the thought of eternal recurrence of the same is the thought of thoughts, then it will be least explicitly portrayed or even named wherever in its essentiality it is to have the greatest impact. If for a certain stretch of time nothing or nothing explicit appears to be said about this thought in Nietzsche's notes, that by no means indicates that it has in the meantime become unimportant or even has been abandoned. We must ponder all these things if we wish to understand Nietzsche's "posthumously published notes" and think them through philosophically, instead of merely piecing together a "theory" out of some remarks we have managed to pick up here and there. . . .

In addition, we must free ourselves straightaway of a prejudicial view. The editors say (XII, 425): "Right from the start two different intentions run parallel to each other; the one aims at a theoretical presentation of the doctrine, the other at a poetical treatment of it." Now, to be sure, we too have spoken of a "poetic" presentation of the doctrine of eternal return in *Zarathustra*. Yet we avoided distinguishing it from a "theoretical" presentation, not because the passages cited from *The Gay Science* and *Beyond Good and Evil* are not theoretical presentations but because here the word and concept *theoretical* do not say anything, especially not when one follows the lead of the editors and of those who portray Nietzsche's "doctrine" by equating theoretical with "treatment in prose." The distinction "theoretical-poetical" results from muddled thinking. Even if we were to let it obtain in general, such a distinction would in any case be out of place here. In Nietzsche's thinking of his fundamental thought the "poetical" is every bit as much "theoretical," and the "theoretical" is inherently "poetical." All philosophical thinking—and precisely the most rigorous and prosaic—is in itself poetic. It nonetheless never springs from the art of poetry. A work of poetry, a work like Hölderlin's hymns, can for its part be thoughtful in the highest degree. It is nonetheless never philosophy. Nietzsche's *Thus Spoke Zarathustra* is poetic in the highest degree, and yet it is not a work of art, but "philosophy." Because all actual, that is, all great philosophy is inherently thoughtful-poetic, the distinction between "theoretical" and "poetical" cannot be applied to philosophical texts.

Heidegger's listeners and readers will no doubt want to know what it means to say that all philosophical thinking is in itself poetic (*dichterisch*) even though it does not spring from the art of poetry (*Poesie*); they will also brood over the ascription of thought to poetry—even though no one would dare call Hölderlin's hymns, Yeats's songs, or Melville's novels and tales, from *Moby-Dick* to "Cock-A-Doodle-Doo!" thoughtless. Yet Martin Heidegger has arguably done as much as any thinker in recent times, with the possible exception of Nietzsche, to pose the question of the essence of poetry and of all written creation, not simply in order to exploit it for the purposes of a metaphorics of being but to attend to the very sake of words, names, and saying, in all language and writing.

Lacoue-Labarthe is right to insist that we know too little about the upsurgence of poetry and the work of art in Heidegger's thought during the 1930s. The move (earlier on) from scientific to hermeneutical phenomenology as fundamental ontology, and (beginning already in 1928) from ontology to meditative thought on the history of being and on the poetic word, remains poorly understood down to the present day. Yet Lacoue-Labarthe's own inquiry here (88–89) seems to me without issue, inasmuch as it fails to follow through on a number of questions concerning the relation of art and truth in the Platonic and Nietzschean perspectives. I myself cannot expatiate on these questions here, but will merely list two of them, once again as incentives for future work.

First, what is the relationship between a work of philosophy—whether it be a *Hauptwerk* that for essential reasons can never be completed or an artistic "antechamber" to such a work—and the setting-to-work, *das Ins-Werk-setzen*, of an artwork? Can the same structures of world and earth be brought to bear on the work that *Thus Spoke Zarathustra* is and does? What would be the relation of such work, that is, the work Nietzsche called transfiguration (*Verklärung*), to the strife of world and earth in the revealing/concealing clearing (*Lichtung*)?

Second, is Heidegger in fact satisfied to declare Nietzsche's philosophy a mere inversion of Platonism, as Lacoue-Labarthe claims (86), or have we not learned by now, in part from Derrida, that we must wrestle with the question of Nietzsche's *Herausdrehung*, his twisting free from the Platonic schema? What does it mean that by some sort of concealed maneuver (as I have called it in my "Analysis" to Volume I of Heidegger's *Nietzsche*) Platonism causes the discordance between art and truth to be a "felicitous" one, enabling the beauty of art to both captivate and liberate us, opening a view onto being, and that Nietzsche's exposure of that maneuver as a ruse or deceit causes the discordance between art and truth to rage and to arouse dread? Lacoue-Labarthe neglects to raise such questions, questions that would further his own efforts to confront Heidegger's thinking of the 1930s.

Of Lacoue-Labarthe's attempt (91–93) to transform Heidegger's question, "Who is Nietzsche's Zarathustra?" into the question "*What* Is Nietzsche's Zarathustra?" I will say nothing here, except to note that Heidegger's own question of the *how?* of Nietzsche's communication goes a long way in responding to the question of *Zarathustra* as a text, and to note, inevitably, that the *what?* question, which is the oldest question of philosophy, is simply unable to perform the deconstructive work that Lacoue-Labarthe demands of it. Far more fertile is his effort (93–99) to bring Nietzsche back to Jena, that is, to focus on an entire series of textual events in German Romanticism and Idealism for possible insight into Nietzsche's own text.[13] Surely Lacoue-Labarthe has here hit upon one of the most important areas for future research. How do the sundry Romantic conceptions of the relation between *Dichten* and *Denken*, or between *Kunst* and *Wissenschaft*, anticipate either (1) Nietzsche's raging discordance between art and truth or (2) Heidegger's own apparently felicitous yoking of thought and the poetic word? Lacoue-Labarthe cites a number of crucial texts in this regard, for example, Schelling's sketches toward *The Ages of the World* and the dialogue *Clara*, Friedrich Schlegel's *Lucinde*, and that bedeviling fragment which we know by the title "The Oldest Program toward a System in German Idealism."[14] Hölderlin's theoretical writings—for instance, his *Grund zum Empedokles*—would have to be added to the list; and from Hölderlin we would be wafted back, as Lacoue-Labarthe fully intends, to the early Greek scene of the contest between philosophy and literature.

To none of this would I take exception. It is only the assertion that such efforts are necessary because Heidegger "refuses to consider the 'poetic' character of Zarathustra" (99), or because Heidegger "at bottom" believes that Nietzsche's *Zarathustra* is purely "Platonistic" (106), that strikes me as ill-considered and indiscreet. Lacoue-Labarthe's thesis in "*Nietzsche Apocryphe*" obliterates too many of Heidegger's own texts to be compatible with the "patient and minute labors" that Lacoue-Labarthe himself so admires. Which brings us to the second of his articles, "*L'Oblitération*."

OBLITERATION

This extended review of Heidegger's *Nietzsche* begins and ends by posing the question of "access." Access to "Heidegger himself," to "Nietzsche himself," and to the *Sache des Denkens* marked by the conjunction Heidegger/Nietzsche. In its opening pages (113–17) it offers what I take to be the very best account in any language of the reception of Heidegger's *Nietzsche* in France, Germany, and the English-speaking world. Lacoue-Labarthe explains how it was possible (and necessary) for Heidegger's "theses" on Nietzsche to be known and to be "refuted" before his massive volumes could be read, how it was possible (and necessary) for philosophers to hasten "beyond" Heidegger's *Nietzsche*, to "surpass" it and leave it safely behind, before they had paused to learn from it. He predicts that the more patient and minute reading, when it comes—and come it will, by its own necessity and law—will prove to be a matter of "urgency." Just as Derrida takes Heidegger's interpretation of Nietzsche to be coextensive with the problem of hermeneutics *tout court*, so Lacoue-Labarthe insists, paradoxically but passionately, that our only access to "Nietzsche himself" is through the "sake" of his thinking as identified by "Heidegger himself" (121). Hence there is no hope of circumventing Heidegger in order to get to Nietzsche, no hope of prying Heidegger/Nietzsche apart, at least not for now and presumably not for some time to come. The reason for this was stated two decades ago by David Allison, in his preface to *The New Nietzsche: Contemporary Styles of Interpretation*, with perfect lucidity:

> Nietzsche's biography is uninspiring, to say the least. Nonetheless, this subject appears to have been the principal source of inspiration for the tiresome array of books that has followed him. The situation changed, however, with the publication of Heidegger's two-volume study, in which Nietzsche finally emerged as one of the prodigious thinkers of the modern age. Perhaps it is a measure of greatness in a thinker that he demands an equally profound critic to recognize the importance of his thought. In any case, the distinction rests with Heidegger for succeeding in this attempt. Not only was Heidegger the first to take up seriously the principal, and most difficult, themes of Nietzsche—Will to Power, Eternal Return, and Overman—but he demonstrated that, together, they formed an integral conception of the entire development of Western thought: of its very ground and highest expression.[15]

However, in "*L'Oblitération*" we once again encounter the Labarthean thesis on Heidegger's ostensible sacrifice of form and literary style for the sake of philosophical content: "Thus to a certain extent . . . , a certain effacement, analogous to an obliteration, animates the very style of interpretation that Heidegger practices . . ." (119). What obliteration means we learn fifty pages later at the close of the review (170–76): to obliterate is to cause an inscription to disappear—or *almost* to disappear (here *Le Robert* is more circumspect than *Littré*),[16] inasmuch as "some traces" of the original inscription always remain—either by erasure, effacement, the ravages of time, the vicissitudes of memory, or by the superposition of a new text. Superposition, the creation of a palimpsest, that is, of marks upon marks, is the action suggested the word's etymology: *ob*, upon, and *littera*, the letters. Obviously, therefore, Lacoue-Labarthe's complaint against Heidegger has to be refined. For both Derrida and Heidegger engage in the conscious practice of writing *sous rature*, that is to say, by means of ob-literation. Yet Lacoue-Labarthe means something else.

Vital to his complaint is what Lacoue-Labarthe calls "the stratagem of un-distancing." *É-loignement, Ent-fernung*, is of course the very theme that pervades Derrida's discourse on Nietzschean "distance" and Heideggerian "proximation" and "propriation." Whether it is a matter of gaining distance from Heidegger's reading of Nietzsche or of Heidegger's own effort to approach yet remain at a distance from the tradition, Lacoue-Labarthe does not underestimate the difficulties: access to "Heidegger himself" (a "fiction" of which Lacoue-Labarthe makes constant and quite conscious use) requires that we understand the opposition of thinking to philosophizing, that is, of Heidegger to Hegel, and that we consider quite carefully what Heidegger means by the "step back" out of metaphysics by means of a *Verwindung*, as opposed to an *Überwindung*, of the tradition.[17] I will not pursue this egregiously complex matter here, but will merely comment that un-distancing (which is also a positive *en*-distancing) refers to the way in which Heidegger tries to think (that is, simultaneously to appropriate and to release) the unthought of past thinkers; his effort is always and everywhere subject to the way in which the oblivion of being as such destines (if the word may be used transitively) thought. For both Hegel and Heidegger, the history of thought and the sake of thinking are the matters at stake. It is not without reason that Lacoue-Labarthe again and again repairs to Heidegger's 1951–1952 lecture course, *Was heißt Denken*? The subject of philosophy and the subject of writing do not entirely obliterate the *Sache* of thought. I shall return to this obstreperous matter later.

Lacoue-Labarthe stresses (139) the importance of the "rupture" in Heidegger's project of being and time, time and being: the way in which contemplation of the work of art comes to replace existential analysis. For it is here that the turn to Nietzsche (as to Schelling and Hölderlin) occurs. Nevertheless, he argues that in some covert way Nietzsche also dominates the strategies of Heidegger's *Being and Time* (143). In a note to his text (number 11, on pp. 178–79) Lacoue-Labarthe suggests that the transition from a hermeneutics of Dasein and an inquiry into the meaning of being to a meditation on the truth of being was occasioned by the failure of Heidegger's "onto-phenomenology"; the latter had been intended to precede and inaugurate the "destructuring" of the history of ontology. That failure—which Lacoue-Labarthe is unable to elucidate, as none of us really are, and which he appears to take for granted, as none of us really should—did not in any sense prevent "the same concept of hermeneutics" from dominating Heidegger's history of the oblivion of being. "The same interpretation of *logos*, of *alētheia*, and of the relation *logos/alētheia*" prevails in Heidegger's thought from beginning to end.

While it is true that Heidegger's early discovery of *alētheia* as unconcealment remains determinative for the rest of his career, the character of *logos* changes subtly: what at the outset lets beings be seen of themselves and from themselves is eventually called "that which lets (beings) lie together before (us)." This subtle change conceals a more consequential one. In fact, Lacoue-Labarthe's claim that the same notion of hermeneutics prevails in Heidegger's thought without alteration from beginning to end is the most serious flaw in his understanding of "Heidegger himself." Lacoue-Labarthe woefully underestimates the shock waves that passed through Heidegger's project during the years 1927–1928; he misses the force of the μεταβολή or *Umschlag*, the turnover or overturning that in those years transformed the entire self-understanding and hermeneutical basis of Heidegger's project. True, it is only the recent publication of the Marburg lectures of 1927 and 1928 that has enabled us to see this; it is churlish to fault Lacoue-Labarthe for not having read what none of us could have read two decades ago. Yet it remains true that without a far more careful examination of these years in Heidegger's "development" we can make no sense either of the "rupture" in the project of being and time, time and being, or of the simultaneous upsurgence of Hölderlin and Nietzsche as veritable watersheds for the inquiry into the history of being.[18]

By now we have arrived at the core of Lacoue-Labarthe's undertaking (143 ff.). Here he formulates his "suspicion" concerning the "*menace* represented by Nietzsche" for Heidegger, a menace that arouses a certain kind of fear and even dread in him. It is the menace of Nietzsche's very proximity to Heidegger, a closeness with which the stratagem of *Entfernung* cannot cope. However melodramatic such a suspicion appears to be, however reductively *ad hominem*, however psychologistic—and it is here that Lacoue-Labarthe himself calls for something very much like discretion: "*Il faut donc observer une certaine prudence*"—Lacoue-Labarthe is, I believe, wise to follow that suspicion. He reviews with considerable thoroughness Heidegger's scattered references to Nietzsche, for example, in "The Anaximander Fragment" and in the introduction to Heidegger's *Habilitationsschrift*. He is too discreet to say why Heidegger in the former piece affirms Nietzsche's "vital relationship" with the Presocratics while denigrating as "superficial" his interpretations of their texts, and why he here selects Hegel as his predecessor.

In spite of his own demur, Heidegger himself always craved such a "vital relationship": early Greek thinking was never a matter of pure scholarship or classical learning for Heidegger, but a matter of intimate and ultimate importance, as it was for both Hölderlin and Nietzsche. In his *Habilitation* thesis Heidegger wrote:

> Purely philosophical talent and a genuinely fertile capacity for historical thinking are found together in one personality only in the rarest cases. . . .
>
> Now, the history of philosophy is not and can never be mere history if it is to belong to the scholarly domain of philosophy. The history of philosophy has a re-

lation to philosophy that is different from, for example, the relation of the history of mathematics to mathematics. The reason lies not in the *history* of philosophy but in the history of *philosophy*. . . .

Like every other discipline, philosophy is said to possess cultural value. At the same time, what is most proper to philosophy is its claim to be valid and functional as a value for life. The philosophical legacy is more than a collection of scholarly materials with which one becomes preoccupied due to some personal preference or the will to further and to help give shape to culture. Philosophy at the same time lives in tension with the living personality, draws its import and its claims from the depth and abundance of life in that personality. Thus it is that every philosophical conception generally has its grounds in a personal position taken by the philosopher in question. Nietzsche found a formula—one that is by now familiar—for the way in which all philosophy is determined in terms of the subject [*dieses Bestimmtsein aller Philosophie vom Subjekte her*], a formula that reflects Nietzsche's relentlessly austere manner of thought and his capacity for vivid and apt depiction. He spoke of the "drive to philosophize."[19]

If the *Habilitationsschrift* soon adopts a tone more reminiscent of Hegel than Nietzsche, it is not because the thinker who is both vivid and relentlessly austere has failed to make his mark. While Heidegger's references to the "living personality" make us think of James and Dilthey, there is something menacing about the fatality of *dieses Bestimmtsein aller Philosophie vom Subjekt her*. That menace (at least in part) gives Lacoue-Labarthe the very title of his collection, *Le sujet de la philosophie*. However anachronistic the title may sound, Lacoue-Labarthe does not doubt that the Cartesian subject is in dissolution: his own theme is in fact the "(de)constitution of the subject" (151). What he is trying to shake is the complacency with which we usually broach the matter of that loss: if the "sake" of thinking is sent by way of some grand dispensation, if it is not Herr Nietzsche who calls on us to think but the issue for whose sake the name *Nietzsche* is spoken and written today, as though that issue were "Nietzsche himself," then the *Geschick des Seins*, the fateful sending of being, seems not so much a fatality as a guarantor. Yet what if the "abundance of life" is lacking? What if the depth of personality, the tension of the bow, turns out to be a matter not underwritten by the assiduous study of philosophy books? What if laughter and folly—and, yes, even madness, if discretion be stretched to the limit—should prove to be as vital to thinking as the sober mien of the *Sache*? As both Bataille and Foucault have taught us, and here Derrida would more than agree, it is not sufficient to *exclude* madness. Indeed, Lacoue-Labarthe believes that to appropriate the unthought is to *conjure* madness (152 ff.). The fatality of thinking is that it escapes the subject, is inevitably out of control, whether we confront the menace of madness directly (*Ecce Homo*: "Why I am a fatality") or invoke, on the oblique, as it were, the Heideggerian sending of being. In words reminiscent of Klossowski's ("Then what is the very act of thinking? . . . What is lucid, what is unconscious in our thought and in our acts . . ."),[20] Lacoue-Labarthe poses the question that we usually associate with the serene sage of Todtnauberg: *Qu'appelle-t-on penser*? What calls on us, as the nowhere voice of no one, and compels us to think? That we are "still not thinking" is not for Lacoue-Labarthe a rhetorical slap on the wrist of our mindless times. "The only possibility granted to us of putting at a distance [*écarter*] the menace of madness, that is, the (de)consti-tution of the subject, would be to think the (de)constitution of thought as the unthought . . ." (157).

Lacoue-Labarthe cites Heidegger's remarks in the 1939 lecture course, "Will to Power as Knowledge," on the absence of a *magnum opus* in Nietzsche, indeed, the absence or an œuvre that would correspond to Kant's *Critiques* or Hegel's *Phenomenology* or Schelling's *Treatise on Human Freedom*. According to Lacoue-Labarthe, Heidegger takes such an absence as evidence of Nietz-sche's tireless struggle with his "unique" thought, to wit, the will to power.[21] Once again, Lacoue-Labarthe's remarks ought to have been tempered by Hei-degger's earlier insistence that while will to power is an "ultimate fact" for Nietzsche, his sole perdurant thought is eternal recurrence: the book *Thus Spoke Zarathustra* is fashioned specifically in order to communicate that thought. These remarks on Heidegger's putative thesis that Nietzsche produces no *Werk* distract Lacoue-Labarthe from what ought to have become one of the crucial points of his entire analysis, namely, the fact that in the 1936–1937 course, "Will to Power as Art," Heidegger claims that Nietzsche's "twisting free," his *Herausdrehung aus dem Platonismus*, is accomplished in and as *the collapse into madness*. In section 24 of "Will to Power as Art" we read:

> During the time the overturning of Platonism became for Nietzsche a twisting free of it, madness befell him. Heretofore no one at all has recognized this reversal as Nietzsche's final step; neither has anyone perceived that the step is clearly taken only in his final creative year (1888). Insight into these important connections is quite difficult on the basis of the book *The Will to Power* as it lies before us in its present form, since the textual fragments assembled here have been removed from a great number of manuscripts written during the years 1882 to 1888. An alto-gether different picture results from the examination of Nietzsche's original manuscripts. But even without reference to these, there is a section of the treatise *Twilight of the Idols*, composed in just a few days during that final year of creative work (in September of 1888, although the book did not appear until 1889), a section which is very striking, because its basic position differs from the one we are already familiar with. The section is entitled "How the 'True World' Finally Became a Fable: the History of an Error" (VIII, 82–83; cf. WM, 567 and 568, from the year 1888).

Nietzsche's "Fable," and everything we have seen Derrida make of it for the question of Heidegger's reading of Nietzsche, ought to have played a cen-tral role in Lacoue-Labarthe's deliberations. Instead, Lacoue-Labarthe again in "*L'Oblitération*" rehearses his thesis that any sense of form and style is bound to menace the essence of thought, and that Heidegger therefore systematically suppresses the poetic and even fictional character of *Thus Spoke Zarathustra*. Lacoue-Labarthe doubtless marshals the evidence that best supports his thesis: Heidegger's disdainful remarks (principally, though not exclusively, in *What Calls for Thinking?*) concerning writers and authors, these penpushers (*Schrift-*

steller) who can never rise to the occasion of thought, along with his telltale nostalgia for the "purity" of Socrates, who did not (have to) write. Perhaps the most striking of these passages (Lacoue-Labarthe notes the "neatness of the gesture" in it) is the following:

> Once we are so related and drawn to what withdraws, we are drawing into what withdraws, into the enigmatic and therefore mutable nearness of its appeal. Whenever man is properly drawing that way, he is thinking—even though he may still be far away from what withdraws, even though the withdrawal may remain as veiled as ever. All through his life and right into his death, Socrates did nothing else than place himself into this draft, this current, and maintain himself in it. This is why he wrote nothing. For anyone who begins to write out of thoughtfulness must inevitably be like those people who run to seek refuge from any draft too strong for them. An as yet hidden history still keeps the secret why all great Western thinkers after Socrates, with all their greatness, had to be such fugitives. Thinking entered into literature. And literature has decided the fate of Western science which, by way of the *doctrina* of the Middle Ages, became the *scientia* of modern times. . . . [22]

It is noteworthy that Lacoue-Labarthe (167) closes the quotation after the word *literature*. The neatness of the gesture (but whose neatness?) is thereby guaranteed. Neither does he allow science to complicate the picture, nor does he permit a word of poetry to be heard—even though the following lines from the second version of Hölderlin's "Mnemosyne" dominate Heidegger's lecture and transition:

> We are a sign, undeciphered,
> We are painless, have all but
> Lost our tongue in foreign lands.

True, the word of poetry *speaks*, as far as Heidegger is concerned. Herr Kolbenheyer,[23] but not Hölderlin, and not Nietzsche—is a *Schriftsteller*. But then Herr Kolbenheyer is no Plato, Kant, or Hegel. We should not forget, as Lacoue-Labarthe apparently does, that Nietzsche scorned penpushers and their "literature" as much as Heidegger did. To Ernst Schmeitzner he protests in 1878, "*Denken Sie, ich sei ein 'Schriftsteller'?*" Three years later, in the famous notebook M III 1 (which will occupy us later, in chapter 8), Nietzsche remonstrates:

> On and on, become the one you are—the teacher and sculptor of your self! You are no penpusher, you write for yourself alone! Thus you preserve the memory of your good moments and you find their interconnection, the golden chain of your self! Thus you prepare yourself for a time when you will have to speak! Perhaps you will have to be ashamed of speaking, just as from time to time you have had to be ashamed of writing—ashamed that it is still necessary to interpret, that deeds and omissions do not suffice to *communicate* you. Oh, yes, you do want to communicate yourself! Some day the attitude will prevail that too much reading betrays bad form: then you will not have to be ashamed of being read; whereas now everyone who addresses you as a writer [*Schriftsteller*] insults you; and whoever thinks to *praise* you on account of your writings gives the sign that he is not very tactful, and

digs an abyss between him and you—he does not have an inkling of the fact that he degrades himself when he thinks to elevate you in *this* way. I know the state human beings achieve nowadays when they *read*: phooey! And to think that some people want to cultivate and create such a state! (11 [297]; 9, 555–56)

Finally, seven years later, to Carl Spitteler, who indeed takes Nietzsche to be an "author": "*Mache ich denn 'Litteratur'?*"

It would perhaps be more fitting to transform Lacoue-Labarthe's complaint into a question: Is there some connection between Heidegger's designations of Socrates as the purest (*reinste*) thinker of the West and of Nietzsche as the last (*letzte*) thinker of the West? Would the as yet unwritten history of philosophical writing, from Plato through Nietzsche (unless the "Envois" of Derrida's *Post Card* recounts precisely that history), tell us something about the wind-shelter (*Windschatten*) that writing may indeed always have been for thoughtful human beings, with all their *doxa, dogma, doctrina*, and *scientia*? Might not Nietzsche's texts—these "cries of calamity," as Heidegger calls them in 1937, and especially the "written cry" of *Thus Spoke Zarathustra*, as he says in 1951–1952—conduct us to the outer limit of a certain textual history? Might not a vast range of texts find their place retrospectively in such a history, texts like Schelling's sketches for and multiple sets of proofs of *Die Weltalter*? Lacoue-Labarthe does not pursue these questions, at least not in "*L'Oblitération.*" And yet there is a sense in which, after a forceful statement of his suspicion concerning "Heidegger himself," Lacoue-Labarthe obliterates that suspicion in order to raise similar kinds of questions. First, the forceful statement, forceful if perhaps misapplied:

> It is necessary [for Heidegger] to cancel [*relever*] the whole of writing and madness. That is why a hermeneutics of the unthought finds in obliteration—in a certain effacement of the letter—its most reliable defense against madness. It is in obliteration that all of Heidegger's operations are ultimately accomplished. . . . Obliteration is the other name for "stratagem of un-distancing"; it is the primitive operation (the maneuver) on which the entire strategy of thought is constructed. If the danger is madness, the enemy is the letter—the thought in the letter or the becoming-letter of thought, in which something worse than death threatens. (168)

However, the obliteration of obliteration now occurs. For if we have access to "Heidegger himself" it is through (reading) the books he wrote, including his massive book about the books Nietzsche did and did not write; through reading, and, if it is not too indiscreet to say such a thing, through *thinking* about all these books. It simply will not do to oppose writing to thinking (173). *Penser, Denken,* "thinking": to be sure, the word is an embarrassment. Perhaps it is even a menace for those who pursue the question of writing.

The closing words of Part One of Derrida's *Of Grammatology* (G, 142), that is, the conclusion of the "theoretical matrix" of deconstruction as such, stresses that "thought of the trace" is both necessary and impossible. Derrida takes Heidegger's word *thinking* as his model, if not mirror, inasmuch as *Denken* is a "transgression" of the field of *episteme*. He tries to use the word neutrally, as though *penser* meant nothing, wanted to say, *veut dire*, nothing.

Yet its power resides in its ability to point beyond the realm of what we know—beyond to the "new science," the science without scientificity, of writing. *Penser, c'est ce que nous savons déjà n'avoir pas encore commencé à faire....* "Thinking is that which we already know we have not yet begun to do...." In his interview (by letter) with Christie V. McDonald, Derrida refers to Heidegger's "thought" of the granting, then adds the following parenthetical remark: "I say 'thought' because one cannot say philosophy, theory, logic, structure, scene, or anything else; when one can no longer use any word of this sort, when one can say almost nothing else, one says 'thought,' but one could show that this too is excessive."[24] Finally, Derrida's concluding words to *Envoi*, a lecture on "representation" and the "sending" or destiny of being, broaches the possibility of our being engaged by a "thinking" that is "altogether different."[25] No, it will not do to oppose writing to thinking, to exclude by written fiat the embarrassment of having to think.

Yet obliteration, even the self-obliteration of a suspicion, does not efface all its traces. And that is its good fortune. For every reader of Lacoue-Labarthe and of "Heidegger himself" will have to pose and sustain the following question: What is it that prevents Heidegger's "step back," out of metaphysics into the essence of metaphysics, from becoming a mere recoil from, and an arrest of, the task of thinking? If one may put the question into German: How are we to distinguish a *Zurückschreiten* from a *Zurückschrecken*, a pensive stepping back from a shrinking back in the face of menace and madness? In a series of five questions at the very end of his review (176–76) Lacoue-Labarthe invites his readers to ask whether the "rupture" of Heidegger's project of being and time, time and being, does not result from a "necessity of writing"; to ask why that rupture leads, by way of Hölderlin and Nietzsche, to the questions of language and poetry as works of art; to ask why Heidegger's own later work is fragmented, and in a sense is merely occasional, so that not only in Nietzsche but also in Heidegger we confront the absence of an *œuvre*, as though an infectious Nietzsche had in some way "contaminated" Heidegger, as though (in Otto Pöggeler's words) a "Sils-Maria wind" blows through all of Heidegger's texts from the 1930s onward, from his *Contributions to Philosophy* to "The End of Philosophy and the Task of Thinking"; and finally, to ask why Heidegger himself is constrained to try his hand at so many different forms and styles of writing (lectures, essays, poems, dialogues, and so on), as though Nietzsche's Plato too, that master of the *mixed* form, had contaminated him. To pursue these questions, any or all of them, would contribute to that fabulous history of philosophical writing that Lacoue-Labarthe has in mind if not altogether in hand.

GLISSEZ

What qualifying considerations allayed his perturbations?
The difficulties of interpretation since the significance of any event followed its occurrence as variably as the acoustic report

followed the electrical discharge and of
counterestimating against an actual loss
by failure to interpret the total sum of
possible losses proceeding originally from
a successful interpretation.
—James Joyce, *Ulysses*, "Ithaca"

Twenty-five years ago it was the "double solicitation" (Ricoeur) to hermeneutics that captivated me. On the one hand, Nietzsche's "School of Suspicion," his genealogical critique of metaphysics and morals, exercised its fascination, as it still does; on the other hand, the abortive "fundamental ontology" and protracted "other" thinking of Martin Heidegger had their own powers of attraction. At the close of my doctoral dissertation, in my "Introduction to a Hermeneutics of Discretion," I asked how long the conjunction Heidegger/Nietzsche could possibly last. So many indicators suggested that the compound was highly unstable and volatile, bound for little if any future.

In the intervening years I have had occasion to reread Nietzsche, reread Heidegger, and take a closer look at Heidegger/Nietzsche. As a result of those rereadings, each of the two *Sachen* for whose sake we write the names *Nietzsche/Heidegger* has gained in stature; at the same time, the bonding of the two has become stronger than ever. Deconstruction and the entire "postmodern" preoccupation, whatever their various intents, do not vitiate but contribute to the strength of that bonding.

Hermeneutics in general, it is true, has taken a beating from deconstruction. Taken a beating from all sides, if the truth be told. Badly battered, it insists that it is ready to get under way again, ready for more of the endless conversation. Who can help but jeer at its limping along? It is still trying to catch up with that fateful conjunction we call *Heidegger/Nietzsche*. Yet if it has not yet learned how to kick its heels in dance it is only because—encumbered by the virtue or vice of discretion—it is still trying to slow the perilous pace of interpretation. *Glissez, mortels, n'appuyez pas.*

SEVEN

"Ashes, Ashes, We All Fall . . ."

Nietzsche, Heidegger, Gadamer, Derrida

When I first sketched out the preceding chapter, "A Hermeneutics of Discretion," I was blissfully ignorant of the Gadamer-Derrida encounter, probably because it never really occurred.[1] John Sallis had asked me to contribute to a collection of papers on the theme of Heidegger/Nietzsche; my indiscreet hermeneutics of discretion was the result. Why indiscreet? Because in that piece I claimed that the issue of hermeneutics as such was bound up with the Heidegger/Nietzsche encounter—as though there were not myriad scenes in which the trials and tribulations of interpretation were being played out. I agreed with Derrida's *Spurs* when it asserted, *per impossibile*, that Heidegger's interpretation of Nietzsche encompassed the question of interpretation *per se*: at stake in Heidegger's *Nietzsche*, I wrote, was the very sake, the *Sache*, of hermeneutics. At the same time, I resisted the minimalist, antihermeneutical strokes of *Spurs*, claiming that even in the case of the forgotten umbrella nothing in Derrida's own text had been left to chance: while deconstruction might eschew the reduction of any text to a semantico-hermeneutical code, its own careful attention to textual strategies seemed to require a crypto-hermeneutics, perhaps an abashed hermeneutics, or at the very least a discreet hermeneutics, a hermeneutics of discretion. I concluded that even if hermeneutics appeared to have taken a beating from deconstruction it was still trying doggedly—and admirably—to catch up with the conjunction Heidegger/Nietzsche. And so I came down, as they say, or slipped and fell, on the side of hermeneutics: *Glissez, mortels, n'appuyez pas*: "Gently, mortals, be discreet."

It should not surprise me that Nietzsche, and Heidegger's *Nietzsche*, crop up again and again in the Derrida-Gadamer nonencounter. And yet it does. Why should Nietzsche, Nietzsche even more than Plato, and Heidegger's *Nietzsche* even more than Nietzsche, occupy the shifting ground of this implausible and perhaps quite impossible encounter? Why does Gadamer refer incessantly to Nietzsche, and to Heidegger's *Nietzsche*, as though to an infallible touchstone? Why does Derrida remain preoccupied with Heidegger's mighty tome when it is obviously a book that arouses his gravest suspicions? Why, when Gadamer encounters Derrida, and Derrida Gadamer, are the two of them encountering Heidegger encountering Nietzsche?

Although neither Gadamer nor Derrida mentions it, Heidegger juxtaposes to his *Auseinandersetzung* with Nietzsche (the *explication*—as the French says—or confrontation with Nietzsche in terms of the guiding question of metaphysics) a "going to encounter in thought," *ein Entgegendenken*, which is not prepared to reduce "Nietzsche" to a unity. Derrida, no doubt, remains skeptical. Gadamer, who ought to embrace thoughtful encounter as the very essence of the conversation he believes we are, never truly celebrates Heidegger's going to encounter Nietzsche. On the contrary, Gadamer announces in almost cavalier fashion, as though it were a secret sin in which he took particular pride, that Heidegger's Nietzsche-interpretation has convinced him utterly.

How odd. It never fully convinced Heidegger.

Both Gadamer and Derrida appear to be convinced that Heidegger was convinced about Nietzsche: convinced that Nietzsche was the last metaphysician rather than the last thinker; that he foundered in value thinking, *Wertdenken;* that a rescue operation of the "innermost will" of Nietzsche's thinking would secure him at and as the outermost point in the metaphysical preoccupation with beings as a whole. Was Heidegger so convinced?

It is no doubt perverse of me to focus on Nietzsche's recurrence in the Gadamer-Derrida encounter—and Heidegger's, and Heidegger's *Nietzsche's.* One rather ought to take up larger and more truly pressing questions, such as the following: Is it not striking that in his 1985 text, "*Destruktion* and Deconstruction," Gadamer cites only two ways other than Heidegger's in which one can avoid the "taming" or "domesticating" tendency of dialectical thinking—his own way and that of Derrida? Of all the encounters Gadamer has had in his long life, would not this "implausible" one, which never took place as such, be decisive for post-Hegelian thought? Would not the urgency of the encounter prompt all sorts of questions *en détail*, questions that the texts of the encounter do little to clarify? Questions, once again, like these: How do the conceptions of text, and especially literary text, differ in Derrida and Gadamer? Why does Derrida decline to take up Gadamer's invitation to discuss textuality; why does he restrict himself to questions of will, power, psychoanalysis, and metaphysics? How successfully does Gadamer resist the charge (or is it a self-accusation?) of logocentrism in his notion of language as speech, and speech as conversation? Does not Gadamer have to suffer a bit more patiently the question as to whether or not his own "conversation" appeals always and everywhere to a certain unity, linearity, encompassment, and closure? And yet does not Derrida's most recent thought on the double-yes, on gift-giving, the *gage*, friendship, sacrifice, mourning, and the secret, have to smile on (not at) Gadamer's insistence that "it is only the answer, actual or potential, that transforms a word into a word" (DD 106)?[2]

Is it not strange how the alignment of the fourfold (Heidegger-Gadamer-Nietzsche-Derrida) shifts in the texts of the encounter? What I mean is: when it is a matter of Heidegger's putative logocentrism, Gadamer aligns himself with the accused against Nietzsche and Derrida; when it is a matter of Heidegger's adventurous odyssey through the Presocratics in search of original words for being, Gadamer takes his distance from Heidegger, who now moves closer to Nietzsche and Derrida; when it is a question of Nietzsche, Gadamer embraces Heidegger (or at least one of the heideggers) and bids adieu to Derrida. With *Nietzsche*, Heidegger's *Nietzsche*, however, all shifting stops. Why is that? Would this whole series of shifts within the fourfold apply to Derrida as well? Or not at all? Is Derrida's position, the position of this notorious shifter, this thinker so many find so shifty, in fact far more consistent and patient than that of Gadamer, who we all thought was Gibraltar?

Why is it that when it comes to *Nietzsche*, Heidegger's *Nietzsche*, the shifting stops? That is the sole question I shall take up. My secret hope is that it will prove important for those larger questions in ways I myself am the least competent to grasp.

GADAMER'S HEIDEGGER'S *NIETZSCHE*

Let me begin by reviewing some of the places in Gadamer's texts where Nietzsche, and Heidegger's *Nietzsche*, become central. In "Text and Interpretation" (1981), Nietzsche raises his mustachioed head as soon as Gadamer invokes the "French scene" he is about to encounter (TI 24).[3] In Gadamer's view, Derrida elects Nietzsche over Heidegger: Nietzsche is "the more radical one" when it comes to abandoning the language of metaphysics. Derrida must therefore totally reject (*ganz verwerfen*) Heidegger's Nietzsche-interpretation. What is that interpretation? It descries and decries Nietzsche's imprisonment in values and value thinking. As soon as Heidegger determines Nietzsche's superficiality ("*Oberflächlichkeit*"—the word, I believe, is Gadamer's, not Heidegger's), he surges beyond Nietzsche in order to enjoin another thinking and a new language. Paradoxically, it is precisely at the point where Heidegger's Nietzsche-interpretation comes to fruition—and it comes quickly, Gadamer will say elsewhere (DD 105), inasmuch as Heidegger and Nietzsche are boon companions only for a brief moment[4]—that Gadamer abandons Heidegger for the stiller waters of Dilthey.

Why must Gadamer abandon not only Nietzsche but also, if one may say so, nietzsche's heidegger, and precisely at the point where the latter is thought to outstrip the former—and presumably, Nietzsche's French avatars as well? If at the end of "*Destruktion* and Deconstruction" Gadamer asserts (112) that his way of escaping Hegelian domesticity goes farther and is more radical than the way of deconstruction, how is it that, pulling ahead of Derrida, with both of them still in Heidegger's wake, Gadamer drops back abruptly and deliberately from the Heideggerian turbulence? Gadamer "can understand" why the "later Heidegger" (and presumably Derrida as well, who is now declared to be at one, *einig*, with Heidegger) would complain that Gadamer is trapped in phenomenological immanence; and Gadamer himself confesses his rootedness in the Romantic tradition of the *Geisteswissenschaften* and the humanistic legacy of that tradition (26). How then can he find fault with Nietzsche's "successors" for having bypassed what both tempts and attempts in Nietzsche's thought, *das*

Versucherische, which, as we heard in chapter 5, is at-temptation itself? Gadamer notes approvingly the profound ambiguity of Heidegger's Nietzsche-*imago* and insists that Heidegger's own attempt surpasses Nietzsche, who putatively remains embroiled in value thinking, by getting back behind the metaphysical provenance of such thinking. Heidegger's own at-temptation leads him back behind—and thus beyond Nietzsche. Not, however, into the light, but into the inexpungeable darkness of being's mystery: as Schelling is to Hegel, so is Heidegger to Nietzsche, except that Heidegger possesses the "conceptual force" that Schelling so conspicuously lacks. Heidegger has it all. And yet Gadamer must surge beyond Derrida in order to fall back behind Heidegger, with whom Derrida, at least in some respects, is *einig*. If my readers find these shiftings confusing, then we are in agreement. Things are seldom clear in an encounter that never eventuates.

In Gadamer's "Letter to Dallmayr" and in "*Destruktion* and Deconstruction," Nietzsche, in the form of Heidegger's *Nietzsche*, is ubiquitous. Gadamer confesses himself a willing sacrificial victim, *ein williges Opfer*, to Heidegger's Nietzsche-interpretation, citing but one aspect of that interpretation: whereas in the earlier lecture, "Text and Interpretation," it was the critique of Nietzsche's metaphysical *Wertdenken* that took center stage, it is now Heidegger's success in "bringing together in thought will to power and eternal recurrence" (LD 94) that prevails.[5] Gadamer finds this *Zusammendenken* "fully persuasive and irrefutable," *völlig überzeugend und durchschlagend*. In his "Letter to Dallmayr" (LD 97), it is the challenge to take Nietzsche "seriously enough" that compels Gadamer to his most concise formulation of the hermeneutician's doubt:

> Here we come up against the central problem resonating in all hermeneutic endeavors, the one that also forms the basis, I think, of Derrida's qualms about my venture in thought: Is there not in hermeneutics—for all its efforts to recognize otherness as otherness, the other as other, the work of art as a catalyst [*Stoss*], the breach as breach, the unintelligible as unintelligible—too much conceded [*eingeräumt*] to reciprocal understanding and mutual agreement?

The Derridian doubt plagues Gadamer's "*Destruktion* and Deconstruction," however confident its rhetoric. And Nietzsche is the carrier of that plaguey doubt or suspicion. Heidegger himself had to absorb the radical risks of Nietzschean thought in order to achieve his own breakthrough (DD 104). At the end of Heidegger's odyssey through early Greek thinking stands Nietzsche as the culminating figure (*Endgestalt*). Nevertheless, as we have already heard, the self-destruction of metaphysics as it occurs in and through Nietzsche can, in Gadamer's view, only result in Heidegger's "becoming a travel companion of Nietzsche's for a short stretch of his own way" (DD 105). Heidegger discovers a new language. And he enables Gadamer to discover the fact that language as such does not represent the Babylonian captivity of thought but the possibility of passing over into the language of the other. However necessary Nietzsche may have been for Heidegger's breakthrough, Gadamer is at pains to lose

Nietzsche in order to find the language that will make himself understood, and to that end to lose Heidegger as well, if necessary, and certainly to lose Derrida. "One must look for the word that can reach another person. And it is possible for one to find it; one can even learn the language of the other person" (ibid.). The formulation is itself awkward, groping, and wholly equivocal: *man kann sogar die fremde, seine, des Anderen Sprache lernen. Seine,* his. His, whose? Not his, meaning one's own, Gadamer would insist, but *his,* meaning the other's, *his* language, the stranger's. We others understand his meaning, do we not? *His.* The stranger's. *Our* stranger's language, which is the language of one's own other's own. Meaning what? And for whom? In and on whose terms?

> Both then were silent?
> Silent, each contemplating the other in both mirrors of the reciprocal flesh of theirhisnothis fellowfaces.[6]

But silent. How long, and with what enormous expenditures of energies, would it have taken Bloom and Dedalus to learn one another's languages—whether Irish, English, French, Hebrew, Greek, or Latin?

In Gadamer's nifty circumvention of Babel, which is neither its destruction nor its deconstruction, a penetrating reading of Nietzsche remains at issue. Gadamer wishes to oppose Derrida's reading of Heidegger's *Nietzsche* and to put his full weight behind Heidegger's own reading of Nietzsche, the one reading that has in fact convinced him altogether, the one reading that is in any case inevitably doubled, being (1) Gadamer's reading of (2) Heidegger's reading of Nietzsche. Presuming that Heidegger's reading is one, and that in the course of Heidegger's *Nietzsche* nietzsche does not read heidegger.

Let us follow quite closely the final paragraphs of *"Destruktion* and Deconstruction" (DD 113). In Gadamer's view, the fourfold Derrida-Gadamer-Heidegger-Nietzsche encounter has but two sides: "On the one side stands the bewildering richness of facets and the endless play of masks in which Nietzsche's bold experiments in thinking appear to disperse [*zerstreuen*] themselves into an ungraspable multiplicity. On the other side, there is the question one may put to Nietzsche, as to what all the play in this enterprise means [*bedeutet*]." On the one hand, play, mask, and dispersion—perhaps the very dispersion that in *Being and Time* threatens the otherwise cohesive span of a resolute, appropriate Dasein.[7] On the other hand, the always coherent, insistently cohesive question, *What does it mean?* As we shall see, that question—in which meaning is pitted against dispersion and play—reverts to a One: one question, one answer, one significance. The very multiplicity and disparity of readings of Nietzsche will prove embarrassing, and will be reduced to a linear progression by means of which one reading becomes altogether convincing and surpasses all others. Nietzsche's own dispersion results from the fact that he fails to discern (*vor Augen haben*) and to grasp conceptually (*in Begriffe fassen*) the "inner connection between the basic principle of will to power and the noontide message of the eternal return of the same." Nietzsche fails to perceive the unity (*Einheit*) of his own (Nietzsche's) thinking. If Gadamer understands

Heidegger correctly (*wenn ich Heidegger recht verstehe*), and if in fact Nietzsche fails to descry the unity of his own thinking, the result is that "these metaphors of his last visions look like mirroring facets with no underlying unity [*hinter denen kein Eines ist*]." Nietzsche's own dispersion, that is, his blindness to the fact that his thought is *not* in dispersion but *is* fundamentally *unified*, "represents the unified, ultimate position [*stelle die einheitliche Endstellung dar*] in which the question concerning being itself forgets itself and loses itself." Eternal recurrence of the same finds its (one) meaning in the (one) era of technology (presumably in the rotary motion of the selfsame, perhaps the least convincing moment of Heidegger's Nietzsche-interpretation) and in consummate nihilism. The claim to think what Nietzsche was unable to think, far from being a regression into metaphysics, represents *Wesen* as a way, as an essential unfolding in which we are able to advance along the path of our own thinking, thus enhancing the conversation that thinking is.

Such conversation seeks new partners, partners of magnitude, partners who are radically other. In 1985, four years after the encounter did not ensue, Gadamer extends the invitation to Derrida to begin. Yet it is an invitation issued as a challenge and a warning, exercising a kind of constraint, making a godfatherly offer that cannot be refused: "Whoever wants me to take deconstruction to heart, and insists on difference, stands at the beginning of a conversation, not at its end" (DD 113).

DERRIDA'S HEIDEGGER'S *NIETZSCHE*

Derrida's "Interpreting Signatures (Nietzsche/Heidegger): Two Questions" adopts a starting point that is markedly different from that of *Spurs*. Whereas the latter accepts Heidegger's own starting point, namely, the will to power as art, the present piece interrogates (1) Heidegger's 1961 foreword to *Nietzsche*, (2) sections 1 and 6 of the 1939 course, "Will to Power as Knowledge," and (3) sections 1 and 12 of the 1937 course, "The Eternal Recurrence of the Same."[8] Presumably, by inquiring into will to power as knowledge and the eternal recurrence of the same Derrida will be touching on that very *Zusammendenken* of the two that Gadamer finds so utterly convincing.

Section 12 of "The Eternal Recurrence of the Same," one of the longest of the 1937 lecture course, proffers a "Summary presentation of the thought [of return]: being as a whole as life and force; the world as chaos." It offers Derrida the chance to focus on a theme that occupies him much of late—that of life, death, life-and-death, or lifedeath—the cosmic economy of ashes [*Aschen*] that Nietzsche introduces. Section 1 of "Will to Power as Knowledge," on "Nietzsche as the thinker of the consummation of metaphysics," will show Heidegger separating off the trivia of Nietzsche's "biography" from the "essence" of his thought; section 6, on "Nietzsche's alleged biologism," will allow Derrida to expose Heidegger's resistance to *Lebensphilosophie*, from whose clutches Heidegger would rescue Nietzsche. This section will also enable him to confront an aspect of Heidegger's Nietzsche-interpretation concerning which

Heidegger himself is least convinced. For Heidegger, *pace* Gadamer, is not convinced about whether one should vote "yes or no" on Nietzsche's putative biologism. He is not even convinced about whether one should cast a vote at all whenever it is a matter of mere catchwords. (One finds oneself wondering whether Heidegger would have found the terms of the present dialogue, for example, *Destruktion, deconstruction,* and *hermeneutics,* among the "catchwords.") His section on "Nietzsche's alleged biologism" ends with the sentence "We must learn to 'read'" (NI, 527/3, 47). Neither Derrida nor Gadamer cites it.

Derrida's two questions concerning the name *Nietzsche* and the notion of *totality* both turn about the issue of unity, the presumptive unity of a signature, and the presumptive unity of metaphysical inquiry into beings as a whole. To be sure, when Derrida puts into question the ostensible unity of the history of metaphysics as the sole backdrop for Heidegger's *Nietzsche,* he comes very close to voicing the objection that Gadamer voices against deconstruction of the metaphysics of presence. (A voice, it must be said, and we will say it again at the end of the chapter, that resembles Derrida's own of late.)[9] The history of being in Heideggerian *Destruktion* (presuming that *Destruktion* and *Seinsgeschichte* eventually coalesce in Heidegger) and the history of metaphysics as presence in Derridean deconstruction—how do they differ? Gadamer does not pose that question, but appears to accept the Heideggerian history, or at least not to challenge it, whereas the Derridean account of logocentrism and oneiric presence arouses his ire. Derrida will later ask: Who said a man carries a single name, and who said there was only one Western metaphysics? Gadamer will reply: You did! Yet he will never accuse the thinker who most at-tempted Derrida in that very direction.

However, it is clear that if the first unity Derrida wishes to challenge is that of "biography" and the "proper name," the second is Heidegger's "general reading of Western metaphysics." These converge in the third postulated unity, that of Nietzsche's own thought, in the interpretation that Gadamer found penetrating, piercing, and all-conquering: *durchschlagend.* Applying to Heidegger a formula that Heidegger applies to Nietzsche, Derrida seeks to think Heidegger's *pensée la plus pensante,* to plumb Heidegger's own *innersten denkerischen Willen.* According to Heidegger's foreword, the *Nietzsche* volumes indicate the path, the unitary trajectory, of Heidegger's thought over the seventeen years that separate the "Letter on Humanism" from the earliest seminars on "the essence of truth." The unities of Heidegger's *Nietzsche* and of metaphysics as such prove to be indissociable from the unity of Heidegger's own *Denkweg,* and for much longer than a brief moment.

The very signature "Nietzsche" is the mark not of a (now defunct) signatory but of a body of thought, a corpus. Of the "two ways" that Derrida sees opening here (curious that here again, as in the case of Gadamer, there are but two), that of his own *Otobiographies,*[10] in which one must take the risk of seeing the name dismembered or multiplied in masks or simulacra, and that of another, which identifies the proper name with the essence of the thought and allows the *particularity* of the individual to fall into oblivion, Heidegger surely wanders the second. However, when Heidegger excludes the empirical and goes for the essential (*"Was liegt uns Herr Nietzsche an!"*) his gesture is classically metaphysical, precisely at the point where it ought to be a matter of the consummation of metaphysics and the commencement of another thinking. The political rationale for Heidegger's exclusion of the psycho-biographo-biological in 1939 is of course clear, and Derrida is never blind to the force of such rationales; yet the reduction of the *who?* to a *what?* remains in service to a One, and is a metaphysical gesture. We recall that the same gesture and appeal loom at the conclusion of Gadamer's "*Destruktion* and Deconstruction," where it is a matter of demanding the One that would lie (truly) behind the Many. In Derrida's view, even the *Zweideutigkeit* of Heidegger's *Nietzsche*, which Gadamer too perceives, derives from Nietzsche's ambiguous position on the crest of the wave of metaphysics, repeating that history, remaining within it, while somehow bringing it to an irrevocable end—which itself, as *the* end of *the* history of being, would be singular.

It is doubtless time to complicate the picture. When Derrida asks of Heidegger whether he is sure that Nietzsche's name and thought are one, when he demands to know who it was who said that Occidental metaphysics is one, would we not have to reply as we imagined Gadamer might? Would it not be easy to comb *Of Grammatology* for references to that profound historical *necessity* by which all the binary oppositions of metaphysics (the one metaphysics) revert to the inside/outside opposition (the one essential opposition), and to one side of that one opposition, the inside of presence, the presence of οὐσία, *Anwesenheit, Gegenwart, Vorhandensein*—as thought by none other than Martin Heidegger? Indeed, who would not fall under the accusation that our language and our thinking (tend to) reduce to a One? When Derrida asks whether the reduction to unicity and to the propriety gathered in and by the proper name is nothing "more" or "something else" than the desire of the proper name, a desire suppressed by Heidegger, as it were, *in media vita*, when he asks whether any conceivable genealogy would not fall under the same monomania, must he not do so from within the selfsame circle of what he calls an "axiomatics"? If Nietzsche's multiplication of signatures, identities, and masks were to be counterposed to unicity as *la chose, la causa* of Nietzsche's thought, as *der Streitfall*, but still applying the definite article, would not a certain resistance to dissemination still be at work in the very counterposition? Derrida's conclusion to his "preliminary remarks" concerning Heidegger's *Nietzsche*, or rather to his own "ulterior" (not "future") reading of that work—his startling image of a fatal rescue operation in which the falling tightrope walker will be dead before he hits the net (remember that in *Thus Spoke Zarathustra* he lived even after smashing against the cobblestones of the marketplace), perhaps the most drastic portrayal of hermeneutic futility, hermeneutic fatality—leaves us with an uncanny suspicion about the chances of either hermeneutics or *Destruktion* or deconstruction. After all, ashes to ashes . . . we all fall.

Which brings us to the second of Derrida's questions, the one concerning totality, the totality of beings as a whole in Heidegger's *Zusammendenken* of will to power and eternal return. This conjoining in thought of will to power and eternal recurrence is at least by half precisely what convinced Gadamer about Heidegger's *Nietzsche*. Is Derrida also convinced that Heidegger's *Nietzsche* is most concerned to convince us of this successful conjunction? Is Derrida the simple obverse of the Gadamerian coinage, is he simply unconvinced? Whatever the case, is it possible to read the 1937 lecture course, "Eternal Recurrence of the Same," quite differently? I shall return to this question in a moment.

Heidegger is of course fully aware that the language of *das Seiende-im-Ganzen* and *die metaphysische Grundstellung* is foreign to Nietzsche, that it is, as Heidegger concedes, a "Kantian" importation. Nor would it be accurate to suggest that Heidegger's ambivalence with regard to Nietzsche's "alleged biologism" arises entirely from his allergic reaction to *Lebensphilosophie*. To be sure, the struggle to liberate his analysis of Dasein from *Existenzphilosophie*, which he needed in order to liberate himself from *Lebensphilosophie*, left its mark on Heidegger long after the 1920s. Nevertheless, throughout the Nietzsche lectures we find Heidegger fascinated by the "new interpretation of sensuousness," with "bodying life," with "some body who is alive." *Dasein lebt, indem es leibt.*[11] Thus Derrida's admittedly surprising revelations concerning the epigraph of Heidegger's *Nietzsche*, which (after Heidegger's excisions) begins with the words "*Das Leben . . .*," should not be too hastily interpreted as Heidegger's suppression of life.[12]

Nor does Heidegger's analysis of the guiding question of metaphysics (*die Leitfrage*: What is the being of beings as a whole?) cause him to suppress entirely the thought of *ashes* in Nietzsche, the thought William Butler Yeats called "life-in-death, death-in-life." True, his "summary presentation of the thought" of eternal recurrence closes by apparently accepting the presupposition that one ought to pursue the guiding question ("—presupposing, of course, that we wish . . ."), to see how chaos is susceptible of recurrence, to demonstrate that doctrine by "proceeding in orderly fashion through the entire labyrinth of Nietzsche's thoughts, mastering that labyrinth as we proceed" (NI, 355/2, 97). Yet is it a matter of pursuing the guiding question, or is it rather the far more questionable grounding question (*die Grundfrage*) that Heidegger wishes to introduce? Is it a matter of demonstration, penetration, and mastery, or of something far more subtle and—to use Heidegger's own word—susceptible? Had Gadamer, for his part, been less convinced by Heidegger's *Nietzsche* he might have invited Derrida to ponder at least two things.

First, the conclusion to Heidegger's reflection on Nietzschean ashes and dreams of totality, a conclusion Derrida neglects to cite:

> Perhaps two different views of the dead are in play here. If that is the case, then the very possibility of contradiction becomes superfluous. If the dead is taken with a view to its knowability, and if knowing is conceived as a firm grasp on what is permanent, identifiable, and unequivocal, then the dead assumes preeminence

as an object of knowledge, whereas the animate, being equivocal and ambiguous, is only a kind—and a subordinate kind—of the dead. If, on the contrary, the dead itself is thought in terms of its provenance, then it is but the ashes of what is alive. The fact that the living remains subordinate to the dead in quantitative terms and in terms of preponderance does not refute the fact that it is the origin of the dead, especially since it is proper to the essence of what is higher that it remain rare, less common. From all this we discern one decisive point: by setting the lifeless in relief against the living, along the guidelines of any single aspect, we do not do justice to the state of affairs—the world is more enigmatic than our calculating intellect would like to admit. (NI, 342–43/2, 85).

Are not Heidegger's thoughts on the cosmic *firebrand* much closer to Derrida's own thoughts on the *brûle-tout* than "Signatures" would suggest? From *Feu la cendre*, "Cinders," one brief extract:

Even so, one must know how to burn. This must be understood. There is also Nietzsche's "paradox"—perhaps Nietzsche is in fact something other than a thinker of the totality of beings—by which the relation of ashes to the whole no longer seems to him to be regularized by the inclusion of parts or by some tranquillizing metonymic logos: "Our whole world is the *ashes* of countless *living* creatures: and even if the animate seems so minuscule in comparison to the whole, it is nonetheless the case that *everything* has already been transposed into life— and so it goes."[13]

The second thing that Gadamer might have brought to Derrida's (and Lacoue-Labarthe's) attention is the fact that Heidegger's "summary presentation of the thought" constitutes a caesura in his thinking of eternal recurrence. Heidegger interrupts his close reading of the *communications* of eternal return in *The Gay Science, Thus Spoke Zarathustra*, and *Beyond Good and Evil* in order to offer a sketch of its configuration, or *Gestalt*, in the unpublished notes. The 1937 lecture course focuses on eternal return not so much as a metaphysical doctrine of totality but as a guarded communication—the telling silence that swathes the figure of Zarathustra. Heidegger himself prevents the thought of the totality of beings from consuming his entire reading of Nietzsche, prevents it here more effectively than anywhere else in *Nietzsche*, by heeding what happens "in the hero's sphere," in Zarathustran solitude, in the gateway *Augenblick*, where transition (*Übergang*) is demise (*Untergang*). A falling to ashes. In Heidegger's own text. "'For at that instant the full moon, silent as death, rose over the house and then stood still, a round, glowing coal . . .'" (NI, 439/2, 177).

NIETZSCHE'S HEIDEGGER/
GADAMER/DERRIDA

Would it not be better for all concerned to be less convinced both by and about Heidegger's *Nietzsche?* For every instance of bold *Zusammendenken* or critical questioning, and for every instance of vigorous reduction to a One, there is in Heidegger's *Nietzsche* a remarkably different gesture: "Yet we must guard against the presumption that we now belong among those who really understand. Perhaps we too are mere onlookers" (NI, 445/2, 181). And, with reference to Nietzsche's *Zarathustra*: "A book for everyone and no one, and consequently a book that can never, dare never, be 'read' complacently" (NI, 289/2, 36).

I do not mean to imply that either Derrida or Gadamer reads complacently. Far from it. These two thinkers belong in the fourfold and let it be: Nietzsche-Heidegger-Gadamer-Derrida—even if one is constantly reminded of Nietzsche's preeminence in the fourfold, his infectious eminence. Whatever shifts occur in that quaternity help us to see who we are encountering here, even if they never manage to meet one another, to wit:

The most impressive *interpreter* of our time, the most zealous and least jealous lover of slow reading, the thinker who remains more perspicuous than anyone else about the hermetic-hermeneutic circle of his own understanding, especially as it expands outward into foreign circles and becomes a passage of frontiers—in short, the supreme *hermeneutician* of the twentieth century: Jacques Derrida.

And the most romantic and adventurous of *readers*, the most flexible and gracious of conceptual thinkers, the one most open to conversation and amiable debate, the one who shifts the instant his position becomes too rigid—in short, the shiftiest and therefore most *French* of contemporary thinkers: Hans-Georg Gadamer.

EIGHT

Eternal Recurrence—of the Same?

Reading Notebook M III 1

I have no intention—especially after two chapters on Heidegger's *Nietzsche*—of arguing that Nietzsche's notebooks contain the essence of his thought or that they are to be privileged in any way over his published work. Yet it remains true that while the thought of eternal recurrence of the same dominates many of Nietzsche's plans, notes, and letters from 1881 through 1888, he himself shied from communicating the thought in his published work. The culmination of Book IV of *The Gay Science* and the heart of Part III of *Thus Spoke Zarathustra* thus remain among Nietzsche's most powerful and mysterious texts. Yet Nietzsche's literary remains are important for many of the thoughts we take to be particularly significant—recall, for example, the late notes on European nihilism. It seems to me that notebook M III 1, dated spring–fall 1881, which contains the first explicit sketches of the thought of eternal recurrence, is an extraordinarily important notebook. In what follows I shall restrict my remarks to the materials found there.[1]

Allow me to observe at the outset what in my judgment makes these initial presentations of the thought of eternal recurrence of the same both very telling and distinctly odd. While many notes cite the thought by name, including the words *des Gleichen*, "of the same," and while still more notes refer to the thought tacitly yet quite affirmatively, a somewhat larger number of notes attack any and every notion of "the same" (*des Gleichen*) or "sameness" (*Gleichheit*) as an unwarranted metaphysical assumption. Nietzsche's thought of eternal return of the same, alone or in combination with the notion of will to power, is often touted as *his* metaphysics. Yet how can Nietzsche, within the space of a few months, weeks, days, or perhaps even moments, both promulgate eternal recurrence "of the same" and decry every appeal to "the same" as the most flagrant of errors? I say the space of a few *moments* because some of the notes in M III 1, as we shall see, both elevate and denigrate *das Gleiche* within the same lines—in the same breath of writing, as it were.

If one is to keep score in this game of thinking eternal recurrence, where one cannot seem to win for losing, I should note that of the 54 notes in which I have found one or other tendency prevailing, 25 notes affirm eternal recurrence of the same, while 29 excoriate any and every notion of the same; finally, five further notes seem to oscillate between the two positions. In order to show the pattern and the juxtapositions of such tendencies, I list below the relevant fragments; those in roman type contain an affirmation of eternal return of the same; those in italic type offer a critique of the concept of the same; those in brackets betray oscillation between these two tendencies:

71, *102*, 121, *132*, *134*, *138*, 141, 143, 144, [148], 149, 152, *156*, *157*, 158, 159, 160, 161, 163, 165, *166*, *185*, [190], 195, 196, 197, [202], [203], 206, 213, 225, *231*, 232, 233, *235*, 237, 245, 254, 262, 265, 268, 269, 270, 281, [292], 293, 305, *308*, *311*, 312, *313*, *315*, 318, 321, 324, 330, 338, 339, 345.

I will not venture to resolve the dispute that has long raged in Nietzsche-interpretation, namely, as to whether the thought of eternal recurrence of the same is a cosmological hypothesis or an existential precept.[2] My focus will be on Nietzsche's strange science, his *cheerful* science, which seems to believe it can and must say very different things about "the same." I hope that by concentrating on Nietzsche's cosmological speculations in M III 1 something will become clearer about the relation of gay science to existence, and about the importance of the thought of eternal recurrence for both. Yet my more modest goal is to follow the faultlines and shiftings in Nietzsche's use and abuse of "the same," *des Gleichen*, both as eternal recurrence of the same and as the eternally contemptible metaphysical boondoggle. Of the 348 notes of M III 1, I will consider only the 60-odd notes that touch on the subject directly. And yet I will hardly be able to do justice to even this group of notes.

If one were to proceed chronologically throughout—although one cannot be certain whether the ordering of notes in the notebook corresponds precisely to the chronology of their composition, inasmuch as Nietzsche often used his books from back to front and front to back simultaneously—a first surprise would be in store for us. For the notes that affirm eternal recurrence of the same are sandwiched in between notes that are devastatingly critical of any use of "the same"; in short, no matter how one conceives of the order in which the notes were written, it seems undeniable that critical *and* affirmative mentions of *das Gleiche* and its derivatives (*des Gleichen, die Gleichheit, die Gleichartigkeit, das Gleichgewicht*, etc.) occur in the closest proximity—indeed, in the selfsame breath, so that sameness appears to be both the life-giving thought *and* debilitating error. I shall proceed chronologically at first, in order to communicate at least something of a *reading* of M III 1, which is anything but smooth, anything but thematically unified. Later I shall drop all pretense of a chronological reading and treat the notes thematically, beginning with those that affirm the same, turning then to those that lambast any appeal to "the same," and concluding with several notes that seem to hang suspended in indecision.

Gleichgültig, "indifferent," "all the same," is the first word of the notebook, as though *indifference* were being spoken prophetically in order to indicate the fate of "the same" in M III 1, and as though indifference were being used in the way Schelling used it, in order to mean not lack of preference but the location of a point prior to and fundamental for every possible future opposition. To be indifferent to praise or blame except within the circle that one cultivates for oneself—*für uns*, Nietzsche underlines—is the goal [1]. That would make us more scientific, inasmuch as the spirit of science thrives only in such profound indifference [110; cf. 10], yet also more autonomous, inasmuch as our naive confidence in what is in-and-for-*itself* is replaced by sensitivity toward what is in-and-for-*me*. The final words of the notebook thus appear to close the circle: instead of the *an und für sich*, Nietzsche invokes the *an und für mich*, adding the unanswered query, "To what end?" "For what?" "—*wozu?*—" [348].

Whatever the answer may be, the thought of eternal return of the same will have to satisfy this paradox or antinomy: it will have to abandon all egoism and complacency, embracing the indifference of the universe, and yet it will also have to embody precisely what is most vital and affirmative for the *me* who utters it. The thought of eternal recurrence of the same will demand radical rethinking and revaluation of life and death both in the *universe* and in and for *me*. For we have allowed our sensibility to convince us that it is superior to all that is insensate, even though we know that sensible pleasure and pain seduce us into every kind of superficiality, including the one that takes "the dead" to be extrinsic, "the living" intrinsic. And so, as though in order to mock those who will take him to be a consistently Zarathustran advocate of life, Nietzsche early in the notebook sings the praises of the dead:

> The "dead" universe! moved eternally and without error, force against force! And in the sensate universe everything false, everything puffed-up! It is a *feast* to move from this world into the "dead world"—and it is the greatest craving for knowledge to hold up against this false world, obscured by pompous thought, the eternal laws that suffer no pleasure nor pain nor deceit.[3] Is this the *self-renunciation* of sensation in the intellect? The meaning of truth is to understand sensibility as the extrinsic side of existence, as an oversight of being, an adventure. For all that, it doesn't last very long! Let us see through this comedy, in order thus to *enjoy* it! Let us *not* think this return to the insensate as a regression! We shall become altogether *true*, we shall be accomplished. *Death must be reinterpreted!* Thus we shall reconcile [ourselves] with the actual world, that is to say, with the dead world. [70]

Immediately following this elegy to death and to the insensate universe is the first foreshadowing of the thought of eternal recurrence:

11 [71]
To the degree that the universe shows itself to be *countable* and *measurable*, hence *reliable*—we bestow *worth* upon it. Prior to this, the *incalculable* universe (of the spirits—of spirit) had worth, and aroused more fear. But *we* see eternal **might** [*die ewige* **Macht**] somewhere else altogether. Our sensibility concerning the universe **is inverting itself: pessimism** of the *intellect*.

Here a third position for humanity seems to be working itself out: instead of either the sacred world of capricious spirits or a single arbitrary spirit—to which we shall have to return at the end of our account—or the profane world that submits utterly to human calibration, Nietzsche promulgates a world in which eternal power is enhanced to an as yet unknown potency. Whatever such enhancement entails, we may be certain that it has to do with that rethinking of life and death in the universe and in us. Herewith, one of the most famous and enigmatic notes of M III 1, a note we saw at work (in a somewhat different translation) in the preceding chapter; the final hiatus of the note gestures in the direction of eternal recurrence of the same: "Our entire universe is the *ash* of numberless *living* beings: and if the living still seems to us to be minuscule in comparison to the whole, it is nevertheless the case that *everything* has already at one time been transposed into life, and so it goes. If we assume an eternal duration, and consequently an eternal mutation of matter—" [84]. The note ends, tantalizing us with possibilities surrounding what will soon be called eternal return. Yet let us not pass this famous fragment by without noticing a difficulty, an ambiguity: " . . . *so ist* alles *schon einmal in Leben umgesetzt gewesen, und so geht es fort.*" Once transposed into life, every being must both quit life (in order to become ash) and continue to remain a part of life: *und so geht es fort— fortgehen* means both to continue and to depart. The cinder or ash Nietzsche is thinking of is not simply the dead universe, but a *trace* of the universe of the living. The thought of eternal return of the same may be a thinking of such traces, remnants of contradictory but coexisting trace elements. In a later note Nietzsche writes: "We can think of *becoming* in no other way than as the transition from one perdurant 'dead' state to another perdurant 'dead' state. Oh, we call what is 'dead' motionless! As though anything were motionless! The living is not the opposite of the dead, but a special case" [150].

Nietzsche has no doubts about the difficulty or about the trouble his thought is in for. The following note, while not mentioning "the same" explicitly, defines the quality of the *error* that "the same" will sometimes prove to be, namely, an error that one cannot put behind one, an error that persists, perhaps as a kind of essential errancy of the living:

11 [102]
　　Wretch! Now you have seen through to the life of the lonely one, the free one: and once again, as before, you have *closed off* the path thither by the knowledge you have gained.
　　I want to list everything that I deny, I want to chant the entire litany: there is no recompense no wisdom no beneficence no purpose no will: in order to act, you have to believe in errors; and you shall act in accord with these errors even after you have seen through them as errors.

From the 1873 "Truth and Lie" onward, as we saw in chapter 2, Nietzsche knows that belief in "the same" is among the cardinal errors.[4] The universe as *chaos* and *ash* is precisely that world in which our concepts, images, and sensations are jumbled by an entirely contingent toss of the dice: the human being remembers what the latest toss has conjoined, as though in promiscuous chemical combination, something "the likes" of which (*ihres Gleichen*) the world has not yet seen; however, it is merely the most recent error, destined to be engorged by the wretch whose life has come to depend on it [121]. Reason itself is Hegelian confidence that the contingent toss of the dice never introduces discord or discrepancy into being. However, Nietzsche's reading of Wilhelm Roux's 1881 work, *The Struggle of Parts in the Organism*, convinces him that because the advance of life depends entirely on the survival of the most minute discrepancies and advantages "in the tiniest things, in sperm and egg," the rational confidence in equality (*Gleichheit*) is in fact "a grand illusion" [132]. If reason takes itself to be the center of the universe, such centralization is a product of reason's fantasy life, *die Einbildung der Vernunft*, and is its greatest eccentricity and most disabling imperfection. Reason is the human being's way of devouring the world, nourishing itself on the foreign by making the foreign its own: assimilation itself is "*making* something that is foreign like unto oneself [*etwas Fremdes sich gleich* machen]," the kind of tyrannizing through dissembling and cruelty that constitutes our ravenous species. No matter how much Nietzsche inveighs against Herbert Spencer in these notes, and no matter how vigorously he criticizes the Darwinian expectation of *progress* through natural selection, the scene of reason in these notes is the Spencerian-Darwinian scene.[5] On this scene, and for this entire system of the mouth (see chapter 9), ingestion or incorporation is a kind of "making the same," and excretion the expulsion of whatever resists reduction to the same, while the mature individual that results from ingestion and growth inevitably reproduces itself by division into two [134]. Reason's devouring and aggrandizing activity is attributable less to imagination, however, than to memory, which is always memory of "the same":

11 [138]
Our *memory* depends on seeing the *same* and taking to be the same [Gleich*sehen und Gleichnehmen*]: thus on seeing *imprecisely*; memory is originally utterly coarse, and sees almost everything as the *same*.—The fact that our representations work as triggering stimuli arises from the happenstance that we always represent and sense many representations as the *same*. Thus it all comes back to our coarse memory, which *sees* the same, and our fantasy, which out of laziness *concocts* the same out of things that in truth are different.— . . .

After two brief critical notes of this sort, we read the note dated "August 1881," which appears to be sketching out a five-part book on eternal return. The title and the fifth part of the sketch specify eternal return as return *of the same*. However, the first three parts of the sketch emphasize incorporation or ingestion, including the incorporation of *errors*. The all-important fourth part, which is the only part the note goes on to elaborate, presumably constitutes a "transition" from sameness as error to affirmative eternal recurrence of the same. The sketch begins as follows:

11 [141]
                    The Return of the Same.
                         Plan.

1. The incorporation [*Einverleibung*] of the fundamental errors.[6]
2. The incorporation of the passions.
3. The incorporation of knowledge, and of the knowledge that knows how to renounce. (The passion of knowledge)

4. The innocent. The individual as experiment. The easing of life; degradation; enervation—transition.
5. The new *burden: the eternal return of the same.* Infinite importance of our knowing, of our erring, of our habits and modes of life for everything to come. What shall we do with the *remainder* of our lives—we who for the most part have spent them in uttermost ignorance? We shall *teach this teaching*—it is the strongest medicament, the one by which we shall *incorporate* it into ourselves. Our kind of felicity, as teacher of the grandest teaching.

Early August 1881 in Sils-Maria,
6,000 feet above sea-level, and much higher above all
human things!—

What seems difficult to the point of undecidability is the question as to whether eternal recurrence of the same is one of those fundamental errors that the race is said to have incorporated or whether the "transition" to a new "center of gravity" or "burden" separates eternal return of the same from all prior thoughts concerning "the same." No matter how we wrestle with "the same," the proximity of Nietzsche's thought of thoughts to his critique of the fundamental errors remains disconcerting. His elaboration of the fourth part of the sketch—which in its movement from "the innocent," through "the individual as experiment" and "the easing of life, degradation, enervation," to "transition" is itself ambiguous—thus gains in import. The opening words of that elaboration take us back to our starting point, the inception of M III 1 as such: "On 4) Philosophy of Indifference [*Philosophie der Gleichgültigkeit*]." What humanity earlier took with high seriousness, what in former ages irritated and stimulated humanity beyond measure, is now to be relegated to mere child's play: a life lived in "untruth" must of course be condemned as a matter of principle; yet it can, and indeed must, also be enjoyed and even cultivated. If knowledge and truth are (known to be) matters of incorporation or ingestion, then one must be able to wait and see whether a kind of humanity can evolve that would live on a steady diet of *knowledge.* The stakes of such an experiment are high: one must either look upon incorporation of all the errors and passions of the past with the eyes of a child at play—no doubt Heraclitus's child, playing games of chance on the steps of the temple—or one must die. Such knowing would know in the first place how to give itself over to life, how to close one eye for the sake of life and how to wink with the other at all the stupidities that have built the race—above all, perhaps, the stupidity that reduces all fine differences to rough-and-ready *sameness*, the stupidity that remembers precisely by means of the eternal return of "the same." An excess of pleasure must be demonstrable in and for such an eye; otherwise we must take the first active step toward the annihilation of an exhausted humankind—we must attend the feast of our own immolation. No wonder Nietzsche's elaboration of point 4 proceeds by way of contradiction and denial:

. . . we must weigh—and *also* outweigh—the past, our own and that of all humankind—no!—this bit of human history *will* and must repeat itself eternally, *this* we may leave out of account, we have no influence on it: even if all the same it should weigh on our compassion and prejudice us against life in general [*ob es gleich unser Mitgefühl beschwert und gegen das Leben überhaupt einnimmt*]. In order not to be overwhelmed by this, our compassion dare not be great. Indifference [*Die Gleichgültigkeit*] must have already worked its effects deep within us, and also enjoyment in looking on. Nor should the misery of future humanity mean *anything* to us. But whether we still *will to live* is the question: and *how* to live! [141]

Nietzsche emphasizes that this projected book of five chapters is to be an intensely personal one. If it summarizes the prior history of the race, it is nonetheless entirely personal in its pathos: " . . . the various *sublime states* I underwent as foundations of the various *chapters* and their material—as regulators of the expression, style, and pathos that hold sway in each chapter—in order thus to gain an imprint of my ideal, as though *cumulatively*. And then to go still higher!" Ironically, the thought that should cause Nietzsche to fly higher than any other is the greatest or the heaviest burden—both an ascensional engine and a kind of ballast. Nietzsche's formulation of it here is reminiscent of aphorism 341 in *The Gay Science*: "If you incorporate the thought of thoughts into yourself, it will transform you" [143]. However, once again, no praise or blame is called for: "If the thought of the eternal return of all things does not overwhelm you, there is no guilt in that; and if it does overwhelm you, there is no merit in it, either" [144]. Nietzsche is therefore *milder* toward his ancestors than they could possibly have been toward themselves.[7] He mourns their incorporated errors, but not their "sin" or their "evil." Again it is *play* and *innocence* that come to the fore in Nietzsche's response to the past:

1. *The mightiest insight.*
2. Opinions and errors transform the human being, and grant him or her drives—or: *the incorporated errors.*
3. *Necessity and Innocence.*
4. *The Play of Life.* [144]

The first extended elaboration of the thought of eternal return as a cosmological hypothesis pits one form of sameness against another. In what follows, Nietzsche argues that the play of forces in the universe never attains equilibrium, *Gleichgewicht* [148; cf. 265]. It is the *lack* of equilibrium that promises something like the circulation or return of the *same*. Nietzsche does not mention *das Gleiche* in what follows, yet "the same" is implied precisely in this universe of eternal disequilibrium:

11 [148]
The universe of forces suffers no diminution: for otherwise it would have grown weak and perished in infinite time. The universe of forces suffers no cessation: for otherwise cessation would have been reached, and the clock of existence would be standing still. Thus the universe of forces never enters into equilibrium; it never has a moment of respite; its force and its movement are equally vast [*gleich groß*] for every time. Whatever state this universe *can* achieve, it must already have achieved it, and not only once but countless times. So it is with regard to this very moment: it was already here once upon a time, and many times, and will recur as it is, with all its forces distributed precisely as they are now: and so it is with the

moment that bore this one and the moment that is the child of this one. Humanity! Your entire life will be inverted again and again like an hourglass, and again and again it will run out—one vast minute of time in between, until all the conditions from which you came to be will converge once again in the world's circulation. And then you will find again every pain and every pleasure and every friend and foe and every hope and every error and every leaf of grass and every glance of the sun, the entire nexus of all things. This ring, in which you are but a tiny grain, glistens always and again. And in every ring of human existence as such there is always an hour in which the mightiest thought will emerge, at first for one, then for many, then for all—the thought of the eternal return of all things—in each case it is the hour of *midday* for humanity.

Yet in the very next breath, or next note, Nietzsche denies that even in an infinite time things recur as the *same*. His example is from chemistry, whose descriptions and formulae cause us to believe that elements dependably combine as the same, time after time. Nevertheless, in the "eternal flux of all things" there is only "eternal change," so that an element like oxygen is "at no moment exactly the same [*genau dasselbe*] as it was before," even if its fluctuating nuances are "too fine for any measurement" [149]. Even so, in this mutable world of fluctuating nuances, the thought of recurrence of the same recurs: "If *all* possibilities in the order and relationship of forces were not already exhausted, no infinity would have flown by. But because it *must have*, there are no new possibilities, and everything must already have been here, countless times" [152].

The repetition of the word *time* in the notes we are now examining suggests that Nietzsche will have to prepare a new interpretation of time. That interpretation will have to clarify precisely what is meant by *eternity, infinity, succession, recurrence, return*, and *repetition*. Precisely how difficult such an interpretation will be is suggested by the following note. In it Nietzsche alters—but does not merely reverse—the order of implication between succession and causality as elaborated, not without pain, in Kant's *Critique of Pure Reason*:[8]

11 [281]
Succession alone produces the representation of *time*. Supposing we sensed not causes and effects but a continuum: we would not believe in time. For the movement of becoming does *not* depend on points at *rest*, on identical stretches of stasis.
◎ The outer periphery of a wheel, like the inner one, is always in motion; in comparison with the inner periphery, the outer one moves more slowly, and yet it is *not at rest*. "Time" does not decide between slower or more rapid motion. In absolute becoming, force can never rest, can *never* be nonforce: "slow and rapid motion of said force" *cannot* be measured on the basis of a unit, for the unit is not given. A continuum of force is *without succession* and *without contiguity* [ohne Nacheinander *und* ohne Nebeneinander] (for this too would presuppose both the human intellect and gaps between the things). Without succession and contiguity there is *for us* no becoming, no multiplicity—we *could* only assert that such a continuum were one, at rest, immutable, devoid of becoming, without time and space. Yet that is precisely a merely human *opposition*.

After an extended note on the impulse to construct experience in such a way as to guarantee a fundamentally fictitious *"uniformity of sensation,"* an impulse that invariably discovers that behind the dream of identifiable and perdurant equal moments there looms the reality of infinitely divisible, infinitely novel moments [156], Nietzsche begins to focus on the thought of the world's circulation, *Kreislauf*, as recurrent. His thoughts eventually come to expression in one of the best known aphorisms in *The Gay Science*, "Let us be on guard!" (FW, 109; 3, 467–69). What Nietzsche here (in M III 1) guards against is the temptation to conceive of cosmic cycles in terms of a striving toward goals. One must even be on guard against circles themselves, which since Plato and Aristotle are invariably circles of the same, whether in the divine head of the otherwise all-too-human body or in the outermost sphere of the universe.[9] In Nietzsche's view, no demiurge comes to order chaotic motion into the regularity of the circle. If there is a chaos of forces, "then that chaos too was eternal, and it recurred in every ring" [157]. The proper model of becoming is not that of celestial bodies or the tides, nor that of the circulation of the seasons, nor the alternation of day and night. The ring of recurrence is twisted at each point of its epicyclical surface.

A twisted circularity doubtless constitutes an odd article of faith, and the next few notes—like the note we shall reproduce at the very end of the chapter—comment on the odd religiosity that surrounds the thought of thoughts. It is a religiosity that grants itself infinite time, as it were, yet also looks to the instant, the moment that is closest at hand.

> 11 [158]
> Let us guard against teaching such a doctrine as an upstart religion! It must sink in slowly; entire generations must cultivate it and become fruitful on it—in order that it may become a huge tree overshadowing all humanity to come. What are the two millennia during which Christianity has survived! For the mightiest thought many millennia are needed—*long, long* must it remain small and powerless!

No matter how many millennia are needed, however, a certain urgency is felt, to wit, the urgency of the moment: "Let us impress the image of eternity on *our* life! This thought contains more than all religions, which despise this life as fleeting and teach us to gaze toward an indeterminate *other* life" [159]. So urgent is the task that it impels us "at every moment": "We should not be on the lookout for remote, unknown felicities and *blessings* and *bestowals of grace*; rather, we should live in such a way that we will to live again and to live *thus* into eternity!" [161]. And again: "My doctrine teaches that the task is to live *in such a way* that you will have to *wish* to live again—you will do so in any case!" [163]. Eternal recurrence of the same thus pertains to the art of life, as the existential precept that the existentialists have always insisted it was:

> 11 [165]
> We want to experience an artwork over and over again! One should shape one's life in such a way that one has this same wish with regard to each of its components! This is the principal thought! Only at the end will we present the *doctrine*

of the reprise of everything that has been, only after the tendency to *create* something has been inculcated—to create something that can *burgeon* and grow a hundred times stronger under the sunlight of this doctrine!

The juxtaposition of the next two notes, both quite brief, indicates once again how jarring Nietzsche's *critique* of "the same" and his *affirmation* of "the same" can be. The first [166] takes us back to Nietzsche's critique of the same as an oversimplified conjoining of merely similar things: "The similar is not a degree of the same: rather, it is something entirely different from the same." The second [167] does not mention the same, but it does refer to eternal return, and its *tendency* is certainly different from the foregoing note: "How can one bestow significance on the closest smallest most fleeting things? (A) By grasping them as the root of our habits. (B) By grasping them as eternal and likewise as conditioning the eternal."

In spite of such jarring juxtapositions, which any reading of M III 1 must learn to negotiate, allow me in what follows to break from the chronological reading and to order the remaining fragments thematically. I will be able to quote only a handful of the relevant notes, but will refer to as many notes as possible. First, to repeat, I shall cite the notes that tend to affirm eternal recurrence of the same; second, I will cite those that offer a critique of the same; third, and finally, I will cite those notes that appear to oscillate between these two positions.

First, the affirmations of eternal recurrence of the same—not that these affirmations are ever entirely devoid of critique. Notes 195–197 present plans and sketches for what will become *Thus Spoke Zarathustra*, under a title that endures throughout the 1880s, to wit, "Midday and Eternity." These plans merit extended quotation:

11 [195]

Midday and Eternity.

Pointers for a New Life.

Zarathustra, born on Lake Urmi, left his home during his thirtieth year, went into the province of Aria, and during the next ten years of his mountain solitude composed the Zend-Avesta.

11 [196]

The sun of knowledge stands once again at midday: and in its light lies coiled the serpent of eternity——it is *your* time, you brothers of midday!

11 [197]

Concerning the "Sketch for a New Manner of Living."

First book in the style of the first movement of the Ninth Symphony. *Chaos sive natura: "On the Dehumanization of Nature."* Prometheus is fettered to the Caucasus. Written with the cruelty of Κράτος, "Might."

Second book. Fleet, skeptical, Mephistophelean. "*On the Incorporation of Experiences.*" Knowledge = error that is organic and organized.

Third book. The most intensely intimate thing ever written, soaring across the empyrean: "*On the Ultimate Happiness of the Lonely One.*" That is the one who has reached the highest level of those who become "autonomous" by escaping from those who merely "belong": the complete *ego*: only *this* ego possesses *love*; at the earlier stages, where supreme loneliness has not achieved a celebration of the self, something other than love prevails.

Fourth book. Dithyrambically encompassing. *"Annulus aeternitatis."* Craving to experience everything once again and an eternal number of times.

Incessant *transformation*—you must in a brief period of time pass through many individuals. The means for that is *ceaseless struggle*.

Sils-Maria   26th of August 1881

(. . .)

The next series of three affirmative fragments consists of one "poetic" and two "scientific" affirmations—if we dare retain such designations at all. First, the dizzying poetic formulation, which will find its way into Book IV of *The Gay Science* and into Part III of *Zarathustra*: "Everything has come again: Sirius and the spider and your thought in this hour and this your thought that everything comes again" [206].[10] Note 213 argues that "an infinitely novel becoming" is contradictory, and suggests that such novelty implies belief in an infinitely waxing force, which would be the force of an "organicist," or what today one might call a "creationist," universe—which Nietzsche rejects. The suggestion is that in a nonliving, finite universe, return of the same must be the rule. Note 225 tries to accommodate the thought of circulation (*Kreislauf*) to that of chaos: the circulation of eternal return is not an expression of purpose or any rational necessity; it is an expression of neither formal nor ethical nor aesthetic freedom. Note 232 argues that although an infinite number of positions of force (*Kraftlagen*) may have occurred, these cannot be infinitely different: a finite and determinate force has only a finite number of possible properties, so that recurrence of the same is assured. Note 245 argues this position at length, but never confidently, and only by once again distinguishing equilibrium of force (*Gleichgewicht der Kraft*) from the states or conditions (*Zustände*) achieved by such force:

11 [245]
If an equilibrium of force had ever been achieved once upon a time, it would still be prevailing: thus it never supervened. The current state *contradicts* the supposition. If one supposes that there was once a state that was absolutely the same [*absolut gleich*] as the current one, such a supposition is *not* contradicted by the current state. Among the infinite possibilities, this case *must* have occurred, for up to now an infinity has already flown by. If equilibrium were possible, it would have to have supervened.—And if the current state was already there, then so was the state that bore it, and the prior state back beyond that one—the result being that the state *was* already *there* a second third etc. time as well—countless times, forward—and backward. That is to say, all becoming moves within the repetition of a determinate number of perfectly identical states [*vollkommen gleicher Zustände*].—Whatever is *possible* cannot of course be left for the mind of man to think through: however, among all possible circumstances, the present state is a possible one, quite apart from our capacity or incapacity to judge what is pos-

sible—for it is an actual state. Thus we must say that all *actual states* must already have had states *the same as themselves* [ihres Gleichen], presupposing that the number of cases is not infinite, and that in the course of infinite time only a finite number can come forward? because reckoned backward from every moment, an infinity has always already flown by? The cessation of forces, their equilibrium, is a conceivable case: but it has not eventuated, and consequently the number of possibilities is greater than that of actualities.—That nothing recurs as the same [*Das nichts Gleiches wiederkehrt*] could not be explained by accident, but only through an intention established in the essence of force: for, presupposing a vast number of cases, the accidental achievement *of the same toss of the dice* [des gleichen Wurfs] is more probable than the absolute never-the-same [*Nie-Gleichheit*]. [245; cf. 305]

If eternal return of the same has been reduced to a shaky probability in a world where actualities are privileged above even the most robust possibilities, Nietzsche realizes that he must rethink the value of possibility. He continues to insist that force is finite, even in an infinite time, and that even if force is eternally active, it can no longer be thought to achieve an endless number of configurations. In short, "it must repeat itself: this is *my* conclusion" [269]. Nietzsche is clear about the fact that his position is in response to a traditional *theological* position: "Whoever does not believe in a *cyclical process of the universe* [*einen* Kreisprozeß des Alls] *must* believe in a God who possesses *the power of free will* [*den* willkürlichen *Gott*]. Thus my way of seeing things is defined in opposition to all prior theistic ways!" [312; cf. 345, on the opposition between the scientific spirit and the "religious spirit that invents gods"]. Nietzsche is also clear, to repeat, that his position requires a new conception of time as recurrent successions of succession. Or, at least, his position requires a rethinking of Aristotle's suggestion (in *Physics* IV, 11; 218b 21–25) that time passes only for the mind (διάνοια) that is vigilant to its (time's) passing:

11 [318]
You believe that you will have a long period of rest before your rebirth—but do not deceive yourselves! Between the last moment of consciousness and the first radiant appearance of your new life "no time" lies—it passes by as quick as lightning, even if living creatures were to measure it in terms of billions of years, or could not even begin to measure it. Timelessness and succession accommodate themselves to one another as soon as the intellect is gone.

As one enters into the final pages of the notebook, the poetic and edifying rhetoric of eternal recurrence—recurrence as a *possibility* of existence—is heard once again, as these two final affirmative notes attest:

11 [338]
Future history: *this* thought will be increasingly victorious—and those who do not believe in it must, in accord with their nature, finally *die out*!

Only those who take their existence to be capable of eternal repetition will *remain*: among *such* existences a state will be *possible* that no utopian thinker has yet succeeded in reaching!

11 [339]

    Are you *prepared* now? You must have lived through every degree of skepticism, must have bathed voluptuously in ice-cold streams—otherwise you have no right to this thought. I will know how to resist facile believers and enthusiasts! I shall *defend* my thought from the outset! It is to be the religion of the most free most cheerful and most sublime souls—an enchanting meadow stretching between gilded ice and crystalline skies!

One might wonder whether and how the "dying out" of those who cannot affirm eternal recurrence of the same relates to the *feast* of death referred to at the outset of the present chapter. It would be ironic if precisely those who cannot survive the chillier universe of eternal return were dispatched—to the feast. Further, one might wonder whether and how the cold bath of eternal return of the same prepares one for that "lovely" or "enchanting" Alpine meadow where Nietzsche invites posterity to dally. Or is eternal recurrence of the same in fact a sunny plateau, a place of consolation, rather than a frigid stream of snowmelt? Is eternal return the most difficult thought, the heaviest burden or does it continue to show strains of what in chapter 3 we called the decadence of redemption?

    Whatever the case, let me now take up those more sober notes of M III 1 that resist and reject any notion of the same, sameness, equality, and so on.[11] Nietzsche argues that, apart from the question of the sequential *circulation* of the same, the simultaneous *coexistence* of same or equal entities is impossible:

11 [231]

The contiguous existence of two things that are entirely the same [*Die Nebeneinander von 2 ganz Gleichen*] is impossible: it would presuppose the *absolutely identical history of existence* [*die* absolut gleiche Existenzgeschichte] back through all eternity. But *this* would presuppose the *universal* absolutely identical history of the origins of all things; that is to say, everything else would have to be absolutely the same through all periods of time; that is to say, all the *rest* would have to repeat itself continually in itself, and *detached* from the two identical things.—But in the same way one can prove absolute difference and inequality in the sequence with only one instance of difference: *detachment* is unthinkable; if one thing changes, the aftereffect passes through everything.

    Equilibrium of forces is impossible because no force is divisible into discrete and equal units; qualities cannot be cut in half, and the "parts" of a force are incommensurable [233]. Because we treat force as though it were mathematically calculable in points and lines, we fall prey to the phantasm of identity or sameness. All theoretical science is ultimately *practical*, and its practice is based on "the fundamental errors of humankind, such that there can be things, and equal things [*Gleiches*]" [235]. Wherever differences of force are "small," we take them to be negligible: the result is that every similarity becomes an "identity": "We should say 'similar qualities,' rather than 'the same'—even in chemistry" [236]. Indeed, Nietzsche now takes blind belief in sameness or equality to be the origin of all experience of frustration and *pain* in the (organic) universe: "There would be no suffering if there were nothing organic; that is, without belief in **the same [Gleiches]**, that is, without *this error, there would be no pain* in the world!" [254].[12] Belief in equality, number, calculable space, and so on, is nothing else than incorporated error [262], the error that culminates in (belief in) the human subject:

11 [268]
In order that there may be a *subject* at all, there must be something perdurant there, and likewise there must be considerable equality [*Gleichheit*] and similarity [*Ähnlichkeit*]. In continuous change, what is *unqualifiedly different* could not be held fast, could be captured in nothing, it would flow like water over a stone. And without something perdurant there would be no mirror upon which extensive and temporal sequences [*ein Neben- und Nacheinander*] could show themselves: the mirror already presupposes something perdurant.—However, I believe that the subject would be able to originate whenever the error of the same [*der Irrthum des Gleichen*] originated; for example, when protoplasm always receives only one stimulus from various forces (light, electricity, pressure), concluding from the one stimulus that its causes are the same [*auf Gleichheit der Ursachen*]; or that in general *it is capable of only one stimulus*, and so *senses everything else as the same* [Alles Andere als Gleich empfindet]—and that is the way things must have transpired at the lowest stage of the organism. Belief in perdurance and equality *outside of us* arises first—and only later do we grasp *ourselves* as something *perdurant and self-identical* [Sich-selber-Gleiches], something unconditioned, in accord with our experience—over eons of time—of things outside ourselves. *Belief* (and judgment) thus must have come to be **before** self-consciousness: in the process of the *assimilation* of the organic this belief is already there—that is, this *error!*—This is the secret: how did the organic come to the judgment concerning the same and similar and perdurant? Pleasure and unpleasure are only *consequences* of this judgment and its incorporation; they already presuppose the customary stimulus of nourishment from what is same and similar!

Note 270 merely confirms this analysis: "*Stimulus* and *occasioning item* confused from the start! The identity of stimuli provided the origin of belief in '*same* things': the *enduringly same* stimuli created belief in 'things,' 'substances.'" The most polished of the critical notes, fragment 293, summarizes Nietzsche's skeptical position as follows:

11 [293]
We must remain forever *skeptical* with regard to all *our* experience. For example, we must say that we cannot assert the eternal perdurance of any chemical quality; we are not sufficiently *refined* to see the ostensible *absolute flux of occurrence*: what *remains* is there only by grace of our coarse organs, which bundle together and lay out on plane surfaces things that do not at all exist in *that* way. The tree is something *new* in each instant: its *form* is something we assert because we cannot perceive the most minute, absolute motion: we read a *mathematical median line* into absolute motion, adding onto it lines and planes in general on the basis of the intellect, which is *error*—the supposition of the same [*die Annahme des Gleichen*] and of perdurance, which we add because we can *see* only what perdures

and because we can *remember* only what is similar (or the same). However, in themselves things are otherwise: we dare not transpose our way of seeing things [*unsere Skepsis*] into the essence.[13]

Nietzsche's reading of the first volume of J. G. Vogt's *Force: A Realist-Monistic Worldview*, the volume impressively subtitled *The Energy of Contraction: The Ultimately Causative, Unified, Mechanical Form of Efficacy in the Cosmic Substrate*, published in 1878, causes Nietzsche to exclaim: "How irregular the *Milky Way* is!" [308].[14] His reading of Vogt, presumably along with J. R. Mayer's 1874 *Thermal Mechanics* and R. A. Proctor's 1877 *Our Position in Universal Space*, also convinces him that his own thought of cycle and circulation, which we examined earlier, must come under suspicion:

11 [311]
Is not the existence of *any form* of difference at all, and the nonexistence of perfect circularity in the world that surrounds us, of itself *sufficient* **counterproof** against a regular, circular form of everything that subsists [*eine gleichmäßige Kreisform alles Bestehenden*]? Whence difference within the circle? Whence the duration of this difference as it passes through time? Is not everything *far too multifaceted* to have originated from *one* thing? And are not the many *chemical* laws and, further, all *organic* species and forms inexplicable in terms of the one? Or even in terms of two?—Supposing there were a regular "contractive energy" in every center of force in the universe: then we would have to ask whence even the slightest difference might originate. In that case, the universe would have to disperse into numberless *fully identical* rings and spheres of existence [*in zahllose* völlig gleiche *Ringe und Daseinskugeln*], and we would have numberless *fully identical worlds* **next to one another**. Is this necessary for me to suppose? For the eternal succession of identical worlds an eternal extension? But the *multiplicity and the disorder* in the *world as known to us up to now* contradicts this; there *cannot* be such universal sameness [*Gleichartigkeit*] of development, inasmuch as a fully regular sphere would have to have been provided for our corner of the universe as well! Is it the case that the origin of qualities is in itself *unlawful*? Can differences originate from the force? Contingencies of any and every kind [*Beliebiges*]? Is it the case that the *lawfulness* that *we* see deceives us? That it is not a primal law? Are the multifaceted qualities in our world too a consequence of the absolute origination of utterly contingent properties? Except that in our corner of the world they no longer come to the fore? Or that they have taken on a *rule* that we call *cause and effect*, without their actually being such things (**a contingency that has come to be the rule,** for example, oxygen and hydrogen, viewed chemically)??? Is it the case that this "rule" is no more than a **caprice** [*Laune*] that has lasted for a considerable time?——[311; cf. 313]

The special significance of this caprice for organic life once again impresses itself on Nietzsche. In the following note he occupies a position quite close to the one that Freud will take up in his 1895 "Project toward a Scientific Psychology," for which the primal scene is not yet that of the Wolfman but still that of the suckling infant searching for—and hallucinating its way to—the nipple of the mother's breast.[15] Once again on his way to a system of the mouth, Nietzsche writes:

11 [315]

There have been countless *modi cogitandi,* but only the ones that conducted organic life forward were preserved—will they prove to have been the most subtle? —*Simplification* is the principal need of the organic; to see relationships in a far more compact form, to grasp cause and effect without a large number of intervening elements, to take much that is dissimilar to be similar—that is what was needed—thus an incomparably *greater search* for nourishment and assimilation resulted because the *belief* that nourishment was there to be found was excited quite often—a great advantage to the growth of the organic! *Craving* enhanced a thousand times by the thousandfold probability of satiation; the organs that *seek are thus strengthened*: groping about and failing to find may soar to incalculability, but the *favorable* graspings will **begin to occur more often!** *"Error"* is the means to *the fortunate accident!*

The question that becomes more and more persistent in these criticisms of "the same" is that of the relation between human presentation, *Vorstellung,* and the being—*Sein* or *esse*—to which presentation responds. Is human presentation crude and approximate, or has it been refined over the millions of years during which organic life has evolved? In other words, if error is in fact a groping for nourishment, is not such groping a perfectible requirement of (our) being, as it were? Is it not "built into" the system as a "transcendental" requirement? Is not *error* mere testimony to the ontological necessity of *trial*— if indeed *there is* life, and if life *must* nourish itself on life? Even if we dare not project our σκέψις onto being, does it not fall out with being in such a way that organic creatures *are there*, and that such creatures will cast the look they have to cast in order, if only for a time, to survive? By means of the bite? Would one not, then, at a certain point in the circuitry and circling of such critique simply have to *affirm* the eternal recurrence of the same as error *and* as being—perhaps what we heard Jean Granier long ago call the *duplicity* of being? Nietzsche seems to be approaching this paradoxical resolution with notes such as the following:

11 [324]

Presentation [*Vorstellen*] itself is *not* the opposite of the properties of *esse:* rather, it is merely the content and the law of being.—Feeling and will are known to us only as presentations; their existence is *not* thereby proven. If they are known to us solely as content of presentation and in accord with the law of presentation, they must appear to us as same similar perdurant etc. Indeed *every* feeling is apprehended by us as something somehow perdurant (a sudden blow?) and not as something novel in itself and unique to itself. It is something similar to [or] the same as whatever else is known. [324; cf. 325]

However, if this compromise position on presentation and presentative *esse* seems sometimes promising to Nietzsche, other notes reassert the predominance of error in and as *our* relation to being. Ironically, such error is emphasized in a note that has as its rubric "fundamental certainty." The reader does not know whether to take comfort in this titular certitude or to go on to plumb the depths of human errancy. At all events, error and errancy are not principally "my" doing; they are nothing that "I" have dreamt up for myself; and to that extent I can count on them as rock-bottom certitude.

11 [330]
Fundamental Certainty [Grundgewißheit].

"I present, therefore, there is a being," *cogito, ergo* est.—That *I* am this presenting being, that presentation is an *activity of the ego*, is no longer certain: just as little as *that which* I present.—The sole being we know is *presentative being [das* vorstellende Sein]. If we *describe it correctly*, the predicates of beings in general must be there. (Yet insofar as we take presentation itself as the object of presentation, will it not be saturated, falsified, made to tremble by the *laws of presentation?*—) *Change* is appropriate to presentation, *not motion*: rather, passing away and coming to be; and in presentation itself all perdurance is lacking; by contrast, presentation poses two kinds of perdurant things: (1) an ego; (2) a content—this belief in the perdurance of substance, that is, in substance's remaining the *same* as itself, which is in opposition to the process of presentation itself. (Even when I am speaking quite generally about presentation, as I am here, I make a perdurant thing out of it.) However, what is *essentially clear* is that presentation is *nothing stable*, nothing identical to itself [and] unchangeable for itself [*nichts Sich selber Gleiches Unwandelbares*]: thus the *being* that alone is granted to us is *changing, not-identical-to-itself*, has *relations* (conditioned, since thinking *must* have a content in order to be thinking).—This is the *fundamental certainty of being*. Now, presentation *asserts* precisely the opposite of being! Yet it does not therefore have to be *true*! Rather, this assertion of the opposite is perhaps merely a *condition of existence* for *this kind* of being, the *presenting* kind! That is to say, thinking would be impossible if it did not *misunderstand* the essence of the *esse* from top to bottom: it must *assert* substance and sameness, because knowledge of something altogether fluctuating is impossible; it has to *conjure up* properties for being, in order itself to exist. *There need not be subject and object* for presentation to be possible; but presentation *must believe* in both.—In short, whatever thinking apprehends as the actual, whatever it *must apprehend*, can be the opposite of what is![16]

If the "fundamental certainty" appears to shut down the possibility of eternal recurrence of the *same* as an occurrence *of being* and to allow it merely as a phantasm of human presentation, as the vicious circle of presentative being and the certainty of error, things in M III 1 are not so certain. We must now finally turn to the notes that seem to oscillate between the two positions we have identified as affirmative of eternal return of the same and critical with regard to every notion of "the same." There are, by my unsteady count, five of them. I have already presented the first of them, note 148, which affirms eternal return of the same precisely by denying the sameness or equilibrium of force in the universe: the impossibility of cessation and lack of *Gleichgewicht* guarantee (the possibility of) *des Gleichen*. Note 190 reaffirms this: "A weak equilibrium comes to the fore in nature as seldom as two congruent triangles. Consequently, there is no cessation of force in general. Were such cessation *possible*, it would already have eventuated!" The following note begins with a similar presupposition, namely, that force is finite *and* unfailing, yet arrives at the apparently opposite conclusion—that there *is* recurrence, but *not* of the same:

11 [202]
The amount of force in the universe is *determinate*, and is nothing "infinite": let us guard against such sweeping conceptions! Consequently, the number of positions alterations combinations and developments of this force, while vast, and in practice *"immeasurable,"* is in any case determinate and not infinite. In contrast, the time in which the universe exerts its force is infinite; that is, force is eternally the same [*ewig gleich*] and eternally active:—up to the present instant an infinity has already run past; that is, all possible developments must already have *been there. Consequently,* the current development must be a repetition, and likewise the moment that bore it and the one that originates from it, and so on, forward and backward! Everything was there countless times, inasmuch as the collective position of all forces always recurs . . .

I interrupt to note what readers will already have recognized: thus far, note 202 recapitulates what we have already heard in the later note 245, presented above; yet it is the turn that is now taken in fragment 202, the turn introduced by the underlined words, *"apart from that* [davon abgesehen]," that surprises us by engaging a critique of "the same"—to repeat, very much in the same breath. I continue the passage:

. . . Whether, *apart from that,* anything the same was ever there is entirely indemonstrable. It seems that the collective position forms the *properties* afresh, down to the smallest details, so that two different collective positions can have nothing the same. Whether there can be something the same in even one collective position, for example, *two leaves?* I doubt it: it would presuppose that they had had an absolutely identical gestation, and that would require that we *presuppose that back through all eternity* something the same subsisted, in spite of all the alterations in the collective position and the creation of new properties—an impossible presupposition! [202]

At this point, a little more than half way through the notebook, it seems that eternal recurrence of the same as a cosmological hypothesis can survive only as a *possibility* that can never be actualized. Moreover, it seems to be a mere possibility of *thought*, which is otherwise a sheer embarrassment in the universe. Even though the periodicity of seasons and tides was earlier rejected as a model for eternal recurrence, it is precisely to the power of the thought of periodicity to which Nietzsche now reverts:

11 [203]
Let us examine how the *thought* that something *repeats itself* has had an impact heretofore (the year, for example, or periodic illnesses, wakefulness and sleep, and so on). Even if circular repetition is only a probability or possibility, the very *thought of a possibility* can shatter and reshape us, not only sensations of determinate expectations! What effects the *possibility* of eternal damnation achieved!

Thus the notes that affirm the *mildness* of the thought of eternal recurrence of the same, its kindness toward all ancestors, contemporaries, and progeny, assume greater importance than we earlier realized. The power of the thought of return would be a subtle power, not a coarse one. That thought would abandon our thinking to a certain oscillation or vacillation with regard to recurrence of the same. It would contaminate our thinking with "periodic illnesses," as though thought itself occurred on the cycle of disease and convalescence, morbidity and (brief) respite, and as though our reading of notebook M III 1 were yet another instance of what one might eventually have to call "infectious reading." For it would recognize in the thought of eternal recurrence of the same a fatal affinity to a very traditional thought of divine creation—if only as the very thought that eternal return desires above all to *resist*. The thought of eternal return of the same would thus culminate not in a fundamental certitude but in a hiatus—which in German is called a stroke of thought, *Gedankenstrich*. Such strokes of thought were important to Nietzsche, as much for his commencements as for his terminations. In a letter to his sister written in Venice on May 20, 1885 (KSAB 7, 52–53), Nietzsche confesses that the "finest degree of understanding" he has ever had from anyone is a vague feeling that there is something "very remote and very foreign" about his thinking. He concludes: "Everything I have written up to now is foreground; for me, things always only get going with hiatuses [*mit den Gedankenstrichen*]." The final note I shall cite from M III 1 will be fragment 292, which appropriately ends with a stroke of thought—a stroke that may paralyze or possibilize our thinking of the same:

> Let us for once go backward. If the world had a *goal*, it must already have been reached: if the world possessed an (unintended) *final state*, it too must already have been reached. If it were at all capable of faltering and petrifying, if there were in its course but one instant of "being" in the strict sense, then there could be no more becoming, thus no more thinking, no more observing, of a becoming. If [by contrast] it were *becoming eternally new*, then it would be posited as something in itself *miraculous* and freely creative, *a self-creating divinity*. Eternal becoming-*new* presupposes that force increase by the power of its will, that it have not only the intention but also the means to *guard itself* against repetition, against reversion to an antiquated form, so that it can survey every motion at each moment with a view to such avoidance—or it presupposes the *incapacity* to wind up in the same position: that would mean that the quantum of force is nothing *firm*, likewise the properties of force. Something *un*firm about force, something undulatory, is altogether *unthinkable for us*. If we do not want our fancy to take flight into the unthinkable, and if we do not want to collapse back into the old concept of the Creator (increase out of nothing, diminution out of nothing, absolute arbitrariness and freedom in growth and in all properties)—[17]

NINE

Two Systems of the Mouth

An Oral Presentation of Novalis and Nietzsche

Who would not be pleased with a philosophy whose germ is a first kiss?
—Novalis, *Vorarbeiten*, 1798; 2, 329

I need *all* my bile in order to pursue science.—
—Nietzsche, M III 1 [120]

Genuine touches are mutual excitations.
—Novalis, *Das allgemeine Brouillon*; 2, 577

Suck dry your state of life and all its contingencies—
and then go on to another one!
—Nietzsche, M III 1 [304]

Eternal recurrence of the same, even and especially as a "fundamental error," remains to be eaten, eaten as what remains, as one of the remnants and leftovers of a long tradition. What sort of mouth can take in the thought of recurrence, not only in order to speak it out but also in order to ingest it and thrive on it? What sort of system can contain it? Or must the thought eventually be excreted? And must one eventually dispose of the eliminated thought before the danger of infection is too great, burning and obliterating all its traces? Yet *can* traces be obliterated? Can they be consumed without remnant?

In Plato's *Timaeus*—the archival belly and bowel of the Occidental mind— the Pythagorean astronomer explains that the universe was created a living sphere complete unto itself. It possessed no organs of any kind, certainly no organs of ingestion and excretion. For when there is nothing else in existence for organs to work on, no "other" to incorporate and excrete, organs are superfluous. Here is but one detail from Timaeus's portrait of the world (at 33c–d): " . . . Nor would there have been use of organs by which it might receive its food or get rid of what it had already digested, since there was nothing that went from it or came into it, for there was nothing besides it. By design [ἐκ τέχνης] it was created thus, its own waste [φθίσις] providing its

own food [τροφή], and all that it did or suffered taking place in and by itself."
Two millennia later, long about 1798, Friedrich von Hardenberg (Novalis)
overhears Timaeus declaiming to a silent Socrates. Novalis interjects: "If every
organic part had the life-duration of eternity, it would need no nourishment in
the stricter sense of the word, no renovation, no elimination."[1] Nietzsche then
interrupts: "The modern scientific pendant to belief in God is belief in the universe as organism: such belief makes me want to throw up."[2]

Timaeus talks so smoothly that we are likely to swallow whole what is
most puzzling about his remarks. Neither Novalis's shy intervention nor Nietzsche's rude interruption disturbs our devouring ears. There *was* nothing besides
the universe, nothing it could have eaten even if it had desired to eat, nothing it
could have desired to eat even if it had desired to desire, unless ᾽Ανάγκη or
Necessity counts, and she does. In any case: no organs of ingestion, digestion,
and elimination. Yet by the demiurge's design (for the demiurge *is*, and is outside the sphere, as are also—and preeminently—the εἴδη "up to" which the
demiurge "looks"), universal waste provides cosmic food. Why? How? Perhaps the sphere could have eaten the demiurge? Perhaps it could have munched
on Forms and sucked out the marrow of god? But no. Timaeus says that the
sphere's "waste" (waste? whence?) provided its own "food" (but, again, why
food, and how?). If there is no food taken in from outside, whence the waste to
satisfy cosmic coprophagia? Why and how food at all for a blessedly self-sufficient economy?

Yet we sense that Timaeus, for all his confusion, is grappling with certain "life requirements." Acting and suffering "in and by itself," present to no
other that it could eat or be eaten by, Timaeus's ostensibly animate universe is
in no comprehensible sense *alive*. It is instead smothered in its own surfeit,
pickled in its own toxins, as it were.

NAUSEA FOR DESSERT

"'Oh, Zarathustra,' the animals thereupon said, 'for those who think as we do,
all things themselves dance . . .'" (ASZ III; 4, 272). Thus commences the most
delightful ditty about eternal recurrence of the same in *Thus Spoke Zarathustra*. It is introduced by Zarathustra's urging his garrulous animals to chatter on:
schwätz also weiter! he cries. For where such delightful chatter fills the air,
the world seems to be a garden. "How lovely it is," exclaims Zarathustra, "that
there are words and sounds: are not words and sounds rainbows and rainbow-
bridges connecting things that are eternally distinct?" "Precisely between the
most similar things [*dem Ähnlichsten*] the radiant rainbow most beautifully
lies; for the smallest gap is the most difficult to bridge." However, Zarathustra
thrives on the prevarication, encourages and cultivates the error for the sake of
his convalescence, which is nurtured by the red and yellow berries his eagle
purveys: "Are not names and sounds bestowed on the things, in order that
human beings may take refreshment from them? *Es ist eine schöne Narrethei,
das Sprechen*: It is a lovely carnival, this speaking: by means of it, human beings
dance over all things."

Novalis's famous *Monologue* of 1798 begins with a very similar remark about language: *Es ist eigentlich um das Sprechen und Schreiben eine närrische Sache*: "Matters touching speaking and writing are really quite carnivalesque. . . ." The garrulity and clownishness of language, *die Geschwätzigkeit, die Narrethei*, impress Novalis and Nietzsche alike, precisely when it is a matter that touches their thought most deeply. To be sure, Nietzsche despises above all else the flapping mouth of Socrates, the prolixity that even hemlock takes so long to paralyze. Novalis too is said to have been an utterly garrulous young man, one who tried the patience of even his most intimate friends. Yet, like Nietzsche, Novalis worries about the gregariousness of the late Enlightenment and incipient Romantic periods: "Our excessive talk—the garrulity of our century is its general characteristic and its fundamental flaw" (*Fichte-Studien I; 2, 60*). However, Novalis concedes that there is something humorous about chatter, citing the works of Jean Paul and Laurence Sterne's *Tristram Shandy (Das allgemeine Brouillon; 2, 524)*, the latter also one of Nietzsche's favorite books from his adolescence on. Perhaps for all their intense and importunate earnestness, both Novalis and Nietzsche would best be read aloud in Shandy Hall?

Systems of the mouth—which is what I am about in the present chapter— include a great deal more than speech. For the mouth is also the portal by which all nourishment enters the body. Concerning this aspect of the system, Nietzsche invents the following catastrophic scene:

"But whatever happened to you?"—"I don't know," he muttered hesitantly. "Perhaps the Harpies flew over my table."—It occasionally happens these days that a mild-mannered, reserved, reticent human being suddenly goes berserk, smashes dinnerware, overturns the table, screams, runs amok, insults everyone present— only in the end to turn aside in shame, furious with himself. To what end? For what reason? In order to starve in isolation, in order to suffocate under the weight of his memory?—Whoever knows the cravings of an elevated and selective soul, one who only rarely finds his table laid and his meal prepared, will be in grave danger at all times. Today, however, that danger is extraordinary. Tossed into a noisy and motley age, in which one does not wish to share one's bowl, one can easily perish of hunger and thirst. Or, if one finally does "dig in," one can perish due to an attack of nausea. Probably each of us has sat down at a table where he or she did not belong; and precisely the most alert of us [*die Geistigsten*], who are hardest to nourish, know of that menacing dyspepsia that arises from sudden insight into and regret concerning our victuals and our messmates—*nausea for dessert*. (JGB, 282; *5, 230–31*)

Of course, the mouth has still other uses. In cases of emergency, we take in air through the mouth by gasping or yawning. In other circumstances, perhaps akin to emergencies, we kiss, with lips and tongue. In other circumstances still, the variety of which approaches infinity, albeit asymptotically, we suck.

In what follows I would like to compare and contrast two systems of the mouth, those of Novalis and Nietzsche, as though only the smallest gap separated the two, the gap most difficult to bridge. In the present case it is the gap between the kiss and the bite. By "system of the mouth" I am thinking of speech and expression, refreshment and nourishment, osculation and regurgitation—the entire corporeal canal and carnival onto which the mouth opens. For the most part, I will restrict myself in what follows to the unpublished notes of Novalis and Nietzsche, the excreta of their respective œuvres. For Novalis, the unpublished scientific-philosophical notebooks of 1795–1800; for Nietzsche, notebook M III 1, dated spring–fall 1881, which we worked with in the preceding chapter.

THE GERM OF THE FIRST KISS

Like Nietzsche, Novalis recognizes in human beings and in the universe in general the existence of a certain expansive force, a certain "drive to completion," *Ergänzungstrieb*: "If the sphere of a particular force expands in a particular way, the necessary result is a drive. Drive is the striving of a force to realize itself" (*Fichte-Studien III; 2,* 134). And, in some sense, the drive to expansion and completion is common to both knowing and ingesting: "How can a human being have a sensibility for something if he does not have the germ of it in himself? What I am to understand must develop organically in me; and what I seem to learn is but nourishment—something to incite the organism" (*Blüthenstaub; 2,* 232–33). Thus even when a philosopher asks for reasons and searches for the *grounds* of a phenomenon, what his or her spirit yearns for is nourishment—the appropriation (*Zueignung*) and assimilation of the object, the absorption of whatever has stimulated one, the transformation of what is *foreign* to something *the same as oneself,* flesh of and for one's flesh (*Vorarbeiten 1798; 2,* 418–19).[3] A later note adduces the rhetorical question "Are the external senses *devourers?*" (*Das allgemeine Brouillon; 2,* 504). Another note from *The Universal Sketchbook* observes the similarity between learning and eating: "Thus learning is quite similar to eating—and a priori knowing is satiety—a nourishing without eating" (*Das allgemeine Brouillon; 2,* 685).

For Novalis, however, the expansive force is as much palpation as it is ingestion; it is as much touch as grapple, kiss as bite, caress as engulf; such expansiveness—what Whitman was to call *dilation*—is philosophizing: "In the most authentic sense philosophizing is—a caress—testimony of the most intense love of meditation, absolute pleasure in wisdom" (*Logologische Fragmente; 2,* 314). For Novalis, there can be no doubt that the kiss is the nascent act of such philosophizing, the *incitement* of nourishment that leads to the embrace of the world. The kiss is therefore the act that communicates or mediates between the systems of nourishment and reproduction. In a long note preparatory to various collections of fragments (1798), Novalis writes:

> We seek the *projection* that suits the world—we ourselves are this projection. What are we? personified *omnipotent points.* However, the execution, as an image of the projection, must also be equal to the projection in its free activity and self-relation, and vice versa. Life, or the essence of spirit, thus consists in the engendering bearing and rearing of one's like [*seines Gleichen*]. Thus, only to the extent that

a human being engages in a happy marriage with itself, constituting a lovely family, is it at all capable of marriage and family. Act of self-embrace.

One must never confess that one loves oneself. Maintaining the secret of this confession is the life-principle of the sole true and eternal love. The first kiss in this accord is the principle of philosophy—the origin of a new world—the beginning of absolute time-reckoning—the completion of an infinitely waxing bond with the self.

Who would not be pleased with a philosophy whose germ is a first kiss?

Love popularizes the personality. It makes individualities *communicable* and *comprehensible*. (Amorous understanding.) (*Vorarbeiten 1798;* 2, 329–30)

The lips of self-embrace in Novalis's system of the mouth, which we will meet once again in chapter 12, may be two, four, or more. They serve as the portals of incoming nourishment and outgoing speech or song. Indeed, Novalis has a particular song in mind—Mozart's "*Wenn die Liebe in Deinen hellen blauen Augen,*" or "To Chloe," Köchel-Verzeichnis 524. Reflecting on the "musical accompaniment" that might suit various "meditations, conversations, and readings," Novalis writes: "I wish my readers were able to read my remark that the beginning of philosophy is a first kiss at the very moment they happened to be listening to Mozart's composition, 'When Love Shines in Your Bright Blue Eyes,' sung most passionately—if indeed they were unable to be in tremulous proximity to a first kiss" (*Vorarbeiten 1798;* 2, 331). Let it be noted that this most innocent of songs, Mozart's "To Chloe," nevertheless proceeds rapidly from first kiss to total exhaustion: *ermattet, ermattet* is the repeated word that resounds at the song's climax.[4] Likewise, Novalis's first kiss is not the last word. It is the overture to a growing warmth, the kindling of a flame, the leaping of a point outside itself in ardor and ecstasy.

The act of leaping out beyond oneself is everywhere the supreme act—the primal point—the *genesis of life.* Thus the flame is nothing other than such an act. Philosophy arises whenever the one philosophizing philosophizes himself, that is, simultaneously consumes (determines, necessitates) and renews again (does not determine, liberates). The history of this process is philosophy. In this way all living morality arises, in order that on the basis of virtue I act against virtue—thus begins the life of virtue, a life that perhaps augments itself into infinity, without ever confronting a limit. The latter is the condition of the possibility of losing its life. (*Vorarbeiten 1798;* 2, 345)

That the first kiss stands in proximity to both the caress and nourishment, both loving and eating, is suggested by the following three notes from the 1798 *Vorarbeiten.* The first asks, "What is the human being?" and answers, "A perfect trope of the spirit." It concludes: "All genuine communication is therefore full of sensuous imagery [*sinnbildsam*]; and are not caresses therefore genuine acts of communication?" (2, 354). The second relates such caressing and kissing to "magical idealism," a term that Novalis sometimes selects as a rubric for his system as a whole.

All spiritual touching is like touching with a magic wand. Everything can become the instrument of enchantment. Yet whoever takes the effects of such touching to be quite fabulous, whoever takes the effects of magical incantation to be quite marvelous, should remember the first touch by the hand of his beloved, the first meaningful glance from her, wherein the magic wand was but a refracted beam of light, the first kiss, and the first loving word—and then he should ask himself whether the entrancement and the magic of these moments too are not fabulous and wondrous, indestructible and eternal? (2, 354)

These thoughts on the refracted gaze, on the caress of light and love, on marriage with oneself and the first kiss—which, as we said, may be a kiss of two lips, or four, or more—these thoughts that are among the most sustained in the *Vorarbeiten*, culminate in a long note on philosophic nourishment:

The philosopher lives on problems, as human beings live on foodstuffs. An unsolvable problem is an undigestible foodstuff. . . . A digestible means of nourishment—that's the way everything should be. As for the condiments with regard to foodstuffs, they are the paradoxes in problems. A problem is truly dissolved when it is annihilated as such. So it is with foodstuffs as well. The gain in both cases is the activity that is stimulated by both. Yet there are nourishing problems, just as there are nourishing foodstuffs—whose elements constitute an augmentation of my intelligence. Through philosophizing, insofar as it is an absolute operation, my intelligence is constantly ameliorated—which is true of foodstuffs only up to a certain point. A rapid amelioration of our intelligence is as dubious as a sudden increase in our weight. The true step to health and improvement is a slow step—even if here too it is true that, as there are various constitutions, there must be various velocities in the sequence. Just as one does not eat in order to attain an altogether novel and foreign matter, one does not philosophize in order to find entirely novel and foreign truths. One philosophizes about why one is alive. If one were ever to achieve a life without any *given* means of nourishment, one would also get to the point where one would not philosophize about any *given* problems. Perhaps a few are already that far along. (*Vorarbeiten 1798*; 2, 354–55)

In the philosophic sequence, Novalis does not stop with the first kiss. He is interested in the ascent of the body and simultaneous descent of the soul, leading to the erotic embrace of coitus, *die Umarmung*, which he calls "the *dy-thiramb* [sic] among sensuous actions," a Dionysian hymn that, if it is to be judged at all, must be judged "in accord with its own natural laws" (*Vorarbeiten 1798; 2, 359*). Indeed, the first kiss implies an entire theory of embodied, erotic language and speech, which the following note develops across a considerable range:

Language to the second power, for example, the fable, is the expression of an entire thought, and it belongs to the hieroglyphism to the second power—in the *imagistic language*[2] [i.e., imagistic language *squared*] *of sounds and written characters*. It has poetic merit and is not *rhetorical*—subaltern—if it is a complete expression, if it is *euphonic*[2]—correct and precise; if, so to speak, it is an expression *that accompanies* and is for the sake of expression, if at least it does not appear as a medium but is itself a complete production of the *higher faculty of speech*.

Language in the genuine sense is *a function of an instrument as such. Every instrument expresses, coins, the idea of its composer.*

If one organ serves another, then it is, as it were, its *tongue*—its throat, its mouth. The instrument that serves spirit most willingly and is most readily capable of manifold modifications, is above all its linguistic instrument—and therewith the language of mouth and fingers.

As though in anticipation of what Nietzsche, from the period of *Human, All-Too-Human* onward, will call *die nächsten Dinge*, the nearest or closest things, Novalis's *Teplitz Fragments* contains notes on daily life—sleep, leisure, and (underlined by Novalis) *food* or *eating* [Essen], and *nourishment* (2, 385; 402). Novalis associates such questions with woman. He devotes several of the fragments to that figure—all of them given the number 17, the original of which reads "Sofie; or, concerning women" (2, 387), noting the name of his defunct fiancée, who died at age fifteen, leaving Novalis with love of wisdom alone. Interspersed among the notes on women are those related to number 8 of the *Teplitz Fragments*, on daily life and *eating* in particular. One of the later notes, a note that most successfully interweaves numbers 8 and 17, encompassing the two themes of woman and nourishment by the ring of *religion*, is the following:

> Eating is but an accentuated living. Eating, drinking, and breathing correspond to the threefold division in the body into things firm, things fluid, and things gaseous. The entire body breathes—the lips alone eat and drink—they are precisely the organ that excretes in manifold tones what spirit has prepared, what it has received by means of the other senses. The lips are so important for sociality; how very much they deserve the kiss. Every soft and gentle elevation is symbolic of the wish to be touched. Thus nature invites us all, elegantly and modestly, to partake in enjoyment—and thus the whole of nature must be female, virgin and mother at once.[5]

"Every soft and gentle elevation. . . ." The upper lip, no doubt, but—given the projections of Novalis's "magical idealism" as a whole—also any other part of the body that invites the lips' palpation. Novalis's "Moral Psychology" concerns itself with such sublime elevations: "The female breast is the chest *elevated to the status of a mystery*—the moralized chest" (*Das allgemeine Brouillon;* 2, 524). Such elevation to the status of a mystery expresses the very relationship of soul, spirit, and matter in the cosmos (see *Das allgemeine Brouillon;* 2, 527). Another of the many "number 8" fragments of the Teplitz group takes this thought in the direction of the eucharist, the meal of grateful remembrance. Yet because memory is unstoppable, the eucharist that commences with Christ the bridegroom ends with the milk[6] of the mother:

> The shared meal is a deed symbolic of unification. All unifications outside of marriage involve actions that take a particular direction, actions determined by an object, actions that are mutually determinative of that object. All enjoyment, appropriation, and assimilation is an eating; or rather, eating is nothing other than appropriation. All spiritual enjoyment can therefore be expressed as eating. In friendship, one eats of one's friend, lives on one's friend. To substitute the body for the spirit is a genuine trope, and in the commemorative meal for a friend we enjoy with a keen supersensuous imagination his flesh in every bite, his blood in every

draft. To our effete age, this seems barbaric—but who says they have to think of raw, corruptible flesh and blood? Corporeal appropriation is mysterious enough to be a lovely image of the way I make something *mine* in spirit. And then, are flesh and blood in fact so repulsive and low? Truly, there is more than gold and diamonds here, and the time is not far off when one will have a more elevated concept of the organic body.

Who knows what a sublime symbol blood is? Precisely what is repulsive in its organic components is what allows us to conclude that there is something utterly sublime in them. We shiver before them, as though before ghosts, and with childish terror we sense in this bizarre mélange a mysterious world, which may turn out to be something like a woman we knew long ago.

But to return to the commemorative meal: may we not think that our friend is now a creature whose flesh could be bread and whose blood could be wine?

Thus we enjoy the genius of nature daily, and every meal is a Mass—an agency for the nourishment of soul and maintenance of body, a mysterious means of transfiguration and deification on earth, an animating intercourse with what is absolutely alive. We enjoy what is nameless in slumber. We wake as a child wakes on its mother's breast, and we know that all this replenishment and nourishment came to us as a free bestowal of love. We know that air, drink, and food are the constituents of an ineffably loving person. (*Teplitzer Fragmente;* 2, 409–10)

The thought of osculation, succulation (to coin a much-needed word), assimilation, and nourishment is an ardent thought, a thought of the flame. It is thereby related to the combustive heat of fermentation, and thus ultimately to digestion and excretion. Among the *Freiberg Scientific Studies* of 1798–1799, the following note develops an expanded notion of excrement as excrescence or product:

4 kinds of flame—1. that whose excreta are the anorganic natures; 2. that whose excreta are plants; 3. that whose excreta are the animals; 4. that whose excreta are human beings. The higher the flame, the more full of *artifice*, the more complex the excrement that is formed.

All devouring is a process of assimilation, binding, generation—
The flame is *that which devours* in and for itself.
Fermentations—excreta too still possess the nature of a flame—they still devour—in the way, for example, that rust devours *metals*.
The metals that *decompose* water surely constitute such groups.[7]

As a thought of flame, Novalis's is also a thought of spirit. Any system of the mouth leads eventually to the thought of soul and spirit, sometimes by the more traditional route of speech and thought, sometimes by way of the thought of liquidity—of salivation, ingestion, assimilation, excretion, and reproduction. A note from the third group of notes for *The Universal Sketchbook* refers to a "simultaneous, mutually related *speaking* and *thinking*" as productive of a miraculous substance—*flame*—which "harmoniously excites and shapes both speech and thought" (*Das allgemeine Brouillon;* 2, 685). Another note from the first group of those notes offers insight into the more foreign reaches of this fiery complex—an uncertain insight, to be sure, inasmuch as the imbibing mouth or receptive orifice is difficult to locate with any assurance: "Semen is a means of nourishment and stimulation for the woman as a replacement for the *menstrua*. Thus in the most authentic sense the man *shares his life* with woman" (*Das allgemeine Brouillon; 2, 554*). Another note, within parentheses, also sheds light on this complex: "(*Life* in general is the genuine, absolute *Menstruum universale*—and the universal *coagulant*.) (There are infinitely many kinds of life. Every organ is *excrement* or *product* of *life*)" (2, 514–15). Yet another note traces out at greater length Novalis's strange itinerary toward an expansive system of the mouth:

> Held over against the life of animals, the life of plants is a ceaseless conception and giving birth; held over against the life of plants, the life of animals is a ceaseless eating and fecundating.
>
> In the way that a *woman* is the *supremely visible* means of nourishment, constituting the *transition from body to soul*—so the genitals are the supreme *external* organs that constitute the transition from the visible to the invisible organs.
>
> The *gaze*—speech—*holding hands*—*the kiss*—*touching the breasts*—*reaching down to the genitals*—the act of embrace: these are all rungs on the ladder down which the soul climbs. Facing it is a ladder up which the body clambers—to the heights of the embrace. *Premonition*—*pursuing the scent*—*the act.* Preparing the soul and the body for the awakening of the sex drive.
>
> Soul and body *touch one another* in the act. Chemically or galvanically or electrically—or *ardently*—the soul eats the body (and digests it?) instantaneously; the body conceives the soul (and gives birth to it?) instantaneously. (*Das allgemeine Brouillon; 2, 497*)

The soul, as animal, devours the body; the body, as plant, conceives the soul. And digests it? And gives birth to it? And excretes it? It is difficult to know what is ascent, what descent, on the ladders of love and nourishment. The only thing that is clear is that for Novalis the eminently spiritual ladder is the body of woman, with the eyes of her breasts the most visible means of nourishment, the folds of her sex embracing the invisible organs that are closest to the unseen soul of what in baby talk used to be called *man*.

A later note, entitled *Physical Doctrine of Meaning*, traces again in barest outline—and thus summarizes—the itinerary that Novalis's *Encyclopedia* was to have pursued, developing a system of the mouth as speech, ingestion, eucharist, and sexual embrace:

> Speaking and hearing are fecundating and conceiving./PSYCHOLOGY. *Shame*—shyness before an announcement—/ART. symbolic, religious mimicry—mimicry within the community—greetings etc. What, for example, does it mean to bare one's head?
>
> Synthesis of man and woman./PHYSICS. Basis of the hospitality of the ancients—*The Last Supper*—communal eating and drinking is a kind of *unification*—a generative act.

No doubt *laughter* is a topic essential to any system of the mouth, and if it were not for extrinsic constraints of space, it would behoove us to consider Novalis's reflections on it.[8] Let us be satisfied with the following brief meditation on excretory thought and the nourishing sensibility: "Is thinking too an eliminating—? Then sensing is perhaps a devouring. Self-thinking thought is perhaps a vital process—a process of devouring and eliminating at once, thinking and sensing at the same time" (*Das allgemeine Brouillon;* 2, 522). Perhaps the strangest of Novalis's thoughts on the system of the mouth, both humorous and profound, is the following note under the rubric "Poetic Physiology":

> Our lips often show great similarity to the two will-o'-the-wisps in [Goethe's] fairy tale. The eyes are the higher pair of siblings to the lips. They close and open a holier grotto than the mouth. The ears are the serpent that hungrily swallows whatever the will-o'-the-wisps let fall. Mouth and eyes have a similar form. The lashes are the lips. The eyeball is the tongue and the gums, the pupil is the gorge.
> The nose is the mouth's brow, and the brow is the nose of the eyes. Each eye has a cheekbone as its chin. (*Das allgemeine Brouillon;* 2, 557)

Tongue and lips—these essential elements of any system of the mouth, including that of Novalis's Mr. Potato Head—are the organs of speech. More than that, they are the prosthetic elements of language as such, reaching across space and time as a sort of primal *telegraph*. Long before the electric telegraph, there were the telegraphs of semaphore and light; it is to these that Novalis refers when he calls tongue, lips, and the other features of the mouth "parts of a telegraph," that is to say, of "an artificial linguistic instrument." He continues: "The eyes are telescopes—the telescopes eyes—the hand, as an instrument of language—acoustic stimulator and nonconductor—as paintbrush—as universal instrument of direction—*lever*, handle—as support, foundation" (*Das allgemeine Brouillon;* 2, 639). Yet the prosthetic, telegraphic aspect of tongue, lips, and hands should not conceal the essentially *eucharistic* and *voluptuous* character of the body and its communications, as the following note suggests:

> Dancing—eating—speaking—communal sensing and working—being together—hearing, seeing, feeling one another, etc.—all are conditions and occasions and even functions—of the efficacy of the *higher*—of human beings who have been brought together—of the genius, etc.

> Theory of Voluptuosity

> It is *Amor* that presses us together. The basis of all the functions mentioned above is voluptuosity (*sym[pathy]*). The genuinely voluptuous function is the one that is most mystical—well-nigh absolute—or the one that compels us toward *totality* of unification (mixture)—the *chemical*. (*Das allgemeine Brouillon;* 2, 666)

When and whether a theory of voluptuosity can fully satisfy its appetite for ardent, chemical unification remains to be pondered, inasmuch as Novalis's *Encyclopedia* never saw the light of day. Novalis approaches something like satiety—the elusive a priori—when his theory brings the systems of assimilation and reproduction to converge on the aperture of the mouth: "On sexual pleasure—the longing for *fleshly* touching—the delight taken in the naked bodies of human beings. Might it be a camouflaged *appetite* for human flesh?" (*Fragmente und Studien 1799/1800;* 2, 771).

INTERLUDE

Thomas Aquinas felt certain that people are better than trees. Trees stand on their heads and suck the earth, baring their nether parts as leaves to the sky. Humans are higher on the stairway to heaven, their heads closer to what Timaeus called the circles of the same. Unless of course those heads go down, in which case they are closer to hell than even the cottonwood. Which reminds me of an old story that comes from Umbria during the High Middle Ages.

Guillermo knew that the Father Superior's accusation against the two friars, Brother Felice and Brother Beatus, was too farfetched to be true. Even so, he had to investigate. That was his job. And so he made the two days' journey from Rome.

The two portly friars were accused of mocking the Eucharist. The fact that they were simple men of the countryside, earthy, pious, and entirely submissive, only increased their Superior's suspicion that it was diabolical possession.

Guillermo had heard of similar cases of possession, sometimes mass possession, evidenced by fits of uncontrollable laughter and lewd dancing. He knew of unspeakable heresies, unthinkable abominations, intermittent since ancient times. His interview with the two, hardly an inquest, occurred in the cell of Father Superior. It was a corner room of the monastery, with the lemon yellow light of the Umbrian morning entering through the two barred windows high overhead. The emaciated Father Superior sat wordless and unmoving in his high-backed chair. Brothers Felice and Beatus shifted from foot to foot, sweat pouring from their brows.

"My dear brothers in Christ," began Guillermo softly. "Perhaps it would be best if you told me in your own words what has happened to you."

Silence.

Then Beatus mumbled something in the dialect of his country, his gravelly voice scarcely audible, his eyes fixed on the stone floor, his mouth working against the guilt of the past and the catastrophe of an imminent future.

"It . . . happens . . . always at chapel, always at Holy Mass. . . . When the celebrant says *Take ye and eat!*"

Without warning, Brother Felice, at the side of Beatus, released a fearful snort. It was more a sneeze or a stifled cry for help than a laugh. He buried his face in the sleeve of his habit. Brother Beatus recoiled in horror, surprised by the inconsolable wail of a stricken cat that issued forth from his own mouth. He doubled over, as an unseen imp savaged his belly and ribs. Father Superior leapt to his feet, knocking his chair against the rear wall of the cell.

"Blasphemers! It is the most sacred doctrine of Holy Mother Church! The son of God offers himself up to you sinners for your salvation—*This is my body!*"

The stricken fratres collapsed to the floor in agonies of unholy laughter. Father Guillermo no longer had the presence of mind to compare the scene to reports he had read in the Holy Office. He had never witnessed such an attack first hand. He tried to calm Father Superior, seeing that the two men who were convulsed with laughter, now rolling on the stone floor, were beyond help.

However, Father Superior refused to be placated. He was mad with rage. Indeed, he raised his hand to strike a blow. Guillermo could not have known that the blow was coming down on him. For the judicious Father Guillermo, called in to grant counsel and render judgment in the case of the errant friars, could not see his own face contorted with the most unexpected and most irreparable of grimacing grins, could not hear the belches of sacrilegious laughter that now exploded from him.

NIETZSCHE'S BITE

The association with Novalis would no doubt have disquieted Nietzsche. True, as a teenager he was fascinated by him. In August 1859, at fourteen years of age, Nietzsche apparently came into contact with the scientific-theoretical notebooks of Novalis in his uncle's library at Jena. In his journal from that summer Nietzsche reports: "In the afternoons I usually read in uncle's library; there I discovered Novalis (whose philosophical thoughts interested me)."[9]

The principal reference to Novalis in Nietzsche's published writings occurs in the first part of *Human, All-Too-Human* (MAM I, 142; 2, 137–38), in the context of an analysis of "the religious life." There he cites one of the aphorisms from the late "Fragments and Studies," dated 1799–1800. Novalis writes: "It is quite curious that over such a long period of time the association of voluptuosity, religion, and cruelty has not made people aware of the intimate relation and common tendency among these three things" (2, 765). Nietzsche takes Novalis to be corroborating—albeit naively, unwittingly—his own thesis that the religious life and saintliness as such consist of certain vices driven to an extreme and camouflaged with piety. What is scorned and despised as vicious in the everyday world is elevated in the religious life to the point of adulation: the will to dominate, the capacity for both self-divination and self-contempt, the periodicity of lassitude and frenetic activity, the gift of transforming total humiliation into total victory, and "a bizarre type of voluptuosity."

However much Nietzsche takes umbrage against Novalis's critique of Goethe, and especially of Goethe's *Wilhelm Meister* (sees the notes at 13, 457 and 496), and no matter how much he derides Novalis's "naiveté," it is clear that Hardenberg is a brother when it comes to questions of voluptuosity and religiosity. This is particularly the case when, as we shall see in the following chapter, these intense movements of the soul are viewed in the perspective of health and illness. For the moment, let us restrict ourselves to Novalis's and Nietzsche's systems of the mouth, turning now to the Nietzschean counterpart.

As we have seen, Nietzsche's notebook M III 1 contains among other things the first stirrings of the thoughts of eternal recurrence of the same and of the universe as chaos and ash. The thought of nourishment or ingestion, *Einverleibung*, is omnipresent there as well. At the outset of the notebook Nietzsche announces his desire to expand the concept of nourishment, *Ernährung*, so that it includes a great deal more than what we call the preservation or maintenance of the body (11 [2]; 9, 441). A large part of that expansion requires that we disabuse ourselves of Kant's confidence in the teleology of nature and the freedom of the will. When we chew, the multiple and highly refined motions of jaw, lips, teeth, and tongue are nothing we ever "represented" to ourselves and then "willed." As Nietzsche says, "the *cleverness* of the tongue . . . far exceeds the *cleverness of our consciousness* in general" (11 [12]; 9, 445). Such teleologies are the final form of our representations of an efficacious creator God in the universe, a God who, Nietzsche now says, is *merciless* but not really very clever—certainly not as clever as a ruminant tongue:

> "I eat in order to have my fill." Yet what do I *know* about such satiety! In truth, satiety is achieved, but it is not *willed.* The momentary sensation of pleasure with every bite, as long as hunger lasts, is the motivation: not the intention "in order to," but the experiment that is performed with every bite, asking *whether* it still tastes good. Our actions are *experiments to determine whether* this or that drive will find its joy, down into the most intricate corners; our actions are playful expressions of a compulsion to act, expressions that our theories of purposiveness misinterpret and misunderstand. (11 [16]; 9, 447)

However, Nietzsche now identifies the craving for such teleologies as itself an expression of our *poetic* or *poietic* force: the images or schemata of our representation and memory *feed* such force and thus *found* our nourishing science: "Every scientific book that provides no fodder for the drive that wills to surmise [what is] bores us: *what is certain does us no good* if it does not want to provide nourishment for that drive!" (11 [18]; 9, 448). It is therefore difficult to say whether in Nietzsche's view the system of the mouth is clever or not: *our* cleverness consists precisely in *not* knowing the work of the tongue, or in our knowing in an abashed way that we do not know it. And our poietic force thrives on the mirage of the will, or on our willingness to let the mirage shimmer. It may all be error, but we bite into it, never achieving our fill. And that is what keeps us going.

In a sense, notebook M III 1 is not at all concerned with speech and language, a word that is mentioned, I believe, only once in its 348 notes. Instead, Nietzsche is here concerned with what transpires prior to all language—if such a concern is practicable or even possible. A note near the end of the notebook places the theme of language in (or *out*) of the context of the buccal system:

11 [323]
How altogether *erroneous* our *sense experience* is! All movements of ours that are derived from sensations are based on judgments—incorporated opinions concerning certain causes and effects, mechanisms, our "ego," etc. But they are all false! Nevertheless, even if we *know better,* as soon as we act practically, we have to act *counter to* our better knowledge, placing ourselves in service to the judgments of our sensibility! That is a *stage of cognition* that is much older than the stage at which language was discovered—a stage for the most part at the animal level! (9, 567; cf. 11 [325]; 9, 567–68)

Two things are happening already. First, a nourishing philosophy is succumbing to a philosophy of nourishment, whereby the science of eating nourishes itself on illusions, apparently thriving on them. Second, Nietzsche is on the (scientific? philosophical?) search for the origins of the aesthetic, cognitive, and moral judgments—and finding them in the gourmandism of that voracious creature whose bark and bite are equally pathetic.

A number of Nietzsche's reflections in M III 1 are strictly dietary in nature. He wonders, for example, whether, once we have measured out our lives with coffee spoons and imbibed our alcoholic beverages for over two millennia, these liqueurs and moccas will prove to have been poisonous (11 [45]; 9, 458). He also ponders the state of our ignorance concerning digestion, which is so much more than an affair of the stomach (11 [230]; 9, 530). He heaps scorn upon the vegetarians of Pythagorean persuasion, who should be consistent enough to refrain from devouring plant life as well (11 [266; 9, 543). Yet these dietary reflections prove to have enormous consequences, even though we usually ignore them. For we always take the short view when it comes to nourishment, not the view of posterity. Nietzsche would not be surprised if in the longer view a fault of nourishment and digestion created the very *ideals* of our culture—which would explain why both our ideals and our culture are so *depressed* (11 [113]; 9, 482). Still other notes go to the core of Nietzsche's famous "perspectivism," and even touch on his thoughts of will to power and eternal return. Indeed, one of the last notes of the notebook cites *will to power* as the instinct of the scientific human being (11 [346]; 9, 575). The drive of the hunter, the drive to nourishment, according to Nietzsche lies at the basis of the drive to private property and the drive to knowledge. The voracious animal is avaricious (11 [47]; 9, 459).

At the basis of all judgments, whether cognitive, moral, or aesthetic in the usual sense, are "aesthetic" judgments in Nietzsche's special sense (11 [78–79; 88]; 9, 471; 474). Preeminent among these primary "aesthetic" judgments is disgust or nausea, *der Ekel*. In the Heroic Age, although not in our own industrial utilitarian culture, the capacity to experience disgust is highly developed (11 [50]; 9, 459). The editors of the historical-critical edition of Nietzsche's works advise us to compare the following note on nausea or disgust with number 59 of *The Gay Science*, "We Artificers," the famous aphorism that leads to Nietzsche's reflection on women and their action at a distance. In the following note, not always coherent, never easy to translate, Nietzsche is searching for the provenance of our puritanism, the origins of our hatred of the body, the birthplace of our nausea and disgust:

11 [53]
    Purification of the soul.—**First** origin of *higher and lower.*
    What is aesthetically insulting in the inner human being, the human being stripped of its skin: bloody clumps of matter, filthy intestines, entrails, the whole sucking pumping monster—shapeless or ugly or grotesque, shocking to the sense of smell. And therefore *thought away into oblivion!* Whatever continues to emerge from the body arouses shame (vomit urine phlegm semen). Women don't even want to hear about digestion. Byron couldn't bear to see a woman eat. (Thus our hinter-

thoughts go their merry way.) This body *veiled* by the skin, the body that seems to *be ashamed* of itself! Cloaking those parts where its essence comes to the fore: or placing one's hand over one's mouth in order to spit. Thus the things that arouse disgust. The more ignorant a human being is concerning the organism, the more the following items are all conflated in his mind: raw meat decomposition stench maggots. The human being, to the extent that he is not a merely formal configuration [*Gestalt*], nauseates himself—he does everything in order *not to have to think about it.*—The *pleasures* that are visibly bound up with this inner human being are taken to be *lower*—an aftereffect of the aesthetic judgment. Idealists of love are enthusiasts of beautiful *forms* [Formen]; they want to deceive themselves, and are often indignant over the representation of coitus and semen.—Human beings have attributed everything shocking pricking provoking to this interior body: they have made seeing hearing and the configurations of thinking all the higher for that. The *nauseating* is thought to be the source of *unhappiness!*—*We shall learn to re-think nausea!*

   Second origin of the distinction between *higher* and *lower*. Everything that in-stills *fear* is taken to be *higher*; everything else is taken to be lower or even contemptible. What is taken to be **supreme** is what instills fear and is nonetheless beneficent and congenial! (9, 460–61; cf. 11 [253]; 9, 537–38)

What Nietzsche calls "aesthetic judgments" are therefore judgments of taste, taste by tongue and nostrils, as though all progress in culture were co-vertly *culinary*, or at least *gustatory* (11 [96]; 9, 475–76). Like Novalis, Nietz-sche too has a doctrine of condiments or spices (*Würzen*). Yet it is neither the superior quality of philosophical nourishment that impresses Nietzsche, nor the invention of unheard-of victuals, nor the surfeit of some sort of a priori, nor even the sweet milk of the breast, but the inveterate *error* of our ingest-ing ways:

11 [112]
   The essence of every action is as revolting [*unschmackhaft*] to a human being as what is essential in every foodstuff: he would rather starve than eat, so power-ful for the most part is his *nausea*. He needs *condiments*; we have to be seduced by every food, as we are to every action. *Taste* and its relations to hunger and to the needs of the organism! Moral judgments are the spices. However, in both cases taste is viewed as *that which decides the value of the foodstuff, the value of the action*: the greatest error!
   How does taste change? When does it become feeble and unfree? When is it tyrannical?—And the same concerning judgments of good and evil; a physiologi-cal state of affairs is the basis of every change in moral taste; but this physio-logical change is not something that always necessarily demands what is *useful* for the organism. Rather, the *history of taste* is a history all its own, and periods of the degeneration of the whole are just as much a consequence of taste as periods of progress. Healthy taste, unwholesome taste—these are false distinctions—there are countless possibilities for development: what always leads in the one direction is healthy; but it can contradict another development. Only when we have an *ideal* in view, an ideal we wish to attain, does it make sense to say "healthy" and "sick." However, the ideal is supremely mutable, even in one individual (the ideal of the child, and that of the man!)—and the *knowledge* we need in order to reach that ideal is almost always missing.

We follow the lead of our *taste* and we baptize it with the most sublime words—duty and virtue and sacrifice. We do not recognize what is *useful* about it; indeed, we are contemptuous of utility, just as we despise the interior of the body. We can bear it all only if it hides under a smooth skin. (9, 481)

For the most part, as I indicated above, our ideal is depressive: what we strive to achieve, what we devote ourselves to, may once have meant victory and its spoils, the pleasures of devouring, voluptuosity, cruelty, and dissembling; yet our madness, our Saint Vitus' dance is now the lurch of a guilty drunkenness, hypersensitivity, laziness, ignorance, aridity of spirit, and *Schadenfreude* (11 [114]; 9, 482). It is a wonder, given such a history, that the species is at all capable of elevated and elevating experiences: "We must always be astonished at a human being who, although he daily has to choke down many poisonous broths, nevertheless knows periods of great sensibility, and is not as a matter of principle nauseated by everything 'great'" (11 [328]; 9, 568–69). Yet precisely what alters our taste in all things remains the fundamental mystery for Nietzsche's system of the mouth:

11 [123]
Whence these changes of *taste* in morality? Do they run deep? Like loss of appetite in questions of nourishment, like the feeling of nausea and of displeasure in proximity to decomposition, smoke, etc.? Is it the case that for a certain state (in a nation, in a human being) its taste stands in relation to what is *purposive*? Or at least in relation to what is believed to be purposive?—Does it express itself in this way: "This is what I *now* need; that other thing I do not need"?—Or are they merely changes in what we are accustomed to, like our taste in foods, evoked by ready satisfaction with this or that thing at hand, so that our growing accustomed to something is born of the stimulus and the craving, whereas the opposite is *felt* in what is foreign and in what *stands opposed*? Or both? (9, 485)

Something like a *politics* of the mouth is implied in all this, a physiological politics based on Nietzsche's reading of Wilhelm Roux, *The Struggle of Parts in the Organism*. Nietzsche spells out this perhaps paranoid politics of incorporation, or excretes a particular form of its system, in the following long note of M III 1:

11 [134]
When we translate the properties of the lowest forms of living creatures into our "reason," the drives to *morality* result. Such a living creature assimilates what is closest to it, transforms it into its own (property is initially nourishment and the storage of nourishment); it seeks to incorporate [*einzuverleiben*] as much as possible, not only in order to *compensate* for what it loses—it is **avaricious.** That is the only way it can *grow* and then *reproduce*—it divides itself into 2 creatures. Growth and generation follow upon the unbounded *drive to appropriate*.—This drive causes the creature to exploit weaker creatures, to compete with those that are equally as strong; it struggles, that is, it **hates,** *fears, dissembles*. Assimilation itself is *making* something foreign the same as oneself, *tyrannizing* over it—**cruelty.**

　　The creature subsumes itself under an order, transforms itself into *functions*, and all but renounces many of its original forces and freedoms, in this way surviving—*slavery* is needed in order to form a higher organism, as are *castes*. The craving for "honor" is—wanting to have its function acknowledged. Obedience is compulsion, condition of life, ultimately a stimulus to life.—Whatever is best able to force other functions to subjugate themselves rules—the subjected functions have their own subjugated functions in turn—their continuous struggles: to sustain these struggles is, to a certain extent, the condition of the life of the whole. The whole, for its part, seeks its own advantage and finds opponents.—If everyone wanted to put "reason" in charge of things, always wishing to exert only as much energy and enmity as is necessary for *life*—then the driving force of the whole would *vanish*: functions of a similar degree struggle, they must continuously be on the *alert*, every weakness is exploited, the opponent *is on the lookout*.—A collectivity must strive for surplus (overpopulation), in order to produce a new collectivity (colonies), in order to break down into 2 autonomous creatures. Any medium that serves to grant duration to an organism *without* the goal of reproduction in view causes it to perish and is unnatural—like the clever "nations" of Europe nowadays.—Every body continuously *eliminates*, excretes what is not *useful* to it in the assimilated creature: what the human being despises, what makes him nauseous, what he calls evil, is *excrement*. However, his ignorant "reason" often calls evil whatever prods and discomfits him—the other, the enemy. He **confuses** what is *unusable* and what is difficult to attain, difficult to conquer, difficult to incorporate. Whenever he "communicates" with others and is "altruistic," it is perhaps merely the elimination of his unusable **feces**, which he *has* to void, in order not to suffer on account of them. He knows that such manure will be *useful* for foreign fields, and thus makes a virtue of his "liberality."—"Love" is a sensibility for property, or what we wish to be property.[10]

It would be important at this point to acknowledge once again that even Nietzsche's "thought of thoughts," the affirmative thought of eternal recurrence of the same, is at least initially thought on this dire scene of "incorporated errors" (11 [144]; 9, 496; cf. 11 [302]; 9, 557). In other words, eternal return is not an antidote or a change of venue, although it may be on a dietician's menu: it is a thought that must be ingested and its nourishing or noxious effects observed. Nietzsche's argument resembles that of Socrates in response to Cratylus: if all being were in flux there would be no knowledge of it, inasmuch as knowledge, ἐπιστήμη, needs something *upon* which it can *stand*—or, in this case, something it can *eat*: " . . . the ultimate truth concerning the flux of things cannot suffer *incorporation*; our **organs** (needed for *life*) are adjusted to error" (11 [162]; 9, 504; cf. 11 [286]; 9, 550–51). If life is the condition of knowledge, error is the condition of life. Yet Nietzsche's twist to Platonism is more than a tweak on the nose; it alters altogether the Platonic-Socratic denigration of art: "We must love and cultivate errancy, which is the womb of knowledge. Art as the cultivation of delusion—our cult." Nietzsche concludes:

To love and to further life for the sake of knowledge; to love and to further errancy and false supposition for the sake of life. To grant existence an aesthetic meaning, *to augment our taste for it*, is the fundamental condition of every passion to know.

Thus here too we discover that both day and night are conditions for *our* life: willing to know and willing to err are the ebb and flow. If *one of them* were to prevail absolutely, human beings would perish, and their capacity to be would be no more. (11 [162]; 9, 504)

Most of the points that have been developed above are summarized in the following note on the history of philosophy as the history of the search for truth, which in fact one might have to call the *history of nausea*, or, alternatively, the *history of happiness*:

So far, the history of philosophy has been quite *brief*: it is a commencement, it has not yet conducted wars and amalgamated peoples; the high point of its preliminary stage was the *religious* wars, and the age of religion is not yet over by any means. Some day one will take *philosophical* opinions to be questions of life and existence, as heretofore religious and political opinions were taken to be such. The taste and the disgust with regard to opinions will be so great that one *will no longer wish to live* as long as another opinion prevails. All philosophy will be experienced before this forum of mass taste and mass disgust. . . . Whatever corresponds to the necessitous life-conditions of the period and of the group will establish itself as "truth": over an extended period of time *the sum of opinions* of humanity will be *incorporated*, those having the greatest utility also having the possibility of the longest duration. The most essential of these opinions, on which the endurance of humanity depends, are those it has long since incorporated, for example, belief in sameness, number space etc. The struggle will *not* turn about *these things*—it can only be an *extension* of these error-laden *foundations* of our animal existence. . . . Thus it will scarcely be a history of "truth"; rather, it will be the history of an organic construction of errors transposed into body and soul, a construction ultimately controlling *sensation* and *instinct*. A continuous selection of what belongs among the living will be exercised. The claim to preservation of life will ever more tyrannically usurp the throne of the "sense for truth"; that is, this claim will *receive* and will refuse to relinquish the *name* of truth.—Let us individuals live our provisional existences; let us leave it to coming generations to conduct wars over our opinions—we ourselves are living at the *midpoint* of human time: **greatest happiness!**[11]

POSTLUDE I

Manger l'autre. "Eating the other." That was the title of Jacques Derrida's lecture course in Paris during the autumn of 1990.[12] The course was not principally about cannibalism, except in a metaphysical Novalisian sense. It all turned about a conundrum: all one can eat *is* something *other*—not just any other, of course, but the *nourishing* other; yet all ingestion of the nourishing other is followed by excretion, the elimination of what even in the most nourishing other cannot be assimilated. One can eat only the other, but the other can be consumed only with remnants, residues, excrement, and leftovers—*les restes*. There are always bits and scraps of *caput mortuum* and effluvium to be purged and hidden away, buried or burned by lime or by fire, or washed away into someone else's backyard.

Yet what is the *system* of such waste production and management? Does this system have anything to do with the other systems of the mouth—all of them touched by Gödel's theorem—systems such as speech and kissing? What would be the remnant of a pristine kiss? What would bring kissing into proximity with waste? Is every aspect of the oral system assimilated in the kiss? Is every aspect of the kiss consonant with the other systems of the mouth? Or are there residues and waste products even here? If so, can there be a wasting of waste, a perfect elimination of all that is unassimilable? Would such wastage be what philosophers pursue when they dream of the *absolute* and the *system*— and even when they dream of the philosophical *fragment* or the trenchant *aphorism*, inasmuch as the one who dreams of fragment or aphorism aspires to wholeness as much as any encyclopedist of philosophical science does?

I will not be able to pursue Derrida's questions here, although anyone who has dined out will understand the significance of the question of waste for all these systems. For every *rest*aurant has its *rest*rooms. Indeed, where does waste begin? With fermentation? With the controlled spoilage of grape juice, beet juice, salted cabbage, cow's and sheep's milk? Consider cheese for dessert, as in France, where a native will demand *un fromage qui pue*, a cheese that evokes a horrified "P. U.!" from an innocent abroad, a wedge of blessed corruption ("Blessed are the cheesemakers . . .") produced by cows who sneer. If you can get it past your nose your mouth will thank you. And will laugh. *Pourrir. Pour rire.*

To repeat, I will not be able to pursue Derrida's questions here. However, because my title, "System of the Mouth," comes from this course of Derrida's, I ought at least to acknowledge with grace the titbits that inform this chapter.

POSTLUDE II

Who will write the great poem of trimethylamine? Who will dream the dream that encompasses the dream of Irma's injection, putting an end to all stuttering and anxiety? The poem will draw us back to the sea, to which the Melvillean metaphysical professor is inevitably drawn; we shall dive in, headlong, head-first, and put our mouth where our money is. To Sándor Ferenczi's thalassal regressive tug, we shall pay more than mere lip service.[13] Not with a cessation of consciousness, but with an enhanced awareness and alertness. The great danger of our time is not contamination and infection but desiccation. Anaximander's "thorny fish" is now stranded, wall-eyed, and hears only the faint sound of pebbles receding on the shore, sensing its own decomposition and outrageous fragrance, the mislaid promise of its own misbegotten body. For the moment, and perhaps for decades hence, anxious about contagion, we shall no doubt prefer to be walruses and seals, preferring to suffer a "geotropic" regressive tug, instead. We now live in memory of cataclysm and catastrophe, and look forward to the impending shipwreck. We shun the sea. Life is killing us.

Who will write the great poem? If it should involve "the age-old intimate connection between the genital impulse and intellectuality,"[14] then let us put our minds to it. Circumscribe my lips, circumscribe my heart, circumscribe my entire face and head. If mouth and eye have a similar form, at least according to Novalis's system of the mouth, then let my mouth meet the face of Medusa, lip to lip. When I was a child, I trembled as a child. Now that I am a man, I tremble as a man. When I was Empedocles—bird, bush, boy and girl in one— I wept because the gods had flown. Now that I am Novalis and Nietzsche, I seek a kiss or bite of communion wherever I may find it.

The molluscular mussel, muscular and fine, with more gates doors portals curtains veils and folds than the many-chambered nautilus, ruddy red to purple, fine-veined, bathed in mother-of-pearl, most beautiful articulation! Novalis would say *the mollusc is the mouth of the thigh, if the thigh is the gorge of the torso, the knee the dimpled chin, the calf the nape of the neck, the foot the five-nippled breast whereon I rest my case.* Let the others go agape for ἀγάπη, I shall go for the upward curving, gentle elevation, the invitation. As we shall see in the final pages of the present book, Nietzsche too—if only as a figure of fiction—will follow Novalis's lead: he need not always bite.

Then let there be meals on wheels out on the town. Let there be underground gourmets. Let there be laughter in the churches, and secret touches, genuine touches.

TEN

Infectious Reading

Health and Illness in Novalis and Nietzsche

> What if I should become the prophet of this art?
> —Novalis, in 1799–1800; 2, 828

> Whoever is not at one with me on this point I take
> to be *infected* [infiziert]. . . . But all the world is not
> at one with me. . . . In all so-called 'beautiful souls'
> there nestles at bottom a state of physiological afflic-
> tion [*Übelstand*];—I won't tell everything, otherwise
> I'd become medi-cynical [*medi-zynisch*].
> —Nietzsche, *Ecce homo*

Infectious *laughter* is catching, highly contagious, and—as Father Guillermo
learned—almost impossible to bring under control. Likewise, I suspect, infectious reading. In what follows I pursue the metaphors of health and illness in
Novalis's and Nietzsche's texts, with brief references to Schelling and Freud.
My object in the present chapter is to pursue the problem of physiological decadence, whether such decadence plays a role in an inventory of genealogical-
critical techniques or in a thinking of eternal recurrence of the same. Once
again I shall call on Novalis for assistance, inasmuch as his meditations on
health and illness anticipate to an uncanny extent many of Nietzsche's insights
and obsessions. I shall focus on Novalis's philosophical-scientific notebooks of
1798–1799 and Nietzsche's *Ecce Homo*.[1]

In the *Poetics*, Aristotle asks what sorts of people are good at writing
tragedies and at creating poetry in general. His answer, at 1455a 21 ff., appears
well before the section on λέξις, or "diction," in which he seems to reduce the
art of metaphor to syllogism. Before the elevation of syllogism and reduction of
metaphor, this is what he says about the talents of the poet and tragedian:

> In constructing his plots and using diction to bring them to completion, [the
> poet] should put [the events] before his eyes as much as he can. In this way, seeing
> them most vividly [ἐναργέστατα], as if he were actually present at the actions, he
> can discover what is suitable, and is least likely to miss contradictions. . . .
> As far as possible, [the poet should] also bring [his plots] to completion with
> gestures. Given the same nature, those [poets] who *experience* the emotions [to be

represented] are most believable; that is, he who is agitated or furious [can represent] agitation and anger most truthfully. For this reason, the art of poetry belongs to the genius [εὐφυοῦς] or the madman [μανικοῦ]. Of these, the first are adaptable [εὔπλαστοι], the second can step outside themselves [ἐκστατικοί].

There is a long tradition, however, that says that those who are most gifted or talented, the supple, subtle, pliant, and plastic geniuses, are precisely those who often "step outside themselves" and succumb to infection, illness, and madness. As though the esemplastic power celebrated by Coleridge were a daimonic force that wrenches a poet out of herself or himself; as though the truly gifted were *vergiftet*; as though the makers of infectious reading materials were themselves infected writers—ecstatics, mantics, manics, and maniacs. Such as Nietzsche. Or those who suffer from deadly infections—for example, tuberculosis. Such as Friedrich von Hardenberg (Novalis).

A POETICS OF THE BANEFUL

Novalis's notes on illness and health appear principally in the context of his *Enzyklopädistik* (1, 477), an ambitious attempt to synthesize—or "symphilosophize"—the findings of all the sciences, whether natural or historical, with a transcendental philosophy and a universal poesy. His dream is to translate all lore, from the fairy tale to the findings of chemistry and physics, into a common code, which he calls the *lingua romana*. In the "Preliminary Studies" (*Vorarbeiten*) of 1798 Novalis writes:

> The world must be romanticized. In this way one will find its original meaning once again. Romanticizing is nothing other than a qualitative raising to the powers [*Potenzirung*]. The lower self is identified with a better self in this operation. Thus we ourselves are a kind of qualitative sequence of powers. This operation is still altogether unknown. Whenever I give the common a higher meaning, the usual a mysterious aspect, the familiar the dignity of the unknown, the finite an infinite appearance, in this way I romanticize it—Opposed to that is the operation for the higher, unknown, mystical, infinite—by connecting these matters we find their logarithms—They receive a customary expression. romantic philosophy. *Lingua romana*. Alternate elevation and degradation. (2, 334)

Between 1798 and 1800 Novalis sketches out his project for "the romanticizing of the world," a project he shares with his friend Friedrich Schlegel.[2] Here the lower and higher elements of the world are viewed as reciprocally and even genetically related, forever in transition from low to high and high to low. A privileged instance of the communication of high and low is, as we learned in the preceding chapter, human sexuality. If philosophy, the love of wisdom, begins with a kiss and is itself the first kiss, its search for the human soul culminates in the sex act, itself conceived of as an ingesting and engendering of soul and body. For Novalis and Schlegel, to be sure, the Roman or Romantic tongue is less what Hegel calls "the prose of the world" than cosmic, universal poesy—albeit poesy of an "algebraic" and "logarythmic" sort. One of the consequences of the project—the only one that I shall develop here, in preparation for a reading of *Ecce Homo*—is the radical relativizing of the concepts of health and illness, illness being "indirect health," and health "indirect illness," each in transition to the other:

> Just as illness is a symptom of health, so must health manifest symptoms of illness.
> 1. *Direct health*—2. indirect health. 3. Direct illness— 4. *indirect illness*.
> No. 1 elides with 4, as no. 3 elides with 2.
> Repeated *indirect illnesses* ultimately elide with direct illness, and vice versa— repeated indirect health elides with direct health. Indirect health follows direct illness as surely as indirect illness follows health. (2, 452)

A note from *Das allgemeine Brouillon* ("The Universal Sketchbook") of 1798–1799 reads: "The utility of illness—*the poesy of illness*. An illness cannot be a life, otherwise the *connection with illness* would have to *elevate* our existence. Continue this bizarre thought" (2, 475). The "bizarre thought" occurs to Novalis that the connection between life and illness might be elevating rather than distressing and depressing. No doubt he is thinking of the imbricated structures of sensitivity, excitability or irritability, and reproduction, as developed in the physiological systems of the Scots physician John Brown and his German disciples Karl Friedrich von Kielmeyer, A. A. Marcus, and J. A. Röschlaub, all associated with Schelling during the period of his influential work, *Von der Weltseele* (1798), a work that both Novalis and Goethe read with enthusiasm.

For the most part, Schelling's *Von der Weltseele* avoids discussion of illness and death.[3] Yet it is clear that when the decline and demise of the individual organism is introduced it will be in the context, and as a consequence, of sexual reproduction. The formation of the reproductive organs and the maturation of the sexual function occur only when the growth of organism is completed, and in many animals—Schelling mentions insects, which are relatively close to plant life—reproduction leads to demise. If growth is continuous individualization, such individualization reaches its zenith in sexual maturity; yet once the zenith is surpassed, only the nadir is left, and sexual maturity ultimately occurs "at the cost of individuality." When living things go to seed, they go to seed. In his next work, *Erster Entwurf eines Systems der Naturphilosophie* (1799), which Novalis also may have read, Schelling elaborates at greater length the sexual function in living organisms. Sexual reproduction seems to him both the "culminating moment" of natural development and the revelation of nature as a sequence of "failed attempts."[4] Whether the sexual function, the establishment of genus and species through two sexes, and the demise of the individual organisms reveal a monistic or dualistic structure in nature is Schelling's undecided and undecidable question. The obsessive and interminable footnotes to the text oscillate back and forth, sometimes toward a monism, but first and last veering away from all monism to a fundamental dualism. For dualism, duplicity, and polarity always gain the upper hand, as Schelling manages to preserve his identity against the one who will become Hegel. Whereas the Hegelian philosophy of nature will culminate in the identification of sexual reproduction as impregnation with the seed of death, and sexual division as original illness, wicked infinity, and the impotence of nature, so that a monistic philosophy of spirit can arise only from the ashes of nature,[5] Schelling refuses to abandon duplicity. Yet relinquish a common, universal cause, relinquish monism once and for all, he cannot:

> Thus a common cause of universal and organic duplicity is postulated. The most universal problem, the one that encompasses all of nature, and therefore the *supreme* problem, without whose solution all we have said explains nothing, is this:
> What is the universal source of activity in nature? What cause has brought about the first dynamic exteriority [*Außereinander*], with respect to which mechanical exteriority is a mere consequence? Or what cause first tossed the seed of motion into the universal repose of nature, duplicity into universal identity, the first sparks of heterogeneity into the universal homogeneity of nature? (1/3, 220)

It is at this point in the *Erster Entwurf* that a long discussion of illness supervenes. While the Brownian trinity of sensitivity, irritability, and reproduction provides the terms for the discussion of illness, a certain ambivalence concerning life in nature shows itself: while life relies on the duplicity of irritability, on the relation of the excitant to the excited, so that health may be defined as the continuous restitution of duality and death as "absolute homogeneity," it also makes sense to say that "life is a continuous illness, and death mere convalescence from it" (1/3, 222 n. 2). Schelling thus anticipates the problem of the "exquisite dualism" in Freud's *Beyond the Pleasure Principle*, which struggles to maintain the impossible distinction between the life and the death drives, impossible inasmuch as drives as such can only be thought of as erotothanatotic, that is, as matters of lifedeath, *la vie la mort*.[6] Schelling defines illness in terms of the graduated relationship between "exciting powers" and the organism's excitability or irritability. While he specifies the inverse ratio of sensitivity and irritability, he neglects to draw the third aspect of the triad—reproduction—into his account, perhaps because in sexual maturity culmination and demise lie too close for comfort. Hegel will not fail to draw the consequences that Schelling allows to hang in suspense, and if Schelling does manage to preserve his identity over against Hegel, it is as the one who never managed to draw the full consequences of that education he got in public. But to return briefly now to Novalis and his "bizarre thought" that illness might elevate rather than depress life—and that malady may lie at the conjunction of high and low, and thus at the heart of the Romantic philosophy.

The equally bizarre thought occurs to Novalis that, no matter how elevating illness in general might be, the soul itself, the very principle of life, may serve to aggravate the worst illnesses of the body. Indeed, Novalis, who knows the secret ambivalence of all φάρμακα, now speculates that the soul itself might be the most poisonous of entities:

> Among all *poisons* the *soul* is the strongest. It is the most penetrating, the most diffuse stimulus. All the effects of the soul are therefore supremely harmful when it is a question of local illness and infection.

A local illness often cannot be cured except by means of a general illness, and vice versa.

Curing *one illness* by means of *another*. (2, 706)

Finally, the utterly bizarre thought occurs to Novalis that sheer *love* of illness can transform malady into "supreme, positive pleasure," that illness may be a means toward higher synthesis, a means of returning to intimacy with nature. To such intimacy the poet gives the name of his dead fiancée, *Sophie*. Such uncanny thinking would involve, to repeat, *eine Poetik des Übels*, a poetics of the baneful and malignant. "Does not the best everywhere begin with *illness*?" Novalis asks, setting for his poetics the theme "On the attractive force of the dire" (2, 628). In one of the final notes, he elaborates as follows:

Illnesses are surely a *supremely important object for humanity*, for they are numberless, and each human being has to struggle with them so often. It is only that we know so little about the art of using them. They are probably the most interesting stimulus to our meditation and our activity. . . . What if I should become the prophet of this art? [*Wie wenn ich Profet dieser Kunst werden sollte?*]. (2, 828)

THE BIOPOSITIVE EFFECTS OF INFECTION

The immediate context for my remarks on Nietzsche's *Ecce Homo* is the second chapter of Pierre Klossowski's *Nietzsche et le cercle vicieux*, on the "valetudinarian states."[7] However, whereas Klossowski raises the question of Nietzsche's thought as a periodic battle with migraine, I wish to relate his thought to the matter of infection. What *is* infection? Even for allopathic medicine, which takes it to be an attack *from without*, an invasion by a bacillus or virus, the threat to the organism is always elaborated *from within*. Infection represents a kind of fifth column, the betrayal or treason of the body, or parts of the body, against the body as a whole. Such betrayal threatens to terminate the body's irreversible life history. Here the Freudian detour becomes the royal road to irremediable demise; here the body goes to meet the primeval Chaos out of which, according to the myth in Plato's *Statesman*, it is said to have arisen and to which it returns. Infection would therefore comprise at least a part of Nietzsche's "secret phantasm," as Klossowski describes it: Nietzsche dreams of investigating a culture that functions according to nonlinguistic forces (*des forces de la non-parole*). Pursuing such investigations and writing up their results would require a *language* that tries to make itself heard and understood at the expense of reason—something like a *lingua romana*, if indeed romance invariably falls in love with demise and death.

Inevitably, Freud's speculations on the economy of lifedeath in the 1895 "Project" and the 1920 *Beyond the Pleasure Principle* form a more distant yet haunting context for any infectious reading. So too do the speculations of biologists such as Eugen Korschelt on the role of disease and decline in the life span of individual plant and animal species. Heidegger cites these speculations at a crucial moment in his *existential* analysis of death, even though fundamental ontology prides itself on the distance it believes it can take from mere biology.[8]

Finally, the speculations of the psychiatrists who have involved themselves in "the Nietzsche case" constitute an irritating, insistent context. The principal sources here are Poul Bjerre, the Swedish psychiatrist writing in 1905, and Karl Jaspers and Wilhelm Lange-Eichbaum, writing in the 1930s. Curt Paul Janz summarizes their findings—and speculations—at the outset of volume two of his three-volume biography. The psychiatrists suggest that there is evidence of "biopositive effects," at least for a poet and thinker such as Nietzsche, of infection with *Lues* or syphilis.[9] Adopting their voice, Janz writes:

> Precisely in the case of luetic infection, as with other infections such as tuberculosis, research teaches us that certain life functions are at least for a time stimulated and enhanced; that an effect similar to that of certain narcotics—alcohol, for example—is produced, such that specific energies and possibilities of fantasy are released, energies and possibilities otherwise suppressed or repressed in the "normal" organism.[10]

Janz's question is: What if the suppression or repression of the energies that are necessary for the "free play of the spirit" were the condition of good health, so that well-being necessitates a dulling of the creative edge, a certain benevolent torpor; what if, from the point of view of the harmonious interplay of the creative faculties at the highest level, after the manner of Kant, robust good health were in fact the genuine psychopathogenic disturbance? Janz embraces the thought that so affrights Jaspers: not that Nietzsche's thought is sick, but that "sick" is impossible to define in sheer opposition to biopositive effects. Whereas Jaspers feels constrained to admit that the factor of illness "not only disturbed but also perhaps even made possible what otherwise would never have come to be"—meaning the writings of the 1880s, from *Daybreak* to the *Dionysos-Dithyrambs*, Bjerre, Lange-Eichbaum, and Janz affirm the biopositive effects of illness with some enthusiasm, albeit with trepidation.

Poul Bjerre had speculated early in the century on "the chronic, mild, intoxicating effect [*Rauschwirkung*]" of luetic infection, as though Dionysian rapture were dependent on noxious chemical secretions of a particular bacillus or spirochaeta, *Treponema pallidum*. From some unknown original moment of infection—whether in the mid-1860s while a student at Bonn or Leipzig, or in 1870 during the Franco-Prussian War, or in 1876–1877 while on ill-health leave in Sorrento, and so on, seemingly endlessly, as the speculations run—up to the collapse on January 3, 1889, the infection would have exerted a biopositive influence, as though both instigating and helping to combat the migraines, the vomiting, and the approaching blindness.

Lange-Eichbaum himself waxes lyrical, even as he diagnoses.[11] He detects "the euphoric mood," the "uninhibitedness," and the "manic traits" of Nietzsche's writings, especially *Ecce Homo*. He appeals to both classical pathology and the tradition of *Existenzphilosophie*, which has taught him that "to the existence of human beings the morbid too belongs, something that acts as a ferment, a stimulus, keeping the living flame in motion, just as sourdough is indispensable for bread, and shadow and the dark for light." It is after all "the inner disquiet in the blood" that spurs thinking and poetry. And, in the midst of the doctor's own sober analysis, armed to the teeth with the technical jargon of the pathologist's *lingua franca*, if not *romana*, the parade of metaphors marches by, and all of them mixed, all of them wildly catachretic: flames that walk, sourdough with chiaroscuro, and disquiet in the blood. Infectious reading is here a delectation for the Thomas Mann of *Doktor Faustus* and *Der Zauberberg*, something for the European twilight and dusk of the 1920s and 1930s.

When the doctors set their metaphors in motion alongside their Latin and Greek germs, we nowadays may be inclined to laugh or to shout, paraphrasing Emerson, "Doctor, infect thyself!" It does seem a mystification, for the usual purposes of manipulation and control, and our "social-critical" and "humanistic" impulses alike rebel.[12] Yet we are unnerved by the doctors even as we shout. For we recall Nietzsche's letter to his doctor, Otto Eiser, in early January 1880 (KSAB, 6, 3–4). After a veritable litany of complaints, the distraught patient adds this postscript: "As a whole, I am happier than ever before in my life." To be sure, no chemical secretion on its own produces either *The Gay Science* or *Zarathustra*. And, at all events, neither the *lingua romana* nor the *lingua franca* of modern medicine is advanced enough to specify the chemical name of the specific intoxicant—assuming there is only one. Lange-Eichbaum does not give us the equivalent of Freud and Ferenczi's trimethylamine, the elixir of "Irma's injection" and of *Thalassa*. Yet it does seem, as both Jaspers and Janz suspect, that especially after 1880 something dismantles "the threshold of inhibition" in Nietzsche; it does seem that something enhances the euphoria and gradually illumines the transfiguration to the burning point. Perhaps some molecular, miasmic Mistral blows in the halcyon skies of Nietzsche's most exhilarating writing?

Admittedly, we have no way to *think* this biopositive impact: either we reduce Nietzsche's creativity to the crudest sorts of objectivist, positivistic determinations, or we idealize his productivity and snatch it away from his body. Worse, after the research and speculations of Weismann, Bernstein, Korschelt, Simmel, and Freud, we hardly know what to make of pathogenesis in general: if death is immanent in and intrinsic to life, if life is the economy of lifedeath, then what *are* infection, disease, dissolution, and demise? If Spinoza's mosquito (carrying malaria, no doubt) imagines itself the center of the universe, what sorts of airs will the bacillus and virus put on—the virus in its free and infectious state being a non-self-replicable yet eminently successful scion of life? Whether we emphasize the allopathic germ theory of disease, with its sepsis, antigens, and antibodies, or the homeopathic account, which lays more stress on the receptivity of the soil than the virulence of the seed, we are unaccustomed to taking seriously the reaction of thought *to* and *in* the diseased body, the body forever ill-at-ease, the body whose mind hovers on the very verge of delirium. Yet if Klossowski is right, this relation is what Nietzsche most wanted to think. If Novalis is the prophet of this new art, Nietzsche is its Messiah, or at least its Anti-Donkey, par excellence.

FIANCÉES, PHYSIOLOGY, AND
INFECTIOUS RHETORIC

Allow me to revert to Novalis, and to the infectious rhetoric of biography. After Sophie's death—two days after her fifteenth birthday, of tuberculosis of the liver and lungs—Novalis is plagued, we are told, by sexual torments. One well-known editor and biographer of Novalis, Gerhard Schulz, cites an apparently laconic yet well-nigh frenzied observation from the notebooks—an observation that is quite representative of Novalis's jottings during the months following Sophie's death: "The voluptuous phantasy of this morning occasioned this afternoon an explosion."[13]

The same biographer now goes on to mix in a curious way sexuality, tubercular infection (of which Novalis himself was to die less than four years later), and the defense mechanisms of a beleaguered spirit (*Geist*):

> We can descry not only in such notes [on the "explosion"] but also in his works the fact that Friedrich von Hardenberg was tortured [*heimgesucht*] in more than usual measure by sexual representations and dreams. That is not unusual or surprising in the case of human beings who, like Novalis, are carriers of the germ of tuberculosis [*den Keim zur Tuberkulose in sich tragen*] and who without surcease have to struggle against a weak constitution. Yet commentators have gladly overlooked the fact that his thought and the world of his poetic representations received strong impulses from the sexual sphere. Above all, one must not forget that his intensified exposure to the pulsional [*das verstärkte Ausgesetztsein an das Triebhafte*] also mobilized the defenses of his mind [*die Abwehrkräfte des Geistes*] against such domination. In many respects, such exposure alone led Novalis to the achievement of his œuvre.

Note the biographer's use of the full family name, Friedrich von Hardenberg, when it is a question of autoerotic torture, and only later the literary pseudonym, Novalis, as though thereby negotiating the mysterious straits between "the man" and "his work"; note also the problematic phrases "tortured in more than usual measure," "carriers of the germ," "weak constitution," "intensified exposure to the pulsional," "the defenses of the mind," and "such exposure alone. . . ." What begins as the tubercular infection of a labile constitution becomes a well-nigh parasympathetic infection through contact with the young woman who can have infected him in no other way, the fiancée whom he once admits loving "precisely on account of her illness," and ends as the achievement of a robust—though besieged and defensive—spiritual production. But let us turn now to Nietzsche.

Two further contexts might be mentioned with regard to Nietzsche's views on health and illness, the first arising from his 1886 prefaces to the second editions of several of his works (the prefaces that we examined in the opening chapters of the present book), the second from letters written during the autumn of 1888. Of course, one could also simply lose oneself in the notebooks from the years 1887–1888, where the themes of health and decadence, the physiology of art, and "the great health" prevail. However, let us examine the well-known prefaces to the 1886 editions of *The Birth of Tragedy, Human, All-Too-Human* (Parts I and II), *Daybreak,* and *The Gay Science,* where questions of health and illness are omnipresent. For such questions involve what Nietzsche calls *die nächsten Dinge,* the closest things, in parody of the eschatological "four last things," *die letzten Dinge.* Nietzsche first mentions "the closest things," I believe, in "The Wanderer and His Shadow," written, as *Ecce Homo* reminds us, at the nadir of Nietzsche's own health—when he truly believed that he was ready to follow in his father's footsteps toward the apocalyptic four last things. Yet diet, climate, locale, and solitude or (more rarely) companionship replace death, judgment, heaven, and hell as the philosopher's ultimate things. For these are crucial not only to the philosopher's health and well-being but also to his or her *thinking* and *writing.*

However, it is high time I introduced the central paradox or double-bind of infectious reading. If Nietzsche's struggle for health enables him to pursue his study of physiological decadence, that struggle dare not abate. If attention to the "closest things" replaces terror in the face of the eschatological "last things," such vigilance dare not replace apocalypse with complacency. The search for health is and remains dalliance with disease and madness. It is not, as both Nietzsche and Klossowski would have it, a *periodicity* of illness and respite, with clearly marked peaks and valleys, but an awful coextensivity, a dreadful contamination. It is what both Schelling and Novalis know as *contagium.*

Indeed, it is high time I reached a bit farther with the thought that was elaborated in chapter 3, "The Decadence of Redemption." If the thought of eternal return smacks of consolation, of piety and piety's ressentiments, it nevertheless has to do with connections that are not so easily broken. Deleuze stresses that we do not know what a human being stripped of ressentiment would look like: *rancune* is not something we can drop from our lives with the application of personal discipline and mental hygiene, a change in diet and a crash course in transcendental meditation. For *res-sentiment* is that which is *felt again,* precisely that which *re-turns.* In other words, we may have underestimated the *structural* relation of ressentiment and return. It may not be a mere contingency that Freud invokes eternal return of the same in the context of re-experiencing trauma. If war neurosis consists in the effort to discharge the excessive energy of the traumatic event through repetition of the original event in active remembrance, if in repetition compulsion the traumatic event is *felt again,* is *re-sented,* it may well be that recurrence is essentially bound up with ressentiment. Not the supreme euphoria of Dionysiac possession can shatter the imbrication—the disastrous dovetailing—of ressentiment and return. Not the grandest of great healths can escape the contagion of chronic indirect illness. Perhaps this is the insight toward which Nietzsche's prefaces to his works of convalescence are headed, however much they may boast of exuberant health.

In his "Attempt at a Self-Criticism" (1, 16) Nietzsche wonders whether madness might be a sign of something other than degeneration or senescence. "A question for the psychiatrists: Are there perhaps neuroses of health [*Neu-*

rosen der Gesundheit]"? Was Plato's *Phaedrus* right when it attributed mortals' best blessings to μανία, divine madness? The preface to the second edition of *Human, All-Too-Human*, Part I, describes Nietzsche's literary corpus to date in terms of convalescence (*die Genesung*). Convalescence consists of recuperation *of* the self *from* the self ("*zur Erholung* von mir," in which the emphatic *von* expresses both the subjective and the objective genitives); convalescence relies on the cunning of self-preservation (*die List der Selbst-Erhaltung*) in the face of the inimical self (2, 14). Nietzsche's very life is an attempt at temptation, tempting health itself in the direction of what he calls "the great [or grand] health" (*die große Gesundheit*) (2, 18). Section 5 of the preface begins: "One step further in convalescence: and the free spirit sidles up to life once again—slowly to be sure, almost in revulsion [*widerspänstig*], almost distrusting." The section ends as follows: "And, to speak seriously: it is a thoroughgoing *cure* of all pessimism (of the cancerous lesions of the old idealists and flagrant liars) to be ill after the fashion of these free spirits, to remain ill a good long while, and then, over a still longer stretch of time, to become healthy—I mean 'healthier.'" As Novalis had prophesied, it is always a matter of one illness battling another, of what one might call *chronic* indirect health. Nietzsche concludes this passage, which mixes the metaphors of health and illness by pitting one form of illness against another, the illness of suspicion—as though suspicion were a free-range scavenger—against the cancer of idealism, with the following remarkable piece of wisdom: "There is a wisdom—a life-wisdom—that consists in prescribing health itself for a long period of time in tiny doses only [*die Gesundheit selbst lange Zeit nur in kleinen Dosen zu verordnen*]" (2, 19).

The preface to *The Gay Science* speaks of the convalescent's gratitude and of the "*drunkenness* of convalescence [*von der* Trunkenheit *der Genesung*]" (3, 345). No wonder so many highly irrational and foolish things come to light in and through a gay science, including the extravagant tenderness the scientist comes to feel for even the spiniest moral-psychological problems. Among the principal problems, Nietzsche avers, is the fact that in the history of philosophy the sick thinkers have prevailed (3, 347). As if anyone could now straightforwardly declare what is healthy, what noxious! *The Gay Science* of 1881, which concludes with Part IV (Part V having been added in 1886 for the second edition), ends with the *Incipit tragoedia* of Zarathustra. Five years later, in 1886, with the second edition, Nietzsche warns us that tragic thinking is in his view and for his practice always a parodic thinking also: "*Incipit parodia*, no doubt." He then writes one of the strangest self-referential remarks in all his œuvre: "*Aber lassen wir Herrn Nietzsche*: pay him no mind: what does it matter to us that Herr Nietzsche grew healthy again?" (3, 347). Yet if by 1886 all the oppositional logic has been purged from the metaphorics of health and illness, is not every assertion touching them—especially the claim of a successful convalescence—essentially parodic and paradoxical, merely tightening the knot of the double-bind? What can it mean that Herr Nietzsche got well? Did he surrender the essential—and essentially noxious—weapons of genealogical critique? Did he get well the way Socrates did, by sacrificing his rooster to Asclepius? Cock-A-Doodle-Doo?

An aphorism on the "health of the soul," in Book III of the first edition of *The Gay Science*, merits our attention in this regard. (No doubt it was an important aphorism for Foucault, who insisted on the auto-da-fé of all knowers.) Here Nietzsche doubts whether virtue constitutes the health of the soul, or whether the health of the soul can be defined at all. "For there is no health-in-itself, and all attempts to define something of that sort are wretchedly misconceived" (FW, 120; 3, 477). There are countless varieties of health in soul and in body. Indeed, the very multiplicity of the states and conditions of health and illness ruins any possible blueprint for health, subverts any regimented regimen, especially for the one who practices genealogical critique:

> Ultimately, we have to leave an important question open, namely, the question as to whether we can *renounce* illness, even for the development of our virtues, and in particular whether our thirst for knowledge and self-knowledge does not need the sick soul as much as the healthy one: in short, whether the will to health, taken by itself, is not a prejudice, a piece of pusillanimity, and perhaps a matter of refined barbarity and atavism [*ein Stück feinster Barbarei und Rückständigkeit.* (Ibid.)

The long penultimate aphorism of the second (1886) edition of *The Gay Science* is entitled "*Die große Gesundheit*" (FW, 382; 3, 635–37). Nietzsche thought so highly of this aphorism that he reproduced it in his account (in *Ecce Homo*) of the gestation of *Thus Spoke Zarathustra* (6, 337–39). It too is a reflection on health and illness in terms of two types of ode—*Tragödie* and *Parodie*. Nietzsche proclaims himself the prematurely born infant of an as yet undemonstrated future, so premature that he will later have to concede the "posthumous" nature of his birth. Yet this posthumous "preemie" has as his most urgent need a new health, a health that is "stronger cleverer tougher more reckless and more hilarious" than any prior sort of health—in a word, "the *great health*." It is a health that always needs to be attained, because it is always and again surrendered during the sea voyages of genealogical critique and transvaluation. As "human-superhuman well-being and benevolence," such health "often enough appears *inhumane*," especially when it poses as "the incarnate, involuntary parody" of everything that heretofore has been held to be sacred. An *involuntary* parody, precisely in its "*great earnestness*," marks the inception (and not the end and cap) of the tragedy. Nietzsche, the genealogist, has a highly developed sense of the extent to which he and all the sons and daughters of Christendom are still pious—which is to say, still infected with ressentiment by and from the origin. He has a highly refined sense of the mutual contamination of biopositive and bionegative effects in genealogical science. His parodic question to his own practice, which is ostensibly always in service to *life*, is whether that practice makes the practitioner worthier . . . to *live*. One is often tempted to think that the multiple voices, the minidramas, and the tropes of even the most prosaic texts of Nietzsche's œuvre are attempts to withstand or to dodge the incessant recoil of such contagious parody, which is always prelude to such relentless tragedy.

INCLUDING THE *ECCE*

Ecce Homo is not the most prosaic of texts. How shall we initiate a discussion of it, or rather, an infectious reading of its discourse on health and illness? Initially, perhaps, by hearing several brief extracts of letters from the period in which it was written, letters that parody, letters that warn.

On 6 November 1888, to C. G. Naumann, Nietzsche's publisher: "Between October 15 and November 4 I carried out an extremely difficult task: I recounted my self, my books, my views, all in fragmentary form, presenting only what was called for. I believe that *this* will be heard, perhaps heard too much [*das wird gehört werden, vielleicht zu sehr*]. . . . And then all would be in order. . . . The new text is called

Ecce Homo
How One Becomes What One Is" (KSAB 8, 464).

On 13 November 1888, to Franz Overbeck: " . . . the manuscript of *Ecce Homo: How One Becomes What One Is* is already at the printer's. This work, of absolute importance, provides some psychological and even biographical materials about me and my literature: they [the readers] will *behold* me all at one go [*man wird mich mit Einem Male zu sehen bekommen*]. The tone of the text is cheerful and fateful [*heiter und verhängnißvoll*], as with everything I write" (KSAB 8, 470).

On 14 November 1888, to Meta von Salis: "For I myself am this homo, including the ecce; the attempt to spread a bit of light *and fright* about me seems to me to have succeeded almost too well [. . . *Dieser homo bin ich nämlich selbst, eingerechnet das ecce; der Versuch über mich ein wenig Licht* und Schrecken *zu verbreiten, scheint mir fast zu gut gelungen*]" (KSAB 8, 471).

Let me now refer to five passages in *Ecce Homo*, proceeding regressively, from back to front. First, a passage from "Why I Write Such Good Books" tells us how, during the period in which *Human, All-too-Human* was written, *circa* 1877–1880, Nietzsche's ill health actually rescued him from his earlier lifestyle and thus contributed to the composition of the œuvre (6, 326). Nietzsche writes:

> At that time my instinct decided relentlessly against any further concessions, collaborations, or confusions-of-myself-for-someone-else. Every form of life, the most unfavorable conditions, illness, poverty—all seemed preferable to me to that undignified "selflessness" into which I had been plunged unwittingly from my *youth* onward, and in which I was later stuck by sheer inertia and the so-called "feeling of duty."—What came to help me, in a way that amazes me more than I can say, and in the nick of time, was that *dire* legacy from my father's side—at bottom, the predetermination to an early death. Illness *slowly undid the fetters*: it spared me every breach, every violent and offensive step. I sacrificed no one's good will toward me, and in fact I gained even more good will. Similarly, illness gave me the right to a complete reversal in all my habits; it allowed me, *commanded* me, to forget; it bestowed on me the *compulsion* of lying still, remaining at leisure, waiting, being patient. . . . But that, of course, is what we call thinking! . . . My eyes alone put an end to all bookwormery—in German, *Philologie*. I was liberated

from the "book," and for years I read nothing more—the *greatest* benefit I ever granted myself! My nethermost self, buried alive, as it were, and silenced by the constant need to listen to other selves (—and that, of course, is what we call reading!), roused slowly, shyly, full of doubt—but in the end *it spoke again*. Never have I been so happy with myself as during the periods of greatest pain and illness in my life: one only has to examine *Daybreak* or "The Wanderer and His Shadow" in order to grasp what this "*return to myself*" implied: a supreme sort of *convalescence* as such! The other convalescence merely followed in its train.—

If illness undid the fetters, it nevertheless remains true that Nietzsche sought recuperation and liberation from his drastic liberator. And if at the end of the passage he appears to collapse back into a traditional spiritualism—with corporeal convalescence "merely following in the train" of the intellectual or scriptural convalescence—it also remains true that illness and the predetermination to an early death mark the very life of this perturbèd spirit.

A second and a third passage (6, 289–90, and 282–84) in "Why I Am So Clever" recount Nietzsche's response to Wagner and his path to "reason" in terms of health and illness. He praises Wagner's *Tristan und Isolde* as the great poison and antidote (*Gegengift*) of his life. "The world is poor for one who has never been sick enough for this 'voluptuosity of hell,'" he exclaims. Further, he condemns Wagner's own convalescence from *Tristan*, with *Die Meistersinger* and *Der Ring*, as sheer regression: those who are as thoroughly decadent as Wagner was should not even try to recuperate. As for Nietzsche's own "cleverness," it arises from his illness, which alone shocked him out of all the bad habits of diet and lifestyle he had accumulated. Illness alone is responsible for Nietzsche's health: "*Die* Krankheit *brachte mich erst zur Vernunft*."

Perhaps the most famous of Nietzsche's reflections on the question "Why I Am So Wise" is the passage in which he declares that he is both decadent and antidecadent at once. It is the passage that serves as the conclusion to the first draft of *Ecce Homo*, the final words of the so-called *Ur-Ecce Homo* (6, 266–67; cf. *13*, 631–32):

> For, apart from the fact that I am a decadent, I am also its contrary [*dessen Gegensatz*]. My proof for this, among other things, is that I always instinctively chose the *correct* medicament against dire conditions, whereas the decadent as such always chooses the medicament that will hurt him. As *summa summarum* I was healthy; as niche, as specialty, I was decadent. That energy for absolute isolation and for the dissolution of customary relationships, that compulsion against myself, not allowing myself to be dithered over, doted on, *doctored* any longer—it betrays an unconditioned certitude of instinct concerning *what it was* at the time that was necessary for me above all else. I took myself in hand, made myself healthy again: the condition for that—as every physiologist will concede—is *that one at bottom be healthy*. A creature that is morbid by type cannot become healthy, still less make itself healthy; as opposed to that, for one who is healthy by type, illness can be an energetic *stimulans* to life, to more life. Indeed, that is how the long period of my illness *now* appears to me: I discovered life anew, as it were, including myself; I tasted all good things, even the most minute, as others could not readily taste them—out of my will to health, to *life*, I made my philosophy. . . . For pay heed to

this: the years of my lowest vitality were the years when I *ceased* being a pessimist: the instinct for self-restitution *forbade* me to embrace a philosophy of poverty and discouragement. . . . And, at bottom, how does one recognize whether a human being has *turned out well* [*die* Wohlgerathenheit]! By the fact that one who has turned out well pleases our senses: that he is carved from wood that is hard, tender, and fragrant. Only what is conducive to him [*ihm zuträglich*] pleases him; his delight, his pleasure, ceases whenever the measure of what is conducive is exceeded. He unearths pharmaceuticals against injuries, uses baneful accidents to his advantage; whatever does not kill him makes him stronger. He instinctively gathers from everything he sees, hears, and experiences, *his* quantum: he is a selective principle, he lets many things fail the test. He is always in his *own* company, whether he tarries with books, human beings, or landscapes: he honors things by *choosing, admitting, trusting.* He reacts slowly to every sort of stimulation, with a slowness that is bred by long-practiced caution and a willed pride—he probes the stimulus that is approaching, far be it from him to approach it. He believes in neither "misfortune" nor "guilt": he knows how to put things behind him, whether they involve himself or others; he knows how to *forget*—he is sufficiently strong to *make* everything serve him for the best.—Well, then, I am the *counterpart* [*das* Gegenstück] of a decadent: for the one I was only now describing is precisely *me.*

If Nietzsche is the contrary (*Gegensatz*) of a decadent, he is also the decadent's counterpart (*Gegenstück*), the σύμβολον of the decadent. The very fortune (*Glück*) of his existence is to be both commencement and decadent; if no "local degeneration" can be found in him, his life is nevertheless convalescence and regression, "the periodicity of a kind of decadence" (6, 265). If Nietzsche is *experienced* in questions of decadence, if he has spelled the word forwards and backwards, if he has developed a finger for nuances and a gaze that sees around corners and down into the secret recesses of the decadence instinct, if, in short, Nietzsche has mastered the optics of the ill (*Kranken-Optik*), then no typology of the "essentially healthy" type, no conceptual procedure, no therapeutic pose, no clever maneuver, no taking-oneself-in-hand will surgically sever the pathogenic from the biopositive effect, no eye will descry and distinguish the peaks from the valleys of periodicity, no nose will know the perfume of hard oak from the sweet corruption of watery cottonwood.

To repeat, *Ecce Homo* is not the most prosaic of texts. How shall we broach a discussion of it? In the first place, no lines of the text lend themselves to a straightforward analysis of health and disease. While one easily spots the inflated, megalomanic, sardonic, or euphoric passages, even the halcyon passages, the passages that are beautifully *composed*, in both senses of the word, must now give us pause. Thus, for example, even the untitled exergue of the book, *An diesem vollkommnen Tage*, which at first perusal seems undeniably in the full flush of exuberant health, slips into an odd state of suspension. In such suspension, questions of *infection* give way to vagaries of *inflection*, and to doubts about whether and how one can *read* the words:

> On this perfect day, when everything is ripening, and not only the grapes are turning russet, a ray of sunlight fell across my life: I looked back, I looked ahead, and never did I see so many things and such good things at once. Not in vain did I

bury today my forty-fourth year: I was *allowed* to bury it—whatever was of life in it has been rescued, is immortal. The first book of the *Transvaluation of All Values*, the *Dionysos-Dithyrambs*, and, for recuperation, the *Twilight of the Idols*, are all gifts of this year, even of its last quarter. *How should I not be grateful to my entire life?*—And so I shall narrate my life to myself.

Is Nietzsche's *vollkommner Tag* a day on the autumnal earth, an earth to which one remains doggedly faithful, or is it a day of *infinite* consummation? A day of mortal harvest or of divine—that is to say, *decadent*—redemption? Are the grapes russet or bronzed? Is it happy birthday or happy burial day? As for Nietzsche's locution, *ist gerettet, ist unsterblich*, one can hardly suppress an "Alleluia, Alleluia." Does something decadent, something reactively nihilistic, something *resentful* and redolent of *rancune* conceal itself in the negative form of the affirmation, *Wie sollte ich nicht . . . ?* Finally, how does one *read* the quasi-reflexive self-recounting of one's own life to oneself? Is the emphasis to fall on the *recounting* or on the *to myself*? Is the question to be inflected liltingly, whimsically? Or defiantly, as though rushing to the barricades? Or piously, that is, paralytically? Or, to end the list, *infectiously*?

CONCLUSION AND POSTSCRIPT

My meager conclusions are these:

1. Novalis's poetics of the baneful moots something like a periodicity of *indirect* health and illness, in which the soul is the most virulent poison, but poison "the most interesting stimulus to our meditation."

2. The biopositive effects of infection may be an invention of hokey medicine, but that invention will haunt those of us who know that in order to do good work you just about have to kill yourself.

3. Infectious rhetorics—for example, in the biographies of literary figures—are nests of prejudices concerning the body, sexuality, and spiritual hygiene. They have to be dirtied.

4. "The great health" is both parodic and tragic. It expresses a double-bind in our reading and writing, including the *ecce*: infectious rhetoric is as unreadable as illness and health "in themselves" are undecidable—at least until death do us part.

Postscript. No doubt there is something vaguely (if not flagrantly) sentimental about this entire venture. Perhaps it only helps us to measure our own distance from the *lingua romana* of Novalis, the Schlegels, and Schelling. By now, long after the 1960s, madness has lost most of its charisma. In *Human, All-Too-Human* (2, 122), Nietzsche himself writes: "Because people observed that an excitation often made the head more lucid and induced lucky inspirations, they came to believe that extreme excitations would enable one to share in the luckiest inspirations and windfalls of the mind: and so they honored the insane as the wise and oracular. At bottom, this was a false deduction."

In the Age of AIDS, tertiary syphilis seems a dose of the old down-home: we can view it with a certain fondness, familiarity, and nostalgia. In the Age of

AIDS, tuberculosis means a mutant, more highly resistant and resilient bacillus, one that defeats the lingering romanticism of "biopositive effects." We never dreamt that when Nietzsche's Zarathustra said, "The human being is something that must be overcome," a highly mobile virus was preparing to undertake the task quite literally, as though it missed the metaphor. Will anything appear in any future of ours that will allow some living creature ages hence to speculate on the "biopositive effects" of AIDS? Or has *our* romance language become a truly *dead* language? And is it the mortification of our romance tongue that best explains why the slightest allusion to sexual desire in our time is grounds for lawsuits, denunciations, and recriminations?

The death of God never troubled us, because we believed that God died so that Eros might live. Now that Eros is in its final throes, not merely poisoned by the culture of Christendom but in our own secular and infectious age administered the lethal dose, one wonders what could possibly keep Thanatos at bay a while longer, what could possibly prolong the detour that is leading us to endless stasis by one more turn, one more round.[14]

ELEVEN

Consultations with the Paternal Shadow on the Altar at the Edge of the Earth

> And the war is not between the sexes, but between
> the sons and their shadows.
> —Luce Irigaray, "*Ecce Mulier?*"

Ecce Homo—is it an autobiography? It is at all events a tale of fathers and mothers, brothers and sisters, loves and execrations. It is also a series of riddles in and about the text. For example, the riddle of an entire section—the third section of Part One, "Why I Am So Wise"—that only recently has been restored to the form that Nietzsche himself, on the eve of his collapse, devised for it. My question is whether this textual riddle (or confusion) affects four compelling readings of *Ecce Homo*, those of Rodolphe Gasché, Jacques Derrida, Sarah Kofman, and Pierre Klossowski.[1]

On 29 December 1888, from Turin, Nietzsche mailed to his publisher C. G. Naumann a large packet of corrections for the manuscript of *Ecce Homo*. Among them was an entirely recast section three of Part One, which Nietzsche instructed Naumann to insert in place of the one in his possession. The revised section came to light in July 1969 among the papers of Heinrich Köselitz (Peter Gast) in the Nietzsche collection of the Goethe-Schiller Archive (*Archiv der deutschen Klassik*) in Weimar. Köselitz had carefully copied Nietzsche's original, which Naumann had passed on to him, before sending it to Nietzsche's mother and sister—who promptly destroyed it. The first version of *Ecce Homo* I, 3, written in October 1888 and present in most editions to date,[2] reads as follows:

Diese doppelte Reihe von Erfahrungen, diese Zugänglichkeit zu anscheinend getrennten Welten wiederholt sich in meiner Natur in jeder Hinsicht—ich bin ein Doppelgänger, ich habe auch das >>zweite<< Gesicht noch außer dem ersten. *Und* vielleicht auch noch das dritte. . . . Schon meiner Abkunft nach	This double series of experiences, this access to apparently quite disparate worlds, repeats itself in every aspect of my nature—I am an alter ego, I also have the "second" sight [or: the "second" face: *Gesicht*], in addition to the first. *And* perhaps the third as well. . . . On the one hand, my very

ist mir ein Blick erlaubt jenseits aller bloß lokal, national bedingten Perspektiven, es kostet mich keine Mühe, ein >>guter Europäer<< zu sein. Andrerseits bin ich vielleicht mehr deutsch, als jetzige Deutsche, bloße Reichsdeutsche es noch zu sein vermöchten—ich, der letzte *antipolitische* Deutsche. Und doch waren meine Vorfahren polnische Edelleute: ich habe von daher viel Rassen-Instinkte im Leibe, wer weiß? zuletzt gar noch das *liberum veto*. Denke ich daran, wie oft ich unterwegs als Pole angeredet werde und von Polen selbst, wie selten man mich für einen Deutschen nimmt, so könnte es scheinen, daß ich nur zu den *angesprenkelten* Deutschen gehörte. Aber meine Mutter, Franziska Oehler, ist jedenfalls etwas sehr Deutsches; insgleichen meine Großmutter väterlicherseits, Erdmuthe Krause. Letztere lebte ihre ganze Jugend mitten im guten alten Weimar, nicht ohne Zusammenhang mit dem Goetheschen Kreise. Ihr Bruder, der Professor der Theologie Krause in Königsberg, wurde nach Herders Tod als Generalsuperintendent nach Weimar berufen. Es ist nicht unmöglich, daß ihre Mutter, meine Urgroßmutter, unter dem Namen >>Muthgen<< im Tagebuch des jungen Goethe vorkommt. Sie verheiratete sich zum zweiten Mal mit dem Superintendent Nietzsche in Eilenburg; an dem Tage des großen Kriegsjahrs 1813, wo Napoleon mit seinem Generalstab in Eilenburg einzog, am 10. Oktober hatte sie ihre Niederkunft. Sie war, als Sächsin, eine große Verehrerin Napoleons; es könnte sein, daß ich's auch noch bin. Mein Vater, 1813 geboren, starb 1849. Er lebte, bevor er das Pfarramt der Gemeinde Röcken unweit Lützen übernahm, einige Jahre auf dem Altenburger Schlosse und unterrichtete die vier Prinzessinnen daselbst. Seine Schülerinnen sind die Königin von Hannover, die Großfürstin Constantin, die

lineage grants me a glimpse beyond all merely locally or nationally conditioned perspectives; no great exertion is required for me to be a "good European." On the other hand, I am perhaps more German than our contemporary Germans—these mere Imperial Germans— are able to be:—I, the last *antipolitical* German. And yet my ancestors belonged to the Polish aristocracy: who knows, that may be the reason why I incorporate so many instincts pertaining to race, up to and including the right of veto. When I think how often during my travels I am addressed as though I were a Pole, and by Poles themselves, and how rarely anyone takes me to be a German, it might well seem that I merely belonged among the *mottled* Germans. Yet my mother, Franziska Oehler, is at all events a very German phenomenon, as is my paternal grandmother, Erdmuthe Krause. The latter lived throughout her youth in the heart of good old Weimar, and not without a connection to Goethe's circle. Her brother, Professor Krause, a theologian at Königsberg, was appointed General Superintendent in Weimar after Herder's death. It is not impossible that her mother, my great grandmother, appears in the young Goethe's diary under the name "Muthgen." She married a second time, taking the hand of Superintendent Nietzsche in Eilenburg; during that vital year in the Napoleonic Wars, 1813, on October 10, the very day Napoleon marched into Eilenburg with his General Staff, she lay in childbirth. Being a Saxon, she was a great admirer of Napoleon's; it may well be that I still am. My father, born in 1813, died in 1849. Before he became pastor of the congregation at Röcken, near Lützen, he lived for several years at Altenburg Castle and tutored the four princesses there. His pupils are now the Queen of Hanover, the Grand Princess Constantina, the Grand Duchess of

Großherzogin von Oldenburg und die Prinzeß Therese von Sachsen-Altenburg. Er war voll tiefer Pietät gegen den preußischen König Friedrich Wilhelm den Vierten, von dem er auch sein Pfarramt erhielt; die Ereignisse von 1848 betrübten ihn über die Maßen. Ich selber, am Geburtstage des genannten Königs geboren, am 15. Oktober, erhielt, wie billig, die Hohenzollern-Namen *Friedrich* Wilhelm. Einen Vorteil hatte jedenfalls die Wahl dieses Tages: mein Geburtstag war meine ganze Kindheit hindurch ein Festtag.— Ich betrachte es als ein großes Vorrecht, einen solchen Vater gehabt zu haben: es scheint mir sogar, daß sich damit alles erklärt, was ich sonst an Vorrechten habe—das Leben, das große Ja zum Leben *nicht* eingerechnet. Vor allem, daß es für mich keiner Absicht dazu bedarf, sondern eines bloßen Abwartens, um unfreiwillig in eine Welt hoher und zarter Dinge einzutreten: ich bin dort zu Hause, meine innerste Leidenschaft wird dort erst frei. Daß ich für dies Vorrecht beinahe mit dem Leben zahlte, ist gewiß kein unbilliger Handel.—Um nur etwas von meinem Zarathustra zu verstehn, muß man vielleicht ähnlich bedingt sein, wie ich es bin—mit einem Fuße *jenseits* des Lebens. . . .

Oldenburg, and Princess Theresa of Saxony-Altenburg. He was full of profound piety toward the Prussian king, Friedrich Wilhelm IV, from whom he also had received his pastorate; the events of 1848 troubled him egregiously. I myself, born on the king's birthday, October 15, received, as was fitting, the Hohenzollern name *Friedrich* Wilhelm. In any case, the choice of this day had one advantage: throughout my childhood my birthday was a holiday.—I regard the fact that I had such a father as a great privilege: it even seems to me that this accounts for whatever other privileges I possess—life, the magnificent *yes* to life, *not* included. Above all, that I need exercise no special intention, but can simply wait, in order to enter willy-nilly into a world of lofty and delicate things: I am at home there, my innermost passion is liberated there alone. That I paid for this privilege almost with my life is, to be sure, no petty exchange.—In order to understand anything at all of my *Zarathustra*, one must perhaps be conditioned more or less the way I am—with one foot *beyond* life. . . .

Nietzsche's revised text, obliterated by his mother and/or sister but preserved by Köselitz, reads as follows:

Ich betrachte es als ein grosses Vorrecht, einen solchen Vater gehabt zu haben: die Bauern, vor denen er predigte— denn er war, nachdem er einige Jahre am Altenburger Hofe gelebt hatte, die letzten Jahre Prediger—sagten, so musse wohl Engel aussehn. Und hiermit berühre ich die Frage der Rasse. Ich bin ein polnischer Edelmann pur sang, dem auch nicht ein Tropfen schlechtes Blut beigemischt ist, am wenigsten deutsches. Wenn ich den tiefsten Gegensatz zu mir suche, die unausrechenbare

I regard the fact that I had such a father as a great privilege: the peasants to whom he preached—for, during his last years, after having lived for several years at the court of Altenburg, he was a preacher—used to say that the angels must look like him.—And herewith I touch on the question of race. I am a pureblooded Polish nobleman, in whom not a drop of ignoble blood has been admixed, least of all German blood. Wherever I search for my profoundest opposite, to wit, incalculable vulgarity

Gemeinheit der Instinkte, so finde ich immer meine Mutter und Schwester,— mit solcher canaille mich verwandt zu glauben wäre eine Lästerung auf meine Göttlichkeit. Die Behandlung, die ich von Seiten meiner Mutter und Schwester erfahre, bis auf diesen Augenblick, flösst mir ein unsägliches Grauen ein: hier arbeitet eine vollkommene Höllenmaschine, mit unfehlbarer Sicherheit über den Augenblick, wo man mich blutig verwunden kann—in meinen höchsten Augenblicken, . . . denn da fehlt jede Kraft, sich gegen giftiges Gewürm zu wehren. . . . Die physiologische Contiguität ermöglicht eine solche disharmonia praestabilita. . . . Aber ich bekenne, daß der tiefste Einwand gegen die "ewige Wiederkunft," mein eigentlich abgründlicher Gedanke, immer Mutter und Schwester sind.— Aber auch als Pole bin ich ein ungeheurer Atavismus. Man würde Jahrhunderte zurückzugehn haben, um diese vornehmste Rasse, die es auf Erden gab, in dem Masse instinktrein zu finden, wie ich sie darstelle. Ich habe gegen Alles, was heute nobless heisst, ein souveraines Gefühl von Distinktion,—ich würde dem jungen deutschen Kaiser nicht die Ehre zugestehn, mein Kutscher zu sein. Es giebt einen einzigen Fall, wo ich meines Gleichen anerkenne—ich bekenne es mit tiefer Dankbarkeit. Frau Cosima Wagner ist bei Weitem die vornehmste Natur; und, damit ich kein Wort zu wenig sage, sage ich, daß Richard Wagner der mir bei Weitem verwandteste Mann war. . . . Der Rest ist Schweigen. . . . Alle herrschenden Begriffe über Verwandtschafts-Grad sind ein physiologischer Widersinn, der nicht überboten werden kann. Der Papst treibt heute noch Handel mit diesem Widersinn. Man ist am wenigsten mit seinen Eltern verwandt: es wäre das äusserste Zeichen von Gemeinheit, seinen Eltern verwandt zu sein. Die höheren Naturen haben ihren Ursprung

of instinct, I always find my mother and sister—if I thought I were actually related to such canaille it would be a veritable blasphemy against my divinity. The treatment I have always received from my mother and sister— up to the present moment—fills me with unutterable horror: here a highly perfected, infernal machine is at work, one that operates with unfailing accuracy at the very moment when I am most vulnerable and most likely to bleed— during my supreme moments, . . . for in these moments one lacks all the energy that would be needed to defend oneself against venomous vipers. . . . Physiological contiguity makes such a disharmonia praestabilita possible. . . . Yet I confess that the most profound objection to the eternal return, that is, to my properly abyssal thought, is always mother and sister.—However, even as a Pole I am an incredible atavism. One would have to go back centuries in order to find this noblest of races ever to exist on Earth exhibiting its instincts as pristinely as I exhibit them here and now. Toward everything today that calls itself noblesse I possess a sovereign feeling of distinction—I would not do our young Kaiser the honor of appointing him my driver. There is one single case in which I acknowledge my equal—I confess it with profound gratitude. Frau Cosima Wagner is the noblest nature by far, and, in order not to leave a single word unsaid, I say that Richard Wagner was by far the man most akin to me. . . . The rest is silence. . . . All the prevailing concepts that govern degrees of consanguinity are unsurpassable physiological nonsense. Even today the Pope insists on trafficking in such absurdity. One is least akin to one's parents: it would be the uttermost mark of vulgarity to be related to one's parents. Higher natures have their origins much, much farther back; with a view to these natures, a

unendlich weiter zurück, auf sie hin hat am längsten gesammelt, gespart, gehäuft werden müssen. Die *grossen* Individuen sind die ältesten: ich verstehe es nicht, aber Julius Cäsar könnte mein Vater sein—*oder* Alexander, dieser leibhafte Dionysos. . . . In diesem Augenblick, wo ich dies schreibe, bringt die Post mir einen Dionysos-Kopf.

great deal had to be accumulated, saved, and hoarded over long periods of time. The *great* individuals are the oldest: I do not understand it, but Julius Caesar could be my father—*or* Alexander, this Dionysos in the flesh. At the very moment I am writing this, the mail brings me a Dionysos-head.

Ignoring most of the intriguing contrasts between these two texts, and setting aside Nietzsche's (bogus) claim to aristocratic Polish ancestry and his (mistaken) great-grandmotherly liaison with Goethe, I wish to stress what is perhaps obvious to any first reading. While the paternal shadow in the revised text may still retain a trace of its foreboding aspect, it is now essentially benign, even "angelic." To have had such a father, both texts proclaim, was a "privilege." Yet the revised text *excludes* the phrase that insists that the *yes* to life does *not* pertain to those privileges inherited from the father. In other words, the revised text, even by its omissions, tends to enhance the position of the father vis-à-vis life. True, the revised text seeks greater distance from *both* parents, to whom, Nietzsche insists, the great individual is *least* related— although it is the infernal machine of mother and sister, itself efficacious precisely because of physiological contiguity and preestablished familial cacophony, that Nietzsche would dearly love to obliterate. Gone altogether from the revised text are the romanzas of the Oehler side, the maternal side, of Nietzsche's family; gone are that "very German phenomenon" of the mother and the dalliance with Goethe on the part of the paternal (great) grandmother, on the Krause side of the family. The revised account leaves us with two profound objections to the eternal recurrence of the same—who are delighted to act as Nietzsche's editors.

What is at stake in these two versions of Nietzsche as *Doppelgänger* and alter ego? Perhaps nothing less than the riddle of Nietzsche's existence, at least in his own estimation. The very first section of *Ecce Homo*, Part One, begins as follows:

> The fortune of my existence, perhaps its very singularity, lies in its fatality: I have— to put it in the form of a riddle—as my father already died; as my mother I am still alive and am growing old. This double provenance, from the highest and the lowest rungs on the ladder of life, as it were, simultaneously decadent and *commencement*—this, if anything, accounts for that neutrality, that freedom from all bias in relation to the entire problem of life, which perhaps distinguishes me. . . . I know both, I am both. (6, 264)

Nietzsche's "riddle," propounded originally as the conclusion to a series of notes we now call the *Ur-Ecce homo* (see *13, 629*), is taken up by Gasché, Derrida, Kofman, and Klossowski in ways that merit careful attention, and it is to these four commentators that I shall now turn. All four have meditated on the riddle of Nietzsche's *double* origin, the nondialectical, neutral, irreducible doubling of high and low, ascendancy and decrepitude, mother and father in Nietzsche's "life." However, may the last-named pair, mother and father, serve as the key to unlock the mystery of the others? Can we—and does Nietzsche—attribute in an unequivocal way vitality to the mother, enervation and death to the father? Can we assume that it is sheer oversight, or the force of a conventional idiom, that causes him to place "highest" and "lowest" in improper sequence in the passage quoted above—inasmuch as everywhere else the paternal legacy appears to be listed first: the father is already dead and forever decadent, but still on the "highest rung" of life's ladder? In short, is Nietzsche's *double* provenance ultimately reducible to a *single* binary opposition? Is the riddle so easily riddled?

All four commentators resist such a reduction, though perhaps not always successfully. Indeed, such resistance is difficult. The bulk of *Ecce Homo*, I, 1 emphasizes the fatality for the son of the father's early demise (*Mein Vater starb . . .*), in such a way that the identification of paternity with ominous shadow appears to be a foregone conclusion. Entropy, decline, and death: are these not the haunting names and negatives of the father?

However, if *décadence* appears to be the paternal legacy, the heritage of vitality and commencement (*Anfang*) cannot so readily be attributed to the mother. The second section of Part One, to which I referred in the preceding chapter, mentions such vitality, attributing it not to her but to Nietzsche's own hand: "For, apart from the fact that I am a decadent, I am also its contrary. . . . As *summa summarum* I was healthy, as niche, as specialty, I was decadent. . . . I took myself in hand [*Ich nahm mich selbst in die Hand*], made myself healthy again. . . . Out of my will to health, to *life*, I made my philosophy. Well, then, I am the *counterpart* of a decadent: for the one I was only now describing is precisely *me*" (6, 266–67). Whether we can take the opposition of *summa summarum* to *Winkel* and *Specialität* as somehow corroborating the equation (mother = life; father = death) is doubtful, unless one insists on identifying the organic niches that gave Nietzsche particular distress (eyes, brain, and stomach) as those organs that suffered most from Nietzsche's paternal, spiritual-intellectual heritage. Yet such distress is more than matched by the anguish induced by that infernal machine of the maternal and sororal presbytery. It may well be that much depends on how we read section 3 of Part One of *Ecce Homo*—and on *which version* we read.

In his article, "Autobiography as Gestalt," Rodolphe Gasché cites these early pages of *Ecce Homo* to which I have been referring. Focusing on Nietzsche's "double origin," he stresses the philosopher's own search for his "nethermost self," the self that is to be found nowhere else than *in physiologicis*. Nietzsche's double maternal/paternal face or sight makes him a veritable *Janus bifrons*. Not simply *in physiologicis*, however: Gasché invokes the gateway *Augenblick*, in which the apparently divergent eternities of past and future "affront one another," as an eminent instance of the double structure in Nietzsche's writing. If the gateway—or, as Heidegger would insist, our *standing in* the gateway—closes the ring of eternity in a moment of decision, then the very "vision" or "visage" (*Gesicht*) of the gateway marks the closure of an infinite past (the dead father) and an ostensibly endless future (the surviving mother).

Although I cannot recount all of Gasché's reading here, I at least want to present his "first transcription" of the solution to the riddle of Nietzsche's double origin—the "riddle" here referring not to the stricken shepherd of "On the Vision and the Riddle" but to the riddle of Nietzsche's *Ecce Homo*. Gasché writes, with the hand of Nietzsche—or, taking Nietzsche into his own hands, or into those of psychoanalysis: "I have killed myself as my own father so that I can commit incest with myself as my mother while as my father I am preventing myself from being born" (282). I shall defer discussion of the first half of Gasché's transcription, at once necrological, Titanic, and oedipal, hence oedipal in the full sense (inasmuch as it would embrace *Oedipus at Colonus*), in order to emphasize the final words: " . . . while as my father I am preventing myself from being born." Here the paternal shadow appears as Chronos doubling as Kronos: Titanic Time jams the mother, as the father who is still untouched by the surgical *legerdemain* of the son.

That Nietzsche bore his father with him always, as though he (Nietzsche, Friedrich) were his own mother, filled by the father, made pregnant by and with him; that Nietzsche felt himself to be reliving the misfortunes and illnesses of the father, waiting for his own brain to ooze, anticipating his mother's tears, the doctor's tragic mien—who can doubt these things? Nietzsche took his chances with such a Titanic father, the fragile *Glück* of his existence, and such chances took him. Unlike the later case of Jean-Paul Sartre, Nietzsche for the first four years of his life *knew* his father, sat on his lap—and in German a lap is a womb: *Schoß*—at the piano and the organ, rapt to his father's improvisations, enthralled by the origins of all music. How could Nietzsche ever have been born or released from such a lap? Only as Dionysos, twice-born, twice buried? Once borne on that paternal bosom, he would in fact never be released, never fully unbound. It is as though in later years his father emerged from the grave to fetch the young son back to his bosom, back to the origins of all music. However, this is to anticipate. Nothing about the paternal shadow seems to follow in good order, generation upon generation; everything seems to anticipate and to presuppose a long and shadowy lineage. On both sides.

To hear with a new ear the names of Nietzsche, Friedrich Wilhelm, *who is himself dead*, and whose very signature is a mark of death—that is the task Jacques Derrida assigns himself in "*Logique de la vivante*." To read with a new eye the "thanatography" of Nietzsche's "biography," to take up again the relation of the "I," signature, writing, and death, as developed, for example, in chapter seven of *La voix et le phénomène*, remains an important part of the task. Yet the present investigation of the logic of the living is less a logic than a gloss on *Glas*, a tolling of the bell, a knell, an obsequy. Derrida's is an essay on "obsequence."

It is Nietzsche's fatality to be both neutral (neither-nor) and doubling (both-and) with regard to his own genealogy, to be *between* the dead and the living, between *le (pére) mort* and *la (mére) vivante*, to be both death, *la mort*, and life, *la vie*, during that stretch of time that he himself, Nietzsche, Friedrich Wilhelm is (was) alive, *le vivant*. Obsequence turns out to be an enigmatic sort of sequentiality, not of generation upon generation, but of multiple and ultimately undecidable first-person existences. Note in the following passage the variety of possible senses and sequences of the je suis, "I am" (from *être*) and "I follow" (from *suivre*): "*En tant que* je suis *mon père, je suis mort, je suis le mort et je suis la mort. En tant que* je suis *ma mère, je suis la vie qui persévère, le vivant, la vivante. Je suis mon père, ma mère et moi, et moi qui suis mon père ma mère et moi, mon fils et moi, la mort et la vie, le mort et la vivante, etc.*"[3]

Derrida's transcription of the riddle doubles up on itself in a way that no English transcription can. One attempt to retranscribe Derrida's transcription—to anglicize the nonlogic of obsequence—is the following:

> Insofar as *I am and follow* my father, I am dead; I am and follow the dead progenitor, I am and follow death. Insofar as *I am and follow* my mother, I am the life that perseveres [cf., by way of contrast, Lacan: *je, père, sévère*], the living male heir, the progenitrix. I am and follow my father, my mother, and me—I who am and follow my father my mother and me, my son and me, death and life, the dead progenitor and the living progenitrix, and so on.

Thus Derrida spins out the riddle into a complex fable of death and living-on, *obséquence* and *survivance*. Yet there is a tendency in Derrida's fable to identify the father with decadence and to acknowledge the mother, without further ado, as she who survives collapse, she who lives on, burying her husband and her second son, she who is the very figure of life for all ontotheology—in Hegel, for example—precisely because she dresses the family corpses for burial. Like Úrsula in García Márquez's *Cien años de soledad*, Franziska would be she who lives on and survives, as the very essence of *Pietà*, precisely in order to bury her son. The son whom Derrida mistakenly calls *le fils unique*. Forgetting Little Joseph. And even if for the moment we are willing to set Little Joseph aside, inasmuch as he died as an infant, some six months after the father's death, we may still ask whether the survival of the mother represents the *survivance* of life or the stasis of deathly obsequ(i)ence.

Of the four readers of *Ecce Homo* that we are discussing here, Sarah Kofman, in "A Fantastical Genealogy: Nietzsche's Family Romance," is the one who most strongly identifies the *maternal* side as the side of death rather than survival. Perhaps that is due to a certain discretion on her part. Or perhaps it is due to the fact that she alone of the four commentators focuses on the *revised* version of *Ecce Homo* I, 3. Kofman notes the shift in Nietzsche's text from a purely "physiological" discussion of consanguinity to a typological, genealogical, or even economic use of blood ties. She hints that such a shift may depend on the intense desire on Nietzsche's part to increase the distance that separates him from the mother and sister: on the one hand, the infernal machine *is* infernal only because it is internal, that is, because of physiological contiguity; on the other hand, Nietzsche wants to deny that his divinity is besmirched by the blood of such infernal, internal *rabble*. Hence the shifts and shiftiness of the text. However, Kofman also wonders about the very intensity of the desire. She notes the fundamental ambiguity vis-à-vis the father, who is an angel and the son's greatest privilege, yet also the decadent who according to the *first* version nearly costs the son his life. While the father guarantees descent from the Polish nobility, hence a distinction of *class* beyond the merely physiological, he also contaminates his son with an incurable morbidity. Thus the father grants the son those poisonous gifts that will lead him to a critique of his paternal legacy—the gifts of the ascetic ideal, which both inform and inflame the son: "Only someone who, like himself, had kept one foot *beyond* life by incorporating the father could have pushed the ascetic ideal and its moral code far enough to make them reverse direction and transform themselves into their opposites" (38). Even the son's fathering of Zarathustra, of the *yes* to life, is attributable to this dubious father, rather than to the despicable, contemptible mother.

Nietzsche exalts his father only to "kill" him, however, and Kofman is intrigued by the subtle variations in the Nietzschean version of the Freudian "family romance," as developed in Freud's 1909 essay, "The Neurotic's Family Novel" (StA 4, 221–26). At first blush, Nietzsche seems to stray far from the model of the Freudian family romance. Whereas Freud emphasizes a boy's resistance to the father and attachment to the mother, Nietzsche must above all resist the mother and sister, relying on an uncanny attachment with the defunct father for support. However, as Kofman indicates, a second glance at Freud's account shows a profound affinity with the basic plot of the neurotic's family novel: in a later phase of the boy's development, writes Freud (225), the *imago* of the father is radically transformed by the boy's fantasies concerning him. The growing boy can accept his father only if the latter's *imago* fuses with the figures of kings, princes, and lords—exalted personages of one kind or another. Thus it is Nietzsche's father who binds the son (in the son's fantasies) by ties of birth and blood to great men of the past—from Friedrich Wilhelm IV back to Friedrich der Grosse, to Napoleon and Goethe, and ultimately back to Julius Caesar, Alexander, and the god Dionysos himself. Perhaps even the young man's sole equal—Cosima Wagner—is an affair mediated by the father, rather than the mother, " . . . in order not to leave a single word unsaid." By contrast, the perspective opened up by the mother and the sister (who ought to be objects of desire, according to the Freudian account) is the perspective—in Kofman's words—of "a froglike worldview, flattening everything lofty and great" (42–43). Venomous vipers, *Gewürm*, the mother and sister are the very image of nausea, the counterimage of the serpent of return, the very picture of the black snake that bites fast inside the shepherd's throat (*Thus Spoke Zarathustra* III, "The Vision and the Riddle"; 4, 201).

Nevertheless, Kofman is surely right to observe that the very intensity of Nietzsche's hatred of his mother and sister—*canaille* or "rabble" in the revised account of *Ecce Homo* I, 3—suggests its libidinal contrary. She cites as evidence Nietzsche's affectionate letters to his maternal grandparents (dated 1 November 1857; KSAB, 1, 12) and to Franziska Nietzsche (2 February 1871;

KSAB, 3, 180). The latter, along with two other "birthday" letters composed by the son for the mother, who is celebrated (jocularly, jovially) as forever young, show something of the profound affection and attachment underlying the (much later) outspoken and even flaunted contempt:

> In honor of February 2, 1871
> [*Basel, presumably January 27, 1871*]

How old, most esteemed Birthday Girl, are you today? As well as I can remember, you go back about to the turn of the century, and it gives me great pleasure to be able to congratulate you on your *seventy-first* birthday, an age you can look upon as a real achievement. . . . This rapid aging of mothers should produce the opposite effect in their children—and, of course, we have the example of our daughter, who can't get beyond seventeen, even though she's been working at it for the past eight years. So, I guess you and I will just have to console one another. I'm content, as you are, although in the meantime I'm suffering the infirmity of old age somewhat more than you, seeing as how I'm celebrating my 87th this year. Maybe it's time I retired. With honors, of course, and a jubilee cup of genuine silver, from which you may sip a nip or two if you like.

> Hearty greetings from your
> Fridericus.
> (KSAB 3, 180)

> [*Basel, January 31, 1872*]

Today, my dear Mother, just the tiniest birthday greeting. . . . At the moment I haven't the time to calculate which birthday it actually is that you are celebrating. Is it a moderate assumption if I should imagine that soon you will be approaching the *middle* of your life?

> In heartfelt love,
> Your Son.
> (KSAB, 3, 283)

> [*Basel*], the last Sunday of January, 1875

My dear and good Mother . . .

I assume that, according to my rough-and-ready calculation, you are now concluding the first half of your life; yet nothing refutes a quite different notion, one you may prefer; for instance, that you have served out only the first third of your life. . . . In the latter case you would still have time to lavish here on the earth until 1973, in the former case, only until 1924. Because I myself have undertaken to grow insufferably old, we might as well get used to looking upon one another as approximate contemporaries. Who knows, perhaps in ten years' time you may look younger than I do! I just about believe it, and I shall not be amazed. At some point, people who know no better will take me to be your older brother (and perhaps Lisbeth, if she continues to mummify herself in her youth, they will take to be our grandchild). The result will be a delightfully inverted world! And whence does it arise? From the fact that Madame Maman refuses partout to grow old. For which on this day I send heartiest congratulations.

> Keep in your love your
> Fritz
> (KSAB 5, 14)

Sarah Kofman does not mention the following letter to Elisabeth (KSAB *1*, 203–204), but it is one that seems to demonstrate her point quite convincingly concerning the sister. Nietzsche, at Schulpforta, writes to his sister in Dresden at the end of April 1862:

Dear Elisabeth!

As I write this I am standing at my lectern, my lectern stands near the window, the window offers a lovely view of the blossoming plane tree and the hills above the Saale bathed in sunlight: but lovely nature reminds me most strongly of Dresden and the pleasant days that I spent there. Of course, in order to remember you, my dear, dear Elisabeth, I do not need such far-fetched levers of remembrance: on the contrary, I think so incomparably often of you that I am almost always doing so—even when I am asleep there is no exception, for I dream quite a bit about you and our being together. . . .

May you fare really splendidly, by the bye, and don't demand any more sentimental outbursts in order to think on your brother, who sends

Much love,
Fritz.

Canaille are invariably roasted upon the long-dying embers of love, ardent and intense love, at least in family romances.

Finally, Sarah Kofman emphasizes what we will soon hear Klossowski affirming, and what we saw notebook M III 1 confirming, namely, that Nietzsche's family romance leads him to affirm *Chaos*, the eternal recurrence of *difference* rather than of *the same* (45). Here the head of Dionysos serves as an amulet or apotropaic device to fend off the head of Medusa, which a number of unpublished notes associate with the thought of eternal return of *the same*.

Pierre Klossowski begins his "Consultation with the Paternal Shadow" by remarking, apropos of Nietzsche's talent for riddles, that to pose a riddle is "to simulate a necessity in order to flee the vacuity of something arbitrary" (12). Nietzsche's own account of the fortune and fatality of his "double origin," the fable of his mother and father, Klossowski therefore calls "the *shadow* of a solution" to the puzzle of his utterly contingent "life." Yet even this shadow is double, multiple, and ultimately undecidable. It is at once the oneiric shadow of the father and the oppressive shadow(s) of the mother-in-mourning and of all the women in the presbytery who raise Little Fritz, the Fritz of their collective heart, *Herzensfritz*, as they call him.

Why is the paternal shadow "oneiric"? Klossowski cites two versions of a premonitory dream that Nietzsche had—presumably at five years of age, about seven months after his father's death—which foretold the sudden death of his younger brother, Little Joseph, *Josephchen*. The first report, composed at Christmas, 1856, some seven years after the event, reads as follows:

At that time I once dreamt that I heard the sounds of the church organ, playing as it had during the funeral [i.e., of Nietzsche's father]. When I perceived what lay behind these sounds a grave mound suddenly opened and my father, wrapped in linen cerements, emerged from it. He hurried into the church and returned a moment later with a child in his arms. The tomb yawned again, he entered, and the cover closed over the opening. The stertorous sounds of the organ ceased instantly, and I woke. On the day that followed this night Little Joseph abruptly fell ill, seized by severe cramps, and after a few hours he died. Our grief knew no bounds. My dream had been fulfilled completely. The tiny corpse was laid to rest in his father's arms.[4]

Note the progression, the obsequence, as it were, of this first account: hearing organ music, seeing nothing as yet, discovering that this is the music of the deceased father—not the improvisations played while Little Fritz sat on his father's lap (sat there *alone*, at least before Josephchen's arrival) but the music of interment—and then the gaping of the grave he cannot in the waking world see. His father hurries into the church and emerges carrying a child, *ein Kind*, in his arms. Which child? Not *Herzensfritz*, presumably, who is observing all this (but from where? and how? presumably from the second floor of the country parsonage that looks out over the church and the adjacent cemetery where, to repeat, his father never was buried: *Ich bin als Pflanze nahe dem Gottesacker, als Mensch in einem Pfarrhaus geboren*—another doubling here, except that if as a human being Nietzsche is born in a parsonage, in the house of the father, then his life as a plant is rooted in God's Green Acres, that is, the cemetery, which would be the mother's), not Little Fritz but *Little Joseph* is the dead man's object. Presumably.

This first account of the dream, written at age twelve, long after the traumatic event, is followed by a second, composed when Nietzsche was seventeen, a dozen years after the event:

Some months later [i.e., following the death of the father], a second misfortune struck me, a misfortune of which I had a premonition, thanks to a remarkable dream. I felt as though I could hear muffled organ music coming from the nearby church. Surprised, I open the window that looked out over the church and cemetery. My father's grave opens, a white figure emerges and disappears into the church. The gloomy, uncanny sounds continue to surge; the white figure appears again, carrying something under his arm that I did not clearly recognize. The grave mound yawns, the figure sinks into it, the organ goes silent—I waken. The following morning my younger brother, a lively and gifted child, is seized by cramps, and a half-hour later he is dead. He was buried right next to my father's grave.[5]

Klossowski notes several deviations from the first account in the second. The music is now muffled, sinister, more resistant to hearing; the dreamer himself opens a window to seek the source of the music, uncanny yet familiar; the "thing" borne under the father's arms is now not readily identifiable; and Josephchen (however, *will* it be he, will it *have been* he, inasmuch as no name is mentioned?) is now, after his seizure with cramps, cramps caused perhaps by the tightening of that paternal grasp, removed from his father's arms (*their* father's arms) and buried *alongside* the father. Klossowski, perhaps recalling chapter four of the Wolfman case, and himself alluding to the "compensatory value of a reconstitution of the traumatism" (*Beyond the Pleasure Principle*, chapters two and three), writes now with the hand of the dreamer himself. And in this second—or third—account of the dream, according to Klossowski's own oneiric hand, which now assumes the "I" of Nietzsche, there is evidence of a *switch* of infants. Klossowski writes:

> I *open* the window and *the tomb* is opened: I open the tomb of my father, who then looks for *me* in the church. My dead father searches me out and carries me off because I am trying to see my dead father [or: trying to see my father dead—*à voir mon père mort*]. I am dead, the father of myself, I suppress my self in order to reawaken in the midst of music. My dead father makes me hear the music. (257)

Although he is looking for "me" in the church, the father finds *Josephchen* instead. Or so the dreamer dreams, and so the writer writes. Little Joseph, if it is he, is not in the house, but has been removed to the church. Who has removed this gay and gifted child to the pale altar at the edge of the earth? Who has exposed him to the lusts of the waxen pastor? Klossowski does not raise this question explicitly. Yet if the oedipal situation applies (recall Gasché: "I have killed myself as my own father so that I can commit incest with myself as my mother . . ."), then it is not only the father but also the second son who must be removed to God's Green Acres. Version one: "Our grief knew no bounds. My dream had been fulfilled completely. The tiny corpse was laid to rest in his father's arms." Version two: " . . . and a half-hour later he is dead. He was buried right next to my father's grave." Note the sequence, the obsequence, up to the perfunctory close: muffled organ music is heard; surprised, I open the window (the infant Wolfman's eyes open of themselves, says Freud, onto the primal scene: it is a matter of attentive, *interested* observation, insists Freud) that looks out onto the cemetery (*Wie lebendig steht noch der Gottesacker vor mir!* exclaims Nietzsche at age fourteen) where I dream that I see my father dead. First my father, then Little Joseph. Our grief knew no bounds. Whose? Ours. Me and Mom's. The two of us finally unencumbered. My dream had been fulfilled completely. Alone at last.

Yet if the first of Klossowski's consultations appears to conform to the usual (oedipal) view—negative identification with the father as decadence, transgression, and guilt—the second consultation (285 ff.) begins to subvert and displace that view. Klossowski stresses the asymmetry and disequilibrium of Nietzsche's "double origin": the mother simply does not embody "commencement," much less the anaclitic object of the child's desire, in the way that the father adumbrates closure. Keeping before him the shadow of the dead father as a kind of shield or amulet, Nietzsche during the course of his lifetime distances himself increasingly from mother and sister, distances himself through his writing, through his texts, such as the new text of *Ecce Homo* I, 3, which no mother or sister ever should have seen. Beneath the forced jollity of a later missive (the last) to Franziska Nietzsche, written on December 21, 1888 (*Meine alte Mutter. . . . Dein altes Geschöpf*), in which he assures her that he is by now *ein ungeheuer berühmtes Tier* ("a monstrously renowned beastie"), we hear overtones that resonate quite distinctly in a letter four days later to

Franz Overbeck: "This does not prevent my sister from writing to me on October 15 [that is, on Nietzsche's birthday, the halcyon forty-fourth birthday commemorated by the exergue to *Ecce Homo*, which we examined at the end of the previous chapter] that I too ought to start to get 'famous'. . . . All the while she calls me 'Darling Fritz,' *Herzensfritz*. . . . This has been going on now for seven years!"[6]

Thus, like the Wolfman, Nietzsche is driven to invert the oedipal situation: he substitutes himself for the mother and the father's daughter in order to become intimate with the father—"as though being," says Klossowski, "*his own mother*."[7] Such inversion or subversion or perversion will not go unpunished. Nietzsche's "real" mother and sister, his "editors," will eventually suffocate him and his text: Klossowski adduces a mordant word on the mother's "mortal compassion for the convalescent son." Indeed, mother and sister represent what Deleuze calls "the second feminine power" (Dz, 24; 214), that is, the reactive impotence of ressentiment. They embody, according to Klossowski as well as Kofman, "Life in its most contemptible form," the sluggish worm and viper—counterimages to the serpent of eternal return.

The consequences of such inversion become increasingly radical in Klossowski's own consultations with the paternal shadow. If the father is detachment from life, if the father—and not the ghost ship of woman—marks the pathos of *Distanz*, then he is also the great healthfulness of the transvaluation of all values. Magnificent health is the father's, the deceased father of all genealogy. Hence "the presence of the dead father as an explanation of Nietzsche's struggle with his own fatality." Klossowski depicts such distance and struggle as Nietzsche's perilous perch on the crest of a wave: from it Nietzsche can descry with "ultimate lucidity" the fatality against which he will shatter—and yet that very perspicacity marks the onset of inexpungible darkness. In the end, the end(s) of Nietzsche himself, Friedrich Wilhelm, the disequilibrium of all origins is radicalized. It is his destiny to replace (to follow *and* to be) the mother, and to insinuate himself with (to follow *and* to be) the oneiric shadow of the father. It is therefore also his destiny to be obsequ(i)ous toward (to follow *and* to be) his younger brother, Josephchen.

The living mother embodies decay of blood, loss of exuberance, the end of adventure, the survival of death alone; the dead father, more a dream about life than life itself, a dream dreamt by at least one of his two sons, embodies— if a shade may be said to embody—the very course and flow (the *sens*) of life. Paternal shadow and gaping tomb become a single sign in Nietzsche's destiny: the sign of *Chaos*. The shadow of the mourning mother, mourning her spouse, mourning Little Joseph, mourning Friedrich Wilhelm before his time, is finally dispersed in what Klossowski calls "automaternity": "Yet in order to rediscover *life itself*, Nietzsche, in so far as he is his *own mother*, gives birth to himself anew [*s'enfante à nouveau*] and becomes his own creature" (260). Hence "the necessity to be born to himself from himself and thereby his tendency to restore himself to a double presence, feminine and virile" (274).

And yet this elevation of the paternal shadow and expulsion of the living mother ought to give us pause. Such "automaternity," such taking-oneself-in-hand: *Wie? Und dies wäre nicht—circulus vitiosus deus?* (JGB, 56; 5, 75). The apparent restoration of what Klossowski here calls a "double presence" and (after Deleuze) "double affirmation" may well be no more than the dream of the "perfect object," the dream of the metaphysics (and the morals) of undifferentiated presence. Such restoration would forget what it most needs to remember, namely, that Nietzsche's great good luck is his double and redoubled fatality, not his automaternity. Automaternity fares no better than autobiography.

Ecce Homo—autobiography? automaternity? consultation with the paternal shadow?

Autobiography doubles up with absences, not presences, and is thanatography. Automaternity, as we shall hear once again in the following chapter, is a usurpation that no mortal man or woman has ever successfully executed. If Nietzsche, Friedrich Wilhelm, is once again with child, is once again himself the child, that child will also follow him, and will turn out to be otherwise. For example, it will be Little Joseph. Doubling up. With stomach cramps, to be sure, but also with the Doppelgänger's uncanny replication.

In the end there will be nothing left for these children—Josephchen, Herzensfritz—but fatal consultation with the paternal shadow, fatal consultation with the maternal shadow: the riddle of an origin that will never cease doubling, sundering, and receding into the infinite distance of all music. That infinite distance opens onto the *lunar night* of all daytime philosophy, which is to say, onto the *other night* of literature, for example, the night of *fiction*.

†

Bellowing bell! Knowing knell! And that growling organ, O my Father! The dark I do not fear, not anymore, but the tintinnabulations and the wheezings terrify me still. Your instruments. They are playing for you, Papi, as always. Your belltower. Your organ. Your tool. Your weapon.

The massive marble slab

To Franz Overbeck in Basel

> *Nice, rue St. François de Paule 26 II*
> *January 9, 1886*

The very first thing I did with the money I received from Schmeitzner was to have my Father's grave covered with a great marble slab. (According to my Mother's wish, it will one day be her own grave as well.)

tastefully decorated in the geometric style, as on a precinct wall at Delphi or Thebes. Symbolism of the tomb. Bachofen. Hot ovens with cold crosses on them. Creuzer. This time with my name incised, Friedrich Wilhelm, just as I inscribed one for you and Little Joseph:

†

Here
reposeth in God
Carl Ludwig
Nietzsche

Pastor of Röcken
Michlitz and Bothfeld
born 11 October 1813
died 30 July 1849
Whereupon followed him into Eternity
his youngest son
Ludwig Joseph
born 27 February 1848
died 4 January 1850
C h a r i t y   n e v e r   f a i l e t h
1 Cor. 13, 8.

I bought the slab, had it inscribed, then slammed it over you so you would never rise and kill again. Forgive me, Papi. I had to secure some time for myself, a longer lease on life for my literature. I mean my philosophy.

To Georg Brandes in Copenhagen

Nizza, December 2, 1887

Honored Sir,
You see the sort of posthumous thoughts with which I live. However, a philosophy such as mine is like a sepulcher—one no longer lives with it. Bene vixit, qui bene latuit, "He lived well, who concealed himself well"—that's what it says on Descartes's tombstone. A grave inscription, no doubt about it!

Yours, Nietzsche.

Your forgiveness too I beg, Little Joseph, brother of my heart. Mooch over a bit, will you? Papi needed something or someone to hold onto, and it was either you or me, Elisabeth being excluded by ecclesiastical decree. Better you than me, you were so cuddly, so cute, all the family adored you so, especially Mama. You would have been so gifted had you lasted. But I carried you into the church that night, the night the organ boomed. It seems pointless now to rue it, irrelevant to regret it, it happened so long ago. A bit more room, please, go ahead and slip right into his arms if you like, I never begrudged you Father's arms, I only wanted a stretch of space, a fragment of time, a piece of his lap, and the music.

The bells reverberate to stillness. Silenced at long last are the stertorous groans of the organ. What did that Russian no not her the composer call it? The beast that never breathes. Instrument of unliving breath, harbinger of undying death. It's awfully quiet up there. Must be waning to twilight, the earliest suspicion, dwindling to dark. Just the three of us here now, darling Little Joseph, my dear Father, and me.

—You mean four, brother dear. You forgot Mamusha, as always.

—No, Little Joseph. Mama's dead. I'm awfully sorry.

To Gustav Krug in Cologne

Genoa, November 16, 1880

We are growing older, and thereby lonelier: precisely that love abandons us which loved us like an unconscious necessity, not because of our particular qualities, but often very much in spite of these. Our past draws to a close when our Mother dies: then for the first time our childhood and youth become re-membrance whole and entire. And so it goes, on and on, the friends of our youth die, our teachers, the ideals of those days—always more solitude; always colder and colder winds assail us.

Devotedly, with heartfelt love,
Friedrich Nietzsche.

Just the three of us, with the serenity of evening before us, the dying summer, and the long night.

To Franz Overbeck in Basel

Sils-Maria, August 5, 1886

Dear Friend,
If only I could give you an idea of my feeling of loneliness! *I have no one to whom I feel related, as little among the living as among the dead. This is unimagi-nably terrifying. Only constant exercise in learning how to bear this feeling, and a step-by-step development from childhood on in my capacity for bearing it— this alone enables me to comprehend how I have not as yet perished on account of it.—For the rest, the* task *for the sake of which I live confronts me clearly: it is a* factum *of unimaginable sadness, albeit transfigured by the consciousness that there is greatness in it, if ever greatness dwelled in a mortal's task. —*

Faithfully,
Your F. N.

A dead man's pallid, waxen hands, phosphorescent in the blackness of darkness, rise and fall in mournful mime of musical rhythm. Fingers spread wide, hands like white spiders pendant on invisible threads descend to the pianoforte keyboard, touch chord upon chord.

— Papi?

Shifting keys, distended harmonies, familiar returns and new departures. The give of your thighs, the smell of soap and sanctity rolling in waves from your face and throat behind and above me, your living breath in my hair. The hardening center below. And the music! O my Father, the music! *Da capo! Da capo!*

†

—Psst!

—What is it, Little Joseph?

—Is Tatus awake? You and I have to talk.

—Papi! Hey, Papi! Not a peep, Little Joseph. Dead to the world. What did you want to talk about?

—Us.

—Us? Well?

—There has been some confusion, you see. It's high time we straightened it out, just the two of us, you and I. You have been operating under a funda-mental misapprehension, mój drogie bracie. So much is true: you are my dear brother, and you always will be, no matter who you are, no matter what your authentic identity.

—What on earth are you talking about?

—Nothing on earth, mój kochany. *Under* it. Souterrain. I'm talking about what's in a name.

—A name? All the names of history I am, all the masks of god. So much for authentic identity. Basta!

—Not so fast. Let us not be overhasty, my dear Joseph.

—"Joseph"? What do you mean, Little Joseph?

—What I mean, Joseph, is that there has been a very specific case of mistaken identity in our holy family, an imbroglio that has lain undetected a good long time now, and you and I are going to achieve some clarity about it.

—I don't follow. Stop it. I am afraid.

—Stop? I've only just begun, Joseph.

—Will you stop that! Call me Fritz, or if you spurn intimacy, call me Friedrich. Friedrich Wilhelm, b. 1844 Röcken, † 1900 Weimar. Can't you read?

—It's no use insulting me, Little Joseph. It's caving in on you, isn't it, the realization? You know the truth now, don't you, darling brother? You were so gifted! So adorable!

—I know no such thing!

—Oh, but you do! I can feel your resistance slipping, the curtain is going up on our aboriginal scene—rather, let us say, the lid of the tomb is gaping once again.

—Bitch's bastard!

—That's right. Now you have it. Now you see it. I thought it would take longer.

—I see nothing! Explain yourself!

—I shall explain *your* self, darling Joseph. That night of all nights was so fraught, how could you be expected to have kept all the details in place—the names, for instance? Your teeth were giving you so much trouble, a martyrdom really, and the colic, and the mounting waves in your brainflow—you were on the brink of convulsion. And I? Friedrich? My sleep disturbed by tremulous organ music, I went to the window. You know what I saw down there, you remember. He went into the church. That is to say: he *came* into the church. By that time you and I were already there. That's why he never spotted you in your bedroom window.

—Liar! Bitch's bastard!

—You were placing me on the hallowed altarstone ever so gently. Through my quilted sleeping sack I could feel the hard cold marble under the altarcloth. Your eyes looked so affectionately into mine as you deposited me there, so ardently, almost hungrily. In the wan light of the earliest suspicion of dawn I saw that triumphant smile spread across your face.

—You're telling me nothing new, Little Joseph. I confessed to it the instant I arrived here at the crypt. What more do you want from me? You want an apology? So, I apologize, I'm sorry.

—It isn't about being sorry, Joseph, it's about being mistaken.

—Will you cut it out I can't stand it I won't stand for it it's wicked nonsense!

—No, not nonsense. It is about what happened, what really happened on the pallid morning of that dim night. Mis-taken is the very word, incidentally, taken by mistake.

—It didn't! It didn't happen! You contradict yourself!

—How rapidly the curtain rises, the resistance in the pulleys has dwindled to next to nothing, and up it glides! Now you can almost see him coming, you can see him out of my own eyes, as it were. You can see him moving up on you noiselessly from behind. Stealth of spirit!

—Stop!

—His immaculate white robes flutter in funereal flight, trailing in the wake of his advance; he floats rather than walks upon those unshod unliving feet. An angel of compassion, hovering behind you, now and forever. And if you cannot see him through my eyes (for your back is turned to him, you have only now placed me on the altarstone, only now gazed ravenously upon me) you can surely feel that gelid musty wind on the rise from the stone floor and you think it is only the draft from the door i left it open i forgot to close it and you try to reassure yourself it isnt him he cant have come this early he promised he would wait till i fled gods mausoleum and ran across gods green acres in through the backdoor of gods parsonage up the creaking stairway to my room into my bed and under my covers shivering sobbing in heartfelt grief by the time he would be coming to get you yet it doesn't reassure you at all for you distinctly remember having closed the broadbeamed oaken portal behind you you remember hearing its iron latch clink reassuringly shut so that no passerby in the twilight would observe someone lurking in the church up to mischief no doubt. But if you cannot see the white flutter of the linen cinctures and cerements or feel the chilly air rising from the granite floor surely you can hear him speaking to you, Friedrich Wilhelm, surely you can hear him calling your name, Friedrich Wilhelm. . .

—No! Ghoul! Back!

— . . . and that voice will stay with me behind me haunting me as a horrific hallucination all my days the night he took you away, Friedrich Wilhelm. . .

—It's only a dream! Wake up!

— . . . for he called you by name, gurgling for your blood *O blessed moment, O savory feast, O unspeakably holy deed! With all my heart, and most profoundly moved, I command:* Bring me now this my beloved child, that I may dedicate him to the Lord!

—But that was my Holy Baptism, when I was given my very own Christian name!

—That is correct, Friedrich Wilhelm, but you abused it: you forfeited your right to both a Christian name and a Christian burial.

—Papi!

—Tatulku! You've been eavesdropping!

—Dreams troubled my sleep, I woke and heard my beloved son, in whom I am mightily displeased.

—Which one of us?

—Which one of us?

—The other one. He is the only one I ever wanted.

—Wait, Papi, wait. This cannot be. This is unreal. What about all my literature? I wrote some catastrophic books: they will last: you can't take them away from me.

To Franz Overbeck in Basel

Cannobio, Villa Badia, April 14, 1887

Dear Friend,

There is nothing more paralyzing or discouraging to me than to travel into today's Germany to take a closer look at those many sincere persons who believe that they take a "positive attitude" toward me. Meanwhile, all understanding of me is lacking. And if my probability-reckoning does not fail me, it will not be any different before 1901. I believe that people would simply take me to be mad if I let it be known what I take myself to be. . . . (This winter I delved into our contemporary European literature, so that I can now say that my philosophical position is by far the most independent one, however much I feel myself to be the inheritor of several millennia. Contemporary Europe hasn't an inkling of the frightful decisions about which my very essence turns, or of the wheel of problems on which I am stretched.—Or that with me a catastrophe is being prepared whose name I know yet will not utter.)

Your faithful friend,
N.

—Books flow from deep wellsprings, boys, not from names on title pages; no one owns them, no matter who signs for them; no product of spirit can be possessed. Your Uncle Hegel was mistaken.

—But they say *Friedrich!*

—But they mean *Joseph!*

—They write only *Nietzsche.* Look at the spine. Embossed in gold and silver: *Nietzsche.* Nothing more.

—Come come, Tatuncio, relent: that would mean that even the Llama could have written them, spitting wisdoms into the wind! Or Mama, who never understood a blessed diabolical word.

—Don't be jejune, son: your Mother was an Oehler, and Elisabeth married a Förster. No oilers or foresters can write *Nietzsche.* It is an affair among us boys.

—But, Papi, that would mean that I was no one in particular, that I was a stand-in, a substitute, an ersatz fritz in a nonoriginal niche.

—Better get used to it, drogy bracie. It lasts an eternity.

—Little Joseph, I cannot be you! You are the incarnation of the pettifogger, the no-sayer, the spirit of rancor, resentment, and revenge!

—At your service, mój kochany. We were both very small when He came to get you.

—However, I became the dancer, the yes-sayer, the very opposite of a no-saying spirit! I never growled like an old bear or howled like a saint in the forest; I blessed life, who was a woman, I said *yes* to every nook and cranny, every shadow and shade!

—Precisely. Which is why you could never weed me out. The most picayune of mortals recurs, and with a vengeance!

—But you weeded yourself out! You autodestructed! You unselected yourself!

—With a little assistance from my dear brother, don't forget. Except that Tatus here knew even then who was destined to do the greater damage, and so he took you with him instead of me, embracing you all through the long long night. As for me, I got my teeth. You have felt them.

—*My* books or *your* books, it doesn't really matter now, I accept that. All the names of history let those tomes go, bequeathing them to all the readers of history: books will have their own fate.

—Indeed they will. And that fate will have nothing to do with yours or mine, Nietzsche.

—For we are dead. Even our names are dead.

—No, boys, not dead: merely confused for a time by the living, though perhaps for a long time, perhaps for all time.

Silence of the grave.

An eternity passes.

Another commences.

The same.

†

The same? The same. That is to say, the eternally, infinitesimally distinct.

TWELVE

Consultations with the Maternal Shadow in the Orangegrove at the Edge of the Sea

Is it too late to touch you, Dear?
We this moment knew—
Love Marine and Love terrene—
Love celestial too—
—Emily Dickinson, no. 1637

Earlier in the volume, I invoked a number of Nietzschean figures of woman: Semele, the mother of Dionysos, the Maenad worshippers, the sailing ship that glides like a butterfly or daimon over the wine-dark sea, life—the woman with whom Zarathustra whispers, the woman who makes him doubt—the piping soprano, Amy Thanatogenous, and—*canaille*. Too many figures to reduce to a common matrix. In what follows I shall try to read Luce Irigaray's *Amante marine de Friedrich Nietzsche* ("She-lover, Sea-lover, of Friedrich Nietzsche") against the backdrop of Nietzschean texts presented some years ago in a book entitled *Postponements: Woman, Sensuality, and Death in Nietzsche.*[1] For Irigaray resists a particular figure of woman that often dominates Nietzsche's texts, the funereal figure that incarnates sensual love as tragic death. She also resists the figure of woman as Maenad, the frenzied lover of Dionysos. Both are figures in which sensuousness and demise converge. The strategies and styles of Irigaray's resistance will be my focus—along with the hopes she invests in the she-lover and sea-lover who rises in waves against the Nietzschean mountain.

Yet one does not merely "focus" on strategies and styles of resistance: one resists them or joins forces with them, or sometimes resists and sometimes joins forces. In any case, one finds oneself caught up in the ἀγών and πόλεμος of "Nietzsche and the feminine." Further, the very style of one's thinking and writing shifts insensibly in such a confrontation. Inasmuch as Irigaray thinks and writes in fragments—they are sometimes extended fragments, but they are always nonetheless nodes of fragmentary writing—it is difficult for a reading of *Amante marine* to submit to the discipline and rigor of an "essay" or extended "commentary." Hence the fragmentary character of this final chapter of mine.

I shall begin with the filiation of Irigaray's "aerial" interpretation of Nietzsche and Gaston Bachelard's "ascensionalist" reading, against which my own *descensional reflection* has been advancing from the outset. I shall then take up the three successive parts of *Amante marine*, "Speaking of Immemorial Waters," "Veiled Lips," and "When Gods Are Born." Finally, in the concluding pages of the book, I will allow my own resistance to many of Irigaray's suspicions concerning the master of suspicion to dissolve—in a way that I hope would intrigue the two philosophers, though not altogether allay their suspicions.

Over fifty years ago Gaston Bachelard published *L'air et les songes: Essai sur l'imagination du mouvement.*[2] He was pursuing his project of a "physiology of the imagination" based on the four elements, fire, earth, air, and water. Because the rarefied element of air rendered very little to the "material imagination," Bachelard proposed to append to the latter a phenomenology or psychoanalysis of the "dynamic imagination" (15–16), that is to say, the imagination of *movement*. Movement through the air he defined as essentially *ascensional*, on the vertical axis that, moreover, organizes human *valorization* as such. "All valorization is verticalization," Bachelard declared, emphasizing that "*of all metaphors, those of height, elevation, depth, abasement, and fall are the axiomatic metaphors par excellence*" (18). Inquiry into the material imagination of air, as a study of the dynamic imagination, would more than any other study expose the *valuative* basis of human psychology. The confrontation with Nietzsche, the thinker of transvaluation—as later with Heidegger, the thinker who resists what he calls "value thinking"—was, or is now, inevitable.

The fifth of Bachelard's twelve chapters offers a detailed study of "Nietzsche and the Ascensional Psychism" (146–85). I cannot now survey in a thorough way Bachelard's methods and hypotheses, even though they are instructive with regard to Irigaray's *Amante marine*. Bachelard examines Nietzsche's poetic works, especially *Thus Spoke Zarathustra*, seeking evidence of the poet and thinker who is "the very type of *vertical poet*, the *poet of summits*, the *ascensional poet*" (147). Bachelard, and Irigaray after him, deny that Nietzsche is a poet of earth and water, even if the cry by which all remember him is "Be faithful to the earth!" (ASZ Vr, 3; 4, 15). For earth itself is a mixture of dust and water, its texture is "spongy," and Nietzsche is not one of the lovers of the porous, muddy earth, lovers whom Bachelard describes as follows: " . . . only a passionate lover [*amant*] of the earth, only a terrestrian affected by a touch of the aquatic, can escape from the *automatically pejorative* character of the metaphor of the *spongy*" (148). If the *mucal* or *mucous* may be associated with the spongy tissues and slimy organs and orifices of the human body, then the filiation of Irigaray and Bachelard at once becomes clear. It is a filiation Irigaray has never wished to deny or conceal.

Why is Nietzsche not a lover of the earth? Because, to repeat, he resists its moist receptivity, accepting the surface only as a platform for action, an action that he alone initiates. Even if Bachelard distorts Nietzsche's relationship to the burrowing mole (*Talpa europaea*, which we met in chapter 5) by characterizing Nietzsche's attitude toward it as a "redoubled contempt," even if he misses the genial fraternity of the groping genealogist and the subterranean mole, Bachelard's account of the essentially aerial Nietzsche is challenging, and has been enormously influential.

Nietzsche insists that the musical *air* be clear and well articulated, that it be an air for dancing rather than swooning or drowning. His polemics against Wagner (and Heidegger joins him in these polemics, thus betraying his own ascensional tendencies), his opposition to the metaphorics of the musical flood, of Wagnerian waves, of the infinite sea of sound (152), clearly expose Nietzsche's aerial, Mozartian preference. Further, Nietzschean air is as bright and cold as Boreas, or Hyperboreas—a piercing arrow forged in solar fire and tempered in polar ice. Bachelard characterizes the joys of the four elements as follows: "*Terrestrial* joy is bounty and weight—*aquatic* joy is mollification and repose—*igneous* joy is love and desire—and *aerial* joy is freedom" (156). Nietzsche's is clearly the joy of the air, the vaunted liberty of a soaring eagle, a brisk wind sweeping across the mountain crag. His is the joy of the predator. "Air is the *infinite substance* that one traverses in a line, with a freedom that is on the offensive, triumphant as lightning, the eagle, the arrow, the imperious and sovereign gaze. In the air one carries off one's victim in the pellucid light of day—there is no place to hide" (157). The bracing air, crisp and void, utterly pure, is the *tonic* of Nietzsche's aerial soul, which is desperate to leave all odors and fragrant memories behind and below. "Chill, silence, height—three roots for the same substance. Cut one root and you destroy Nietzsche's life" (161).

If Zarathustra's enemy is the spirit of gravity, Nietzsche's war is fought to gain the high ground. To go *over man* in order to fulfill the earth's promise. To rob the temples, to flee and fly, to evaluate: *voler, voler, évaluer*. Nietzsche's is thus not a reversal of Platonism in any sense, according to Bachelard, and certainly not a twisting free; it remains a Platonism of the *will* (167). The Nietzschean hierarchy is thus less Heraclitean than Platonic (and once again Heidegger would concur with Bachelard): "Earth over water, fire over earth, air over fire—such is the utterly *vertical* hierarchy of Nietzschean poetics" (173).

My own work, from start to finish, has wanted to resist the force of Bachelard's psychopoetics of Nietzsche's ostensible ascensionalism. In the first three chapters of the present book, I resisted the ascensionalist view of truth in Nietzsche as developed by Jean Granier. I insisted instead on a kind of "descensional reflection," the word *descensional* having been chosen precisely in order to counter Granier and Bachelard.[3] Perhaps I have been emphasizing the obvious, to wit, that Nietzsche's mountain heights remain on the earth's surface, and that the old mole of genealogy needs the ethereal affirmation of eternal return precisely in order to sustain him or her in an underground no-saying and no-acting. While I cannot deny the powerful metaphorics of ascension in Nietzschean poetics, it seems important to stress the terrestrial and aquatic base—the point from which all flights depart and to which they return, without any hope of limitless soaring. When we accuse Nietzsche of a traditional form of ascensionalism, say, that of anamnesic ascent to the divine banquet in Plato's *Phaedrus*, or ascent up the ladder of love or the divided line in *Symposium* and *Republic*, or ascent toward the Kantian starry heavens or the Hegelian self-knowing spirit, I wonder whether we are simply failing to take the measure of what Nietzsche had to oppose, ignoring the earthbound labors of the subversive mole.

At the very end of his chapter on Nietzsche, Bachelard alters his thesis slightly. He suggests that Nietzsche's "aerial life" is less a flight from the earth than "an *offensive* against the sky" (178). He intimates what we heard Albert Camus arguing strongly for in *L'homme révolté*, namely, that Nietzsche is forever in rebellion against the agents of the heavens. Nietzsche's voluntarism is his only flight plan: *vouloir* and *voler* revert to the same *volo* (180). And yet, Bachelard now concedes, "there is no eternal climb, there is no definitive elevation" (181). For Nietzsche, as for Heraclitus, the way up is the way down, and not for nothing is *Thus Spoke Zarathustra* dominated by the rhythm of ascents *and* descents. Not for nothing does it begin and end with descent rather than ascent. In the end, Bachelard concedes, "Nietzsche is not an alpinist." "His poems were often composed *on climbing back down* from the heights, returning to the valleys where human beings dwell" (184).

The "double perspective" of height and depth results in something both more and less than a traditional ascensionalism: alongside the *élan* of Nietzsche's aerial offensive we find a *volonté de richesse*, an affirmation of the bounty of the *earth*. Exposure to Nietzsche's text, to Nietzsche's poetics, thus tempers to some degree the Bachelardian judgment so confidently pronounced at the outset.

From Bachelard's *L'air et les songes* one retains many impressions, and many questions. For example: If Nietzsche's ascensionalism tempers its aerial quality with an affirmation of the bounteous earth, is the bounteous *sea* nowhere to be found on Nietzsche's earth? And, after all, does not Nietzsche prefer an air that, far from being empty and utterly pure, is redolent of pine and wildflower, or of seaweed and brine, an air of mixed fragrances, "full of smells" (KSAB 5, 425)? One also retains a haunting sense of the inadequacy of all one-sided judgments here, the inappropriateness of all polemic. Indeed, Bachelard's own visions and revisions raise a suspicion: Does not the desire to shoot arrows—whether *in* Nietzsche or *at* Nietzsche—itself reflect an essentially aerial, rather than an aquatic, imagination?

Irigaray's *Amante marine*, to repeat, consists of three parts. The first, "Speaking of Immemorial Waters," responds to Nietzsche's *Thus Spoke Zarathustra*. Here the she-sea-lover addresses the man-in-the-mountain, inviting him to return to the sea. The second part, "Veiled Lips," is a meditation on the central Nietzschean theme of *sich geben als, se donner pour*, the self-giving of truth and woman that is always at the same time *dissimulation*. The third, "When Gods Are Born," muses on the births and destinies of Dionysos, Apollo, and the Christ. There can be no question of doing justice to Irigaray's text in any one of its three parts. The worst injustice would be to try to encapsulate her text in "arguments" or "theses." However, my own scattered remarks here should not be taken as signs of *Irigaray*'s incoherence: the rhythm of her fragmentary writing works as waves on the shore, for while her thoughts are never predictable, they show a remarkable regularity and insistence. They inundate as well as instruct. They constitute a plea as well as a case, and neither case nor plea should be ignored. I will have to leave to other voices a more coherent account of her challenge to Nietzsche and a more sensitive appreciation of her plea on his behalf.

Irigaray counterposes midnight to midday. The ugliest man alone thinks eternal recurrence as an affirmative thought, and he thinks it as the midnight thought, behind Zarathustra's back, as it were. Nietzsche's affirmative thought cannot be a thought of gold, possession, the sun, or the same. Nor will it be a lunar reflection of solar light. It will be dark. Even as the hollow fold or pocket in a delicate membrane, beyond the master's reach. However, the affirmative thought is precisely for that reason the heaviest burden. "For hollows mean only the abyss to you. . . . The membrane was not yours to have. We formed it together. And if you want it for yourself, you make a hole in it just because I lack any part. And don't you make God out of that absence?" (13–14/7).

Why the suspicion against volume, possession, solidity, and helio-theiomorphic gold? Because they always seem to serve as compensation for a lack that is both feared and desired. "Isn't your sun worship still a kind of ressentiment? Don't you measure your ecstasy against the yardstick of envy? And isn't your circle made of the will to live this irradiation—there will be no other but me?" (21/15). One is reminded of the very first stage in the "true world" fable ("I, Plato, *am* the truth!"), and of the helio-basileo-patro-theology of *Phaedrus* as analyzed in Derrida's *Pharmacy*.[4] The legacy will always be passed from father to scion, from sun to son. Even though Pharmacia herself is anything but one of the two.

Irigaray repeats Gaston Bachelard's complaint, albeit in a remarkably different voice:

> . . . you teach the overman: the meaning of the earth. But do you come from earth or sea to announce the news? Is it fluid depths or solid volume that engendered you?

Are you fish or eagle, swimmer or dancer, when you announce the decline of man? Do you want to flow or climb? Overflow or fly? And in your entire will for the sea are you so very afraid that you must always stay up so high?

Perched on every mountain peak, hermit, tightrope-walker, or bird, you never dwell in the great depths. And as companion you never choose a sea creature. Camel, snake, lion, eagle, and doves, monkey and ass, and. . . . Yes. Yet *no* to anything that moves in the water. Why this persistent wish for legs or wings? And never gills?

And when you say that overman is the sea in whom your contempt is lost, that's fine. That is a will that is wider than man's own. But you never say: overman has lived in the sea; that is how he survives.

It is always hot, dry, and hard in your world. And to excel for you always requires a bridge.

Are you truly afraid of falling back into man? Or into the sea? (18–19/12–13)

When in Plato's *Phaedrus* Socrates is displeased by the words that have at that moment rolled off his tongue, he compares the bitter taste they leave in his mouth to the taste of brine, and says that he will wash his mouth out with sweet water. Later, in the course of his *second* speech, his panegyric on the winged steeds of the aerial soul, he compares the soul of mortals to an oyster imprisoned in the shell of the body. Why doesn't Socrates like oysters? Why does he identify the salt sea as bitter? Why does Plato's Socrates prefer pegasus to pearls? Cocks to waterfowl? In the end, is Nietzsche simply one more victim of the Socratism he otherwise so deftly portrays?

What Irigaray pleads for is a certain fidelity of embodied memory. For example, the memory of water in the mouth, as Sartre's Roquentin recalls it in *La nausée*. Yet here, in Irigaray, with a notable difference in taste:

So remember the liquid ground. And taste the saliva in your mouth also—notice her familiar presence during your silence, how she is forgotten when you speak. Or again: how you stop speaking when you drink. And how necessary all of that is for you!

These fluids softly mark the time. And there is no need to tap, just listen, in order to hear the music. With very small ears! (43/37)

As a boy Nietzsche was afraid of the water. When he finally learned to swim at Schulpforta it changed his life. Nothing made him happier, not even riding. He describes it in letters and journals—giving his body over to buoyancy. During the year at Sorrento with Malwida von Meysenbug and Paul Rée, he swam quite often in the bay below the orangegrove—after that year he wanted to divide his whole life seasonally between the sea and the mountains, between salt air and pine breeze. The most agonizing day his mother had with him after he was released from the Jena Institute for the Care and Cure of the Insane was the day they closed the local swimming pool for repairs. He raged. He ran off and discovered another place where he could strip and swim. A policeman found him.

Not that it can ever be a question of Nietzsche "becoming woman," or even "writing with the hand of woman." Bad politics joins bad writing in such a presumption, no doubt.[5] It is rather a question of not ignoring the resources in and of the *other*. "Why are we not, the one for the other, a resource of life and air?" (37/31). It is a question of finding the courage for pleasure beyond the death principle. "But you will never have pleasure [*jouir*] in woman if you insist on being woman. If you insist on making her a stage in your process. There is nothing like unto women. They go beyond all simulation. And when they are copied, the abyss remains. Well on this side of your measurements, the women, the abandoned ones, take place" (45–46/39).

Yet Nietzsche wants eternity alone for his wedded wife, desires eternity alone to be the mother of his children. Irigaray suspects that the cost of such nuptials is extravagant: "And for your only wife you want eternity. For in her, finally, you can give yourself up wholly. Though dead" (49/43). It is as though in the thought of recurrence Nietzsche wants to give birth to himself, to mother himself through all eternity, to take his birth into his own hands—*s'enfanter à nouveau*, as we heard Pierre Klossowski put it in the preceding chapter.[6] Yet that thought is madness, a mere parody of eternal recurrence:

> Forever you lose hold of the place where you take body. And to repeat your own birth is simply impossible. And by wishing for it, you choose to die. Finding again that dark home where you began to be once upon a time. Once and for all.
> That event does not happen twice. That necessity and that chance, horrendous and wonderful as they are in the blind term of their meeting.
> And, as you enter into the eternity of your recurrence, you cut yourself off from that unique occasion when you received life. All powerful, perhaps, for a fleeting moment; until the thread breaks that connected you to the earth. Then begins the decline. (63/57)

It is once again as Úrsula, in *Cien años de soledad*, knows: only one century, one saeculum, is granted to mortals: " . . . *porque las estirpes condenadas a cien años de soledad no tenían una segunda oportunidad sobre la tierra* [because lineages condemned to one hundred years of solitude had no second chance on the earth]."[7] Eternal return must engage that realization each time it is thought. It must be thought in the way Heidegger insisted—as *downgoing*, as anything but ascensional. Thus it is a matter of overcoming our anguish—"The danger of immersion in primary matter endlessly feeds your anguish, your forgetfulness, and your death" (73/66)—by means of whatever resources of life and air the other affords us. Resources of life and air *immersed* in fluid matter. Thus the thinking of recurrence subverts the thought of *the same*. Nietzsche knows that: as we saw in chapter 8, the notebook in which he first elaborates the thought of return contains his most trenchant critique of the metaphysics of the same, *des Gleichen*. Indeed, the thinking of eternal recurrence must learn to get along without recurrence itself, so that Nietzsche would affirm *with* Irigaray, "Become other, and without recurrence" (75/69).

Yet Irigaray remains unconvinced. If there is a "final judgment" expressed in the first part of *Amante marine*, it is something like this: One expects to find in Nietzsche an encounter with radical otherness, but, at least in terms of the other as *woman*, the expectation is disappointed. At the very end of her book Irigaray reiterates as follows: "Nietzsche—perhaps—has experienced and shown what is the result of infinite distance reabsorbed into the same [*le même*], has shown the difference that remains without a face or countenance" (200/187). If his "thought of thoughts" or his "Idea" is eternal recurrence of the same, his resistance to the same does not rescue him from the thought itself. "The sacrifice he makes to the Idea is inscribed in this—that he preferred the Idea to an ever-provisional openness to a female other [*l'ouverture, toujours temporisante, à une autre*]" (ibid.). The other is (in) the feminine. Such temporisation, which is more than merely "provisional," I would now define less as a being in *postponement* than as the need to persist *on the verge*. In a sense, Nietzsche was too impatient, was too anxious to absorb the other into his own experience. Irigaray's complaint:

That he refused to break the mirror of the same [*du même*], and over and over again demanded that the other be his double. To the point of willing to become that female other. Despite all physiology, all incarnation. Hermit, tightrope-walker, or bird, forgetful of the one who bore him, accompanied him, nourished him; in a solitary leap he leaves everything below him or in him; the chasm becomes bottomless. . . . (201/187–88)

What, precisely, is missing? "Rhythm and measure of a female other [*une autre*] that endlessly undoes the autological circle of discourse, thwarts the eternal return of the same, opens up every horizon through the affirmation of another point of view whose fulfillment can never be predicted. Always at risk? A gay science of the incarnation?" (201/187–88). Yet the very demands of the gay science of incarnation prevent one from closing the Nietzsche case too hastily. Indeed, one must respond to Nietzsche as a lover, not petulantly, but importunately.

Like Klossowski and many others, Irigaray (79–80/72–73) appears to accept the view that Nietzsche's rejection by Lou von Salomé was the fatal source of his ressentiment against woman. A look at the letters confirms that Nietzsche would never be the same after this near miss with the other, although, as Sarah Kofman would want us to remember, it is the way in which "Naumburg" (that is to say, sister and mother) became implicated in the Rée-Lou fiasco to which the letters most eloquently attest. Perhaps it is inevitable that the biographical *argumentum ad hominem* be trotted out against Nietzsche: that the one who inveighed against the human, all-too-human should all-too-humanly fall in love, and that his love should be spurned—who can suppress a rancorous chuckle, a poke in the ribs, a knowing wink? Yet what does one gain by such not very subtle aggression and reduction? An ephemeral sensation of power, Nietzsche would have said; a remarkably brief victory over one who otherwise always carries the day; winning the lover's quarrel, losing the lover's war.

A final suspicion or question with regard to Irigaray's reading of *Zarathustra*. Is it entirely certain that the sea and the sea-lover constitute the ultimate and unequivocal "other" to Nietzsche's thought? Entirely certain that the sea—the shroud of the sea that rolls on as it rolled five thousand years ago—is altogether without metaphysical consolations, devoid of romanza, liberated from illusions? Or might the sea be the very milieu of eternal recurrence of the same in its most consolatory guise? Might the sea—the wine-dark, life-giving sea—be the counterelement to transiency; might it be the symbol of the eternity sought for all things? Recall Nietzsche's note from the winter of 1887–1888, examined in chapters 3 and 5, which identifies the sea as a source of consolation (*Trost*): "Ought one to pour the costliest unguents and wines into the sea?—My consolation is that all that was is eternal:—the sea spews it forth again."[8] The sea: shroud or cornucopia, white shark or bounteous coral reef? And, whatever the case, what if the pretension to *gills* were the very pretense of birthing oneself anew, as though one could will such a thing, could will the obsolescence of lungs? Whether in the case of the *homo* or the *mulier*, including the *ecce*, is there not something fishy about birthing oneself anew as the (self-proclaimed, always selfsame) "other"?

Part II of *Amante marine*, "Veiled Lips," offers a devastating reading of *The Eumenides*, with Pallas Athena sprouting from the head of Zeus and testifying in the courtroom in such a way as to fulfill all her Father's wishes. "The cunning of the father, of the God? Rape/rob the female one so that the other can indefinitely produce doubles for him" (114/106). Part II also offers telling responses to those famous passages of Nietzsche's *The Gay Science* (FW, 59–60; 3, 422–25) on women and "naturalness," as well as their "action at a distance." The response to FW, 59 is particularly powerful, and I shall reproduce some passages from Nietzsche's text, followed by Irigaray's reply.

> We *Artificers*!—When we love a woman we may well fly into a rage against nature, thinking of all the repulsive naturalnesses [*Natürlichkeiten*] to which every woman is exposed. . . . Here one stops up one's ears against all physiology and secretly decrees for oneself: "I want to hear nothing about human beings' consisting of anything more than *soul and form*!" The human being "under the skin" is for all lovers a horror and an abomination, a blasphemy against God and against Love. . . . It is enough for us to love, hate, desire, sense anything at all—*immediately* the spirit and force of the dream comes over us and we climb the most hazardous winding ways, open-eyed, coolly confronting every danger, up to the rooftops and turrets of fantasy, without a hint of vertigo, as though we were born to clamber—we somnambulists of the day! We artificers! We concealers of naturalness! Moonsick, Godsick! Relentless wanderers, still as death, along heights we perceive not as heights but as our level plains, our securities!

In this passage the "we" is captivating. It oscillates somewhere between an outwardly directed analysis of the moonsick artist-artificer and the most painful sort of recoil, recoil back onto the genealogist of unnaturalness himself. Or herself. Irigaray replies less acerbically than one might have expected, perhaps in appreciation of the recoil already at work in Nietzsche's own text.

> Nature can be loved only if she is concealed: as if in a dream. No sooner do they sense nature than the men of yesterday and today climb high onto the roofs and towers of fantasy. They are born to climb—to rise up. And they feel not the slightest giddiness, provided their climb is concealed from them. These night-walkers by day, these God-struck ones, these moonstruck men with eyes open, see nothing in it but art.
>
> Their dream: to cover the natural with veils. To climb ever higher, get farther and farther off, turn away from nature toward certainties that they can no longer see, as an escape onto dangerous heights—their plains, their plans. As a way to rid their thoughts of the disgusting things to which nature subjects every woman (?). (115/108)

It is difficult, if not impossible, in the sense of *unreadable*, to separate out Nietzsche's own contribution to Irigaray's reply, that is to say, to delineate the ways in which that reply remains indebted to the Nietzschean analysis: it cannot be a matter of mere mockery here, no matter how severe the recoil on "Nietzsche" "himself" may be. Lack of generosity would soon prove to be lack of perspicacity. Nietzsche's greatest gift/*Gift*, as we saw early on, is his ability to *let* his genealogical analyses *recoil*, in this way helping his readers to their own responses. If Nietzsche did not wield the φάρμακον that makes of him a φαρμακός, no one would bother to reply to him—or to love him. Yet can one learn such recoil and such reckless generosity from Nietzsche? Can one presume to love him?

In this second section of *Amante marine* Irigaray presents the maternal-filial romanza of Demeter and Kore, rather too predictable in its contours: " . . . the mother's daughter, and the nearness they shared. . . . The end of the young girl, torn from her mother's arms, carried off into death. . . ." (121/113). When *Postponements* first appeared, I asked a psychoanalyst friend whether Nietzsche's misogyny troubled her. Her reply silenced me. "It doesn't trouble me at all," she said. "Whenever Nietzsche uses the word *woman* I substitute the words *my mother*, and then I have no difficulty accepting what he says." Sometimes Kore prefers life in hell.

Once again in these pages Irigaray reproduces her rhapsody of the lips, the one and the other in absolute intimacy, the lips of woman touching each other in perfect self-embrace (91/85). Perhaps this is what we heard Novalis calling the beginning of philosophy, the first kiss. Of course, Irigaray senses the danger of such a claim, a familiar danger, a danger she always wants to avert: "And she does not oppose a feminine truth to the masculine truth. Because this would once again amount to playing the—man's—game of castration" (92/86). There nevertheless follows the by now familiar gothic tale of these lips' generously and altogether gratuitously setting aside their self-sufficiency in order to embrace the violent ingrate, "him":

But because, through the reembrace of her lips—both passive and active, experienced without ressentiment—she still remains familiar to the other, she is disposed to receive him again and yet again into her. She does not take him *into* her. The other is not, here or there, taken into the whole of herself. She "wills" herself only with the other. She takes endless pleasure in ensnaring [*d'enlacer*] the other. Always moving inside and outside at the same time, passing between the edges, thriving in the depth and thickness of the flesh, as though outside the universe, more or less removed from it. She goes and comes, in herself and outside herself, ceaselessly. According to at least four dimensions: from left to right, from right to left, from before after, from after before, the threshold of the inside to the outside of the body.

Thus is ceaselessly engendered the expansion of her "world," which does not develop within any square or circle or anything else, and which remains without limit or boundary. Anything occurring in that world is wedded in movement, if it remains an other that self-embraces. Passive and active, feeling without ressentiment. (123/115)

Activity and passivity, self-embrace, generosity without need, sheer altruism or sly Sirenic ensnaring, but in any case always pure spontaneity: she is the Demiurge *redivivus*, without a demisemiquaver of either desire or need, except perhaps the desire to find hands outstretched to receive her proffered honey. Irigaray's is more Zarathustra's solar desire, more a yearning for the aerial realm, "which remains without limit or boundary," than the receptive generosity and nocturnal languor of Schelling's desirous God, who is on the verge of discovering that He is betimes a woman. (That may be bad politics on Schelling's part, or on the part of his God, but it is the only interesting theology.)

Feeling. Without feeling ressentiment. That is the key. While the arrow of ressentiment is deflected back again and again upon Nietzsche, which is precisely where the genealogist himself or herself always needs to have it deflected, Irigaray expresses the truth or the desire-of-the-truth to have been utterly devoid of ressentiment. The interiorized cruelty that Nietzsche identifies as the energizing force of ascetic ideals should have, must have, can have, nothing to do with woman. No ascetic priestesses, not ever. Yet when the arrow is deflected back at Nietzsche one must wonder whether it is not the same aerial arrow that Nietzsche shot from *his* bow. Indeed, deflection and reaction would not be the motion of the sea; it would not suit the sea to shoot or deflect arrows and accusations. After writing of ressentiment as though it were a sentiment quite beneath or altogether outside of woman, perfectly phallically foreign, Irigaray writes the concluding words of "Veiled Lips":

And if the latest fashion is to will that she be phallic, she will prove to you that she is phallic, that you are right to believe it. Piling it on, until the phallus, and all the rest, go to their ruin.

Since, of course, all the perspectives that have already been fixed, all the shapes already outlined, all the boundaries already laid down, appear to her as merely a set in a game. That will entertain her—perhaps? But only for a moment. For as long as it takes to feel the limit, and start her operation again.

> Unless she has been dead since birth. An immortal virgin, because never a little girl. A flower hypostasized into truth, appearance, semblance. . . . According to your will, the necessities of your power, the historical moments. Everything at the same time, every woman at the same time, in order to please you.
> Stop, dead stop, without end. [*Arrêt, et de mort, sans fin.*] (127/119)

Without ressentiment, yet with all the accusatory pathos of one who has received the death sentence; piling it on, in the desperate gamesmanship of Death Row, giving itself (out) as (if) without ressentiment, as though for a moment's entertainment. *Se donner pour, sich geben als. . . .*

Part III, "Where Gods Are Born," offers a remarkable reading of the birth and (shared) character of Dionysos, Apollo, and the Christ. Surprisingly, the readings become more generous as they proceed, so much so that one discerns a shadow of Mariology hovering over the final pages of Irigaray's book. The response to Nietzsche's analysis of the hypersensitivity of the Redeemer type (as we saw it, in chapter 1, analyzed in *The Antichrist*) and the outspoken preference for a secular Jesus, is more generous to the Crucified than to Dionysos. For Christianity is putatively a matter of purity of origins betrayed by a "tradition":

> Was he like that? Or has tradition made him like that? The place of his loves is rendered virgin, or childlike, or adolescent. Must the Christic redemption mean that the advent of the divine has never taken place in the incarnation of an amorous relationship with the other? Must this messenger of life neglect or refuse the most elementary realities? Must he be a timid or morbid adolescent, too paralyzed to realize his desires, always attentive to his Father's edicts, executing the Father's wishes even to the point of accepting the passion and the Father's desertion . . . ?
> Who interpreted him in this way? Who abominated the body so much that he glorified the son of man for being abstinent or castrated? (189/177)

The generosity that underlies the critical questions is that of *The Last Temptation of Christ* or of the Dutch theologians—the latter in distant memory of and nostalgia for Vatican II. "Search for traces of the divine in anything that does not preach, does not command, but enacts the work of the incarnation" (182/170).

Most ironic and intriguing in Irigaray's treatment of the Christ is her reflection on the lance-wound in the side of the Crucified. As though in reply to the ancient Gnostic sects, who argued that the Glorified Body of every deceased Christian woman must be outfitted with a Christic phallus before it can be assumed into heaven,[9] Irigaray calls this wound a *vagina* (177/166). She does not speculate that it may be the very sheath from which the rib of Adam was removed.

In general, Irigaray's treatment of Apollo equates the Delphic god with what Nietzsche calls *Socratism*—the death of the tragic thought. There is no discussion of the meeting and mating of Apollo and Dionysos, the intermittent coupling that produces the miracle of tragedy, no discussion of Apollo's "removing the weapon" from the hand of the Lydian god (1, 32), no discussion of their productive difference(s). Irigaray focuses instead on the ostensibly identical genealogy of these two apparently male gods:

> Apollo does not exclude Dionysos. They complete each other in Zeus, but never reproduce his unity. Apollo hands down the celestial patrimony of the mantic, the light, measured restraint, justice, the organization of the city. Dionysos inherits his father's thunderous excesses, the gift of seducing women in drunkenness and ecstasy, the attraction for water, the possessive and devastating passion of night.
> The two—couple of false twins?—must coexist as incarnations of the power of Zeus. Even if one surpasses the other in power, the division of possessions, here, cannot be closed. The whole will no longer belong to any one. It is up to the brother-men, without resorting to bloody warfare, to divide up the Father's attributes. Including those he has stolen from the ancestress or the mother. (170–71/159)

One can understand the desire to abnegate whatever the sons of Zeus have touched. Including Ariadne, who is here surrendered to Gilles Deleuze's interpretation: "Ariadne—double of the male" (125/117).[10] However, if Dionysos is, as Irigaray writes, the god of excess, the one who seduces women (but how? what kettle logic will explain it, or explain it away?), the god who displays "an attraction for water," which is something the sea-lover should know about, and "the possessive and devastating passion of the night," which is at least not altogether solid and solar—then one might expect a rather different response to Dionysos. A response to Dionysos as Zagreus, fragmented and eaten by at least two systems of the mouth, but without ressentiment. A response that would lower its weapons and become multifaceted, manifold.

Even if one remains within the confines of Olympian genealogy, the sons of Zeus have at least something to do with the *downfall* of the Father. What else is Aeschylus concerned with, especially in his *Prometheus Bound*, than the inevitable demise of Zeus? If the bloody passage of power from Ouranos to Kronos to Zeus is something that tragedy is well aware of, then perhaps the *birth* of tragedy in the (intermittent, intromissive, incomprehensible) mating of Apollo and Dionysos has something to do with the collapse of the *Deus*? That Nietzsche—wandering amid the ruins of fallen gods and the toppled statue of Pan—sought out the ways of the *mothers* in his first major work, that he sought out the ancestress or the mother from whom the Father stole "his" attributes, suggests that a reading of *The Birth of Tragedy* and the unpublished texts surrounding it ought to have lain at the heart of *Amante marine*, "When Gods Are Born." They do not.

Both Hölderlin and Nietzsche were convinced that the very essence of tragedy involved—in addition to the downfall of the Father—the figure(s) of woman and sensuous love. Even though tragic poetry could never be confused with sentimental poetry, Panthea and Delia (originally *Rhea*) are powerfully present in Hölderlin's *The Death of Empedocles*. Nietzsche's own plans for an Empedoclean drama locate the sensuous love of man and woman at the very center of the action. To the extent that these *Empedocles* plans dovetail with later plans for *Thus Spoke Zarathustra*, we can say that they reveal something very near the displaced core (or ecstatic center) of Nietzsche's concerns. Now, the figure of Empedocles is at the heart of Irigaray's own response to Heidegger— in *L'oubli de l'air*.[11] One might therefore have hoped to follow the thread of Irigaray's response to the Dionysian in the direction not of the genealogy of the (false) twin gods but of Love and Strife in the Empedoclean sphere—the tragic sphere. Yet Irigaray everywhere resists the Dionysian and the Maenadic, resists the tragic thought that is so much a thought of the sea. The enthusiasm of the Maenads is in her view too violent, too destructive (132/124). Irigaray thus accepts, in a straightforward—that is, altogether negative—way, Heraclitus's identification of Dionysos and Hades. Her suspicion of the god who has down on his cheeks is this: "In calling us once again to desire, does he not destroy the body?" (137/129). That is the very accusation brought against this foreign god by Pentheus. Ironically, Irigaray's suspicion of the Maenad throng reduplicates that of the Theban King, the primal Father of the city. However, no messenger comes to reassure her about the Dionysian women:

> . . . Starting out from the mountains, the women are worshippers of the phallus. Leaving their sea clan far behind, they are caught up and carried out of themselves by their eternal betrothals to the god who is coming. And their desire becomes a chorus of suppliant women in exile, the convulsive rites and dances of women in a trance. And the throbbing music of the summons to a wedding that is forever deferred pours out of them, like a fluid that the women still breathe out but is already bent to the rhythm of the man-god and therefore no longer flows in them. Or between them. The whole thing is driven by the very cult of the phallic effigy.
>
> Their madness is still visible. And their pain. The violence of their passions. Exasperated to the point of destroying life. Still wild, but a kind of wildness already inspired by the beyond. A wildness in which the women become impassioned, lose their wits, their energies, move out of their natal element. In the grip of movements too swift to last. Between rhythms, finding no passage, losing the harmony. And they collapse onto the ground from weariness at the conclusion of their intoxication [*ivresse*]. (149/140)

Each complaint finds its parallel in the complaint of the king, and each is contradicted by the shepherd messenger who has actually seen the Bacchae at their revels. Irigaray's nightmare vision mirrors that of Pentheus: convulsive rites of women entranced, women poisoned, women intoxicated and betrayed by promises of a wedding that will never take place; madness, pain, and violence mar their passions, which are passions destructive of life; women without wits, women driven out of their element, women deprived of the fluidity that is their birthright, like fish out of water; women whose rhythms now lack harmony, whose convulsive pleasures will not last, whose frenetic movements will gain them no sure eternity; women worshippers who ignominiously collapse to the ground in weariness, frustration, and exhaustion.

Oddly, Irigaray adopts a position close to that of *one* of the Nietzsches, namely, the medi-cynical Nietzsche who fears and derides the Maenads. "I know these lovable Maenads. . . . Ah, what dangerous, insidious, subterranean little predators! And so pleasant all the while! . . . (EH; 6, 306). Yet there is another Nietzsche, one who is closer to the Maenadic throng, and whom Irigaray herself resists. This other Nietzsche embraces the message of the one who has seen the women, rather than the fantasies of the solar-aerial king who fears them: in the unpublished essays surrounding *The Birth of Tragedy* Nietzsche tells us that the women unite in their midday dream extreme sensitivity and passionate suffering with "the most luminous contemplativeness and perspicacity" (1, 591; cf. 31 and 555–56, repeated at 583). The only life they will destroy is that of Pentheus, who resists and oppresses them. As I indicated in chapter 3, Pentheus is the first cousin of the god—for their mothers are sisters—and is himself the next reincarnation of Dionysos. The god is always doubled, masked, and remarked, and always from his mortal mother's side. True, it is the mourning (πένθ[ε]ος) that Irigaray objects to, the sense of loss that surrounds the god from the moment of his violent birth: "But the primitive whole is already destroyed. And Dionysos shows more signs of sadness confronting that disappearance than of rejoicing in a new harmony" (139/131). It is his mourning, she says, that drives the women to distraction: "From him to whom they give life, they receive death. If he is son of the God. For now the women kill the little children of simple mortals, in their madness" (151/142). To repeat, however, the only child the women kill is the manchild Pentheus, "grief" and "mourning," the proud, doomed patriarch whose opposition to the Maenads is startlingly similar to Irigaray's.

By what were the Maenads seduced away from the sea? By the mountain wine—away from the wine-dark sea? By the flowers and herbs inland? By the statue of Pan, not yet toppled? By the thyrsos, wound by ribbons and ivy? By the phallus? Thus commences the kettle logic of seduction—a seduction that is both impossible and inevitable. What can never have interrupted the intrinsic self-embrace of the lips except by sheer extrinsic violence now becomes *seditious*, subverting from the *inside*, as it were, and thus contaminating the perfection of the female inside/outside. Perfection succumbs to infection. Whence the fifth-column phallus? The male phallus is carved from driftwood, which, admittedly, is wood of the sea. Whence the potency of the phallus, whence its power to seduce creatures who are perfect without it? Its potency too is from the sea, presumably, the sea that long ago left its calcareous remnants on the coral atoll and alluvial mountain—indeed, *as* the alluvial mountain, inasmuch as the (masculine) mountain is nothing other than the alluvium of the sea-lover, she-lover. Irigaray riddles on the riddle of such a seduction by the murderous phallus:

> Since he is not yet a god, Dionysos shows the way. And one of his favored masks is the phallus. Carved out of hard wood, supposedly taken from the sea.

Mask of birthing [*génération*]? Supernatural birthing? Of desire? One already modeled by the law of the Father of the gods? Effigy of love among the living (men) [*vivants*]? Interdict of happy relations with mortal women? Petrified potency fished out [*repêchée*] of the great depths after the mother's murder?

Power that still shows its ambiguity. Phallic Dionysos grants drunkenness [*ivresse*] and ecstasy. Calls beyond. Sets absence within and between bodies. Desire becomes an exodus toward death, sign of its approach. Erection commemorating its fulfillment. A monument to crime in its cadaveric stiffness, fascination of a ghost [*revenant*] that is/is not in the depths, evanescent rising of one who survives only in the anxiety of disappearing, in the terror of vengeance. The mask covers the whole thing over—in a format larger than life. (141–42/133)

Each word resounds with ambivalence, even where a massive univocity of revulsion seems to prevail: the proscription of the phallus, which always and everywhere is ruinous of "happy relations with mortal women," *all* mortal women, differences in preference or taste or individuality notwithstanding; ostracism of the Maenads, who are revoltingly drunk with the god's juice, besotted, beside themselves; condemnation of erection, with its deadly entelechy, its fulfillment in inevitable demise. The erect penis, itself insecure and anxious, donning the brave phallic mask, is declared outlaw, criminal, and cadaverous— in view of its very rigor, not to say vigor. The sea-lover finds the driftwood dry, and pours contumely upon it:

In wetness the seed of the living (men) [*la semence des vivants*] finds its fecundation. Not in phallic erection, its mask. Frozen parodic appropriation. Where one believes the seed resides, although it does not. Always under every surface, in the fluid depths. Short of any form that is already visible. Short of or beyond all erection. Sterile.

Except for seducing into drunkenness [*la séduction dans l'ivresse*]. Involving ecstasy—outside the body. Summoning dance and music. Recalling and forgetting the flesh as it remains in the movement of its becoming. The rhythm is too fast and goes beyond the natural beat [*la mesure naturelle*]. Exaltation that tears away from the roots. Attracts one out of the self, upward. Finding a place high up, on the very peak. Coming to it by moving away from it. Having no element but the one that exaltation opens up at the peak of its elevation. Always ecstatic. Always beyond one's own body. Always in exile from one's own completeness. (145–46/137)

Why contumely, when wetness is desired? Why the arid, scathing sarcasm of "frozen parodic appropriation"? To what does the isolated word *Sterile* refer? To the erection, or to the seed in the fluid depths? What will keep that word in its place? The phallus dependably impotent and without possible effect. A sort of dildo, the "woman's best companion," advertised in the back pages of men's magazines. Risible. "Except for seducing into drunkenness." Why this exception? Why the Biblical anathematization of drunkenness? "Summoning music and dance," as though to Geneva, for trial? And *how* does the seduction work its effects, however risible, however scandalous?

In contrast, the messenger says that the women are not drunk, not in their cups, not sloppy, not witless, as the king imagines them to be. Why the insistence that Maenadic ecstasy is *outside* the body? Uprooted from its native soil—a soil, to be sure, that belongs to the sea only in catachresis? Why the presumption that every woman's body, once it is infected by wine or by the phantasm or fluid of the phallus, once that it tastes that particular exaltation, can be denigrated in this prescriptive way? Who says there is no Socrates among the women, the imbibing yet serene Socrates portrayed by Alcibiades? Who dictates the rhythm of becoming? Who possesses the measure of the "natural beat"? Whose is the Mariological or Pentheic or Pausaniac wisdom that will appropriate all nature and propound the measure? Who will prohibit ecstasy or restrict it within bounds, the oneiric bounds of "one's own completeness"?

Nothing is less certain, according to some contemporary archaeologists and classicists, than the intoxication and frenzy imputed to the Maenads. Nothing is less certain than the effects of the phallus on the women worshippers of Dionysos. It is therefore not surprising to find at least one contemporary classicist who goes even further than Euripides' shepherd messenger in shattering the assumption that the Bacchae have been driven out of their minds and morals: "Maenads are inviolable . . . , as chaste as they are sober."[12] Furthermore, there is "no symmetry of masculine and feminine around Dionysos: it seems that when a woman is associated with the *phallos*, she is not Dionysiac, and when she is Dionysiac, she is not associated with the *phallos*."

If one thinks through the disconcerting association of Irigaray with Pentheus—both of whom challenge Dionysos because of his putative reduction of woman to an alienated plaything of (masculine) desire, outside herself, a fish gasping on the strand—one arrives at the doublings, duplicities, and doublebinds of what one might call *Pentheic projection*. Can one utter *anything* about the god and "his" effects on "the women" without holding up the mirror of Dionysos to oneself—to one's own fragmented, distorted, and distorting self? Would not one be less inclined than ever to shoot arrows, or throw boomerangs, at such projected images?

"One's own completeness"? Whose completeness, whose first and final kiss, in the mirrorplay of whose dreams? Always the claim of perfection, plenitude, self-embrace. Always the concomitant condemnation of ecstasy. Always an insistence on the *interiority* of one's own womanly body, or on the readily negotiated frontier of one's own *inside/outside*, utterly sufficient unto itself, untouchable and impenetrable, ultimately as inconcussible as the truth of the cogito. Always the return to the allegorical island-fortress of metaphysics. Always the accusation of crimes committed by the (readily identifiable, always dependably selfsame) other and the victimization of oneself. And the cry, Pity me, Pity me, who nevertheless am invincible, except when I am drunk or doing kettle logic. Pity me—and feel the piercing of my arrows. Shot without ressentiment.

Always the arrows—arrows not unrelated to these very arrows I am aiming here, in these very words of mine now—shot back in anger and frustration and anxiety. Perhaps even in ressentiment. Shot back—as though refutation could touch erotic difference(s) or diminish one's love of a person who instills doubt.

Who owns the phallus? Why the presumption that its signification is "male"? Need the phallus always be desiccated? Need it always be surface elevation, without depth? Why does Irigaray never mention the niches carved into the driftwood, niches containing figurines, niches that certainly would have fascinated all the Nietzsches? Does not contumely aggravate the desiccation that creates the brave mask, the hated phallic scepter and dildonic verge? Is it not possible, or often quite likely, that the tumescent organ of the man is the creation of a woman, born of the wet, maintained—insofar as it ever can be maintained—by the wet? Does not that organ too bespeak the brine, stammering of the salt sea? Never an architectonic erection, never the phallic edifice, never a mask that is not a molding of multiple hands and mouths. Perhaps Lacan is right when he confesses that the cock of the walk is a woman, and that if there is only one libido it is the jouissance of the godhead; perhaps Schelling is right when he speculates that the godhead is (also) of woman. In any case, it is not always easy or advisable to make clearcut gender or genital divisions in matters of eggs and lips, buttons and stems, depths and surfaces, and liquids that smack of the sea. Only the bird's eye view, only the dizziest aerial view, would ever try to distinguish what the sea is happy to commingle.

They say that when Nietzsche celebrated his fiftieth birthday in 1894 Paul Deussen came to visit. He presented chrysanthemums and chocolates as Nietzsche's mother lit the candles on the cake. Nietzsche himself had trouble concentrating. At the word *birthday* he could think of only three things: one of the final sets of pageproofs he had corrected, proofs of a text he had begun to write on his forty-fourth birthday, the last birthday he could really remember, mixed up with memories of a much earlier time when he felt very close to Jesus but realized that Jesus was in some sense the credulous son of a prison warden, and, finally, mixed up with phantasms of what he called "birthing." It was all muddled in his head. Proofs. Jesus. Birthing. Mums. He would have wanted to jot it all down in his fictional autobiography. Proofs and mums and chocolates. He remembered too a woman who used to visit him in secret many years before, somewhere in Italy, somewhere near the sea where he bathed and the smell of oranges. It was now the fifth year of his insanity, everything was higgledy-piggledy and yet oddly, intensely, unbearably focused, everything in uncanny repose. Sometimes you have to get that muddled before you can think clearly about the sea-lover.

•

happy birthday to me poring over pageproofs. my way of birthing. i wrote very beautiful things once upon a time mama i kept working on them until they were printed and even while they were being printed because i loved the smell of paper and ink intoxicating mama. it was like birthing. read me some of them dont be shy i know that secretly when no one is watching you admire them. open one of them mama and read to me in the night when no one is there to interrupt us birthing. it can happen more than once mama birthing and it can happen backwards in reverse. getting your tongue around the words. corinna calina i dont remember very well the stiffening stiffens my memory. i was writing it was evening no not yet evening i remember the late afternoon sun slanting in through the window on my left i was writing about what i dont remember wait a prison and the warden that was my father mama and the son thats what i was writing with great joy smoothly easily even though calina corinna i dont remember was there all that afternoon in ree myself. she was no longer singing not even humming softly as she always did just sitting quietly i didnt even notice her mama giving birth parturing me and what i was writing making me her own son not the wardens son i dont know how she did it i cant remember i can only see the oblique rays redorange lighting laving her skin it was all she wore mama sitting on a hardwood straightbacked chair pressed up against the whitewashed wall. nice? no. rapallo? no. portofino? i dont know. fino molto fino italia somewhere in ree. sitting slouching ever so slightly mama her head turned hard to the right away from the sun her gaze relentless on the floor. rose marble. that place near naples with ree in ree malwida and brenner consumption all consuming in the orangegrove yes that was it the smell of ink and oranges not nice at all not rapallo not portofino not torino it will come back to me in a moment mama. her inky hair in careless tresses hanging the uneven tips of it brushing the swollen indolent brown nipples near naples yes chocolates mamas huge puffy bittersweet setting suns burning in the late afternoon sun. she paid me no mind i was writing she was birthing me and my writing it came so smoothly so easily the warden and his only begotten son no not capri not ligure not levanto i cant remember i see only corinna calina her slouch her gaze fixed averted her hands lopped lazily over her raised knees opening like the wings of a butterfly in the warm rees of the afternoon sun. her heels poised on the very edge of that straightbacked hardwood chair her feet wide apart each foot pointing down and away the long delicate toes the second toe much longer than the big toe beside it botticelli feet corinna calina i cant for the stiffening neck the throbbing head mama cant remember anything now not mesopotamia not messina not sicily not acragas empedocles agrigentum not herculaneum ashes cast in plaster i looked up from my writing just as the wardens son was suffering the jeers of the prisoners disbelief looked up and over to her she was absent to me to herself hands draped hands so beautifully busy before mama now like the folded wings of a swan vain and languorous the bubs of swollen unmistakable for anything else flesh and below the cupped weight and swagger of breasts her belly folding in the slouch and sloth of bellybutton omphalos center of the earth the great cleft beneath tartaros the burning black bush where moses put down his rosen steel tip pen replaced the rubber stopper in the inkbottle pushed back the cane chair it creaked and scraped the floor she never moved her head mama hardright the tendon at the base of her throat distended taut an animal would have seized her there what am i mama im not an animal am i but without moving her head without hinting she might have heard the creak and scrape heard my noiseless tread felt it through the floor of roses and slowly infinitely slowly lowered her hands between her knees her thighs and joined thumb to thumb and index to index forming a diamond windowframe about her smiling notmouth her notclosed lips her ragged gaping vertical smile no thorns no agave mother do you know it only colors more colors in the redorange burntsienna light no not sienna than ever were in the white incandescence of noon the purple veins almost jetblack. sparkle of sequins dans la saison des fleurs. i was on my knees now mama i was as close as birthing mama not yet praying not yet whispering no longer writing only seeing rapt observant inquisitive beholding the infinitesimal porphyry veins of the rose wall wet with the underground spring the font of castalia corinna calina kali phosphoricum trimethylamine all the walls watery wet with lambent mother of pearl opal of seawash breath of brine and orangeblossom birthing it was the same flow as writing mama descrying where the setting sun could penetrate no longer she was sinking now in the ponient waters nothing there in that noplace was dark not even at the crease where the light glistened but could not penetrate no dark beneath the scrub i would have thought there was dark there mama but there was no dark until i closed my eyes and my head went into the gesture of reception like the boys and girls at the communion rail in the italian churches mama tasting god and for a very long time i was not afraid i was not anything or anywhere to be seen my face in a world that gave way but never budged withdrew but never retreated surrendered but never capitulated a face that never denied or abnegated never affirmed or asserted anything but only sighed hissed yes yes yes yes. birthing. happy birthing. i slake no horses. i can remember nothing mama not rimini not deiva marina not serendipity not papi not sorella read to me o please mama what i wrote birthing read me remind me because i am on the very verge of remembering without being able in the end to remember calina corinna whatever became of you sorella how can you not be here when i am there now again yes here and now in mind and mouth of you in not even surrender sorrento yes sorrento of course it was sorrento the orangegrove outside the house above the bay perfume of oranges rising off the page on the haze of evening overpowering even the fragrance of the sea the grotto the cavern where————sorrento dido the orange fire smoldering into purple night and i was lost at sea the wardens son no more i was an other that orangeblossom evening pledging endless inky promises yes yes yes yes sorella sorrento.

Notes

I cite Nietzsche's works in the *Kritische Studienausgabe* (KSA), edited by Giorgio Colli and Mazzino Montinari, in 15 volumes (Berlin and Munich: Walter de Gruyter and Deutscher Taschenbuch Verlag, 1980), with the volume in italic, page number in Arabic; most references are preceded by the initials of the specific work cited, according to the code below. Nietzsche's letters I cite in the KSAB, that is, *Sämtliche Briefe in 8 Bänden, Kritische Studienausgabe*, edited by Giorgio Colli and Mazzino Montinari (Berlin and Munich: Walter de Gruyter and Deutscher Taschenbuch Verlag, 1986). I cite Nietzsche's early writings, those not contained in the KSA, in the edition by Karl Schlechta, *Werke in drei Bänden* (Munich: Carl Hanser Verlag, 1965); *Der Wille zur Macht*, edited by Elisabeth Förster-Nietzsche and Peter Gast (Stuttgart: Kröner Verlag, 1964), I cite as WM, with aphorism (not page) number. The code by which I cite individual works by Nietzsche is as follows:

GT	= *Geburt der Tragödie*
UB I–IV	= *Unzeitgemäße Betrachtungen*, I to IV
MAM I, II	= *Menschliches, Allzumenschliches*, Parts I and II
M	= *Morgenröte*
FW	= *Die fröhliche Wissenschaft*
ASZ I–IV	= *Also sprach Zarathustra*, Parts I to IV
JGB	= *Jenseits von Gut und Böse*
ZGM I–III	= *Zur Genealogie der Moral*, treatises I to III
GD	= *Götzen-Dämmerung*
A	= *Der Antichrist*
EH	= *Ecce homo*

Abbreviations for works by other authors are given in the notes in which the works are first cited.

ONE. *CRITICA GENEALOGICA I*

1. According to Max Scheler, *Vom Umsturz der Werte*, 2 vols. (Leipzig: Der neue Geist, 1919), esp. *1*, 45–236, "*Das Ressentiment im Aufbau der Moralen*," Nietzsche makes this French word a *terminus technicus*. The French word suggests (1) an emotional response that is directed toward another but plunges into the core of personality, deep beneath the zones of expression and normal intercourse, a response that is re-experienced and relived, and (2) a negative response, "containing a movement of animosity." Scheler suggests as a possible translation of the French word the German *Groll*, a sulking, grudging, resentful ill-will against others. Ressentiment is a paralyzing hatred, independent of the control of the ego, which spreads through the personality in the way a poison invades the bloodstream. Elsewhere Scheler defines ressentiment as "a psychic poisoning of the self" (51). One of its characteristics is an impulse to revenge that never succeeds in arousing attack: ressentiment is the feeling of incapacity and impotence that causes all hatred to boil and bubble without hope of expression (52). As far as Scheler's own work is concerned, one may say that the first section of the work, "Toward a Phenomenology and Sociology of *Ressentiment*" (48 ff.) is helpful; the rest of the work is a clumsy polemic in defense of "Christian love" against the Nietzschean slur of ressentiment. Scheler's wall of piety successfully prevents an adequate understanding of Nietzsche's notion of ressentiment; his awkward "refutation" of Nietzsche makes for painful reading. Like his prolific "metaphysics of German war," Scheler's attempts at Nietzsche-refutation must be set aside, with no small amount of embarrassment, as relics of an epoch that has vanished.

2. Jean Granier, *Le problème de la Vérité dans la philosophie de Nietzsche* (Paris: Seuil, 1966), p. 339; cited henceforth in the body of my text as Gr, with page number. Nietzsche's analysis of the body constitutes an introduction to the phenomenological philosophy of Merleau-Ponty, especially the theme of *le corps propre*. It was one of Merleau-Ponty's chief tasks to show that metaphysical idealism and scientific empiricism alike were children of an inadequate metaphysics. See Maurice Merleau-Ponty, *Phénoménologie de la perception* (Paris: Gallimard, 1945), chap. 4, pp. 64 ff.

3. Thus, at any rate, Walter Kaufmann, in *Nietzsche: Philosopher, Psychologist, Antichrist* (Cleveland: Meridian Books, 1956), pp. 159–60; I shall cite Kaufmann's book from hence as Kf, with page number. Note Nietzsche's use of the phrase with regard to "the scientific human being" in notebook M III 1, dated spring-fall 1881 (11 [346]; 9, 575), discussed in chap. 9, below.

4. Herman Melville, *Moby-Dick: or, The Whale* (Boston: Houghton Mifflin, 1956), pp. 84–85.

5. Gilles Deleuze, *Nietzsche et la philosophie* (Paris: Presses Universitaires de France, 1962), p. 17; cited hereinafter as Dz, with page number.

6. Granier, 95, cf. FW, 348; 3, 583–85.

7. *Méditations I*, in Descartes, *Œuvres et lettres*, ed. André Bridoux (Paris: Gallimard-Pléiade, 1953), p. 267; cited from hence in the body of my text by page number in parentheses.

8. JGB, 19; 5, 31–32. Actually, Nietzsche says this about *willing*, but inasmuch as "I will" is, at least in terms of its assertory nature, interchangeable with "I think," a critique of the one encompasses the other as well.

9. WM, 483; 11, 598. For further discussion, see chap. 9.

10. Immanuel Kant, *Kritik der reinen Vernunft*, ed. Raymund Schmidt (Hamburg: F. Meiner, 1971), A 1; cited hereinafter as KrV, or simply by the pagination of the first (A) or second (B) editions; translated by Norman Kemp Smith as *Critique of Pure Reason* (New York: St. Martin's Press, 1965).

11. Cf. the first of Leibniz's "24 Theses," reprinted in Martin Heidegger, *Nietzsche*, 2 vols. (Pfullingen: G. Neske, 1961), 2, 454–57, esp. ". . . *quod nihil fit sine ratione. . . .*"

12. Melville, *Moby-Dick*, pp. 409–10.

13. Nietzsche, letter to Georg Brandes dated January 4, 1889; in KSAB, 8, 573.

14. William Butler Yeats, *Collected Poems* (New York: Macmillan, 1956), p. 161.

15. *Thus Spoke Zarathustra*, Part III, "Das andere Tanzlied"; 4, 285–86.

TWO. *CRITICA GENEALOGICA II*

1. Eugen Fink, *Nietzsches Philosophie* (Stuttgart: Kohlhammer, 1960), p. 7; henceforth cited as Fn, with page number, in the body of my text.

2. Deleuze, p. 2; Deleuze continues: "Genealogy is opposed to the absolute character of values, as also to their relative or utilitarian character. Genealogy signifies the differential element of values, from which their value itself derives. Genealogy thus means origin or birth, but also difference or distance in the origin" (pp. 2–3). Granier writes: "Genealogy is not only research into the origin of values, but also an appreciation of the value of the origin" (p. 164).

3. Deleuze, p. 3, referring to *Thus Spoke Zarathustra*, Part III, "On Passing By," and Part I of *Ecce Homo*, sections 6–7.

4. Michel Foucault, "Nietzsche, Genealogy, History," in *Hommage à Jean Hyppolite* (Paris: Presses Universitaires de France, 1971), pp. 145–72; English translation in Michel Foucault, *Language, Counter-Memory, Practice*, ed. D. F. Bouchard (Ithaca, NY: Cornell University Press, 1977), pp. 139–64. In what follows I will cite in the body of my text the page references to the English translation. See also Foucault's *L'ordre du discours* (Paris: Gallimard, 1971); English translation in *Social Sciences Information*,

vol. 10, no. 2, April 1971), 7–30; also as an appendix ("The Discourse on Language") to Foucault, *Archaeology of Knowledge,* trans. A. M. Sheridan Smith (New York: Harper Colophon, 1976), pp. 215–37.

5. On *la discontinuité de l'être,* see Georges Bataille, *L'érotisme* (Paris: Minuit, 10/18, 1957), pp. 15–30.

6. The book that best captures the sense of such recoil, and that best expresses the frustrations that any Foucauldian militia (almost always, strangely, in U.S.-American fatigues) encounters, is Charles Scott, *The Question of Ethics* (Bloomington: Indiana University Press, 1990), esp. chap. 3, pp. 53–93. One must also note here another extraordinary American genealogist, Alphonso Lingis. See, for example, his "Vicious Circles," in *Deathbound Subjectivity* (Bloomington: Indiana University Press, 1989); "Black Stars: The Pedigree of the Evaluators," in *The Graduate Faculty Journal,* New School for Social Research, vol. 15, no. 2 (1991), 67–91; and *The Community of Those Who Have Nothing in Common* (Bloomington: Indiana University Press, 1994). (My thanks to Joel Shapiro and Ferit Güven for help with these references.)

7. If Granier's approach to a Nietzschean ontology possesses a fatal flaw, it is this: "Becoming itself *is,* it did not become" (Gr, 355). A fatal flaw, for this is what cannot be uttered—even if, as we shall see in chap. 8, many of Nietzsche's notes in notebook M III 1 approximate precisely this impossibility. Granier's success is to have subordinated all approaches to a Nietzschean ontology to the discipline of a new *hermeneutics,* for which his unfortunate term "meta-philosophy" is inadequate. *Kata-philosophy* would be better. I also want to resist Kaufmann's interpretation of will to power (see esp. Kf, 173, 182 ff., and 204 ff.), which is ultimately moralizing. A genealogical critique is fascinated to discover that it is this moralization of will to power that enables Kaufmann to conjoin will to power and eternal recurrence in order to construct a Nietzschean ontology, even a "monism," in which Apollo and Dionysos become identical twins. A further irony is that even though Kaufmann fumes and froths over Heidegger, his reading of Nietzsche ultimately succumbs to the least thought-provoking of Heidegger's theses. Kaufmann's paean to "self-control," which used to be a category on children's school report cards, only reinforces Nietzsche's suspicion that all ontology rests on hidden moral prejudices.

8. The version in WM contains many misreadings that disrupt the sense of the text; here it is particularly important that readers have access to the version in the KSA.

9. Granier actually makes the central theme of his work not a *threefold* sense of truth but the *dual* character of truth in Nietzsche's philosophy. Granier argues that Nietzsche's "passion for philological probity" is the expression of a will to knowledge that is radically distinct from the "vital pragmatism" by means of which Nietzsche demolishes idealistic metaphysics (498; cf. 515–17, where Granier qualifies his thesis admirably). As Nietzsche was himself suspicious of dualisms, so should we be. Every bit of evidence one can muster contradicts Granier's thesis. No one knew better than Nietzsche himself that his own occupation of genealogical critique was itself an expression of will to power. More than that, Nietzsche suspected that genealogical critique shared with all other sciences the "piety" afforded them by their metaphysical parentage; he suspected that genealogical critique was an expression also of the ascetic ideal, the most decadent and sickly form of will to power in all history; finally, he suspected the virtue of "probity" of becoming a new stupidity of free spirits—by no means was he united to it by "an unconditional loyalty" (499). It would not be difficult to take each piece of evidence cited by Granier and show that, far from supporting his thesis, these quotations within their context speak against his theory; it would not be difficult, but it would be time consuming. It would be better to introduce more positive evidence to support the three theses we oppose to Granier's: (1) genealogical critique shares the dubious "piety" of all other analytical sciences; (2) genealogical critique suspects itself of an asceticism that is inimical to the will to life; (3) philological probity is at best a virtue of free spirits whose will to knowledge is affirmative of life, at worst a "stupidity" and "sanctity" that are inimical to the will to life.

10. From Paul Ricoeur, *Philosophie de la volonté, Finitude et culpabilité II: Symbolique de mal* (Paris: Aubier, 1960), p. 300.

11. Jean-Paul Sartre, *Les mots* (Paris: Gallimard, 1964), p. 25; cited in what follows by page number in parentheses.

12. GD; 6, 77, quoted by Granier, p. 100, who develops the contrast between Nietzsche and Hegel in this regard.

13. In the edition by Karl Schlechta, see *3*, 199; 206. See also Nietzsche's complaints, in "We Philologists," about the current state of the philologists' profession, especially its inability, despite all its linguistic scholarship, to reach the world of the Greeks, *3*, 323 ff.

14. In the edition by Karl Schlechta, *3*, 157.

15. See Granier, pp. 355–56n; see esp. pp. 606–7: "What definitively hinders the displacement of this problematic [of language] is the insufficiency of Nietzsche's conceptions touching the ontological meaning and the functions of language."

16. G. W. F. Hegel, *Phänomenologie des Geistes*, 6th ed. (Hamburg: F. Meiner, 1952), p. 82. Cf. Ludwig Feuerbach's acerbic criticism of this passage in his *Principles of a Philosophy of the Future*, in *Werke in sechs Bänden*, ed. Erich Thies (Frankfurt am Main: Suhrkamp, 1975), §28; 3, 289–90.

17. Hegel, *Phänomenologie des Geistes*, pp. 558–59.

18. See *Beyond Good and Evil*, no. 36; *5*, 54–55; cf. *11*, 610 and *14*, 727, along with WM, 1067; see also Kaufmann, pp. 187–88, for the quotation.

19. R. J. Hollingdale, *Nietzsche* (Baton Rouge: Louisiana State University Press, 1965), p. 67.

20. Hollingdale, p. 207.

21. Hollingdale, p. 96.

22. Stefan Zweig, cited in Walter Kaufmann, *The Portable Nietzsche* (New York: Viking, 1954), p. 104.

23. Melville, *Moby-Dick*, pp. 58–59.

24. The above extracts are from Books XXI and XXII of Herman Melville, *Pierre: Or, the Ambiguities* (New York: New American Library, 1964), pp. 320–46.

25. This, I believe, is what Kaufmann does in his *Nietzsche*. He argues that the contradiction of yes-saying and no-saying is "merely verbal," and that even though the philosopher discloses a "cancerous growth" in human existence, he can still accept the cancer as "a *fait accompli*" (see p. 94 and pp. 348 ff.). However, in the case of Nietzsche, no contradiction is "merely verbal," but is a *contraction* or a *recoil* that strikes back hard against the thinker. One cannot cite *Ecce Homo* as though it were a source of evidence or proof for this or that thesis: the book is a riddle, every word of it, and as a text it goes nowhere but *down*.

THREE. *CRITICA GENEALOGICA III*

1. GD; 6, 96–97; cf. WM, 765, that is, *13*, 422–26; cf. also Joan Stambaugh, *Untersuchungen zum Problem der Zeit bei Nietzsche* (The Hague: M. Nijhoff, 1959), pp. 161 ff.; I shall refer to Stambaugh's book in the body of my text as St, with page number.

2. Euripides, *The Bacchae*, trans. William Arrowsmith (Chicago: University of Chicago Press, 1959), ll. 89–94; cited from hence in the body of my text by line.

3. Albert Camus, *L'Homme révolté* (Paris: Gallimard, 1951), pp. 94–95; cited henceforth as Cm, with page number, in the body of my text.

4. Melville, *Moby-Dick*, p. 186.

5. Heinz Heimsoeth, *Die sechs grossen Themen der abendländischen Metaphysik*, 5th ed. (Darmstadt: Wissenschaftliche Buchgesellschaft, 1965), pp. 59–60.

6. Heimsoeth, pp. 24–25.

7. EH; 6, 339; see the earlier version of Nietzsche's account, dropped from the published version of *Ecce Homo*, at KSA *14*, 496–97.

8. EH; 6, 339. In this regard, the Schlechta edition of *Ecce Homo* contains an interesting misreading: it takes Nietzsche's description of his "complete ecstasy," *vollkommnes Ausser-sich-sein*, as an "incomplete ecstasy," adding an *un-* where the holograph clearly does not even hint at it. It is as though the editor(s) of that edition had Nietzsche's insistence on the *incompleteness* of possession too much in mind. See the Schlechta edition, II, 1131, l. 4 from the bottom; cf. KSA 6, 339, l. 24; finally, see the facsimile edition of the holograph, that is, the printer's manuscript, prepared by Karl-Heinz Hahn and Anneliese Clauss (Leipzig: Edition Leipzig, 1985), folio sheet 70, l. 7, for confirmation of "complete ecstasy."

9. Alphonso Lingis, *Excesses: Eros and Culture* (Albany: State University of New York Press, 1983), pp. 1–16.

10. GT, 1–2 and 12; *1*, 25–34 and 82; see John Sallis, *Crossings: Nietzsche and the Space of Tragedy* (Chicago: University of Chicago Press, 1991), passim.

11. W. B. Yeats, "There," from "Supernatural Songs," in *Collected Poems*, p. 284.

12. I am thinking of my remarks in *Daimon Life: Heidegger and Life-Philosophy* (Bloomington: Indiana University Press, 1992), pp. 6–8.

13. Karl Löwith, *Nietzsches Philosophie der ewigen Wiederkehr des Gleichen* (Stuttgart: Kohlhammer, 1956), p. 67; henceforth cited as Lw, with page number, in my text.

14. Albert Camus, *Le mythe de Sisyphe* (Paris: Gallimard, 1942), p. 15.

15. ASZ II; 4, 177–82. My account here follows Stambaugh's, pp. 68–78, and Löwith's, pp. 81 and ff.

16. St, 140 ff., citing WM, 635; *13*, 258–59.

17. Mircea Eliade, *Le mythe de l'éternel retour: Archetypes et répétition*, revised ed. (Paris: Gallimard, 1969), p. 30.

18. See the discussions by Granier, pp. 567–68, and Kaufmann, pp. 124–25.

19. Merleau-Ponty, *Phénoménologie de la perception*, p. 484.

20. Melville, *Moby-Dick*, p. 431. The preceding quotation, on "the tornadoed Atlantic of my being," appears on p. 303.

21. Maurice Blanchot, "*Passage de la ligne*," *Entretien infini* (Paris: Gallimard, 1969), pp. 215–27.

22. Pausanias, *Guide to Greece*, 2 vols., trans. Peter Levi, S. J. (Harmondsworth: Penguin Books, 1971), Book IX, section 39; *1*, 392–95. Translation modified slightly.

23. Martin Heidegger, "Letter on Humanism," in *Wegmarken* (Frankfurt am Main: V. Klostermann, 1967), p. 182; English translation by Frank Capuzzi *et al.* in *Basic Writings*, revised edition (San Francisco: HarperCollins, 1993), p. 254.

FOUR. THE COCK

1. The first version of the present chapter, written some twenty-one years ago, appeared in *Topic: A Journal of the Liberal Arts* (published by Washington and Jefferson College, Washington, PA), no. 28 (Fall 1974), pp. 33–49. I am grateful to R. Lloyd Mitchell for inviting me at that time to write it, and to John Sallis, who made it possible. I cite Plato by Stephanus pagination, using Friedrich Schleiermacher's translations and the Greek text established by Édition Belles Lettres, Paris: *Platons sämtliche Werke*, 10 vols. (Frankfurt am Main: Insel Taschenbuch Verlag, 1991). The intrusions in the chapter come from one of the most bizarre of Herman Melville's *Piazza Tales*, "Cock-A-Doodle-Doo!"

2. It is difficult to convey the excitement that John Sallis's courses on Plato in the late 1960s and early 1970s aroused. Sallis read Plato with the attention to detail of a Straussian, but with none of the piety and reactionary politics. Indeed, he read Plato

with a "provocation" for which Nietzsche was largely responsible. To be sure, Hegel and Heidegger provoked the reading as well; yet it was Nietzsche who sent Sallis (and now us, his students) back to the drama—the *ergon* and the *mythos* as well as the *logos*—of the dialogues. See the second edition of Sallis, *Being and Logos: The Way of Platonic Dialogue* (Atlantic Highlands, NJ: Humanities Press, 1986), and his forthcoming, long-awaited book on the χώρα of Plato's *Timaeus*.

3. Jacques Derrida, *La carte postale de Socrate à Freud et au-delà* (Paris: Aubier-Flammarion, 1980), pp. 13–14; cited henceforth simply by page number. An English translation by Alan Bass appears in the University of Chicago Press series, published in 1987. The remarks by Heidegger on Socrates are to be found in his *Was heißt Denken?* (Tübingen: M. Niemeyer, 1954), p. 52.

4. See D. A. F. Sade, *Les cent vingt journées de Sodome*, in *Œuvres complètes du Marquis de Sade*, ed. Annie Le Brun and Jean-Jacques Pauvert (Paris: Pauvert, 1986), *1*, 200, 256, and 371.

5. In the edition by Karl Schlechta, see *3*, 333–48.

6. H. Gauss, *Philosophischer Handcommentar zu den Dialogen Platos*, II/2 (Bern: H. Lang, 1956), pp. 33–34: "Philosophizing, rightly understood, . . . is always a meditation on death. . . . Therefore, there is but one alternative: either we will never come to know what is right, or we will do so first of all after death. Hence philosophy is nothing other than a perpetual attempt to purify oneself from sensuous influences, and . . . a systematic preparation for death. Whoever cannot greet death as a friend is no philosopher. . . .'"

7. Melville, *Moby-Dick*, p. 271.

8. See Jacques Derrida, *"Apories: Mourir—s'attendre aux "limites de la vérité,"* in *Le passage des frontières: Autour du travail de Jacques Derrida* (Paris: Galilée, 1994), pp. 309–38; English translation, *Aporias*, trans. Thomas Dutoit (Stanford, CA: Stanford University Press, 1993). If Plato is concealment, then Heidegger would no doubt have to modify even more than he does in "The End of Philosophy and the Task of Thinking" his thesis concerning the "shift" that occurs in the history of truth, from unconcealment to correctness of assertion or adequation of representation to state of affairs. See esp. "Plato's Doctrine of Truth," in *Wegmarken* (Frankfurt am Main: V. Klostermann, 1967), pp. 109–44; see also *Beiträge zur Philosophie (Vom Ereignis)*, Martin Heidegger Gesamtausgabe vol. 65 (Frankfurt am Main: V. Klostermann, 1989), §§ 208–11 and 231–33, pp. 331–36 and 358–61; for "The End of Philosophy and the Task of Thinking," see Heidegger, *Zur Sache des Denkens* (Tübingen: M. Niemeyer, 1969), pp. 61–80; English translation in *Basic Writings*, revised ed., Reading XI.

FIVE. *DER MAULWURF*/THE MOLE

Anmerkungen zum deutschen Text

1. Zur Maulwurfsliteratur aus einer linkspolitischen Perspektive s. Alfred Opitz und Ernst-Ullrich Pinkert, *Der alte Maulwurf: Die Verdammten (unter) dieser Erde, Geschichte einer revolutionären Symbolfigur*, Berlin, 1979. Die Auszüge aus Marx, Schopenhauer, Filbinger und Eich in dem vorliegenden Kapitel stammen aus der Opitz/Pinkert'schen Sammlung. Die Rolle des Maulwurfs bei Kant, Hegel und Nietzsche wird in diesem Buch freilich nicht behandelt.

2. Immannuel Kant, *Kritik der reinen Vernunft*, herausgegeben von Raymund Schmidt, Hamburg, Felix Meiner Verlag, 1971.

3. Dem Aufsatz von Professor Sallis, den ich im Manuskript lesen konnte, verdanke ich jede Menge Maulwurfsmulm. S. jetzt J. Sallis, *Spacings—of Reason and Imagination in Texts of Kant, Fichte, Hegel*, Chicago, 1987, S. 1–22. Auch den folgenden Mannheimer Mitwühlenden möchte ich hier herzlich danken: Ulrich Halfmann, Friederike Born, Burkhardt Allner, Elisabeth Hoffmann, Thomas Müller, Werner Reinhart, Margarete Seidenspinner, Jupp Schöpp und Jochen Barkhausen.

4. G. W. F. Hegel, *Werke in zwanzig Banden,* Frankfurt/Main, Suhrkamp, 1971, XX, 455.

5. Selbstverständlich sind alle Zitate aus den *Vorlesungen über die Geschichte der Philosophie* nur vorläufig als Hegels Wortlaut zu akzeptieren. Man darf auf die verschiedenen kritischen Ausgaben, die zur Zeit in Frankreich, Italien und Deutschland in Vorbereitung sind, gespannt sein.

6. Vgl. die beiden letzten Seiten der *Phänomenologie des Geistes,* über "Er-Innerung." S. jetzt D. F. Krell, *Of Memory, Reminiscence, and Writing: On the Verge,* Bloomington, Indiana University Press, 1990, Kap. 5.

Notes to the English-language column

1. For an account of the literature on the mole in Germany, especially from a leftist political stance, see Alfred Opitz and Ernst-Ullrich Pinkert, *The Old Mole: The Damned of/under This Earth: History of a Revolutionary Symbol* (Berlin, 1979). The extracts from Marx, Schopenhauer, and Filbinger stem from the Opitz/Pinkert collection. Nevertheless, the monograph says nothing about the mole's role in Kant, Hegel, and Nietzsche.

2. Immanuel Kant, *Critique of Pure Reason,* trans. Norman Kemp Smith (New York: St. Martin's Press, 1965).

3. I owe mountains of molehills to John Sallis, who generously sent me his "Tunnelings" in manuscript; see his *Spacings—of Reason and Imagination in Texts of Kant, Fichte, Hegel* (Chicago: University of Chicago Press, 1987), pp. 1–22. And let me also thank the following among the milling moles of Mannheim: Ulrich Halfmann, Friederike Born, Burkhardt Allner, Elisabeth Hoffmann, Thomas Müller, Werner Reinhart, Margarete Seidenspinner, Jupp Schöpp und Jochen Barkhausen.

4. G. W. F. Hegel, *Werke in zwanzig Bänden* (Frankfurt am Main: Suhrkamp Verlag, 1971), 20, 155.

5. All references to Hegel's *Lectures on the History of Philosophy* must, however, remain provisional. Whether they represent his own words we simply do not know. The critical editions now being prepared in France, Italy, and Germany will, I trust, be of aid in this respect.

6. See the final two pages of Hegel's *Phenomenology of Spirit,* which treat *Er-Innerung,* self-internalizing remembrance; see also chap. 5 of my *Of Memory, Reminiscence, and Writing: On the Verge* (Bloomington: Indiana University Press, 1990).

SIX. A HERMENEUTICS OF DISCRETION

1. D. F. Krell, "Nietzsche and the Task of Thinking: Martin Heidegger's Reading of Nietzsche," Ph.D. dissertation, Duquesne University (Ann Arbor: UMI, 1971).

2. See Jacques Derrida, *Éperons: Les styles de Nietzsche* (Paris: Flammarion, 1978), which I shall refer to in the body of my text by page number. "*L'Oblitération*" is a later title for Lacoue-Labarthe's review article on Heidegger's *Nietzsche* in *Critique,* no. 313, "*Lectures de Nietzsche,*" published in June 1973. For both articles see Philippe Lacoue-Labarthe, *Le sujet de la philosophie: Typographies I* (Paris: Aubier-Flammarion, 1979), pp. 75–109 ("*Nietzsche Apocryphe*") and 111–84 ("*L'Oblitération*"). This text too I shall cite in the body of my text by page number.

3. See Martin Heidegger, *Nietzsche,* 2 vols. (Pfullingen: G. Neske, 1961), I, 43. I shall cite the German text as "NI" or "NII," with page number. See the four English volumes of Heidegger's *Nietzsche,* now in two paperback volumes (San Francisco: Harper-Collins, 1991), which I shall cite as "Ni," with volume and page number. Here see Ni *1,* 33.

4. Nick Land, *The Thirst for Annihilation: Georges Bataille and Virulent Nihilism (An Essay in Atheistic Religion)* (London and New York: Routledge, 1992), passim.

5. Blanchot, *Entretien infini* (cited in note 21 of chap. 3), pp. 205–8.

6. *"Geschlecht"* appears in Jacques Derrida, *Psyché: Inventions de l'autre* (Paris: Galilée, 1987), pp. 395–414; an English translation appears in vol. XIII (1983) of *Research in Phenomenology*, pp. 65–83. The theme of *"Geschlecht"* is anticipated in a long footnote added to *Éperons* in 1978 and in the opening lines of the section entitled *"Le coup de don."* See *Nietzsche aujourd'hui?* (Paris: Union Générale d'Éditions, "10/18," 1973), *1*, 263 (where the footnote was later to be inserted) and pp. 270–71. Cf. *Éperons*, pp. 75, 84, and 88. In addition, see "Choreographies," a postal interview with Jacques Derrida by Christie V. McDonald, in *Diacritics* vol. 12 (1982), pp. 66–76, which is devoted to this theme. For *Aporias*, see Derrida, *"Apories: Mourir—s'attendre aux 'limites de la vérité,'"* in *Le passage des frontières: Autour du travail de Jacques Derrida*, pp. 309–38; in English, *Aporias*; both are cited in note 8 of chap. 4.

7. Jacques Derrida, *"Envoi,"* now also in *Psyché*, pp. 109–43; English translation of a part of *"Envoi"* by Peter and Mary Ann Caws, "Sending: On Representation," in *Social Research*, vol. 49, no. 2 (Summer 1982), pp. 294–326.

8. See D. F. Krell, *The Purest of Bastards: Works of Mourning, Art, and Affirmation in the Thought of Jacques Derrida.* (Chicago: University of Chicago Press, forthcoming), passim.

9. See Jacques Derrida, *La voix et le phénomène* (Paris: Presses Universitaires de France, 1967), chap. 7, esp. pp. 105–8; see also my *Purest of Bastards*, forthcoming, chaps. 1 and 4.

10. Jacques Derrida, *De la grammatologie* (Paris: Minuit, 1967), p. 99. I shall refer to this text as "G," with page number.

11. See section I of Nietzsche's 1886 foreword to the second edition of *The Gay Science* in the *Kritische Studienausgabe*, *3*, 346.

12. See chap. 4 of my *Postponements: Woman, Sensuality, and Death in Nietzsche* (Bloomington: Indiana University Press, 1986).

13. A weakness in Lacoue-Labarthe's analysis here is that he says nothing of Heidegger's nascent insight into the relation of Nietzsche to Schelling—Heidegger's lectures and seminars on Schelling always fixed one eye on Nietzsche. See Martin Heidegger, *Schellings Abhandlung über das Wesen der menschlichen Freiheit* (1809) (Tübingen: M. Niemeyer, 1971), for example, pp. 224–25. No doubt the connection between what Schelling calls the *split* in God between "existence" and "ground of existence" and what Nietzsche will announce as the *death* of God has to be elaborated quite carefully, as does the connection between such matters and the fate of a fragmented, mutilated *logos*. I will make a gesture toward the connection between Nietzsche and the Jena Romantics in chaps. 9 and 10, on Novalis (Friedrich von Hardenberg) and Nietzsche.

14. See my presentation of this text in *The Owl of Minerva*, vol. 17, no. 1 (Fall 1985), 5–19. Lacoue-Labarthe dates the text 1794, probably incorrectly: the closing weeks of 1796 now seem the most likely time of its composition.

15. David B. Allison, ed., *The New Nietzsche: Contemporary Styles of Interpretation* (New York: Delta Books, 1977), p. ix.

16. See Derrida's use of the term *oblitération* early in Part Two of *De la grammatologie*, pp. 159–61.

17. See Lacoue-Labarthe, 122–38. Lacoue-Labarthe's reading of Heidegger's texts on Hegel, especially "The Onto-Theo-Logical Constitution of Metaphysics" (in *Identität und Differenz* [Pfullingen: G. Neske, 1957]), is highly perceptive. See also Michel Haar, "Structures hégéliennes dans la pensée heideggerienne de l'Histoire," in *Revue de la métaphysique et de morale*, vol. 85, no. I (January–March 1980), pp. 48–59. See also D. F. Krell, *Intimations of Mortality: Time, Truth, and Finitude in Heidegger's Thinking of Being* (University Park: Pennsylvania State University Press, 1986), chap. 7.

18. See chapters 2, 3, and 6 of *Intimations of Mortality*.

19. Martin Heidegger, *Frühe Schriften* (Frankfurt am Main: V. Klostermann, 1972), pp. 136–38; cf. Lacoue-Labarthe, 147–48.

20. Pierre Klossowski, *Nietzsche et le cercle vicieux*, revised ed. (Paris: Mercure de France, 1969), p. 13.

21. Lacoue-Labarthe, 162; see NII, 481–87.

22. Martin Heidegger, *Was heißt Denken?* (Tübingen: M. Niemeyer, 1954), p. 52; translated as *What Is Called Thinking?* By Fred D. Wieck and J. Glenn Gray (New York: Harper & Row, 1968), pp. 17–18. Recall the discussion of this passage in chap. 4, above.

23. A protofascist author ridiculed by Heidegger in his 1934 lecture course, *Hölderlins Hymnen "Germanien" und "Der Rhein"* (Frankfurt am Main: V. Klostermann, 1980), p. 27.

24. See "Choreographies" (cited in note 6, above), p. 70.

25. See "Envoi," p. 143; English translation, p. 326.

SEVEN. "ASHES, ASHES, WE ALL FALL . . ."

1. Chap. 6 was originally published in *Research in Phenomenology*, vol. 15 (1985), 1–27.

2. "DD" will be my abbreviation for Hans-Georg Gadamer, "*Destruktion* and Deconstruction," in Diane P. Michelfelder and Richard E. Palmer, eds., *Dialogue and Deconstruction: The Gadamer-Derrida Encounter* (Albany: State University of New York Press, 1989), pp. 102–13.

3. "TI" will be my abbreviation for Hans-Georg Gadamer, "Text and Interpretation," in *Dialogue and Deconstruction*, pp. 21–51.

4. Is the Heidegger-Nietzsche encounter only a brief one, or does it begin in the early 1900s and end only in 1976? See Krell, *Intimations of Mortality: Time, Truth, and Finitude in Heidegger's Thinking of Being* (cited in note 17 of chap. 6), chaps. 6 and 8.

5. "LD" refers to Hans-Georg Gadamer, "Letter to Dallmayr," in *Dialogue and Deconstruction*, pp. 93–101.

6. James Joyce, *Ulysses*, ed. Hans Walter Gabler et al. (New York: Random House, 1986), p. 577, ll. 1182–84.

7. See Martin Heidegger, *Sein und Zeit*, 12th ed. (Tübingen: M. Niemeyer, 1972), sections 64 and 72; on *Zerstreuung*, see esp. pp. 56, 129, 172, 310, 323, 347, 371, and 389–90. See also Jacques Derrida, "Geschlecht: Différence ontologique, différence sexuelle," in Michel Haar, ed., *Martin Heidegger* (Paris: Cahiers de l'Herne, 1983), pp. 419–30; also available in *Livre de poche*, pp. 571–95, and *Psyché: Inventions de l'autre* (cited in chap. 6, note 6), pp. 395–414. English translation in *Research in Phenomenology*, vol. 13 (1983), 65–83.

8. Jacques Derrida, "Interpreting Signatures (Nietzsche/Heidegger): Two Questions," in *Dialogue and Deconstruction*, pp. 58–71. For the sections of Heidegger's *Nietzsche* cited here, see NI, 9–10/1, xv-xvi; NI, 255–59/2, 5–8; NI, 339–56/2, 82–97; NI, 473–81/3, 3–9; and NI, 517–27/3, 39–47.

9. See Jacques Derrida, "*Lettre à un ami japonais*," in *Le Promeneur*, no. 42 (Mid-October 1985), 2–4; translated in David Wood and Robert Bernasconi, eds., *Derrida & Différance* (Evanston, IL: Northwestern University Press, 1988), pp. 1–5.

10. Jacques Derrida, *Otobiographies: L'enseignement de Nietzsche et la politique du nom propre* (Paris: Galilée, 1984).

11. See the references in *Intimations*, p. 190 n. 16, but add to them *Hk*, 234/146. On this entire question, see now Krell, *Daimon Life: Heidegger and Life-Philosophy* (cited in note 12 of chap. 3).

12. Notice that Gadamer's reference (105) to the motto chosen for "The Will to Power as Art" (NI, 11/1, 1), "Well-nigh two thousand years and not a single new god!" is *not* the motto for Heidegger's *Nietzsche-Rezeption* as a whole. As for "*Das Leben . . .*": I confess that I did not check this opening epigraph from *In media vita* when I translated NI almost two decades ago, nor in the intervening years, so that Heidegger's excisions caught me by surprise. I did manage to indicate a far more serious case, involving *Will to Power*, no. 617, KSA 12, 312–13; see NI, 27/1, 19 and NI, 466/2, 201–2. Yet I would

resist Derrida's suggestion—as I resisted Lacoue-Labarthe's in chapter 6—that Heidegger generally neglects or even "effaces" the more subtle aspects of a text, such as its punctuation (see "Interpreting Signatures," in *Dialogue and Deconstruction*, p. 66). Quite often in *Nietzsche* Heidegger insists that we read every mark of punctuation, every piece of italic, and so on. As usual, with Heidegger the matter is complicated.

13. "*—Encore faut-il savoir brûler. Il faut s'y entendre. Il y a aussi ce 'paradoxe' de Nietzsche . . .* etc." See Jacques Derrida, *Feu la cendre* (Paris: Des femmes, 1987), pp. 51–53; translated as *Cinders* by Ned Lukacher (Lincoln: University of Nebraska Press, 1991). Note that the text of GOA, XII, no. 112 (= KSA, M III I [84] 1881), cited by both Heidegger and Derrida, has not been translated well in my translation of *Nietzsche* (NI, 342/2, 84): " . . . that everything has already been transposed into life and so departs from it." The German text reads: " . . . *so ist alles schon einmal in Leben umgesetzt gewesen, und so geht es fort*" (KSA 9, 473, ll. 1–2). *Fortgehen* can of course mean departure; but the *so* suggests that the sense here is one of *continuance*, as in the verb *fortsetzen*. The French edition has " . . . *et continuera de l'être ainsi.*" The translation now proposed tries at least to preserve the ambiguity: " . . . that *everything* has already been transposed into life—and so it goes." Finally, the passage ends with a sentence-fragment that all concerned have heretofore omitted: "If we assume an eternal duration, and consequently an eternal mutation of matter—"[.] If we do so assume, would the whole of being be the eternal return of the same? Let us not forget that notebook M III 1, which we shall consider in chap. 8, contains Nietzsche's most vigorous critique of the presupposition he regards as eminently metaphysical, that of *des Gleichen*. For Nietzsche it remains a matter of ashes. (See pp. 260–62 of my "Analysis" at the end of vol. 2 of the English edition of Heidegger's *Nietzsche*.)

EIGHT. ETERNAL RECURRENCE—OF THE SAME?

1. I shall refer to the fragments of M III 1, which has the Mette-no. 11, in square brackets—at the beginning of the note if it is cited in its entirety, at the end of the note if it appears only in part. The notes are to be found in the KSA at 9, 441–575. In the translations I have tried to respect the anomalies of Nietzsche's (non)punctuation, which are important for the style of his thought.

2. See, for example, Karl Löwith, *Nietzsches Philosophie der ewigen Wiederkehr des Gleichen* (cited in note 13 of chap. 3), passim; Eugen Fink, *Nietzsches Philosophie* (cited in note 1 of chap. 2), esp. pp. 82–118; Bernd Magnus, *Nietzsche's Existential Imperative* (Bloomington: Indiana University Press, 1978); Harold Alderman, *Nietzsche's Gift* (Athens: Ohio University Press, 1977); and Joan Stambaugh (cited in note 1 of chap. 3), among the many works on this subject.

3. On the value of death for life, cf. Novalis, *Das philosophisch-theoretische Werk*, ed. Hans-Joachim Mähl, in *Werke, Tagebücher und Briefe Friedrich von Hardenbergs* (Munich: Carl Hanser, 1978) 2, 756 (June–December 1799): "Death is the romanticizing principle of our life. Death is the minus, life the plus. Through death life is strengthened." Of this *feast* or *festival* of death, Nietzsche's M III 1 elsewhere notes: "To be redeemed from life and to become dead nature again can be sensed as *feast*—by the one who wishes to die [*vom Sterbenwollenden*]. To love nature! Once again to esteem the dead! It is not the opposite but the womb, the rule that makes more sense than the exception: for irrationality and pain are to be found merely in the so-called 'purposeful' universe, in the living" [125]. The third portion of note 82 extends the thought of the feast to what *Thus Spoke Zarathustra* will call "free death": "3. Suicide as the usual kind of death: new pride of the human being, who posits an end for himself or herself, and who invents a new kind of *festival*—demise." The dead as the womb of life, the ash as the ember of ardor—such is the demand of Nietzsche's thought of the

trace of ash. Yet the thought of eternal recurrence of the same, as we shall see, is thought to be precisely a cultivation of life, of life *against* death, as it were, so that only those who are *incapable* of thinking the thought will die out, passing over to the feast they will never have enjoyed.

4. "Let us think in particular of the formation of concepts: every word immediately becomes a concept, not when it is used for the singular and altogether individualized primal experience to which it owes its gestation, in order thus to serve as a kind of re-membrance, but when it must immediately serve for numberless more-or-less similar things—that is to say, strictly speaking, things that are never the same [*niemals gleiche*], thus for a whole range of nonidentical [*ungleiche*] cases." KSA 1, 879–80. For other criticisms of *Gleichheit* in the context of organic life, see *Human, All-Too-Human*, I, nos. 11 and 18, and II, nos. 11 and 12 (KSA 2, 30–31, 38–40, and 546–48); see also *The Gay Science*, nos. 111 and 335 (KSA 3, 471–72, and 563). To be sure, Nietzsche is not the first in the history of philosophy to be suspicious about the origins of "sameness": in a number of notes from the years 1796–1798, Novalis ponders the importance of "sameness" for oppositional thinking of any kind. See Novalis, 2, 90, 105, 134, and elsewhere.

5. Herbert Spencer's *Ethics*, in German translation since 1879, is an important ele-ment in Nietzsche's reading at this time.

6. The editors of the KSA advise us to examine section 1 of *Ecce Homo*'s account of *Thus Spoke Zarathustra*, 6, 335, which refers in a dramatic way to this note as a whole. On the "primitive, incorporated, fundamental errors," see *Die fröhliche Wis-senschaft*, no. 110, KSA 3, 469–71. See also *Beyond Good and Evil*, no. 230 (5, 167–70). Finally, one should extend the thought of incorporation, ingestion, and nour-ishment to Nietzsche's discussion of diet in *Ecce Homo*, "Why I Am So Clever," 6, 279; see also chap. 9 in the present book.

7. Later [160] Nietzsche will note: "This doctrine is mild toward those who do not believe in it; it has no hellfire, no threats. Whoever does not believe has a *fleeting* life in his consciousness." Later still [331], Nietzsche notes: "We *are milder* and more humane. Yet all mildness and humanity consist in our calling *circumstances* to account, and in our no longer laying everything at the feet of the person! and in our allowing egoism to assert itself, no longer taking it to be evil and culpable (as the *community* takes it to be). Hence the *easing up* of our belief in the absolute responsibility of the person and the culpability of the individual is what constitutes our progress beyond barbarity!"

8. See Immanuel Kant, *Kritik der reinen Vernunft*, esp. the Schematism, A 137–48; however, Nietzsche's note is of equal importance for the second analogy of experience: see A 190–211. According to Kant, "an application of the category to appearances be-comes possible by means of the transcendental determination of time, which as the schema of the concepts of the understanding mediates the subsumption of the appear-ances under the category" (A 139). According to Nietzsche, such transcendental determination of time is not a "mediation" but an inevitable falsification, projecting per-durance and sameness onto what only in retrospect and in irony can be called "appearances." Nietzsche would agree with Kant that in the Schematism we are dealing with "an art concealed in the depths of the human soul, whose true manipulations [*deren wahren Handgriffe*] nature is hardly likely ever to allow us to discover, and to have open to our gaze" (A 141). Now, the schema of causality depends upon "the suc-cession of the manifold, in so far as that succession is subject to a rule" (A 144). Nietzsche may therefore be taken as reinterpreting the form of inner intuition, the Schematism, and also the first two of Kant's analogies of experience. The first analogy (A 182–89) develops the principle of the permanence (*Beharrlichkeit*; cf. Nietzsche's *Be-harren*) of substance. The second (A 189–211) develops the principle of succession in time in accordance with the law of causality. Nietzsche would agree with Kant that all change in time "would have to be viewed as a mode of the existence of what remains and

persists" (A 183); it is only that the scene of such "having to view" would shift dramatically in the move from Kant to Nietzsche from the properly regulative to the utterly *tyrannical* use of reason. To the second analogy, Nietzsche would object, not that Hume's "habit" vitiates the analogy, but that the "necessary order" of "objective succession" is, as Kant well-nigh concedes, utterly dependent on "subjective succession": "We can extract clear concepts of them [i.e., space and time] from experience, only because we have put them into experience, and because experience is thus itself brought about only by their means" (A 196). Further, Nietzsche would object that *belief* in objective succession underlies the *confidence* that an a priori rule of causality can be distinguished from an a priori requirement for survival through (self-) deception. I bite, and the living thing then dies. That Kant's second analogy *must* revert to the first, that is, that causality itself depends on permanence of substance (see A 205), only confirms Nietzsche's analysis of the fundamental error of perdurance as *sameness*. The battle between Kant and Nietzsche would continue to rage, with the "Refutation of Idealism" (B 274–79) as perhaps the scene of the final engagement. Of course, there is no possible Nietzschean rejoinder to the *Hegelian* objection—that Nietzsche himself remains embroiled in transcendental arguments—nor to the *Kantian* objection—that his speculations remain (possibly) *dogmatic*. The thing's dying when I bite is not a response to an objection, of course; but then neither is my bite a dogmatism like any we have ever known.

9. I am thinking of the demiurge's desire to transform all chaotic rectilinear motions into perfect circular motion, and his praise of the roundness of the human head, which contains "the circles of the same." See Plato's *Timaeus*, 33b, 36c–d, 44d–e, 62d, 69b–70a, 75c, 90a–d, and elsewhere. I am also thinking of Book Λ of the *Metaphysics*, in which Aristotle discusses *unceasing circular* motion as most divine, and hence most proximate to philosophical thinking. See Aristotle, *Metaphysics* Λ, chaps. 7–8. Finally, for a contemporary appreciation of the temptations that lie in such circles, see Jacques Derrida, "Ousia et grammè," in *Marges—de la philosophie* (Paris: Minuit, 1972), pp. 31–77; English translation by Alan Bass (Chicago: University of Chicago Press, 1982), pp. 29–67; on the circle, see esp. pp. 60–61/52–53.

10. It is worth noting that this fragment would lend a great deal of support to the thesis of Pierre Klossowski, *Le cercle vicieux*, chap. 3, "The Experience of Eternal Return." For Klossowski emphasizes the periodicity of anamnesis and amnesia in the thinking of this thought: if the exhilaration of the thought is to be experienced again and again, a kind of oblivion must intervene between "this hour" and "this your thought that everything comes again." Only the periodicity of memory and oblivion could account for the exhilaration we experience in *thinking* the thought—one more time—each time we think it. Thus the following fragment [326] too supports Klossowski's reading: "I am learning more and more that what *distinguishes among* human beings is *how long* they can preserve for themselves an *elevated mood* [*eine* hohe Stimmung]. Many can sustain it for scarcely an hour; and for some, one must doubt whether they are ever capable of elevated moods. There is something physiological about this."

11. Nietzsche's *political* objections to equality (equal treatment, rights, and so on) would be a theme for itself, yet one that is no doubt related to his *critique* of all notions of sameness; in M III 1, see esp. fragments 185 (cf. 12 [213]; KSA 9, 613), 274, 279, and 303. One of the keys here would be the role that sameness and equality play in the formation of (belief in) the *subject*; see esp. note 268, considered later. For the most splendid rhetoric of ridicule with regard to "sameness," in connection with the human will as *free* will, see aphorism 12 of "The Wanderer and His Shadow," entitled, "The fundamental errors": 2, 547–48.

12. Fragment 321 further refines the relationship of *pain* to *error*. In this note Nietzsche speculates that pain, frustration, and error must somehow be necessary—must derive from being, as it were. He writes—in a syntax that at a certain point suddenly gets out of hand: "Untruth must be derivable from the 'proper, true essence' of things:

diremption into subject and object must correspond to the actual state of affairs. *Not* knowledge pertains to the essence of things, but error. Belief in the unconditioned must be derivable from the essence of the *esse*, from the universal state of being conditioned! What is baneful and painful [*Übel und Schmerz*] pertains to what is actual: but not as perdurant properties of the *esse*. For the baneful and painful are mere *consequences* of presentation [*des Vorstellens*], and that presentation is an eternal and universal property of all being, whether it can provide perdurant properties at all, whether becoming does not exclude everything that would be the same and all perdurance [*alles Gleiche und Bleibende*], except in the form of error and appearance, whereas presentation itself is a process *without* things that are the same and that perdure? — Did error *originate* as a property of being? Then to err is continuous becoming and transformation?"

13. See also fragment 306; cf. my own note 8, above, on Kant.

14. Whether Vogt's "contractive energy" derives from F. W. J. Schelling's concept of *contraction* (as opposed to *expansion* or *dilation*) in the universe remains a question for future research. Nietzsche's own question in fragment 11 [311], discussed later, as to whether contractive energy would not prevent all forms of *differentiation* in the universe, is quite close to Schelling's own question concerning the origin of motion and difference in the universe. See, for example, Schelling's *Erster Entwurf einer Philosophie der Natur*, cited in chap. 9. Finally, whether either Vogt's or Schelling's contraction has to do with the "contraction" that I contrasted with "contradiction" in the first three chapters of the present book remains to be thought. At all events, when I first sketched out the first three chapters I was unaware of Schelling's and Vogt's "contraction."

15. In his section on "Cognitive and Reproductive Thought" in the 1895 "Project," Freud offers but one example of a cathected desire—where dynamic image, judgment, and perception coalesce in a successful action. "For example, the desired mnemic image is the image of the mother's breast and its nipple in full front view, and the first perception is a lateral view of the same object without the nipple." See Sigmund Freud, *Aus den Anfängen der Psychoanalyse*, ed. Ernst Kris (New York: Imago, 1950), p. 413. Freud continues: "In the child's memory an experience may be found, an experience it had accidentally while sucking, that with a certain turn of the head the full front image is transformed into the lateral image. The lateral image now in view leads to a movement of the head; a first attempt shows that its opposite must be executed, and the perception of the full front view is achieved." Without that *contingent* or *accidental* mnemic image that results from the infant's earlier turning of the head, and the perhaps somewhat less contingent kinesthetic sense of turning the head in the opposite direction, the famished human race would have become extinct long ago. Such is what Freud calls *die Not des Lebens*, "the exigency of life." For further analysis, see chap. 3 of my *Of Memory, Reminiscence, and Writing: On the Verge* (cited in note 6 of chap. 5), esp. pp. 134–35. See also, once again, the following chapter of the present book, "Two Systems of the Mouth," in which I return to the breast.

16. Nietzsche's embrace here of "presentative being" invites a return to Heidegger's Nietzsche-interpretation, especially his critique of *Vorstellen* in Nietzsche's thought. See Martin Heidegger, NII, 141–92; in English, see vol. 4 of the four-volume translation, sections 15–20. Whether Heidegger here and elsewhere fully comprehends the importance of Nietzsche's critique of presentational perdurance and sameness for his own (i.e., Heidegger's) critique of the traditional meaning of being within metaphysics as *ständiges Anwesen* or *Beständigkeit*, perdurant presencing or constancy, remains a decisive question. It may well be that Heidegger underestimates Nietzsche's own criticism of presentation and appreciation of the intricate problem of "presentative being" as "fundamental certitude." It may be that Nietzsche's position is not wholly ensconced in Platonism or Cartesian modernity. Yet it remains the case that Heidegger's aletheiological challenge to Nietzsche's interpretation of the world as *chaos* is vital: if being as

a whole *shows itself* to Nietzsche as a presentative error, that is, as falsehood and ty-rannical commandeering by the living species that we *are*, then that *self-showing* nonetheless remains as problematic as it ever was. Indeed, Heidegger's understand-ing of truth as ἀλήθεια, revealing *and* concealing, disclosedness *and* errancy, poses an unheard-of challenge to Nietzsche—or perhaps, quite to the contrary, offers Nietzsche an unheard-of opportunity for the further development of his own position. With regard to Heidegger's reading of eternal recurrence of the same in the second of his lec-ture courses (taught in 1937; see vol. 2 of the English translation), the following must be said: Heidegger does *not* emphasize as I am doing here the discomfiting proximity of Nietzsche's *affirmation* and *critique* of "the same." Nor does Heidegger's insistence on the distinction between sameness and identity—that "the same" is not to be confused with "the identical"—really shed much light on the problems we are raising in the present chapter. However, the importance of Nietzsche's "thought of thoughts" for Heidegger's own project of a thinking of being and propriation must be reaffirmed. So too must the thesis that Heidegger's lecture course on eternal return represents the high point of his own *reading* of Nietzsche. Finally, with regard to the still-current, facile criticisms of Heidegger's use of the *Nachlaß*, one must once again confirm Heidegger's *careful* insertion of these unpublished materials into his reading of Part III of *Thus Spoke Zarathustra*. (Once again, see vol. 2 of the English translation, and my "Analy-sis" of the 1937 lecture course.) Heidegger's rejection of any division of the unpublished notes into "scientific-theoretical" versus "poetic" materials, discussed in chap. 6, is confirmed by my own reading of M III 1 here—indeed, it may be that I have fallen into the trap that Heidegger wishes me to avoid, inasmuch as I have continued to use these rubrics. Still compelling is Heidegger's account of Nietzschean being as a whole as *chaos*. Heidegger's account of eternal recurrence of the same as a *possibility for mortal thinking in our time* remains in my view one of the most profound of contemporary interpretations of Nietzsche. (On the question of the unpublished notes, see my "Analy-sis" to vol. 2, esp. pp. 241–42, 246–51, and 259–68. I would now alter the final two lines of p. 261, continuing onto p. 262, so that these lines read as follows: " . . . a pos-sibility. A considerable range of notes support the 'conclusion' that recurrence of the same is plausible, but a still greater number of notes cast doubt on the entire matter.")

17. It is difficult not to succumb to the temptation of a long postscript on the fate of the thought of eternal recurrence of the same after the period of M III 1 (autumn 1881). Without attempting anything like a survey of the dozens of notes on eternal return from this period through 1888, the following generalizations may perhaps be justified. After 1881 Nietzsche tends to drop the words *des Gleichen*, "of the same," from his references to *eternal recurrence*, although it is difficult to see whether the mere disap-pearance of "the same" alters anything: what could "recurrence" mean without (at least tacit) reference to recurrence *of the same*? At all events, in the many plans and sketches in which this thought serves as a culmination, it is not so much cosmological or scientific hypotheses that prevail—thoughts concerning forces and circulation in the universe—as the question of *belief* in the thought as a selective principle, or as the *tragic* thought par excellence. In the spring of 1884 eternal return is called a "soothsay-ing," and is associated with "Dionysian Dances and Festival Songs," but also with "discipline" in regard to future humanity, such that those who cannot withstand the thought will be "driven out" (*11*, 9, 73, 85); in the summer and fall of 1884, in a note that emphasizes the "inequality [*Ungleichheit*]" of the superior human beings, as discussed in *Thus Spoke Zarathustra*, Nietzsche writes: "(Dionysian wisdom) The supreme force *to feel that* everything imperfect and suffering is necessary (*worthy of eternal repetition*), as an effulgence of creative force, which must always and again shatter, which must choose the most audacious, most difficult paths (Principle of the greatest possible stupidity, God as devil and symbol of audacity)"; here the thought of eternal recurrence prevails in the context of the superior human beings and the overman (*11*, 214, 281). In June and July of 1885, eternal return is thought in the com-

peting contexts of will to power and Dionysos: see esp. the famous note "And do you also know what 'the world' is to me?" which appears variously as no. 36 of *Beyond Good and Evil* (5, 54–55) and as the concluding note (no. 1067) of the second edition of *The Will to Power* (in the KSA see 11, 610–11 and 14, 727). The late note that is perhaps most reminiscent of eternal recurrence of the same as thought in M III 1 is the Lenzerheide fragment on "European Nihilism," dated 10 June 1887 (12, 211–17). Here Nietzsche thinks recurrence as the "most frightful thought" and "the extreme form of nihilism," at once "the *most scientific* of all possible hypotheses" and a thought that only a particular form of humanity would dare "believe." For an indication of the fact that the tension, paradox, and contradiction of eternal return in M III 1 do not abate in later years, one need only recall the note taken up as no. 617 in *The Will to Power* (12, 312–13), from 1886–1887: "That *everything recurs* is the extreme *approximation of a world of becoming to that of being: peak of the meditation.*" It is an approximation, however, that may well be the epitome of a "*twofold falsification*," and not merely of an epistemological sort: eternal recurrence is the thought that will usher in "the tragic age" of European humanity (12, 388). Finally, another reminiscence of the thought of "the same" occurs in a note from the period of November 1887 to March 1888 (13, 34–35): "If cosmic motion had a final state [*Zielzustand*] it would have been reached. However, the sole fundamental *factum* is that it has *no* final state. . . . Becoming is of the same value [*werthgleich*] in each of its moments: the sum of its value remains selfsame [*sich gleich*]: *in other words, it has no value*, for there is nothing against which one might measure it and with respect to which the word *value* would have any meaning." To be sure, the subtle alterations of Nietzsche's "thought of thoughts" cannot be reduced to a note, not even an unforgivably long one, but must remain material for future strokes of thought—.

NINE. TWO SYSTEMS OF THE MOUTH

1. Throughout I cite Novalis, *Werke, Tagebücher und Briefe*, 3 vols., ed. Hans-Joachim Mähl and Richard Samuel (cited in note 3 of chap. 8), with particular reference to vol. 2, *Das philosophisch-theoretische Werk*, by page number in the body of my text. In the present instance: *Das allgemeine Brouillon; 2, 563*. I have also checked my quotations against the historical-critical edition initiated by Paul Kluckhohn and Richard Samuel, revised in 1981 by Richard Samuel and Hans-Joachim Mähl (Stuttgart: Kohlhammer, 1981), vols. 2–3.

2. Notebook M III 1, no. 11 [201]; KSA 9, 522.

3. On the process of nourishment as a process of *organization* and *crystallization*, see the later note of *Das allgemeine Brouillon; 2, 562–64*; in the "Fragments and Studies" of 1799–1800 Novalis writes: "It is with spiritual *enjoyment* as with bodily eating: much depends on the stomach, the health, age, time, custom, etc." (*Fragmente und Studien III; 2, 841*).

4. My thanks to Elizabeth Hoppe, who provided our graduate seminar on Novalis at DePaul University with a recording of Mozart's song. It was a departure from the songs that regularly concluded our sessions—Richard Strauss's *Vier letzte Lieder*, sung by Jessye Norman. This chapter is dedicated to my students of "Novalis, Schelling, and Nietzsche": Kelly Coble, Brodie Dollinger, Ferít Güven, Elizabeth Hoppe, Elaine Miller, Bernie Mizock, Bob Vallier, and Anna Vaughn.

5. *Teplitzer Fragmente; 2, 407*; the theme of the eucharist—which is about to be broached—has its classical source in the seventh of Novalis's *Spiritual Songs*, entitled "Hymn"; see *Geistliche Lieder; 1, 188–90*.

6. "If milk and the demulsifying agents serve as antidotes, diminishing the effects of toxins in organs, they can be such only to the extent that the toxins augment those organs—and this would be their so-called *involutive* effect" (*Das allgemeine Brouillon;*

2, 576). As a chemist, Novalis would have been familiar with the antitoxic effect of milk. Further, what he calls the *involutive effect* of toxins may be related—if only by way of opposition, inasmuch as Novalis's text is difficult to unravel here—to what in chapter 10 we shall call the *biopositive effects* of infection.

7. *Freiberger Studien, Physikalische Fragmente;* 2, 453; cf. the following from *Das allgemeine Brouillon;* 2, 498: "The philosophy that allows nature to proceed from minerals to mankind is the theory of fire with regard to nutrition, positive combustion; the philosophy that lets things unfold in the reverse direction is the theory of secretion with regard to fermentation, negative combustion." Novalis's nourishing philosophy therefore always remains a thinking of excrement. Perhaps recollecting the account of the self-sufficient universe in Plato's *Timaeus*, with which we began, Novalis asks, "Could someone survive by devouring his excrement?" Later he asks, "Should not *filth* lend itself to being used again?" (*Das allgemeine Brouillon;* 2, 504; 680). Freud and Derrida would concur—here we are close to one of the recurrent dreams of philosophers, the dream of total absorption in a system, without remnants.

8. See the long note in *Das allgemeine Brouillon* at 2, 521–22.

9. See Friedrich Nietzsche, *Jugendschriften 1854–1861*, ed. Hans Joachim Mette (München: Deutscher Taschenbuch Verlag, 1994; a reprint of the historical-critical edition published by C. H. Beck in the years 1933–1940), pp. 147–48.

10. M III 1 [134]; 9, 490–92; cf. [156], [164], [182], [241], [296], [316], and [335]; 9, 500–502; 505; 509–512; 532, 555, 563–64, and 572.

11. 11[262]; 9, 540–41; cf. 11 [273] and 320; 9, 546; 565–66.

12. The title is particularly difficult to render in English: it did not contain the word *autrui*, the existential and ethical Other that has been the rage for decades now, especially in the English-speaking world, but the neuter/neutral word *l'autre*, other with a small "o."

13. Sándor Ferenczi, "Versuch einer Genitaltheorie" (1924), in *Schriften zur Psychoanalyse*, 2 vols. (Frankfurt am Main: Fischer, 1972), 2, 317–400; English translation by Henry Alden Bunker, *Thalassa: A Theory of Genitality* (New York: W. W. Norton, 1968), passim.

14. Ferenczi, 2, 379; English translation, 71.

TEN. INFECTIOUS READING

1. I shall continue to refer to Novalis, *Werke, Tagebücher und Briefe Friedrich von Hardenbergs*, 3 vols., especially vol. 2, *Das philosophisch-theoretische Werk*, ed. Hans-Joachim Mähl (cited in note 3 of chap. 8). On the question of health and illness in Novalis's theoretical work, see the important study by John Neubauer, *Bifocal Vision: Novalis's Philosophy of Nature and Disease* (Chapel Hill: University of North Carolina Press, 1971), passim. As for Nietzsche, a word about editions of *Ecce Homo*, the composition of the work, and related materials in the notebooks. No other work of Nietzsche's is as complex in its printing history as *Ecce Homo* is. No single edition, not even the historical-critical edition by Giorgio Colli and Mazzino Montinari, suffices. The most useful edition is a facsimile of Nietzsche's holograph, with a transcription and commentary: F. Nietzsche, *Ecce homo, Faksimileausgabe der Handschrift, mit Transkription und Kommentar*, ed. Anneliese Clauss, Karl-Heinz Hahn, and Mazzino Montinari, Edition Leipzig, 1985. For details on the printing history of the text, see the extensive and authoritative account in the *Kritische Studienausgabe*, 14, 454–512. Nietzsche composed and corrected the text in six main phases, beginning on October 15 and finishing by the end of December, even though the bulk of the writing was completed by November 4. The most important alteration was the substitution of an entirely new section 3 for Part One, "Why I Am So Wise," mailed to C. G. Naumann on December 29, 1888. There are surprisingly few related materials in the notebooks,

apart from the so-called *Ur-Ecce Homo*. The final page of notebook 23 (Mette-Nr.) contains the untitled exergue of the work, *An diesem vollkommenen Tage*. Fragment 1 of notebook 24, some eighteen pages, presents the *Ur-Ecce Homo*. The material there corresponds for the most part to *Ecce Homo* Part Two, "Why I Am So Clever," although sections 1, 2, and 4 of Part One are also sketched out here. Let this one passage offer something of the flavor of these notes. It is 24 [6] (*13*, 633):

> The perspicacity of my instinct consists in my sensing the truly calamitous conditions and dangers for *me* as such.
>
> likewise, in my surmising the means by which one avoids them *or* arranges them to one's own advantage and reorganizes them, as it were, about a *higher* intention.

Finally, fragment 6 of notebook 25 offers a first draft of Part Four, "Why I Am a Destiny," which begins "*Ich kenne mein Loos . . .*" In sum, to repeat, the relevant notebooks are 23–25, in KSA, *13*, 613–35.

2. See esp. no. 116 of Friedrich Schlegel's 1798 *Fragmente*, which begins: "Romantic poesy is a progressive universal poesy," and which ends: " . . . for in a certain sense all poesy is or should be romantic." Friedrich Schlegel, *Werke in zwei Bänden* (Berlin and Weimar: Aufbau Verlag, 1980), 2, 204–5.

3. F. W. J. Schelling, *Von der Weltseele, eine Hypothese der höheren Physik zur Erklärung des allgemeinen Organismus* (1798), in *Sämmtliche Werke* (Stuttgart and Augsburg: J. G. Cotta, 1856), Abteilung 1/2, p. 534.

4. See *Sämmtliche Werke*, Abteilung 1/3, pp. 44–65 and 220–40.

5. See G. W. F. Hegel, *Enzyklopädie der philosophischen Wissenschaften (1830)*, ed. Friedhelm Nicolin and Otto Pöggeler (Hamburg: F. Meiner, 1969), §§367–76.

6. I have cited the sources and discussed them in some detail in chap. 7 of my *Daimon Life: Heidegger and Life-Philosophy* (cited in note 12 of chap. 3).

7. Pierre Klossowski, *Nietzsche et le cercle vicieux*, p. 40. The quotations appear on pp. 40 and 51.

8. Once again, see chap. 7 of *Daimon Life*.

9. The term *lues* arises from an early designation of the particular germ that was thought to cause syphilis: *Cytorryctes luis*. The more commonly accepted term for the bacillus is *Treponema pallidum*. See on all these questions Claude Quétel, *History of Syphilis*, trans. Judith Braddock and Brian Pike (Cambridge, England: Polity Press, 1990), passim.

10. Curt Paul Janz, *Friedrich Nietzsche Biographie*, 3 vols. (Munich: Deutscher Taschenbuch Verlag, 1981), 2, 10.

11. Wilhelm Lange-Eichbaum and Wolfram Kurth, *Genie, Irrsinn und Ruhm: Genie-Mythus und Pathographie des Genies*, 6th ed. (Munich: Ernst Reinhardt, 1967 [first ed., 1927], pp. 244–46.

12. Yet no matter how "social-critical" we are, we no doubt prefer the humanistic explanations of creativity, which keep illness, whether physical or psychological, at arm's length. See, for example, Albert Rothenberg, M.D., *The Emerging Goddess: The Creative Process in Art, Science, and Other Fields* (Chicago: University of Chicago Press, 1979), passim; see esp. pp. 135–36 and 351–57 (on the distinction between creative processes and psychopathological symptoms), and pp. 142–44 on the creativity and "great healthiness" of Nietzsche. However, whether or not the proximity of genius and illness occurs only in extreme or "dramatic" cases, as Rothenberg avers, the question of the biopositive effect of *infection* remains altogether undiscussed by him—although the material on "anxiety and arousal" (pp. 351–57) might well lend itself to an infectious reading. (I am grateful to Professor Carl Hausman for recommending Rothenberg's text to me.)

13. Gerhard Schulz, *Novalis* (Reinbek bei Hamburg: Rowohlt Monographien No. 154, 1969), pp. 66–67.

14. A thoughtful critic at the University of Toronto, where I presented a version of this chapter as a paper in May 1994, rightly noted that AIDS should not be used as material for a peroration—that it must stand at the *front* of a paper and be confronted more directly and courageously. I accept that criticism. All it will take on my part to do that is more insight into what has changed for us in this terrible time, and more courage in order to face it. At all events, my gratitude to that unknown critic, who will rightly find it even worse that I have reduced this matter to an endnote—meant, however, as a promissory note, a hostage to our common endangered future.

ELEVEN. CONSULTATIONS WITH THE PATERNAL SHADOW ON THE ALTAR AT THE EDGE OF THE EARTH

1. Rodolphe Gasché, "Autobiography as Gestalt," originally published in *boundary 2*, IX, 3 and X, 1, 1981; this double issue of *boundary 2* has been published as *Why Nietzsche Now?* ed. Daniel T. O'Hara (Bloomington and London: Indiana University Press, 1985); see pp. 271–90 for Gasché's contribution. Jacques Derrida, "*Logique de la vivante*," appears in two places. First, in Derrida, *L'oreille de l'autre*, ed. Claude Levesque and Christie V. McDonald (Montreal: VLB-Editeur, 1982), pp. 13–32; second, in Derrida, *Otobiographies: L'enseignement de Nietzsche et la politique du nom propre* (cited in note 10 of chap. 7), pp. 33–69. Sarah Kofman, "A Fantastical Genealogy: Nietzsche's Family Romance," appears in Peter J. Burgard, ed., *Nietzsche and the Feminine* (Charlottesville and London: University Press of Virginia, 1994), pp. 35–52. And Pierre Klossowski, *Nietzsche et le cercle vicieux*, pp. 251–84. All these texts will be cited by page number in the body of my text. I regret that the chapter does not engage with the remarkable text by Philippe Lacoue-Labarthe, "L'écho du sujet," in *Le sujet de la philosophie* (cited in note 2 of chap. 6), pp. 217–303, which is explicitly on the theme of autobiography and music—something that plays a major role in my own more modest efforts here. I would especially like to have been able to reply to "La clôture maternelle," pp. 296–97. Nietzsche's autobiographical sketches, not contained in Colli-Montinari, I cite from the edition by Karl Schlechta. The story of the textual confusion of *Ecce Homo* I, 3, is recounted by Mazzino Montinari in *Nietzsche-Studien*, Band 1, 1972, 380–418. The first account in English of this important textual matter appears in Tracy B. Strong, "Oedipus as Hero: Family and Family Metaphors in Nietzsche," in *Why Nietzsche Now?* (cited earlier in this note), pp. 311–35. Strong presents the revised text of *Ecce Homo* I, 3 on pp. 327–28 of his article, which also contains an excellent discussion (pp. 322–26) of Nietzsche's dream, discussed in this chapter. (On October 15, 1994, Sarah Kofman died in Paris. In memory of a conversation we once had on "exquisite pain," and Freud's "exquisite dualism," this chapter is dedicated to her.)

2. I cite the edition by Karl Schlechta, 2, 1073–74.

3. In *Otobiographies*, p. 62.

4. See the Schlechta edition, 3, 17. Frau Pastorin Simone Kant pointed out to me a first inconsistency in the dream: from no room of the house where Nietzsche spent his first five years is the *south* side of the church visible, the side on which, as far as we know, his father's grave was always located. Thus Nietzsche sees his father emerging from some other grave, a grave that is not his, or displaces himself to an impossible position of observation. For from his bedroom window the boy *can* see the church cemetery below, where, to repeat, his father and younger brother were *not* buried. See the account and the photographs in D. F. Krell and Donald L. Bates, *The Good European: Nietzsche's Work Sites in Word and Image*, forthcoming from the University of Chicago Press.

5. See the Schlechta edition, 3, 93. The insistence that Nietzsche can *see* his father's grave is stronger here than in the first recounting. The *displacement* at work in the

dream, or in the *accounts* of the dream, is nothing short of bizarre. Only from the interior of the church itself could the boy have seen his father's grave, adjacent to the outside wall; yet even from inside the church, looking down the wall on the southern side, the windows are too high, there is no purchase. Not even if one stands on the altar.

6. KSAB *8*, 542–4; 549 (letters 1204 and 1210).

7. In the second session of the "Double Séance," Derrida (see *La dissémination* [Paris: Seuil, 1972], p. 301n.) cites Freud's references to such inversion in the Wolfman case: "The phantasm of a second birth was thus here an abbreviated and bowdlerized version of phantasms involving homosexual desire. . . . The rending of the veil is analogous to the opening of the eyes, to the opening of the window. . . . To be born of his father . . . to give him a child at the cost of his own virility . . . homosexuality here finds its supreme and most intimate expression." See Freud, *Studienausgabe, 8*, 231. See the long note on Nathanael's homosexual posture toward the imago of his beloved father, in *"Das Unheimliche," StA, 4*, 255–56.

TWELVE. CONSULTATIONS WITH THE MATERNAL SHADOW IN THE ORANGEGROVE AT THE EDGE OF THE SEA

1. I came to know of Luce Irigaray's book (through the kindness of Gary Shapiro) only when my own book was on its way into print—time enough only to extract an epigraph (see *Postponements*, p. 71). In the remarks that follow I will refer to the French/English versions of her remarkable book: Luce Irigaray, *Amante marine: De Friedrich Nietzsche* (Paris: Minuit, 1980; translated as *Marine Lover of Friedrich Nietzsche* by Gillian C. Gill (New York: Columbia University Press, 1991); I shall cite them by page without any further designation, first the French, then the English.

2. Published by Librairie José Corti (Paris, 1943).

3. See the final section of chap. 4, "Descensional Reflection"; see also chap. 7, "Descensional Reflection and the Hermeneutics of History," in my *Intimations of Mortality: Time, Truth, and Finitude in Heidegger's Thinking of Being* (cited in note 17 of chap. 6), pp. 115–25.

4. See Jacques Derrida, "La pharmacie de Platon," in *Dissémination* (Paris: Seuil, 1972), esp. sections 2–3; trans. Barbara Johnson (Chicago: University of Chicago Press, 1981). I have discussed this heliocentrism in *Of Memory, Reminiscence, and Writing: On the Verge*, chap. 4, esp. pp. 187–204.

5. See the response to *Postponements* by Kelly Oliver in *International Studies in Philosophy*, vol. 22, no. 1, pp. 118–19; see also her "Nietzsche's Abjection" and Benjamin Bennett's "Bridge: Against Nothing," in *Nietzsche and the Feminine*, ed. Peter Burgard, pp. 53–67 and 289–315, respectively. Yet neither Oliver nor Bennett is as informed by Nietzsche's own texts as is Claudia Crawford, *To Nietzsche: I Love You: Ariadne* (Albany: State University of New York Press, 1994), passim.

6. Pierre Klossowski, *Nietzsche et le cercle vicieux*, p. 260. Birthing himself anew, taking his life into his own hands: such would be the obsessive reading of an obsessional phrase in *Ecce Homo* (KSA 6: 266): "*Ich habe es jetzt in der Hand, ich habe die Hand dafür. . . . Ich nahm mich selbst in die Hand. . . .* [I now have it in hand, I have the hand for it. . . . I took myself in hand . . .]."

7. Gabriel García Márquez, *Cien años de soledad* (Barcelona: Plaza & Janes, 1975 [originally published in 1967]), p. 383; trans. Gregory Rabassa as *One Hundred Years of Solitude* (London: Jonathan Cape, 1970), p. 422. See also chap. 6 of my *Lunar Voices: Of Tragedy, Poetry, Fiction, and Thought* (Chicago: University of Chicago Press, 1995).

8. Mette no. 11[94]; *13*, 43. Taken up as aphorism no. 1065 into the second edition of *Der Wille zur Macht*.

9. Leo Steinberg, *The Sexuality of Christ in Renaissance Art and in Modern Oblivion* (New York: Pantheon/October Books, 1983), p. 131.

10. See Gilles Deleuze, *Nietzsche et la philosophie*, pp. 16–24, 199, and 213–22; see also his more recent reflections on Ariadne, summarized in Deleuze, "Mystère d' Ariane," *Magazine littéraire*, no. 298 (April 1992), pp. 21–24. As far as I can see, these more recent reflections resolve none of the dilemmas I discussed in *Postponements*, pp. 28–31. The problems with Deleuze's thesis that I discussed in *Postponements* are by no means resolved or even ameliorated by his "revisions": his thesis on eternal recurrence—"that the thought of eternal return is consolatory, while eternal return itself is selective" (24)—seems a mediocre compromise, like a redoubled wishful thinking; and the thesis on Ariadne as the necessary supplement to Dionysian affirmation as *double* affirmation seems to me now even weaker than when I responded to it in *Postponements*. In every respect, Pierre Klossowski's reading of Nietzsche in *Le cercle vicieux* seems to me superior to the reading by Deleuze; indeed, Klossowski's is one of the finest meditations on Nietzsche ever written. The fact that (as far as I am aware) it is not yet translated into English, whereas Deleuze's book has been available for a decade, is a scandal. And, once again, for an energetic, independent-minded Ariadne, see Claudia Crawford's *To Nietzsche . . . Ariadne*.

11. Luce Irigaray, *L'oubli de l'air chez Martin Heidegger* (Paris: Minuit, 1983). I have discussed this remarkable text in my *Daimon Life*, chap. 9. On the Empedoclean dramas of Nietzsche and Hölderlin, see chaps. 1 and 2 of *Lunar Voices: Of Tragedy, Poetry, Fiction, and Thought*.

12. François Lissarrague, "The Sexual Life of Satyrs," in *Before Sexuality: The Construction of Erotic Experience in the Ancient Greek World*, ed. by David M. Halperin, John J. Winkler, and Froma I. Zeitlin (Princeton: Princeton University Press, 1990), pp. 63 and 65–66. In this same collection, see the excellent article by Anne Carson, "Putting Her in Her Place: Woman, Dirt, and Desire," chap. 5 of the collection. The second quotation in my text is also from Lissarrague.

Index

aesthetics, xvi, 37, 39, 45, 57–58, 67–68, 71–72, 127–28, 168, 190–91, 193; *see also* will to power as art

affirmation, xiv, xvi, 17, 21, 30, 49, 53, 57–58, 60, 62–64, 66–67, 69, 72–77, 117, 129, 158–60, 162, 164, 168–70, 173–74, 193, 211, 215, 217, 221, 223, 227, 233, 238, 240–41, 257n. 9, 262n. 10; *see also amor fati*

AIDS, 272n. 14; *see also* infection, syphilis

Allison, David B., 138, 262n. 15

ἅμα, *hama,* simultaneity, 70

amor fati, 60, 66, 72, 117; *see also* affirmation, fatality, fate, Russian fatalism

Ἀνάγκη, 178; *see also* necessity

Anaximander, 195

Apollo, xviii, 38, 59–60, 66, 81, 97–98, 238, 245–46, 257n. 7

archaeology, 93, 250

Ariadne, 21, 67, 246, 274n. 10

Aristophanes, 77, 90, 93, 98

Aristotle, 50, 70, 166, 169, 197–98, 266n. 9

art, xv, 7, 36–40, 46, 52, 58–60, 66, 68–71, 84–85, 88, 100, 126–27, 135–37, 139, 145, 150, 166, 185, 193, 197, 201, 203–204, 242–43, 265n. 8; *see also* aesthetics, will to power

ascent, ascensional reflection, xv, xviii, 2, 4, 15, 24, 29, 35–36, 39–40, 64, 72, 75–82, 108, 117, 134, 164, 182, 185, 218, 235–37

asceticism, ascetic ideal, xiii, xiv, 3–4, 12, 16–17, 30, 33, 57, 62, 68, 221, 240, 244, 257n. 9; *see also* ressentiment, revenge

ashes, the universe of, 35, 97, 147, 152, 154–56, 161, 188, 200, 264n. 13, 264–65n. 3; *see also* becoming, nature

Augustine, 117

autobiography, xiii, xvii, 213, 227, 251, 272n. 1

Bach, Johann Sebastian, 92, 96

Bachelard, Gaston, xviii, 72, 81, 235–38

Bataille, Georges, 27, 30, 133, 141

becoming, 2, 14–15, 34–35, 37, 40, 44, 47–49, 63, 65, 69, 71, 73, 75, 87, 116–17, 161, 165–66, 168, 171, 174, 176, 250, 257n. 7, 266–67n. 12, 268–69n. 17; *see also* ashes, drives, forces, nature

being, xvi, 13, 27–28, 36, 39–40, 42, 45, 47, 49, 56, 63, 65, 71, 73–74, 87, 91, 96, 115, 126–31, 136–37, 139–41, 145, 149, 150, 152, 160–61, 173–74, 176, 193, 264n. 13, 267n. 12, 267–68n. 16; *see also* becoming, duplicity, metaphysics

belief, 77, 116, 134, 161, 165, 168–74, 178, 265n. 7, 265–66n. 8, 268–69n. 17

biology, biologism, xvii, 152–53, 155; *see also* body, health and illness, medicine, physiology

bipolar standard, *see* will to power

Bjerre, Poul, 202

Blake, William, 104

Blanchot, Maurice, 75, 128, 133, 259n. 21, 261n. 5

body, the human, xvi, 3, 10, 16, 28–29, 30, 62, 81, 84, 87, 94–96, 99, 166, 183–87, 189–95, 198, 201, 203, 207, 211, 236, 239–40, 244–45, 247, 249–50; *see also* physiology

Brandes, Georg (Morris Cohen), 20, 228

Brown, John, 199–200

Busch, Wilhelm, 118–24

Cadmus, 58

Camus, Albert, 60–61, 66–68, 80, 237, 258n. 3, 259n. 14

chaos, 35, 71, 152, 155, 161, 166–68, 188, 201, 223, 226, 266n. 9, 267–68n. 16; *see also* ashes, becoming, drives, forces, nature

Christianity, 4–5, 9, 16–18, 25, 56, 61, 63, 66–67, 84–85, 89–90, 97, 166, 207, 212, 231, 245–50; *see also* Jesus

circle, the, 166, 172–73, 175–76, 186, 238, 241, 266n. 9, 268–69n. 17; *see also* eternal recurrence

cock, the, xv, 82–83, 89–93, 96–100, 207, 239, 251; *see also* Melville, Socrates

cogito, the, 3, 8–12, 19, 44, 49, 70, 79, 174, 250; *see also* Descartes

Coleridge, Samuel Taylor, 198

comedy, xv, 93–94, 99, 160

commanding and obeying, 10, 13, 34–35, 42, 70, 193, 208, 245, 267–68n. 16; *see also* will to power

commencements, 194, 210, 217–18; *see also* origins, provenance

consciousness, 64, 77, 109, 111, 189, 195

consolation, xiv–xv, 72–73, 76–77, 80, 116, 170, 242, 274n. 10

contraction, contradiction, 50, 79–80, 267n. 14; *see also* recoil

convalescence, 23, 97, 134, 176, 178, 200, 205–206, 209–10, 226; *see also* decadence, health and illness, medicine

Crucified, the, 20–21, 25, 67, 245; *see also* Christianity, Dionysos, Jesus

Daedalus and Icarus, 78, 81

daimon, the, 68, 82, 87, 198, 234, 259n. 12

Darwin, Charles, 17, 162

Special thanks to David Thomas for his work on the index.

DAVID FARRELL KRELL is Professor of Philosophy at DePaul University. He is the author of *Lunar Voices: Of Tragedy, Poetry, Fiction, and Thought, Daimon Life: Heidegger and Life-Philosophy, Of Memory, Reminiscence, and Writing: On the Verge, Postponements: Woman, Sensuality, and Death in Nietzsche,* and *Intimations of Mortality: Time, Truth, and Finitude in Heidegger's Thinking of Being;* coeditor (with David Wood) of *Exceedingly Nietzsche;* and editor and cotranslator of works by Martin Heidegger, including *Basic Writings, Nietzsche,* and *Early Greek Thinking.*

Lightning Source UK Ltd.
Milton Keynes UK
UKOW06f1543280317

297728UK00001B/56/P